Public Access

V

Public Access

Literary Theory and American Cultural Politics

◆

MICHAEL BÉRUBÉ

VERSO

London · New York

First published by Verso 1994
© Verso 1994
All rights reserved

Verso
UK: 6 Meard Street, London W1V 3HR
USA: 29 West 35th Street, New York, NY 10001-2291

Verso is the imprint of New Left Books

ISBN 0-86091-424-0
ISBN 0-86091-678-2 (pb)

British Library Cataloguing in Publication Data
A catalogue record for this book is available from the British Library

Library of Congress Cataloging-in-Publication Data
A catalog record for this book is available from the Library of Congress

Typeset in Baskerville by NorthStar, San Francisco, Calif.
Printed and bound in Great Britain by Biddles Ltd, Guildford and King's Lynn

For Janet Lyon,
Nicholas Bérubé, and James Bérubé

Contents

Preface

As its subtitle suggests, this book attempts to describe the relations between literary theory and American cultural politics in the 1990s. For reasons I explore in the first third of the book, these relations have lately been understood under the capacious sign of 'political correctness': a new breed of academics, we are told, has provided the intellectual foundation for campus speech codes, anti-harassment guidelines, racial polarization, grade inflation, America-bashing, and most of all, chants of 'hey, hey, ho, ho, Western Culture's got to go.' I write to contest this account, and I write not to deny that literary theory has had important social effects on and off campus, but to assess its effects in more reliable and serious a fashion than your average well-funded right-wing demagogue has done to date.

Because most of the public press, too, has indiscriminately tarred literary theory with the PC brush, this book starts by scouring off the tar before moving on to provide alternative descriptions of contemporary scholarship in the humanities. The PC wars, however, are important in their own right, both for themselves and for what they tell us about the difficulty of sustaining legitimate intellectual exchange in a culture more accustomed to waging mass-media smear campaigns than to fostering substantive debates on historicism or the Voting Rights Act. The smear campaign against contemporary scholarship in the humanities has successfully set the terms for further public discussion on the subject; and as I argue in my introduction, such campaigns, however dishonest, can be devastatingly effective whether they focus on deconstruction or the writings of Lani Guinier.

Yet the phrase 'political correctness' was indeterminate from the start; in its current usage, it refers variously to liberal hypersensitivity, leftist dogmatism, or ludicrous euphemisms (such as 'vertically challenged'). You can be labelled PC for worrying about the rainforest, reading Jacques

Derrida, disliking Rush Limbaugh, or just saying 'African American' in daily speech. What's most important about the term 'political correctness' in the long run, however, is that its continued use gives American conservatives a monopoly over the discussion of cultural values – by casting liberalism as doubly *void* of values, at once relativist and totalitarian. On the cable channels you can hear Dan Quayle or Pat Buchanan railing against the liberal cultural elite for their alleged mockery of 'values'; on the networks you can hear Rush Limbaugh and William Bennett railing against the liberal cultural elite for their alleged 'political correctness'. In other words, liberals and leftists don't have 'values'; instead of values, we have PC. The right has values. The consequences of this rhetorical sleight of hand can be quite serious insofar as they help shape the terrain of public deliberation and public policy. Professing 'family values', for instance, does not mean being concerned that one in five American children are born into poverty; it means supporting anti-gay rights ordinances and opposing 'family leave' policies. Likewise, believing in 'traditional' values is no barrier to defunding battered women's shelters, shredding the Constitution in order to fund *contras* in Nicaragua, or advocating – as did William Bennett during his term as drug czar – the beheading of drug dealers.

Since I believe that American conservatives' rhetoric of 'values' belies their profoundly amoral conduct of social policy in the eighties, and since I also believe that contemporary literary theory has everything to do with cultural values even when it's not defending itself from the PC onslaught, I was tempted to take as my title *The Book of Virtues* rather than *Public Access*. Unfortunately, the intrepid Mr Bennett grabbed the title at the last second. Perhaps that's just as well for me and my title, for any investigation into the relations between literary theory and American cultural politics has to ask itself whether academic literary theorists can write in a 'public' voice in the first place, and whether the 'public' will be willing to lend an ear should theorists try to open a public access channel. The essays in *Public Access* are, in principle, accessible to a wide generalist reading audience; two of them once had a reported circulation of 775,000 in the *Village Voice Literary Supplement.* But it remains to be seen whether 'public access' to cultural analysis (or, more generally, to American higher education) will become a central concern of teachers and scholars in the humanities – or whether wide generalist reading audiences will want to concern themselves with essays on American higher education and cultural analysis.

Three of the essays in this volume address the polemics over PC and the culture wars; the remaining essays provide surveys, analyses, and examples of recent scholarly work on postmodernism, cultural studies, deconstruction, multiculturalism, new historicism, and 'political' readings of literature and film. The book opens with an autobiographical essay on theory in the humanities, as I encountered it in graduate school from 1983 to 1989; and the book closes with an essay on the importance of the humanities (and the centrality of 'theory') to our textual and political lives as humans. These are sometimes weighty matters, and since I think they deserve better treatment than they've gotten lately, I do try to deal with them as seriously and responsibly as 'public' presentation necessitates or admits. At the same time, though, I try to keep in mind the question that permanently changed the way I write. It was asked of me not long after I finished my dissertation, when my wife and I paid a visit to her Aunt Judy, a feisty, wisecracking Cape Cod year-rounder; upon being informed that I had written a dissertation and was trying to turn it into a book, Aunt Judy fixed an eye on me and snapped, 'What's your book like? Is it funny?'

Well, *that* was a stopper, since I had not in fact written the dissertation with such a question in mind. But I gradually decided that it was a fairly important question to consider if I ever wanted to write for people other than my dissertation committee and their colleagues. My fondest hope, therefore, is that this book might actually be not merely enlightening to my readers but, at some points, entertaining as well. I suppose that too remains to be seen.

I wrote these essays over the course of two years, without any of the usual forms of institutional support. In other words, my family basically wrote this book with me. Portions of it were composed wholly on the graveyard shift, 12 to 4 in the morning, or whenever the kids agreed to occupy themselves. None of them could have been written without Janet Lyon, the world's craftiest writer, editor, teacher, mother, spouse, and soulmate. But most of them also required the active cooperation of Nick and James, who would rather use the computer for other purposes, and who continue to regard their parents' work as a complex mechanism designed for the generation of scrap paper.

Jim Arnold, Larry Gallagher, Sarah Higgins, Bud Lyon and Mark Rykoff, as crucial components of my nonacademic control group, kept me honest – and intelligible. Stacey D'Erasmo and M. Mark at the *VLS* were ideal and ideally challenging editors, as were Wahneema Lubiano, Bruce Robbins and Jeff Williams as readers of my more academic essays, and Michael Sprinker as a reader/critic/interlocutor on every page. To Lisa Duggan and Mark Edmundson I owe thanks for helping to get me started; to Amanda Anderson, Nina Baym, Gerald Graff, Allen Hance, Gregory Jay and Cary Nelson, thanks for keeping me going, either with a shot in the arm, an idea in a pinch, or a kick in the knees. Craig Fischer and Rick Powers were gracious and generous enough to set me straight on *2001* and anything else I needed to talk with them about, as were Barry Faulk, Robert McRuer and Michael Stowe-Thurston on other essays. From the National Association of Scholars, I have learned most by way of constructive and illuminating exchanges with Barry Gross and Gary Saul Morson. Finally, I need to thank the friends and colleagues I met in Brazil in 1993, whose hospitality and multicultural acuity I will always remember: Sergio Bellei, Carlos Daghlian, Margarida Gandara Rauen, Laura Izarra and Rita Terezinha Schmidt.

'Winning Hearts and Minds' originally appeared in the *Yale Journal of Criticism*, vol. 5, no. 2 (1992); 'Disuniting America Again' was first published in *The Journal of the Midwest Modern Language Association*, vol. 17, no. 1 (1993); and 'Bite Size Theory: Popularizing Academic Criticism' appeared in *Social Text,* no. 36 (1993). I am grateful to these journals and their respective publishers – Basil Blackwell, the Midwest MLA, and Duke University Press – for permission to reprint the essays here. Among the previously published essays whose copyrights reverted to me, 'Just the Fax, Ma'am' and 'Pop Goes the Academy' appeared in the *Village Voice Literary Supplement* in October 1991 and April 1992, respectively; 'Discipline and Theory' was first published in *Wild Orchids and Trotsky: Messages from American Universities,* edited by Mark Edmundson (Viking Penguin, 1993); and a substantially different version of 'Exigencies of Value' was published in *the minnesota review,* no. 39 (1992–93).

All the infelicities, errancies and weaknesses here are mine, and without a doubt they all crept into the manuscript at some point between 12 and 4 in the morning.

Champaign, Illinois
February 1994

We realize every day more strongly that we can never hope to
get hold of the 'man in the street'; we are too damned intellectual.
Beatrice Webb,
Fabian Socialist

For a privileged minority, Western democracy provides the leisure,
the facilities, and the training to seek the truth hidden beneath the veil
of distortion and misrepresentation, ideology, and class interest
through which the events of current history are presented to us.
Noam Chomsky,
Media Celebrity
and Presidential Candidate

Culture is the Ho Chi Minh trail of power;
you surrender that province and you lose America.
Patrick J. Buchanan,
Public Intellectual

Introduction

American Political Culture

and Cultural Politics

Public Opinion and Political Hypocrisy

On 13 October 1992, ninety million Americans and I tuned into the vice-presidential debate among Dan Quayle, Al Gore and James Stockdale. Not long into the debate, as its viewers will recall, Quayle charged that Gore had called for spending $100 billion in taxpayers' money to clean up the environment in foreign countries. When Gore denied having proposed such a thing, Quayle accused him of 'pulling a Clinton' – saying one thing and doing another – and cited page 304 of Gore's book, *Earth in the Balance,* as proof that Gore had in fact made the proposal he was now denying. Quayle didn't cite a specific passage, but his mere reference to a page number was, for the moment, convincing enough to persuade many people that he had his facts in order, and that Gore was backpedaling from an indefensible pair of positions, environmentalist 'extremism' and tax-and-spend liberalism.

The next morning, though, one of CNN's periodic 'reality checks' told a different story: page 304 of Gore's book made no specific spending proposals. According to CNN, Quayle had misstated Gore's record repeatedly, both on the environment and on the Caribbean Basin Initiative. For his part, Gore had falsely claimed that Clinton had created high-wage jobs while governor of Arkansas; but whereas Gore's stretcher simply credited his running mate with more than was his due, Quayle's claim, by contrast, came close to being a direct lie about Gore's written words. And when Gore denied the charge, Quayle's response labeled him a waffler and a hypocrite as well as an extremist. Gore had no similarly fraudulent claim about Quayle's record, and therefore no opportunity to turn a Quayle denial to his advantage; all he had was his indignation and his demurrals, which weren't especially convincing.

1

I had not been a fan of Mr Quayle before the debate, but I had been willing to see him as most of the American media had portrayed him – a bumbler, a harmless right-wing extremist who lacked the political credibility that would make him dangerous. More or less the way centrists and liberals saw Ronald Reagan in the mid to late 1970s, to their downfall. Now, however, I changed my mind. The Quayle who had accused Gore of hypocrisy was no bumbler: he was something worse. It was Quayle, after all, who later in the same debate gave Bush credit for passing the Clean Air Act of 1990, even though at the Republican convention in Houston that August, he had triumphantly defended his own Council on Competitiveness, which had managed to vitiate or undermine most of the act's regulations. And it was Quayle, too, who took on the job of challenging Clinton's Vietnam record, even though Clinton had avoided fighting in a war he opposed, while Quayle had avoided fighting in a war he supported. The primary outcome of this Quayle–Gore exchange, I thought, would be to obscure and confuse still further the meaning of political hypocrisy for all those millions of citizens who don't pay meticulously close attention to the positions, records and intellectual careers of their candidates and leaders. I recalled a similar impasse in the 1984 electoral campaign, when Republicans declared that Geraldine Ferraro had embarrassed her ticket by claiming that Ronald Reagan wasn't a good Christian, and later in the fall, Barbara Bush got herself a small story on page 29 of the *New York Times* of 8 October:

> In a gibe at Geraldine A. Ferraro, Barbara Bush said today that she and her husband, the Vice President, had no intention of obscuring the fact that they are wealthy and enjoy it, 'not like that four-million-dollar – I can't say it, but it rhymes with rich.'[1]

This was, of course, before Barbara Bush had been made over into America's favorite grandma, when she could still call (or not call) a vice-presidential candidate a bitch with something like impunity. But the political impact of the episode was precedent-setting: as of 1984, 'hypocrisy' didn't apply to wealthy people professing Christianity and practicing class war; it applied to wealthy people professing concern about the poor instead of enjoying their money. From that point on, apparently, Quayles became plausible critics of the 'hypocritical' service records of Clintons; and they enjoyed their money, too.

Of all the sorry exchanges in that slightly surreal debate, though, it was the claim about Gore's book that really got me. Quayle's gesture here, and his willingness to cite a page number to support himself, struck me as something right out of the PC debates as conducted by *Newsweek* or the

Wall Street Journal. For a moment, I actually felt some sense of kinship with Al Gore – as if he'd written a scholarly article for *Critical Inquiry* that had been excoriated by *U.S. News & World Report,* or as if he'd found his carefully composed words mangled by the likes of Christina Hoff Sommers or Dinesh D'Souza. Suitably incensed, therefore, I wrote an opinion piece about the debate. The premise had to do with my son Nick, then six, and his admiration for Gore, which was based on his belief that Gore was the best friend to animals among the six principal players in the debates. When Nick had heard Bush mocking the Democratic ticket for its reputed love of spotted owls, he had immediately chosen to root for Clinton, in the hope that Clinton, like himself, appreciated how great is the number of endangered species on the planet. I informed Nick that Clinton's record was nothing to be pleased about on this score, whereupon he then asked about Gore, who, I admitted, had a demonstrable concern about the environment.

But I'll admit I didn't write the op-ed just to give voice to Nick. By the time the debate was more than a day old, Republican spin doctors had had some measure of success in selling Quayle's performance as a triumph, as evidence of the maturation of the candidate who had been so unimpressive against Lloyd Bentsen in 1988. Feeling powerless, therefore, at not being one of the molders and shapers of what's known in the industry as 'public opinion', I took an evening and wrote seven or eight hundred words about how Quayle's bulldog tactics were familiar to me from my campus experiences with the New Right, and how I'd had some difficulty explaining the debate to Nick – first the claim that Gore was untrustworthy, and then the CNN report that Quayle had been seriously in error. As the op-ed put it, 'When I picked up Nick from school the next day, I had news for him. Mr Quayle had been bluffing. But since Nick didn't understand "bluffing," I had to use the L-word: lying.'

I knew that an op-ed by a private citizen didn't have a snowball's chance in hell. Since all the debates were taking place in the space of ten days, the opinion mill was working overtime; every pundit and talking head right, left and center would be charting or redirecting the spin of events. My own piece was a little too long, much too partisan, and probably too late. But miraculously, the piece was placed within a few hours by the Illini News Bureau: the *Atlanta Journal-Constitution* ran it that weekend (along with a picture of me and Nick) on a page chock-full of opinion on the debates, under the audacious headline, 'Face the Truth, Son: Quayle Lied'.

I learned quickly that one does not publish such a thing a month before the election in a crucial swing state like Georgia and remain unnoticed. Within days I received a package from Richard W. Porter, counselor to the vice president. It included a two-page letter to Nick, a six-page document on Gore's positions on abortion and the Caribbean Basin Initiative and, most important, a four-page, single-spaced document entitled '*Earth in the Balance*, Page 304: *A Rorschach Test for Media Bias*'. In it, the 'Gore Facts Research Office' branch of the Bush-Quayle campaign laid out their reading of *Earth in the Balance*, concluding not merely that Gore lied about his own work, but that – and this is the organizing theme of the piece – Quayle had exposed Gore, and now the liberal media 'are trying valiantly to save him': 'The press is "pulling a Clinton" when it refuses to accurately report Gore's plan for "bold" action.' Cannily, the Quayle team accuses the press of *not reading*: 'If the press actually were to read the pages leading up to and following page 304, it would become clear that Al Gore is proposing an immense new US initiative that would cost about $100 billion.'[2]

The following two pages of the memo were devoted to excerpts from Gore's book, noting Gore's comparison between the Marshall Plan and the multinational cleanup he envisions. Taken on their own, the excerpts seem to bear out the Quaylist interpretation of *Earth in the Balance,* and therefore lend credence to the claim that the media were whitewashing Gore's radicalism and stifling legitimate conservative critique of Gore's position as well. I can't do justice here to the argumentative complexity of the memo, which turns Gore's words against him with a real sense of style and tonal nuance, but I can say that I managed a brief rebuttal on the central point.

I pored over the last chapter of *Earth in the Balance,* filled in the context of Gore's comparison to the Marshall Plan, and concluded that in the passage cited by the Quaylists, Gore was using the $100 billion figure as an indication of how substantial are the obstacles that prevent the United States from embarking on such a plan. The first of the relevant passages runs as follows:

> The two donor participants in the Marshall Plan, the United States and Great Britain, had established a remarkably close working relationship during the war, which was then used as a model for their postwar collaboration. Today, of course, the *United States cannot conceivably be the principal financier for a global recovery program and cannot make the key decisions alone or with only one close ally* [emphasis mine]. The financial resources must now come from Japan and Europe and from wealthy, oil-producing states.[3]

Gore then notes that the prospects for this kind of international cooperation are not bright, since the environmental records of Japan and Germany are so poor and the United States itself has an enormous budget deficit. The passage cited by Quayle's staff comes at the end of a paragraph enumerating the financial and political hindrances to a global environmental cleanup:

> [W]e are not nearly as dominant in the world economy as we were then [in the late 1940s], and that necessarily has implications for our willingness to shoulder large burdens. And our budget deficits are now so large as to stifle our willingness to consider even the most urgent of tasks. Charles Maier points out that the annual US expenditures for the Marshall Plan between 1948 and 1951 were close to 2 percent of our GNP. A similar percentage today would be almost $100 billion a year (compared to our total nonmilitary foreign aid budget of about $15 billion a year). (p. 304)

Noting that all of Gore's specific, substantive proposals come later in the chapter (where Gore calls his agenda the 'Strategic Environmental Initiative' and eschews dollar figures), I concluded, as I imagined any reasonable person would, that Gore intended to cite the $100 billion figure as a barrier rather than a spur to action, and that Gore had not called for the US to undertake global cleanup alone. The Quayle camp, though, while admitting 'there is language that Senator Gore can point to that indicates that he intends this program to be a joint program' (p. 4), went carefully through Gore's text and plausibly developed the opposite interpretation, which, with the help of careful editing and a well-placed ellipsis, they framed thus:

> On pages 304–305, Senator Gore concludes his comparison to the Global Marshall Plan he proposes and the original Marshall Plan he is emulating by pointing out: 'the annual US expenditures for the Marshall Plan between 1948 and 1951 were close to 2 percent of our GNP. A similar percentage today would be almost $100 billion a year (compared to our total nonmilitary foreign aid budget of about $15 billion a year) . ... With the original Marshall Plan serving as both a model and an inspiration, we can now begin to chart a course of action.' He clearly intends to set this as a reference point for the amount of US taxpayer money he believes is necessary for 'saving civilization'.

In my little op-ed, I had written of my disbelief that Quayle could have declared 'that his staff would issue proof of his unprovable claims', but I truly had no idea that the Quayle staff was ready to hand in the equivalent of an eight-page term paper on *Earth in the Balance,* complete with thesis and supporting textual evidence. Despite my conviction that the Quayle camp's 'Rorschach test for media bias' was even more deceptive than Quayle's claims on their own, I closed out this episode with a measure of respect for the textual conduct of the Bush-Quayle team. The Quayle reading is mistaken, I think, and Quayle's debate claim was certainly a misstatement of fact, since Gore's book does not contain the proposal Quayle said it does; but on the whole, as 'political' readings go, this one isn't bad. It's not nearly so outrageous as the Reagan administration's reading of the 1972 ABM treaty that held crucial components of the Strategic Defense Initiative to be authorized by the terms of the very treaty that banned such undertakings – and it gets the words in the right order, too. I considered returning it to the White House with commentary, suggestions for improvement, and a grade of B plus.

It almost made one nostalgic: in the bad old days, creepy Republican electoral campaigns simply stole Ed Muskie's stationery and sent out fraudulent letters, or wiretapped hotel rooms, or stole their opponents' debate notes. In the 1990s, it would seem, the New Right engages in no such unsavory and criminal behavior for mere elections (though they're not beyond rifling through State Department files in a pinch), reserving that stuff for high-priority foreign policy matters. Instead, their campaign staffs are lined with column after column of skilled textual manipulators. And in a country half of whose adult population cannot be counted on to read carefully and competently, such textually sophisticated conservatives can be battled only by SuperReaders: journalists with the patience and acuity of the late I. F. Stone or, in their stead, left-leaning academic literary critics.[4]

PC Inside and Outside the Academy

I'm being facetious. As events have fallen out over the past few years, literary critics have been especially weak and ineffective opponents of the tactics used against them, partly because, although much in their careers depends on delivering subtle and sustained critiques of other peoples' readings, they are simply not ready to play this game the way the Beltway Bunch plays it when the stakes are high. In academe one grows used to having the time and leisure to engage in critical debates with 'antagonists' whose worldviews, in the context of the American political spectrum, are not dramatically divergent from one's own. We were not equipped for an all-out textual assault from the hard right, nor were we prepared for the nastiness, cynicism, and imperviousness to fact with which that assault was carried out. And where the Clinton camp had its banks of faxes ready to flood print and TV media with instant rebuttals of Bush-Quayle claims, we had only quarterly journals in which we could conduct analyses of the PC wars on our own terms long after the specific charges had receded from public memory, long after the public image of loony-left humanities professors had been solidified in national news media.

The right's conduct in the Quayle–Gore episode is, I think, symptomatic of the tone, method and purpose of the right's PC onslaught against higher education as well. But it's both more and less than a battle over PC, for it also reminds us that although the New Right's demonization techniques have been impressive at eroding nonacademic liberal and nonpartisan support for leftist professors, these techniques have more immediate and dangerous effects in the political culture at large than they do on campus. Starting with its claim that children's-rights advocate Hillary Rodham Clinton was a wild-eyed radical who equated marriage with slavery, the right won some support, notably from Christopher Lasch, for the proposition that she was an anti-family force who would further fray the national fabric.[5] Clinton's victory, moreover, did not mean defeat for the smear campaigns of the far right: far from it. Within weeks of the inauguration, the right had done a quick, redbaiting PC number on Spelman College president Johnnetta B. Cole and then, flushed with early success, went after female African American nominee number two, Lani Guinier.

The anti-Guinier campaign followed the path of the PC attack with military precision, beginning in the pages of the *Wall Street Journal* (conducting itself in this regard like a postgraduate version of the *Dartmouth Review*), fanning out to the *US News & World Report,* spreading quickly to right-wing outposts at *Newsweek* and the *New Republic,* and culminating in a triumphal march down the editorial page of the *New York Times.* According to Kathleen Quinn, the feeding frenzy was started by Boston University adjunct professor of education Abigail Thernstrom, a veteran of the culture wars against liberal academe and thus no stranger to the 'politicized' university; Thernstrom alerted conservative activist Clint Bolick to the nomination, and the rest is history.[6] Completing the neocon daisy chain familiar to PC-watchers, Thernstrom then trashed Guinier in the pages of the *New Republic,* grotesquely distorting Guinier's position on 'authentic representation'. After running through a few of Lani's loony claims, such as 'whites who need black votes still ignore black constituents', Thernstrom drove the stake home:

> In fact, in Guinier's world, black constituents can lack representation even if their elected officials are black. If the officeholders are not 'community-based', 'culturally rooted' and politically and psychologically 'authentic', then they're 'tokens' – contaminated by white support. Thus neither Virginia Governor Douglas Wilder nor Andrew Young counts as a 'black advocate'; they are too 'assimilated' into the political mainstream. The authentic black

has a 'distinctive voice' and a level of group consciousness incompatible with white enthusiasm.[7]

Responsible citizens may know by now that Guinier does not advocate this position. Yet Thernstrom's almost-random use of scare quotes creates a kind of 'citation effect', leading one to believe that she's paraphrasing Guinier – unless one knows better.

No matter. Guinier's actual beliefs and positions were not the issue at hand anyway. The real issue, as the *New Republic* made clear in its editorial the same week, was that Clinton was succumbing to Negrophilia: 'There is one issue, central to Bill Clinton's electoral appeal and to the remaking of the Democratic Party, on which the signs are truly alarming. That issue is race.' Where Clinton had heretofore sagely distanced himself from 'the politics of Jesse Jackson and the Afrocentric fringe', he was 'now in danger of losing this mantle.' Three signs seemed especially ominous to *TNR*:

> Welfare reform is, we are told, on a very distant back burner. Sheldon Hackney, who as president of the University of Pennsylvania supported codes to limit the free speech of students, is the nominee for the National Endowment for the Arts [sic]. And now Lani Guinier, whose published support of equal racial outcomes is spelled out on page 16, is the nominee for assistant attorney general for the civil rights division in the Department of Justice.[8]

The editorial's mention of Hackney seems unwarranted, unless one believes that Hackney (like Jackson, Guinier, Leonard Jeffries, and the rest of the Afrocentric fringe) harbors a radical civil rights agenda favorable to welfare queens; and because facts and other little details are irrelevant to this fulsome neoliberal diatribe, *TNR* does not bother to find out that Hackney had actually been nominated to the National Endowment for the Humanities.

Had the *TNR* staff waited for the 14 June issue of *Time*, however, they could have found the vital Guinier-Hackney link they needed, courtesy of noted civil rights advocate Patrick Buchanan, who called Hackney 'a politically correct leftist like Lani Guinier – a virtuecrat, out of touch with Middle America.' The *Time* article on Hackney, interestingly, was entitled 'The Next Lani Guinier?' Three weeks earlier, *Newsweek* had titled its story on Guinier 'Crowning a "Quota Queen"?'[9] The question marks in these uncannily intertextual titles, needless to say, are our postmodern guarantee of media objectivity: *Time* and *Newsweek* are simply presenting the news as it's been presented to them. Likewise, those scare quotes around 'quota queen' are there to let us know that *Newsweek* is simply citing the *Wall Street Journal*'s tag for Guinier, and not really *calling* Guinier a quota queen (or, as *TNR* might suggest, a welfare queen). But then these questions should provoke some questions in return. Does the *Newsweek* headline deconstruct the opposition between 'use' and 'citation'? Are 'mainstream' print media framing these people and issues in terms taken directly from the hard right? Can rhetorical questions be performative utterances? Do smear campaigns work? If you answered yes to all the above, congratulations: you're a virtuecrat, out of touch with Middle America.

For its part, the *New York Times* editorial against Guinier sounds strikingly like a condemnation of literary theory, charging that Guinier's 'ponderous prose' produced articles that are 'poorly written, provocative and easy to caricature'. One suspects that Guinier's status as a 'critical race theorist' made her doubly unattractive to the *Times* (radical, and academic too), thus facilitating its editorial decision to join forces with conservative ideologues. The president 'had good reason to drop' Guinier's nomination, opined the *Times,* because her writings suggested that 'she was not the right person to be Washington's civil rights enforcement chief.' Should this seem circular, the *Times* added that her work 'alarmed moderate readers, including longtime supporters of the Voting Rights Act, who feared her extreme-sounding enforcement notions would discredit and imperil that valued law.'[10]

Of course, it's true that Lani Guinier alarmed moderates – as long as their time constraints or substandard reading skills prevented them from reading the Voting Rights Act for themselves. When David Broder of the *Washington Post* claimed in an editorial post-mortem that Guinier was 'clearly groping for an authenticity yardstick beyond just the ability to win elections',[11] Elaine Jones, the director of the NAACP's Legal Defense Fund, replied to Broder within days:

> if such 'groping' is a disqualifying factor, then anyone who has ever litigated a Voting Rights Act case or has supported federal voting rights legislation is disqualified. From its inception, the Voting Rights Act has focused on the responsiveness of elected representatives to their African American constituents. ... The Voting Rights Act prohibits electoral practices that 'result' in racial and linguistic minorities having 'less opportunity than other members of the electorate to participate in the political process and to elect representatives of their choice.' Those are Congress's words, not mine or Lani Guinier's. The act is explicitly race-conscious and focuses on the results of the political process.[12]

Years from now, perhaps academic feminists, civil rights lawyers, critical race theorists and leftist political activists will show just how badly the

Post and *Times* were snookered by Thernstrom, Bolick, and their anti-Guinier henchmen, just as a similar amalgam of progressivist forces helped shift public opinion of Anita Hill well after it was too late to influence the Senate Judiciary Committee. But in the meantime, the right can count on a comfortable lag time between conservative smear campaigns and critical analyses that expose them. SuperReaders travel much more slowly than speeding bullets.

All of these recent exercises in the new methods of right-wing textual manipulation share features in common, but they have met with widely various results. The attempt to hang 'radicals' with their own paper trails largely failed with Al Gore, and met only moderate success with Hillary Rodham Clinton, but was spectacularly effective in keeping Lani Guinier from taking the first step towards the Justice Department – all of which suggests that the right's PC tactics have a likelihood of success directly proportional to their target's positional distance from the straight-white-male norm.[13] Most important, all these 'hit' assignments sought the same goal, the goal of Reaganite hegemony since 1981: to constrict the bounds of legitimate social debate by painting moderates as radicals. For as any reader of *Earth in the Balance* would know, Gore is no radical environmentalist. He's surely a sincere, intelligent and conscientious fellow, which puts him radically far left of the Reagan-era EPA, but from the perspective of Greenpeace or Earth First, Gore stands squarely in the middle of the road: he's an environmentalist who believes that global cleanup can only be accomplished with moderate governmental reform and the cooperation of private industry. By the time election year 1992 drew to a close, however, President Bush was screeching nocturnally that Gore, whom he now called 'Mister Ozone', was 'crazy, way out, far out, man'.[14] Again, although the right lost that specific battle, it did set the terms for discussion of Clinton's infant presidency in 1993, precisely by having already narrowed the political options open to the new administration – and, incidentally, by having put the mainstream press so insistently on the defensive about its 'liberal' bias that it dared not present Clinton's 'controversial' initiatives and appointments in a favorable (or even neutral) light.

Defending Gore, then, can be a strange task for an academic lefty, just as defending nonradicals such as Stanley Fish or J. Hillis Miller may seem a curious enterprise to their academic critics, who are more apt to critique them for their inattention to the social consequences and implications of their work. But that's what's involved in maintaining the center *as center* when it's mischaracterized by the extreme right: for when the center will not hold, some of the political work of left intellectuals consists of nothing more rewarding or 'progressive' than keeping left-like positions alive and thinkable via the circuitous route of legitimating the center. Environmental awareness and cleanup will get nowhere so long as Gore's positions are construed as 'radical', just as the civil rights division of the Justice Department will remain toothless so long as Guinierian positions are construed as antithetical to (rather than consonant with) Madisonian warnings about the abuses of majoritarian rule. Though legitimating the center means running as hard as you can just to stay in the same place, I think it's a demonstrably necessary exercise at the moment – and that's why much of my work in these pages is devoted to examining why innocuous positions in academe are so readily ridiculed by otherwise centrist commentators in media.

In its conduct of the Washington branch of the culture wars, the right has rarely been so triumphant as when Clinton decided to withdraw his nomination of Guinier before she had been given so much as a public hearing. Guinier was gone, Clinton was (rightly) seen as gutless, and debate over the composition of the Department of Justice remained fixed on how far Clinton could safely stray from the benchmark set by Edwin Meese and William Bradford Reynolds. Yet where Senate confirmations are concerned, the academic front of the culture wars has recently afforded the right a similar satisfaction: as we 'radicals' are increasingly pressed into service to defend moderately liberal positions on cultural criticism, the moderates seem to have engaged in a kind of intellectual fire sale, unburdening themselves of 'controversial' ideas and positions with which they can no longer afford to be associated. Thus when Sheldon Hackney finally appeared before the Senate Committee on Labor and Human Resources, he assured his questioners that he was not the kind of irresponsible nihilist-PC academic they had been reading about in the papers:

> Asked about political correctness at the hearing, Mr Hackney said it could be 'a serious problem if it were to capture a campus, if it were to become the orthodoxy shutting out other points of view.'

He said he was particularly troubled by 'the intellectual form of political correctness' – scholarly fields like deconstruction and post-structuralism – that, he said, maintain 'that every thought is a political thought, that every statement is a political statement, so that there can be no objective tests for truth.'[15]

And so Sheldon Hackney avoided becoming the next Lani Guinier.

In the face of the PC onslaught, it is understandably tempting for some university faculty members and administrators to try to placate the forces of reaction by throwing a few unruly colleagues to the wolves: surely they'll be left alone if they just get rid of – or at least show themselves willing to criticize – some of the people catching the most heat, be they gay or lesbian scholars, Afrocentrists, deconstructionists, radical left critics or loudmouthed young turks. Perhaps Hackney would not have given this kind of testimony if his tenure as president of the University of Pennsylvania had not been embroiled in controversies. Having presided over an incident in which an Israeli student, Eden Jacobowitz, was nearly expelled for calling black female students 'water buffalo', and another incident in which black students hijacked an issue of the campus conservative paper, Hackney doubtless had to find some way of making himself look suitably critical of something associated with 'political correctness', and found poststructuralism to be the lowest card in his hand.[16] But his choice of discard should be alarming nonetheless, for it signals two ways in which the cultural right had, by 1993, significantly altered the terrain of American cultural politics. First, it had successfully linked in the public mind four disparate areas of debate: affirmative action, recent Continental philosophy, curricular revision, and speech codes. Second, it had created a political climate in which certain Clinton nominees to 'sensitive' domestic policy posts (which prior to the Reagan era did not normally include the National Endowment for the Humanities) could not be confirmed by the Senate unless they discovered some way to sound vaguely similar to Bush nominees.

Thus, by my lights, this political victory fully deserved the self-congratulatory response it drew from the right. Stephen Balch, president of the National Association of Scholars, called Hackney's appearance before the Senate 'a red-letter day in the humanities' and seconded his testimony strongly: 'To hear Dr Hackney censure scholarly theories that argue that all knowledge is political, and to explicitly name deconstruction and poststructuralism, is immensely significant.'[17] I will not belabor the bitter irony that Hackney's and Balch's statements are thoroughly political even in a pre-poststructuralist sense, geared only to setting the rhetorical prerequisites for the confirmation of Clinton nominees. But gauged by intellectual standards rather than by the measure of factional wins and losses, Hackney's harried defense of objectivity was a sorry moment. Imagine, if you will, a nominee to the National Science Foundation who, for 'political' reasons, found herself obliged to tell the Senate she would have none of those modish quantum mechanics or Kuhnian histories of science, because these things were reputed to put 'objective knowledge' into doubt. For although it certainly can be argued that Cartesian objectivity or Platonic presences really are put in question by deconstruction and poststructuralism, the idea that a federal nominee would therefore have to reject recent Continental philosophy as illegitimate is as appalling as the idea that a nominee to the National Endowment for the Arts could not be confirmed unless he testified to the degeneracy of modern art, regardless of whether that testimony were delivered in English or German.

The Right's Declining Standards

I do not mean to imply that my relation to poststructuralism is without ambivalence, any more than that I have an unequivocally positive response to Al Gore. Poststructuralism can very well be debated in the terms academics normally employ, whereby it may be found to have too limited an account of agency, or an account of language too close to the Sapir-Whorf hypothesis that language is completely coextensive with thought, or too sketchy an account of how humans might come to have seen themselves as 'positional', 'contingent', and 'constructed' in the first place. I myself am critical of strong poststructuralisms in some of the essays that follow, primarily on the last of these grounds, since I believe that many of poststructuralism's challenges to positivist history and the determinacy of meaning are equally well mounted by hermeneutics, and, moreover, that hermeneutics actually requires a more fully 'situational' account of understanding than poststructuralism insofar as it demands not just a realization of one's own contingent, unprivileged position in relation to the past (or to others), but a concomitant realization of how one's own position has been in part produced by the past's relation to *us* (or the prior relation of other people(s) to us). The point here, however, is that it's important for *all* academics, and nonacademic intellectuals of whatever political stripe, to remember that Sheldon Hackney's testimony was not produced by careful, thoroughgoing critiques of poststructuralism. It was produced by Beltway hardball, by a campaign of Cheneyan misstatements about 'theory'; and only when that fact is sufficiently realized will 'traditional' scholars and intellectuals – especially, but not exclusively, those hostile to poststructuralism – realize how foolish it is to applaud or condone the tactics of the people who waged that campaign simply because it wound up delegitimizing an intellectual movement they weren't fond of.

This may seem an obvious enough point, but I've lost track of the number of times I've been warned by critics and colleagues of my own foolishness and naïveté in not realizing the full extent of the danger posed by the forces of PC. If I would only look around honestly, I'm told – or if I were older and had more experience – I would come to realize the peril presented by evil feminists who construe all male sexual conduct as rape, extreme Afrocentrist scholars whose only concerns are spreading black self-esteem and hatred of whites, fascist queer theorists who demand special rights, and nihilist radicals who would jettison the canon and substitute Harlequin romances and music video. I'm not going to pretend that versions of these caricatures don't exist in American universities. But I'm also not going to pretend, as so much of the commentary on PC has done so far, that these characters constitute the kind of threat to higher education – and, more widely, to honest debate – that the cultural right has posed to date. They may be nuisances, embarrassments, and occasionally worse, but any academic who's watched the PC debates unfold so far will know they do not present the unified front attributed to them by the right, and that academe is in fact rife with internal criticism of speech codes, identity politics, affirmative action policies, curricular revisions, and contemporary Continental theories. (The idea that conservatives on campus or elsewhere are somehow prevented from criticizing affirmative action is an especially strange notion, since in reality, criticism of affirmative action is one of the salient mating rituals of American conservatives, perhaps the primary means by which they recognize each other and bond *as* conservatives.) More important, however, is the corollary point: there has been considerable self-criticism and soul-searching among the so-called campus Thought Police, with no similarly substantive self-criticism on the right. On the contrary, the right's most vocal critics of liberal academe are also the people least likely to engage in self-criticism – and least likely to abide by standards of 'evidence' and 'rationality'.

Lest this seem an overstatement, allow me two illuminating illustrations. In *Telling the Truth,* her final salvo from the bully pulpit of the NEH, former chair Lynne Cheney singled out a passage from an article Donald Lazere had published in *College English,* in order to brand Lazere as a doctrinaire campus radical practicing a pedagogy of intimidation. Lazere had proposed that students such as his, who are overwhelmingly conservative and middle class, be introduced to 'a critical awareness of the constrictions in their own class position'; to foster such critical thinking, he proposed that students 'be exposed to sources delineating the gross inequities between the upper class and themselves' in order to challenge their economic and cultural 'manipulation by the elites controlling big business, mass politics, media and consumership, in large part through the rhetoric of public doublespeak.'[18] Normally, if one is educating students for participation in a democracy, one wants them to be able to steer their way around rhetorical strategies of mass manipulation. But since this task involves combatting the 'common sense' with which students arrive in class, Cheney wastes no time in construing Lazere's pedagogy as political coercion:

> This faculty member is determined to convert his students to his point of view. He has no intention of introducing them to other perspectives. He wants students to embrace his conviction that the United States is a closed and class-ridden society, and he intends to bring them to this realization while they are in his English class.[19]

This last clause might be superfluous, since it's unlikely that Cheney would applaud such a strategy if she came across it in political science class. But Lazere's argument earlier in his essay contradicts Cheney directly: 'Conservatives are correct in insisting that it is illegitimate for teachers to advocate a revolutionary or any other ideological position in a one-sided way and to force that position on students – and despite the tendentious exaggerations of conservative critics about the tyranny of left political correctness, this sometimes does occur' (p. 11). Unfortunately, though it hints at Cheney's own ability to tell the truth, Lazere's encounter with *Telling the Truth* also demonstrates how futile it is to cede a rhetorical point here and there when one is dealing with the hard right. To gauge by this exchange, crediting conservatives with correctly advocating anti-coercive pedagogies won't win academic leftists any better treatment from their opponents. It's not as if Cheney will read Lazere more closely someday and write, 'Golly, I had you folks all wrong! You're really supporters of open debate after all!' By the same token, Bill Clinton could decide to execute severely mentally impaired African American felons with his bare hands, and to chastise Sister Souljah once a week – but that wouldn't prevent the *New Republic* from casting him as a Negrophile anyway.

The Lazere passage is characteristic of *Telling the Truth*, which not only recycles the right's standard war stories about Stephan Thernstrom's 'ordeals' at Harvard and the radical freshman composition program at the University of Texas at Austin, but which also steadfastly ignores all evidence that these stories just aren't true.[20] The Lazere passage, in this light, is merely a characteristically unprincipled miscitation of academic work. But in this case, the egregiousness of the distortion prompted the editor of *College English* herself, Louise Smith, to write to Mrs Cheney at the American Enterprise Institute, asking for a public apology to Lazere and to the journal. That much is to be expected (and admired) in any responsible editor of a scholarly journal, but unfortunately, Louise Smith was not dealing with an interlocutor for whom admission of wrongdoing is politically desirable.[21] And apologies and retractions are out of the question when one cannot even get one's opponent to admit she has anything to apologize for in the first place. All the more appropriate, then, that Cheney's booklet is called *Telling the Truth* and that elsewhere she has accused her critics of engaging in Orwellian tactics.[22]

Similarly, despite the innumerable factual errors and deliberate mis-statements contained in Dinesh D'Souza's *Illiberal Education,* there has as yet been no serious reassessment of D'Souza from his allies on the right – not even so much as a strategic retreat, whereby one might say D'Souza got some of the story wrong but offers a useful and worthy critique of academic extremism all the same. Today's cultural right gives no such ground. On the contrary, the most recent treatment of D'Souza's recep-tion in *Academic Questions,* the official journal of the National Association of Scholars, reads D'Souza's critics, including myself, as proof positive that D'Souza's direst warnings have all come true:

> The response to *Illiberal Education* is more significant than the book itself. D'Souza raises serious questions about the direction higher education has taken. More often than not, however, those questions have been met not with answers but with invective. D'Souza's evidence has not been discredited, ex-cept on the ground that it reaches a politically 'incorrect' conclusion.[23]

Just as the press coverage of Gore's *Earth in the Balance* only proves the media's liberal bias, so too when D'Souza's critical readers find evidence that D'Souza's accounts are either misinformed, distorted, or fabricated, they too serve only to testify inadvertently to the liberal stranglehold on American cultural politics.

Accordingly, what underwrites my major caveat to Gerald Graff's well-known exhortation to 'teach the conflicts' (about which I have more to say in Chapter 3, 'Exigencies of Value') is the right's willingness to close ranks and suppress all criticism from within. It's not only their well-documented indifference to fact that's at issue; it's their refusal to abide by common, civilized standards of criticism and review, as well. As Abigail Thernstrom said when asked what lesson academic critics should derive from the mor-ally questionable tactics with which she savaged Guinier, 'Grow up.'[24] Thus, if it seems outrageous to us that we be criticized by such people for having 'politicized' education and abolished the concept of 'truth', then we should take Thernstrom's words to heart: *grow up.* Nobody around here really believes in 'truth', dearie.

Now, in principle I don't consider it impossible to have a reasoned debate with Cheney, D'Souza or the rest of the Beltway PC crew – as long as the debate involves direct confrontation rather than monologic battles in print media. Apparently, Stanley Fish has found it possible, and others may as well. But my experience to date leaves me less than sanguine. In-deed, I learned to be extremely wary of D'Souza from the moment I en-tered the fray over the PC wars, when he asked the *Village Voice* for a retraction of my claim that he had, during his editorship of the *Dartmouth*

Review, published stolen correspondence from members of Dartmouth's Gay Student Alliance. For D'Souza's behavior, like Cheney's, Quayle's, and Thernstrom's, leaves me skeptical as to whether the political opponents of the cultural left can be reached by appeals to 'intellectual honesty' at all.

The episode itself dates from 1981, but it is D'Souza's conduct in 1991 that principally concerns me here. Here's how things fell out. On 13 May 1991, David Corn reported in the *Nation* that D'Souza had maliciously 'outed' some gay students at Dartmouth, and that he had later gloated over having done so at the New York Athletic Club. Corn was right about item one, and wrong on item two; D'Souza wrote to the *Nation* asking for a full retraction and got a partial retraction instead. This prompted a second letter from D'Souza, who by now had grown nasty: 'My friends tell me not to waste my time because I should expect lies from the "loony left"' he wrote. 'I hope I am not naive in holding you to a higher standard.'[25] He sent Corn faxes of documents he believed would clear his name, and also wrote to the *Village Voice,* in more measured tones:

> Michael Bérubé, in a June 18 article, alleged that while I was the editor of *The Dartmouth Review,* I 'proudly published the stolen private correspondence of Dartmouth's gay and lesbian students.' This claim, which was first printed by *The Nation,* is false. Indeed, when presented with the facts, *The Nation* retracted the claim.
>
> What really happened was this: the *Review's* article concerned the Gay Student Association [sic] as a college-recognized and -funded group. The article named the five officers of the group who were listed with the college's Committee on Student Organizations [sic]. Such listing is a requirement for funding and the names are open to public scrutiny. No other names or identities were revealed, and all the information in the article came from the public file.
>
> Later, one of the officers named claimed he was not affiliated with the group, and had been erroneously named. Apparently, the young man was not openly gay, but made the error of accepting an officer's position with the group, thus putting his name on the public record. The *Review* was in no position to know this and regretted in print having named the young man.[26]

By the time the *Voice* apprised me of D'Souza's letter, I had gotten in touch with both David Corn and Victor Navasky of the *Nation,* wanting to know the status of their initial report and what they called its subsequent 'clarification and amplification'. Corn sent me copies of the documents D'Souza had sent him, and I dug up an old story I recalled having been published in the *New York Times* about the time I graduated from college. And here's where the story gets weird.

D'Souza's third paragraph to the *Voice* was gratuitous, since I had written nothing about any subsequent exchange between the *Dartmouth Review* and the Gay Student Alliance. But stranger still, his entire letter was contradicted *by the very documents he had sent to Corn,* which clearly showed that the *Review,* in an article under D'Souza's name, had in fact published excerpts from students' correspondence – as well as photocopies of official and unofficial GSA documents, whose legal-pad scrawls revealed the name and official position of the student who had requested that the *Review* not associate him with the GSA. I then made a few phone calls to Dartmouth, and soon I had the text of my reply to D'Souza, which ran as follows:

> What really happened was *this:* D'Souza's May 18, 1981 *Review* article also included anonymous excerpts from what he called 'personal letters from students confessing their gay sentiments.' *The New York Times* revealed D'Souza's source later that year, when it reported that some 'membership and correspondence files of the Gay Student Alliance disappeared from the College Center, and ... were printed in the *Review.*' Dolores Johnson, former director of Dartmouth's Council on Student Organizations, confirmed to me that none of D'Souza's information could have come from a 'public file', because 'no administrative office keeps lists of the membership of, or letters to, any student organization.' (David Corn, in the July 8 *Nation,* retracted his earlier 'Correction and Amplification'.) And what D'Souza can possibly mean by saying the *Review* 'regretted in print having named the young man'? D'Souza offered no apology; on the contrary, he *intensified* his previous allegation – *by publishing facsimiles of the stolen documents.* His only sentence of regret was 'We are sorry that it has come to this.' I cannot guess why D'Souza has now chosen to heap one distortion atop another. But I fail to see how any responsible person can continue to take D'Souza seriously. Conservatives should begin shopping around for a more credible representative.

Because of the *Voice*'s strict space limitations, I could not go on to say that the 1982 *Times* article had also reported that one named student contemplated suicide as a result of the *Review* story;[27] nor could I explain that, for whatever reason, D'Souza himself had provided David Corn with precisely the material I needed to contradict the claim in his third paragraph.

Within a few days, I got a call from Paul Berman inviting me to reprint my article in his collection *Debating P.C.* I gratefully accepted the invitation, whereupon Berman informed me that I would have to strike the reference to D'Souza and the Gay Student Alliance, since D'Souza was contesting that allegation – again, despite having just released proof that the allegation was quite true. When it became clear that Berman would not consider reprinting the piece unless the 'questionable' allegation was dropped, I dropped it. Only to include it again here, of course, with suitable commentary.

First, let it be noted that D'Souza, however unwittingly, drove a fellow student to contemplate suicide because of his article on the Gay Student Alliance (this alone, today, would be enough to qualify him for a position at the *Wall Street Journal*). Second, let us acknowledge that in the ten years between that event and his exchanges with the *Voice* and the *Nation*, D'Souza learned that his behavior in 1981 was a grievous political liability, and would have to be met with nothing less than complete denial. Third, let us marvel at the cockiness with which D'Souza demanded a retraction from the *Nation*, proclaiming his knowledge that he would meet with 'lies from the loony left'. Fourth, let us wonder what the Sam Hill is going on with a character who sends his critics the evidence that convicts him, presumably in the belief that it exonerates him. And last, let us reflect on the words of Jon Weiner, who did an investigative report on the so-called 'Thernstrom case' at Harvard in which he noted that 'D'Souza represents the finest flower of a vast neocon talent search, one that began in the early Reagan era, when right-wing foundations like Olin set up and funded a network of conservative student newspapers, the flagship of which was the virulently racist *Dartmouth Review*.'[28]

I suppose I will be accused of shooting the messenger, though the essays that follow should leave no doubt that I take both the messenger and the message seriously. I still don't know just what I think of my own unpleasant introduction to the world of PC polemics and professionalized political hypocrisy, but I suggest that the mentality that gave us a D'Souza to attack academe is the same mentality that gave us a Clint Bolick to attack Lani Guinier on issues of racial justice, and a Quayle to attack Clinton's 'hypocrisy' over Vietnam. We could call that mentality Atwaterian or Ailesian – or Animadversian, if we wanted to stress its commitment to fairness. Whatever our terminology, the point is clear. Academic critics must, when attacked, engage the arguments of their attackers, and we can even give them credit where credit is due, when they criticize something worth criticizing. But it's well to remember that in Republican Washington, circa 1981–93, and on the D'Souza-Cheney axis of the culture wars, 'debate' is conducted by rules that most academics – and most responsible citizens – don't recognize. I'll return to this theme in some of the essays that follow, but I think it helpful, by way of introduction, to explain where I got my conviction that the right's leading PC people are playing either with loaded dice or with something less than a full deck.

Higher Education and American Liberalism

To this point I've addressed only those people who could conceivably be persuaded that the PC attack on American academe has been conducted in a fundamentally unethical manner; that it has created a toxic climate in which it is impossible to call unproblematically for 'debate' with conservatives on higher education and the public sphere; and that it is intimately tied to broader attacks on leftists, liberals and moderates in the culture at large. Many of my readers will not need convincing on any of these counts. But others, I trust, may be inclined to believe, with John Searle, that 'long-term assaults on the integrity of the intellectual enterprise' have been more likely to come from inside the universities themselves than from conservative newsweeklies and Washington think tanks.[29] It is difficult for academics to remember, moreover, that for a larger constituency spanning the cultural spectrum from Dittoheads to Deadheads to department heads, the Cheney-D'Souza attacks are nothing more than the just desserts of stuffed-shirt professors, snooty intellectuals and Lexus-driving Marxists who had it coming anyway. And if the attacks play a little fast and loose with the record, hell, that's politics. Grow up.

Yet the larger context of the culture wars debate cuts curiously across the interests of this constituency. For it has to do with the politics of higher education, the 'failings' of elementary and secondary education, and the reprivatization of culture and industry pursued with malice aforethought during the Reagan era. The PC debates on campus, as the overheated polemics of 1991 made clear, are of a piece with conservative assaults on public education, public television, and public funding for the arts. In these struggles, too, college professors are often seen as liabilities by their potential allies: where millions of ordinary citizens can see the point of rallying to keep 'Sesame Street' on the air, or creating safe and well-run public schools, or allowing 'controversial' artists to put body parts on wallpaper in the name of freedom of expression, few can find it in themselves to get worked up about the possibility that Lynne Cheney's NEH may not have given a fair hearing to grant proposals concerning poststructuralism or multiculturalism. Add to this the extraordinary ease with which anyone can ridicule or demonize college professors, largely because no one outside academe has any clear idea of what professors do inside or outside the classroom, and you can see that conservative criticisms of higher education have greater chances of success – particularly among self-described 'liberals' – than their criticisms of public education, PBS or Karen Finley's performance art.

Nevertheless, the right has begun to discover that it cannot delegitimate higher education in toto simply by casting aspersions on college professors. In an economy where college graduates stand a healthy chance of raising their standard of living in the midst of their nation's gradual economic decline, while nongraduates are likely to lose ground with each passing year of their lives, 'college' – as an ideological sign and as a credentializing mechanism – remains freighted with the hopes of millions of Americans who see it as their only chance for a life better than that of their parents. What results is a class schizophrenia concerning colleges and the people who run them: professors are widely distrusted and loathed for their cushy working conditions, but colleges as institutions remain widely respected as gatekeepers of the promise of better working conditions for their graduates.

It must be said that some of this class antagonism is imaginary – and routinely fostered by both right- and left-wing forces outside the university for their own various purposes. As Fredric Jameson has recently pointed out, progressive academics may be populists, but populism often includes a hatred or distrust of professors and intellectuals, who are seen as upper-class regardless of their income (as in the Quaylist phrase 'cultural elite').[30] This may seem strange to young professors in the humanities, who wonder why they've put in six to ten years of postgraduate education and are still making less than many an entry-level car or insurance sales rep, or half the salary of first-year lawyers and stockbrokers. One reason for public distrust of the professoriate, assuredly, is tenure, which offers its recipients a job security found in few American workplaces outside the federal judiciary. (Tenure is also thought by both left and right to be antithetical to political progressivism; hence the force of Roger Kimball's title, *Tenured Radicals,* which compactly accuses us hypocritical 'radical' academics – as Barbara Bush might have said – of *not enjoying our money.*) Another is that professors have sometimes consciously traded financial reward for workplace autonomy – flexible schedules, lenient dress codes, decent health care and a considerable measure of control over the content of their own work.

This aspect of professors' lives is often exaggerated, but because it contrasts so vividly to the conditions of workers who have little or no insurance benefits, vacation time or workplace autonomy, it can be readily exploited whenever state legislatures begin deciding where this year's cuts will fall most heavily. In other words, though the generals in the PC wars have made professors look dangerous, foolish, and absurdly privileged in the light of the manufactured 'common sense' of the 1980s, they cannot delegitimate higher education all by themselves – even to Dittoheads – because they cannot undermine the popular investment in college as a means of upward mobility: even a radical lesbian feminist deconstructionist multiculturalist can still give you an 'A' and help you toward a career in which you'll outearn her. Unless, that is, the American economy bottoms out so dramatically as to render college diplomas more useful for kindling than for credentializing.

What truly endangers the future of higher education, then, are the PC wars in tandem with the growing mad-as-hell taxpayer outrage at the professional autonomy of faculty, an outrage most effectively expressed as the demand that universities curtail professorial research and require more undergraduate instruction from their employees. Now, there's nothing outrageous about that demand per se. But the emphasis on teaching at the expense of research, like the class resentment over professors' wages and workplace autonomy, overestimates the size of its target by focusing exclusively on the elite of the academic profession to the exclusion of all those who are already teaching three or four classes a semester, working part-time at $1500 to $2500 per course without benefits, or employed in non-tenure-track jobs that require them to relocate more often than most American workers.[31] These teachers, whose numbers are growing as universities continue to 'downsize', must remain invisible to the public if the attacks on PC teachers and useless, tax-dollar-devouring researchers are to succeed. So far, they have been invisible indeed; and when there is no public outcry over the exploitation and betrayal of workers at Hormel, Caterpillar or General Motors, it's safe to say that no one will stop traffic at the realization that almost two-fifths of the country's college teachers are working part-time for pitiful wages.

Clearly, the cultural right is attempting to diminish public opinion of universities by fostering negative public opinion of the people who work there. As Paul Starr pointed out in his review of Martin Anderson's 1992 anti-academic book, *Impostors in the Temple*, 'Mr Anderson seems to want to do for the universities what [Newt] Gingrich and his confrères have done for the Congress: bring the institution into such disrepute that conservatives, long stuck in minority status, will have a chance at gaining power.'[32] Admittedly, professors themselves, like Representatives and Senators, are sometimes their own best arguments against their institutions; for that matter, the modern form of conservative distrust of American colleges can trace itself all the way back to William F. Buckley's *God and Man at Yale*. Yet what makes the cultural right's strategy so dangerous now, aside from the state of the national economy (for which education has only rarely been an important budget priority), are the fissures the right has discovered and exploited within American liberalism: tensions between its individualist philosophies and its programs for social action, and related tensions between its faith in education and its ambivalence toward affirmative action and speech codes.

The tussles over affirmative action and speech codes are largely beyond the purview of this book; I'm more immediately concerned with the public impact of relatively more arcane phenomena like interpretive theory and curricular change. I probably should say, though, since I've just noted that the right has managed to string all these disparate things together, that I'm generally opposed to speech codes, strongly supportive of affirmative action (not the paternalist, fake-liberal version that thinks of affirmative action as 'lower standards' for minority students or faculty, but the progressive version that gives the nod to minority candidates who *on balance* – and not just on paper – are as qualified as their white counterparts), friendly to curricular change (*and* an advocate of core courses in Western Civ, if only we could get the engineering and business majors to take them), and somewhere within shouting distance of nihilist things like deconstruction and poststructuralism. I realize, for instance, however strong my distaste for Dinesh D'Souza's *Illiberal Education,* that his call for a class-based rather than race-based affirmative action is a proposal with some merit, not to be quickly dismissed. But by the same token, I note that it is workable only for students (about whom colleges already collect so much financial information), and nonsense for faculty.

Hence, the fissure within liberalism that's of greatest moment to me is the gap between liberal individualism and post–New Deal liberal reliance on governmental remedies to social impasses. This fissure has proven troublesome for liberal debates over abortion, pornography, and affirmative action, where social constructionists and democratic socialists may wind up on the same 'side' as libertarians, but for vastly different reasons. In debates over theory and higher education, by contrast, the relevant struggles between libertarianism and left social policy have to do with liberal resistance to poststructuralism and liberal aversion to 'anti-Americanism', as that aversion is coded in terms derived from the Cold War. In this tangle of issues, 'America' is considered to be the repository (and sometimes the terminus) of 'Western' values, and thereby construed as the guardian of an individualism threatened formerly by Communism (the opposite number of 'the West') and currently by Continental poststructuralism (the intellectual opponent of individualism).

Take, for instance, John Searle's curious defense of the Western canon in the 'The Storm over the University'. I call it 'curious' because although I agree with Searle that some left critiques of required Western Civ courses as 'ethnocentric' or 'hegemonic' are in fact misplaced, I would not predicate a defense of such courses on the argument that the Western canon is already so superbly self-critical that it has made all further Western self-criticism unnecessary. Searle's version of this reasoning follows his rather unreliable précis on 'those who think that the traditional canon should be abandoned', who allegedly 'believe that Western civilization in general, and the United States in particular, are in large part oppressive, imperialist, patriarchal, hegemonic, and in need of replacement, or at least of transformation' (p. 94). Searle concludes:

> There is a certain irony in this in that earlier student generations, my own for example, found the critical tradition that runs from Socrates through the *Federalist Papers,* through the writings of Mill and Marx, down to the twentieth century, to be liberating from the stuffy conventions of traditional American politics and pieties. Precisely by inculcating a critical attitude, the 'canon' served to demythologize the conventional pieties of the American bourgeoisie and provided the student with a perspective from which to critically analyze American culture and institutions. Ironically, the same tradition is now regarded as oppressive. The texts once served an unmasking function; now we are told that it is the texts which must be unmasked. (pp. 94–5)

Searle rightly suggests that the Western 'canon' is not identical with 'the stuffy conventions of traditional American politics and pieties', thus provoking us to ask specifically how 'we' as a nation can be construed as the product of Western Culture after all. And that's not all there is to agree with here, either; one can easily imagine the first two sentences being ripped from the context of Searle's essay and adduced by some future D'Souza as evidence of rampant campus radicalism. (That phrase about 'demythologiz[ing] the conventional pieties of the American bourgeoisie' will not stand Searle in good stead when the Robertson-Buchanan brand of the Cultural Revolution comes to call.) Still, the principal idea is that the West already contains all the tools you'd ever need to develop a critical attitude, so there's clearly no reason to go and develop a critical attitude toward the West.

I will examine another, much cruder version of this line of thought in 'Winning Hearts and Minds', where the late Allan Bloom celebrates the superiority of the West's 'openness' (relative to the non-West), only to turn with fury on Margaret Mead for her 'openness' to other cultures. Searle's vindication of Western self-criticism is far more subtle, yet open to the same charge of self-contradiction: if criticism of our critical traditions is in fact a distinctly Western characteristic, then why is this latest round of Western self-criticism to be considered a violation rather than a continuation of that tradition?

The answer, I suggest, is unintelligible outside the context of Cold War cultural politics – which, significantly, seem quite capable of surviving the Cold War itself. Searle's argument is the genial Western Civ counterpart to the standard conservative argument against American dissenters: because American society (Western thought) is the locus of freedom, and already enables dissent from within, it is unnecessary to engage in actual dissent. More than this, such dissent is the stuff of treason rather than patriotism, since – so the argument goes – the enemies of Western thought (the Soviet Union specifically, international Communism generally) themselves would not permit the dissent that American dissenters take for granted. In recent years the specific content of 'that which is not the West' has shifted somewhat, and now that its referent cannot so clearly be Communism, 'Western' will sometimes take, as its implied opposite term, 'Islamic'. Still, the general opposition is the same: we self-critical American-Western individuals are locked in struggle with evil empires and terrorist rings made up of groupthinkers with no traditions of self-criticism, and therefore we must suppress our capacity for self-criticism and present a united front if we are to prevail over totalitarian philosophies.

My own attitude toward political freedom, like that of most of the American left, is exactly the opposite: because I live in a country where my public criticism of the vice-president will be met with a media packet rather than with death squads intent on removing my brain before the next sunrise, I try to avail myself of the right to dissent whenever it becomes necessary to do so. I consider this an unremarkable attitude, entirely in the American grain from Martin Luther King, Jr to Susan B. Anthony to Frederick Douglass to Henry David Thoreau to Thomas Jefferson and Thomas Paine. And yet even among Americans who recognize the legitimacy of judging American political practices by the standard of American political ideals, there remains strong resistance to similar criticism of 'the West' in Western terms.

This slippage between 'West' and 'America', Communism and poststructuralism, is fundamental to Paul Berman's introduction to *Debating P.C.,* where Berman credits academics whose 'radical instincts are closer to Michael Harrington than to Martin Heidegger' but nevertheless casts PC as a threat to Western traditions.[33] Drawing for his critique of poststructuralism chiefly on the work of Luc Ferry and Alain Renault, Berman portrays poststructuralism as a form of linguistic determinism that conceals a malignant strain of totalitarian thought:

> Currently we have a lot of academic terms like 'difference', 'diversity', 'the Other', 'logocentrism', and 'theory', that are intended to be consonant with humanist traditions of the liberal left. But these words willy-nilly hark back to a cultural theory that has its roots in the anti-humanist intellectual currents of a generation ago, and buried within those terms may be certain definite ideas that are anything but liberal. [When I say 'theory' in this book, then, I unwittingly mean 'totalitarianism'.] There is the idea that we are living under

25

a terrible oppression based on lies about liberal humanism, and that with proper analysis the hidden vast structure of domination can be revealed. There is the temptation to flirt with irrationalist and racial theories whose normal home is on the extreme right. ... Dwight Macdonald defined 1930s fellow-traveling as the fog that arose when the warm ocean currents of American liberalism encountered the Soviet iceberg. Political correctness in the 1990s is a related syndrome. It is the fog that arises from American liberalism's encounter with the iceberg of French cynicism. (pp. 23–4)

In Berman's account, American poststructuralists are not merely jejune, ignorant of whom they're getting in bed with; depending on how one reads this partisan review (or Macdonald's partisan review) of fellow-traveling, they may be a threat to American freedoms as well. That is, if fellow-traveling was in fact as naively dangerous an enterprise as Berman and Macdonald suggest, then PC American poststructuralists, as the unwitting precipitates of Continental cryptofascism, really are the kind of dupes who don't know they're in the service of a hostile foreign power – or a hostile foreign theory.

It's crucial that the definition of fellow-traveling here remain vague, for Berman does not want to damage his credibility by suggesting that the defenders of the second Spanish republic were a bunch of Stalinist patsies or that Stephen Greenblatt is carrying around a Leninist virus that spreads through his system every time he writes 'circulation' or 'power'. There are additional problems with Berman's account, no doubt: his equation of poststructuralism, identity politics, and obsessive PC terminology cannot bear the light of day, partly because the PC politics of style that gave us 'Congressperson' and 'Black' predates the American reception of Foucault by some years, and partly because poststructuralism and identity politics are more usually antagonists than allies – as any responsible follower of the debates over 'social constructionism' would know. All the same, though we can shoot holes in Berman's polemical link between poststructuralism and fellow-traveling, we cannot necessarily weaken the ideological power of the link just by arguing that it relies on a simplistic account of complex social and intellectual phenomena. (And as I'll argue in the opening pages of Chapter 8, 'It's Renaissance Time', there is a sense in which strong forms of Continental poststructuralism can be understood as 'anti-American' after all – though not in the Cold War sense.) For the ideological power of the link has little to do with the actual practice or meaning of fellow-traveling, poststructuralist or otherwise, and everything to do with liberal resistance to all postmodern intellectual developments that seem to challenge the sovereignty of individualism.

The terrain of American cultural politics, in short, is laced with contradictions; so much so that, despite the frequency with which the directional terms 'cultural right' and 'cultural left' appear in this book, I want to argue that the meanings and constituencies implied by these terms are neither obvious nor stable, just as they can be neither disentangled from nor directly mapped onto the correlative terms 'political right' and 'political left'. What I've tried to show in this section is how these contradictions shape the cultural moment of the essays in this book: American higher education maintains broad public support as the ticket to economic security, even as Americans are rightly anxious as to whether that support is justified. College professors, especially those in the humanities, do not inspire the same faith. 'Politically correct' campus policies such as affirmative action and curricular revision are often defended by a coalition of traditional liberals and centrists, but literary theory and speech codes draw fire from liberals and conservatives alike; 'theory', for its part, is both embraced and rejected by different factions among nonacademic feminists, gay activists, and various 'minority' social movements. In the political culture at large, the very terms 'liberal' and 'conservative' are increasingly contested, as the Clinton White House often finds it either undesirable or impossible to break decisively with the Reagan-Bush policies of the 1980s, while Republicans, given four years to regroup, remain alternately embarrassed and energized by the 'cultural war' wing of the right, which, since floating major candidates in the 1988 and 1992 elections, has come to coalesce around a social agenda advocating the repression and occasional beating of gay and lesbian citizens, the murder and terrorization of abortion doctors and family planning workers, and (underwriting these) the moral superiority of Christian culture.[34] The postwar American consensus has plainly unraveled, Cold War definitions of 'American' seek a new Other on which to predicate a national Us, and American higher education (its postwar growth heretofore dependent on its usefulness to Cold War research and development) anxiously waits to discover whether its numerous intellectual investments in nonvocational training – the more speculative social sciences, the humanities, and the 'studies' programs spawned by the 1960s – will find any base of public support other than those grounded on the purely economic and credentializing functions of 'college'. It is not an easy task to try to discover one's potential allies and opponents in such a foggy atmosphere as this (damn all these icebergs!), but it is not a dull time to be a cultural critic in the United States.

Public Access

Seven of the ten essays collected here have been previously published in the US, though I've revised and coordinated them where possible or necessary. The first, 'Discipline and Theory', was requested by Mark Edmundson for his collection *Wild Orchids and Trotsky: Messages from American Universities*. Mark told me that the volume would contain essays by Richard Rorty and Nancy Miller and Frank Lentricchia, and that it would be modeled along the lines of intellectual autobiography. Since I considered these people's intellectual biographies more substantial and interesting than my own, I decided to base my narrative on the fact that I would be one of the few contributors who actually attended graduate school in the Age of Theory. I composed it with Robert Alter and David Lehman in mind: Alter for his claim that 'many young people now earning undergraduate degrees in English or French at our most prestigious institutions have read two or three pages of Lacan, Derrida, Foucault, and Kristeva for every page of George Eliot or Stendhal',[35] and Lehman for his belief that 'the student with an authentic literary vocation may be the one who feels least at home with the academic orthodoxies of our day.'[36] Since my graduate school experience consisted of eleven courses in literature and three in theory (one of these in Plato and Aristotle), and since my literary vocation has been confirmed as 'authentic' by a team of independent vocation consultants, I decided to try to convince people that the acquisition of 'theory' in graduate training involves no indoctrination into a whirl of outlandish ideas – just an introduction to engaging yet rather unexceptional propositions about the world, facilitated by a little intellectual curiosity here and there.

The next two essays are my briefs on PC circa 1991–92. The first, 'Winning Hearts and Minds', which appeared in the *Yale Journal of Criticism*, is a heavily rewritten version of an article I published in the *Village Voice* in the summer of 1991 under the title 'Public Image Limited'. Since I didn't think there was much point to complaining in an academic journal that academics weren't getting a decent hearing in public, I responded to the *YJC*'s request for a modified *Voice* article by providing a vest-pocket historicization of the rise of the cultural right, and demonstrating the continuity of rightist rhetoric from the 1960s to the 1980s. 'Exigencies of Value', which first appeared in *the minnesota review*, is an extended follow-up on one strangely effective component of the right's attacks, the claim that academic critics in the humanities have abandoned their sworn obligations to make distinctions among books – and, by extension, among students and cultures as well. This is foremost among the claims that have enabled D'Souza and his friends to smear deconstruction, canon revision, affirmative action and multiculturalism with a single all-purpose brush. What's noteworthy about this strategy, though, is that it managed to win over a number of commentators who really should have known better, including C. Vann Woodward and the late Irving Howe. I've rewritten the first half of this essay for inclusion here, since in its *minnesota review* incarnation it addressed itself specifically to the cultural terrain of 1992.

The next section is written in a slightly different voice – the voice of public presentation. The first two essays appeared in the *Voice Literary Supplement:* 'Just the Fax, Ma'am', on modernism and postmodernism, was the assignment I drew from the *VLS* after my initial article on PC was published in the *Voice*. I had little idea how to present debates on postmodernism in such a publication so as to be intelligible for nonacademics (many of whom, if they're *VLS* readers, know a great deal more about some aspects of pomo than I), yet reasonably interesting and substantive for academics already sick to death of the subject. Most of my nonacademic friends had a hard time with it, and the only response I've seen in print came in an article in the *Boston Review* that took me to task for not mentioning Clarence Thomas and Anita Hill, whose drama hit the TV screens a few weeks after the *VLS* went to press.

As for me, my only misgiving is that the opening couple of paragraphs are a bit too emphatic about the capacity of the American culture industry to incorporate and circulate anything it has a mind to. I say this now not just because *Twin Peaks* turned out not to fulfill its early promise to confound the narrative logic of the television series, but more because Midwestern commercial radio has proven to be much more resistant to hip-hop than it seemed to be in 1991. At the time I wrote 'Just the Fax, Ma'am', it was possible to hear some mild rap on central Illinois radio, such as L. L. Cool J's 'Mama Said Knock You Out' and Monie Love's retake of 'It's a Shame'. Since then, however, the station that dared to play those tunes has run screaming from rhythmic urban music to the safe haven of 'adult contemporary', offering its listeners all the stuff they can't hear anywhere else, like Mariah Carey, Phil Collins, Rod Stewart and Billy Joel. On the other hand, this past summer I heard the local mall muzak playing Heavy D. and the Boyz' 'Now That We Found Love', which not only proved to me that you can't keep the hip-hop from leaking into the cornfields somehow, but also afforded me my strangest muzak experience since I was subjected to the Mantovani rendition of 'The Ballad of John and Yoko' in 1981. So I'm letting the intro of 'Just the Fax' stand just the way it is.

The next essay, 'Pop Goes the Academy', originally an essay on Routledge's 1992 volume *Cultural Studies*, was at first supposed to be a book review of about two thousand words, but gradually grew into a cover essay five times that length as the editors of the *VLS* asked me to narrate a brief history of cultural studies and to include more excerpts from among the book's forty essays. I had misgivings about presenting myself as the 'subject supposed to know' all about cultural studies, since much of the work in the collection is well beyond my ken, but I feared that the conference and book would be so overwhelmed by all the carping in the academic undertow that its version of 'cultural studies' would never get the public airing it deserves. Moreover, I thought the *VLS* was in many ways the ideal forum for this work, particularly since the Illinois conference brought together people like Simon Frith, Douglas Crimp and Michele Wallace, all of whom would be familiar to *Voice* readers.

My worries about the academic undertow have proven to be well-founded. In the past three years I've read and heard the strangest things about the Illinois staging of cultural studies, all of which leads me to believe that part of the academic left is never so happy as when it gets to eat its own. The conference could hardly have drawn more fire had it been organized by Orrin Hatch and Rush Limbaugh – but then, one senses that some wings of the academic left, armed with intricate critiques of What Is Insufficiently Oppositional, haven't seen an antagonist further right than Al Gore in a long, long time.

The last essay in this section, 'Bite Size Theory', more or less comments on the aspirations of the first two. It was an MLA talk that grew, with the help of a little nasty water from John Leo of the *US News & World Report,* into an essay I submitted to *Social Text* in early 1993. My main concern, in condensing for an academic audience the little lessons I learned in writing for the hybrid readership of the *VLS,* was to make the case that the relevance and power of contemporary theory is partly a function of its mimeticism, and that theory's practitioners therefore have the opportunity to speak in several hybrid languages about the work they do – including languages that speak to the various people we do our work *on.* But since there's no professional 'reward' for doing so even in those disciplines in the humanities in which there are professional *imperatives* to do so, I propose that we consider basing our evaluations of faculty merit (and promotion) less exclusively on publications in peer-reviewed journals, and take into consideration humanities professors' 'public' work as well, whether this work consists of teaching, community service, presentations to K–12 schools, or articles and op-eds on academic subjects in the popular press. These areas of faculty activity are no substitute for scholarship, of course, but they can be judged by one's peers nonetheless. And such a state of affairs, however potentially chaotic and open to abuse, would have numerous advantages over a narrowly professionalist regime in which peers adjudicate the merit of each others' work simply by counting their 'professional' publications (and gauging their relative prestige of lo-cation) instead of reading them.

The final three essays include one reading of a fictional text, one talk delivered to Brazilian teachers of English and American literature, and a discussion of multiculturalism and public schools. 'Paranoia in a Vacuum', an examination of Stanley Kubrick's *2001: A Space Odyssey,* is meant in part to provide a demonstration of the kind of close rhetorical reading-slash-cultural criticism that draws instant derision from American newsweeklies; it also establishes some of my concerns with the functions of interpretation, ignorance, and silence, all of which are crucial to my closing essay – as well as to Kubrick's *2001* and to academic cultural criti-cism. Like the two essays that follow it, 'Paranoia' reflects on critical American articulations of the American national character. But it's also here because I want to include at least one example of the kind of 'read-ing' I do when I'm not popularizing academic criticism or taking up arms in the culture wars.

'It's Renaissance Time' is doubtless as uneasy a piece as either of the two *VLS* essays, written in the same spirit of fear that its content would be too foreign to its immediate audience and too old-hat to my academic colleagues in the field. The essay owes a great deal to the work of Gregory Jay and Russell Reising, as well as to the debate between Frederick Crews and Donald Pease over the constitution of the American Renaissance. The conclusion will probably sound triumphant if not worse, full of happiness and good cheer about the American public sphere, but I should be careful to point out that the talk was, after all, delivered in Brazil, and that most of my audience had spent their entire academic careers – if not their entire adult lives – under the military dictatorship that governed the country until 1986. Since the essay addresses the pertinence of Foucauldian anayl-sis to absolutist monarchy (in the English Renaissance) and to incomplete democracy (in the American Renaissance), I figured it behooved me to say a few words about how Foucauldian analysis itself circulates more freely in the latter than in the former. And since my listeners and I tended, on the whole, to prefer flawed representational democracies to monar-chies and military juntas, I decided it would be a good time to reflect briefly on the subject.

My considerations of the meaning of American identity and American democracy dovetail most fully in the final essay, 'Disuniting America Again' – which, as the title suggests, takes on the subject by way of Arthur Schlesinger's *The Disuniting of America.* While I've been working and re-working this essay since I wrote it in fall 1992, Schlesinger has also been hard at work; when last I saw him, he was on NBC's cable channel, CNBC, fooling Vladimir Posner and Phil Donahue into believing that he's an earnest supporter of 'moderate' multiculturalist reforms that don't cave in to 'ethnic separatism'. So far, I haven't heard any Schlesinger interviewers on radio or television, including Posner and Donahue, who know that *Disuniting* itself was a rejection of the moderate multiculturalism called for in the New York 'Rainbow Curriculum' (which has since been eighty-sixed by conservatives organizing around the issues of condom distribution and the toleration of gay sexuality rather than the issues of ethnic separatism and American assimilationism).

I dread including the essay here, though, because every time I try to present its closing Kozolian argument about the politics of public school funding, something bad happens in the world of public school funding. In November 1992, a few days before I presented it as a paper to the Midwest Modern Language Association, the citizens of Illinois narrowly rejected a ballot proposition that would have established a 'right to education' for every resident of the state (the measure needed the approval of 60 percent of voters, and drew support in the high 50s). Then the next spring, three days before I reworked the talk for a presentation on campus, my Champaign neighbors voted down a modest property tax increase earmarked for building a new elementary school. And finally, as I prepared it for inclusion here, the state legislature of Michigan voted to cut property taxes by 65 percent. This last item may seem to be an insane gesture on the part of Michigan, abandoning the state's schools or leaving them ripe for corporate takeover at the hands of Christopher Whittle, but the way I figure it, the vote makes perverse sense. The state legislature was so embarrassed in late March 1993, when the national media reported that one public school in Kalkaska, Michigan was ending its year two months early for lack of funds, that it has presumably decided to close the public schools altogether – thus eliminating the possibility of being further disgraced by stories of 'early' closings. One hears that Michigan is in the vanguard of this issue, searching (as I suggest legislatures should do) for alternative ways to fund public education that do not set childless homeowners against their neighbors, or the elderly against the young. But then again, one also hears that Michigan is proposing hikes in cigarette and sales taxes to recoup what it's lost from property owners. So perhaps the 'vanguard' for the 1990s will consist of finding ways to pay for public education by means of the most regressive taxes available. Surely some audacious libertarian will soon propose a similar 'education' tax on food stamps and the WIC program.

My epilogue, 'Harvesting the Humanities', sums up the major concerns of the book by explaining why I find education in the humanities an enterprise all the more worthy of undertaking in the midst of the multiple crises of American cultural politics. I don't let all my chips ride on the traditionalist account of 'critical thinking', but neither do I rest my faith entirely in the cultural left's belief that demystification and activism in equal parts can change the world. And since I hope that some of my readers will be wondering, by this time, about the function of specifically 'literary' works in the cultural landscape I describe, my narrative about cultural values, cultural legacies and cultural capital proceeds by way of James Weldon Johnson's brilliant 1912 novel, *The Autobiography of an Ex-Colored Man.*

Although these essays were composed with different kinds of readers in mind, they all assume a general hypothetical audience relevant to the collection as a whole. Throughout the book, I want to reach those academics who still think the culture wars won't really affect them or their livelihoods; I want to address the broad group of nonacademic liberals and centrists who have been hitherto all too susceptible to anti-academic public relations work from the right; and I want to challenge, provoke and engage in any way possible those relatively responsible social conservatives sincerely committed to some variations on the ideals of liberty and justice, and to appeal to their sense of chagrin at (and difference from) the thuggish tactics of their nominal associates on the hard right. As for me, I consider myself, for official statisticians' purposes, a lefty middle-innings pitcher, keenly aware of living in a time when New Deal liberalism marks the leftward border of the thinkable in the United States, and committed to a pragmatic politics of the most fairly regulated markets this society can produce or imagine.

This includes combatting the fraudulent anti-tax mania by which the right has captured the middle-income electorate and which has exacerbated the evils of the most inequitable tax code in the industrialized world; and it also therefore includes swimming upstream against practically every outlet of 'public opinion' and policy analysis, making the case that European varieties of democratic socialism have produced the political and economic systems most congenial to ordinary working people. It's distressing to hear conservatives and libertarians extolling the unregulated free market as if there were something about the American economic landscape from 1870 to 1930 that we need to get back to now, but one hopes that people with a sense of history will help their fellow citizens recall that neither wholly planned nor wholly free economies have created just societies to date. Still, however much I may draw on Marxist criticism (or democratic socialism) for an understanding of culture and society, I expect my nation's policy debates not to produce revolution – or to guarantee workers a living wage and affordable healthcare and day care – but to haggle over ways of fiddling with the mixed economy.

Critique is useful for me only insofar as it helps people to live their lives in such a way as to realize (or even only to imagine) the really radical imperatives of democracy: full and equal participation in education, in cultural conflict, in political discourse. Once the entitlements and obligations of citizenship have been conceived on egalitarian terms, there's no going back on the promise – which is why Enlightenment rhetoric and rights, though conceived in violence, slavery, and sexism, can still be invoked by the oppressed against their oppressors. Capitalism hasn't proven to be all that amenable to the idea of 'free and equal participation', and its adversary for the past seventy-five years has been so sorry and brutal an 'alternative' as to keep us all thinking that the alternative to monopoly capital is simple totalitarianism. So because mixed, planned, and free economies don't usually promote radical democracy on their own, they have to be nudged and nagged by a chorus of egalitarian voices inside government and out.

All that sounds liberal enough, and in practical political terms it is. My position in the world of cultural politics, though, is somewhat different, since it's easier to define than one's position in the world of social policy; and it's in cultural politics that the fissure between liberals and the cultural left is both real and increasingly problematic. For that matter, as I noted above, our terminology is extremely unhelpful. As Bruce Robbins recently put it,

> with the disintegration of the socialist states and the intensifying of North/South confrontation, with the increasing importance of knowledge and information to the economy, the decline of union radicalism, and the rise of political movements in the name of race, gender, environment, sexual orientation, and so on, the meaning of a metaphor based on Parisian seating arrangements two hundred years earlier can no longer be assumed.[37]

Still, we know what's most feared by the country's reactionary and anti-democratic forces, for it underwrites their obsessive and indiscriminate hatred of the 1960s: political and cultural alliances among progressive university intellectuals, students, 'new social movements' (including the ones enumerated by Robbins), traditional liberals, and fairminded fencesitters. It was a weird and shaky coalition then, and its bonds are even looser today, but the very fact that the right is trying to divide progressive academics from their potential nonacademic political constituencies is our best indication that we cannot give up on the hope that cultural criticism can do some work in the world.

In cultural politics it's at once easy and necessary to call oneself a 'radical democrat', committed to the full and long-overdue realization of the principle that democracy entails the creation and maintenance, by whatever 'artificial' means, of equal opportunities and equal access to public resources (such as education) across the board of citizenship without exception. It's harder to be a radical democrat in the world of practical policy, when one confronts the possibility that a majority of Americans would strike the Fourth Amendment from the Constitution, thus choosing expanded police powers over their own civil liberties. But being a radical democrat in the world of cultural criticism still leaves one with two intractable difficulties, around which all the following essays continually pivot: the 'liberal', whoever this creature might be, remains at once the potential political ally and the potential rhetorical opponent of the 'radical' academic. On the one hand, argument with liberal critics leaves left academics in the all-too-familiar position of squabbling over a narrow patch of turf with their immediate political cognates, whence arise all those critiques of how liberalism is insufficiently oppositional (which, however valid, are not necessarily productive, and certainly not useful in proportion to the numbers in which they're churned out these days). On the other hand, liberal constituencies are among the most likely to be persuaded that egalitarian conditions for the exercise of power do not yet exist and must be brought into being; in fact, one of the reasons feminist and radical cultural criticism has earned its berth in the academy is that it gradually managed to convince previously hostile liberals and centrists of the merits of its claims.[38]

I don't mean to suggest in the previous five paragraphs that cultural politics and practical politics are unrelated; far from it. They are complexly intertwined, as Pat Buchanan's moral crusades have recently shown. Yet there is a difference between the two political registers, and the failure to recognize that difference leads to a critical slippage between two meanings of 'politics', broad and narrow. It leads the cultural left to think it's more subversive than it is, and it leads the cultural right to affect outrage that literary and cultural critics are engaged in 'politics', as if we were interfering with trade agreements or filibustering a jobs bill. Hence the paradox that when cultural critics claim to be 'politicizing' their fields, they mean they're making them more relevant and accountable to the world in which we live – whereas when professional politicians say that an issue is 'politicized', they mean that it cannot be adjudicated honestly because the need for party loyalty has superseded all other policymaking imperatives. For us it means behaving like responsible citizens; for them it means ceasing to behave like responsible representatives.

Yet cultural politics in many ways underwrites practical politics at the most basic conceptual level, affecting our deepest conceptions of human agency, subjectivity, knowledge, and social interdependence. It is the realm of Shelleyan unacknowledged legislators and their interpreters, where shifting language games, hegemonies, paradigms and discursive formations make possible vast changes in human understanding and cultural value – which eventually, in concert with changes in material conditions, make themselves felt as new forms of social and political organization. Progressive cultural politics today – the kind I analyze and practice in these pages – chiefly has to do with the creation and circulation of cultural value; and progressive cultural critics, by interpreting and reshaping the relations between culture and society, hope to forge new understandings of subjectivity – and new formulations of the status of *political* subjects in their interactions with other political subjects – in which 'radical democracy' in the discursive realm will aid and abet the spread of radical democracy in practical policymaking.

Radical democratic critics in the university, then, are faced with the task of presenting their 'liberal' and uncommitted auditors with an uneasy combination of stringent critique and rhetorical persuasion. This much should be uncontroversial. All the same, it doesn't seem to me that a lot of persuasion is going on in contemporary left academic criticism. Public gatherings of the academic left are singularly deficient in this regard: one cannot get out of an academic conference without hearing X number of appeals to a politics of coalition and alliance, but then one usually cannot get out of the same academic conference without hearing a great deal of hostile if not contemptuous criticism directed at academe's potentially closest allies in the culture at large. We appear to have developed an academic subculture that can theorize 'hegemony' up and down the historical bloc, but that in practice proves less skilled at cultivating actual political alliances and coalitions than at pissing off contrary factions in faculty meetings. Perhaps that's because, as Gerald Graff argues, the university structure is such that no school of thought ever has to confront and directly engage its severest critics. I, for one, can recall speaking before only one or two academic gatherings in which a majority of the audience was to the right of Al Gore. Or perhaps (to take the other side of the same coin) the academic left has been so socially marginal for so long that it no longer considers persuasion important. I write these essays in the hope that it ain't so.

I make this point here because I think it accounts for some important differences in tone and approach in the essays that follow. When I write for audiences composed largely of the academic left, in the pages of *Social Text* and the *minnesota review,* I tend to sound a cautionary note about the efficacy of the academic left, particularly with regard to its rhetorical relations with nonacademic liberals. Likewise, when I first delivered 'Disuniting America Again', it was for a panel on 'cultural diversity' entitled 'Liberal Pluralism and the Ideology of the Melting Pot', in which it would have been the easiest thing in the world (and therefore undesirable) to take liberal pluralism to task for its ideology of the melting pot. In Brazil, in *Wild Orchids and Trotsky,* or in the *VLS,* by contrast, my primary concern lay in establishing the legitimacy and intelligibility of left academic scholarship and theory in the humanities, and my tone was consequently far less cautionary. But because the cultural context for academic work is usually so constricted, I suspect that where my work registers dissent from the academic left in strongly leftist forums, it may seem instead that I've been preaching to the choir just where I meant (as in 'Bite Size Theory' and 'Disuniting America Again') to be exploring ways of simultaneously criticizing and building coalitions with liberals and centrists.

It is this dilemma, provoked by the dual need for critique and for coalition with which every progressive academic is well acquainted, that leads me to argue that the political, cultural, and social context of academic 'theoretical' debates needs to be broadened and 'popularized'. *They* (those ubiquitous third-person plurals) need to do a better job of listening carefully to *us,* and *we* have to start behaving as if we really could be talking to *them* (rather than to the colleague down the hall whose work is brilliant and insightful but insufficiently oppositional in that it reinscribes the hegemonic practices it decries). As I'll say again in these pages, this is no wild-eyed faith that the American public is just waiting for progressivist academics to come along and take the culture by storm. But if we're going to be PC, politically committed, then we'll also have to be PI, persuasively inclined. Despite what Kissingerian conventional wisdom has had to say on the subject, the debates in universities are fierce precisely because there is so *much* at stake: jobs, tenure, institutional locations, the power to speak *from* institutional locations, the power to shape curricula, to shape our understanding of the culture, to produce knowledge for future generations.

None of that power will matter, though, if we speak only to ourselves, or if we allow higher education to follow the market logic that gave us our tiered health care system – the best services in the world for those who can afford them, tolerable services at inflated prices for the moderately comfortable, and whatever can be patched together, or nothing at all, for everybody else, all based on the criterion of ability to pay. If you're interested in democracy, in or out of the academy, you have to be concerned with the question of which constituencies American universities will continue to serve and how, and whether universities will work to reduce socioeconomic inequities in American life, or whether they'll work to exacerbate them. That's what the stakes are, finally. Conservatives, liberals, traditionalists, and Weberians of all stripes may believe what they want about universities as citadels for the untrammeled pursuit of truth, and because some political attacks on politicized scholarship ultimately threaten academic freedom, it's worth noting that academic 'autonomy' is not necessarily the evil, irresponsible thing the left so often assumes it to be. But the pursuit of truth in the humanities is always a pursuit of truth *about humans* (as opposed, say, to the pursuit of truths about four-dimensional spheres), and as such it will always have 'social' and 'political' consequences even when it is pursued with every sincere interest in disinterestedness.

We need not pretend otherwise, nor need we reply to the Weberians by pointing out that most of the university, and research in the applied sciences especially, pursues only those truths for which corporate or governmental funding is available. We need merely attend, as responsible scholars and citizens, to the social consequences of our pursuit of contingent, human, historically specific truths. And that means acknowledging that there *are* social consequences of our scholarship and teaching, consequences we must account for. The decisive issue in the academic culture wars is the issue of public access: public access to university education, in the first place, and public access to the academic criticism and theory in which some of the most interesting, provocative, and rewarding university education is currently taking place. To enable public access, we need, among other things, to have a public address system. These essays represent my initial attempts to help set up the PA.

Notes

1. 'Bush's Wife Assails Ferraro, But Apologizes', *New York Times*, 8 October 1984, p. A29.

2. For a corollary to the Quaylist response to criticism based on factual evidence rebutting Quaylist charges, see David Brock's response to critics of *The Real Anita Hill* (New York: Free Press, 1993). Having made a number of unsubstantiated, poorly researched, and sometimes downright false assertions about Anita Hill, Brock now blames liberal media bias for much of the criticism he's received; as he puts it, 'apparently I may not appear on television unless acompanied by someone who will brand my book a lie at the very moment it is being presented to the public' (quoted by Kathleen Sullivan, 'The Hill-Thomas Mystery', *New York Review of Books*, 12 August 1993, p. 15). Thus Brock frames the discussion of his book as one in which liberals have already framed the discussion of his book to their advantage.

3. Albert Gore, *Earth in the Balance: Ecology and the Human Spirit* (Boston: Houghton Mifflin, 1991), p. 303.

4. See the 1993 survey on literacy issued by the US Department of Education, as reported in William Celis III, 'Study Says Half of Adults in US Can't Read or Handle Arithmetic', *New York Times*, 9 September 1993, p. A1.

5. See, e.g., Christopher Lasch, 'Hillary Clinton, Child Saver', *Harper's*, October 1992, pp. 74–82.

6. Kathleen Quinn, 'Author of Her Own Defeat: Lani's Lesson for Academia', *Lingua Franca*, vol. 3, no. 6 (September/October 1993), p. 54.

7. Abigail Thernstrom, 'Guinier Miss', *New Republic*, 14 June 1993, p. 18.

8. Editorial, 'Withdraw Guinier', *New Republic,* 14 June 1993, p. 7.

9. Buchanan was quoted in Bonnie Angelo, 'The Next Lani Guinier?' *Time,* 14 June 1993, p. 29; see also Bob Cohn, 'Crowning a "Quota Queen"?' *Newsweek,* 27 May 1993, p. 67.

10. 'The Lani Guinier Mess', *New York Times,* 5 June 1993, p. A20.

11. David Broder, 'Here's Evidence Clinton Was Right to Drop Guinier', *Washington Post,* 16 June 1993, p. A21.

12. Elaine R. Jones, 'Broder v. Guinier', *Washington Post,* 20 June 1993, p. C7.

13. By contrast, liberals' successful attempt to block the confirmation of Robert Bork to the Supreme Court in 1987 may have provided conservatives with a sense of outrage that will last them through the end of the century, but only gave the nation a William Kennedy as associate justice in Bork's place. Guinier, as part of Clinton's Justice Department, would not have held a lifetime post, and would have been confined, in any case, to carrying out Clinton's own policies. Unlike Bork, Guinier could be fired by the president at any time – if she turned out to be as radical as her extremist critics claimed.

14. Michael Wines, 'Bush, Buoyed by Polls, Scrambles to Rebuild Winning Coalition', *New York Times,* 30 October 1992, p. A1. Although it was not noted at the time, Bush's rhetoric of 'way out, far out, man' shows just how thoroughly the pernicious 'tune in, turn on, drop out' hipster-Yippie ideology of the 1960s has permeated the highest echelons of American politics.

15. Stephen Burd, 'Hackney Attacked and Praised for Criticizing Literary Theory', *Chronicle of Higher Education,* 14 July 1993, p. A21.

16. See Stephen Burd, 'Hackney Clears Hurdle in Run for the NEH', *Chronicle of Higher Education,* 7 July 1993, pp. A26, A33.

17. Quoted in Burd, 'Hackney Attacked and Praised', p. A21.

18. Donald Lazere, 'Back to Basics: A Force for Oppression or Liberation?' *College English,* vol. 54, no. 1 (1992), pp. 18–19.

19. Lynne V. Cheney, *Telling the Truth: A Report on the State of the Humanities in Higher Education* (Washington, D.C.: National Endowment for the Humanities, 1992), p. 13.

20. Compare Cheney's outrageous account of English 306 at Austin, pp. 30–34, with Linda Brodkey and Shelli Fowler, 'What Happened to English 306', in *Beyond PC: Toward a Politics of Understanding,* Patricia Aufderheide, ed. (St Paul, Minn.: Graywolf Press, 1992), pp. 113–17.

21. For a more detailed narrative of the exchange among Lazere, Smith and Cheney, see Lazere's article, 'The Mugging of the Academic Left', excerpted in the second issue of *Democratic Culture,* the newsletter of Teachers for a Democratic Culture, and forthcoming in the *Yale Journal of Criticism.*

22. Lynne V. Cheney, 'Reader's Forum', response to Joan W. Scott, 'The New University: Beyond Political Correctness', *Boston Review,* vol. 17, nos 3–4 (June 1992), p. 31.

23. Heather MacDonald, 'D'Souza's Critics: PC Fights Back', *Academic Questions,* vol. 5, no. 3 (1992), p. 20. Earlier in the essay MacDonald admits that D'Souza sometimes engages in *ad hominem* argument. But that's all, folks.

24. Quoted in Kathleen Quinn, 'Author of Her Own Defeat', p. 55.

25. Dinesh D'Souza, letter to *Nation,* 8 July 1991, p. 38.

26. Dinesh D'Souza, letter to the *Village Voice,* 9 July 1991, p. 5.

27. Dudley Clendinen, 'Conservative Paper Stirs Dartmouth.' *New York Times,* 30 May 1982, p. 23: 'One student named, according to his friends, became severely depressed and talked repeatedly of suicide. The grandfather of another who had not found the courage to tell his family of his homosexuality learned about his grandson when he got his copy of *The Review* in the mail.'

28. Jon Wiener, 'What Happened at Harvard', in Aufderheide, ed., *Beyond PC,* p. 105.

29. John Searle, 'The Storm over the University', in Paul Berman, ed., *Debating P.C.: The Controversy over Political Correctness on College Campuses* (New York: Dell, 1992), p. 87. (Hereafter cited by page number.)

30. See Fredric Jameson, 'On "Cultural Studies"', *Social Text,* no. 34 (1993), pp. 17–52, esp. pp. 39–46.

31. See Paul Lauter, "'Political Correctness" and the Attack on American Colleges', in Michael Bérubé and Cary Nelson, eds, *Higher Education under Fire: Politics, Economics, and the Crisis of the Humanities,* forthcoming from Routledge.

32. Paul Starr, 'Pummeling the Professors', review of Martin Anderson, *Impostors in the Temple* (New York: Simon and Schuster, 1992), *New York Times Book Review,* 9 August 1992, pp. 10–11.

33. Berman, 'Introduction: The Debate and Its Origins', *Debating P.C.,* p. 22. For a still less trustworthy account of the relation between the academic left and American political traditions, see John Patrick Diggins, *The Rise and Fall of the American Left* (New York: Norton, 1992), esp. pp. 277–306, 342–83. Diggins starts with a cartoonish portrait of the New Left's relation to academe in the 1960s and 1990s: 'with the ambition of yuppies, many veteran New Leftists turn out the same kind of dense scholarly verbiage as other professors in a competitive effort to climb the greasy pole of promotion' (p. 290). Since Diggins proceeds to complain, *sans* evidence, that this left has frozen out liberals, who now have 'about as much chance of getting hired on some faculty as Woody Allen of starting as point guard for the Knicks' (p. 291), it would seem that Diggins considers academe appropriate for liberals but not for leftists. Diggins concludes, in a surprise move, that 'PC has become a new loyalty test reminiscent of McCarthyism' (p. 297).

34. The hard right resists such characterizations of itself, but is finding it increasingly enjoyable – and politically profitable – to indulge its fascist fringe. For an amazingly forthright defense of anti-gay discrimination on the grounds that it prevents 'waverers' from becoming gay, see E. L. Pattullo's 'Straight Talk about Gays', *Commentary,* vol. 94, no. 6 (1992), pp. 21–4; for extremism in defense of extremism (and the moral superiority of Christians), see Pat Buchanan's 1993 speech to Pat Robertson's Christian Coalition, as reported by Thomas B. Edsall, 'Buchanan Warns GOP of Schism on Abortion: Christians Told Not to Abandon "Culture War"', *Washington Post,* 12 September 1993, p. A8.

35. Robert Alter, *The Pleasures of Reading in an Ideological Age* (New York: Simon and Schuster, 1989), p. 11.

36. David Lehman, *Signs of the Times: Deconstruction and the Fall of Paul de Man* (New York: Poseidon, 1991), p. 29.

37. Bruce Robbins, *Secular Vocations: Intellectuals, Professionalism, Culture* (London: Verso, 1993), pp. 5–6.

38. See Gregory Jay, 'The First Round of the Culture Wars', *Chronicle of Higher Education,* 26 February 1992, p. B2: 'Over the last 20 or 30 years, scholars in the humanities have used the traditional legitimation procedures of their profession – the refereed article, the scholarly monograph, the conference presentation, the tenure and promotion process, the classroom dialogue – to produce an astonishing body of new knowledge about how cultures treat those groups and individuals who are branded as *not* belonging to the dominant society. ... It is a testimony to the soundness of the legitimation procedures that such modes of criticism became fairly widespread and respectable, despite the fact that most tenured faculty members initially disagreed with them.'

PART I

PC and the Humanities

1

Discipline and Theory

Scorn the sort now growing up
All out of shape from toe to top.

W. B. Yeats

It's a beastly rough crowd I run with. No doubt about it, junior faculty are getting out of shape and out of hand. 'The grimmest and most orthodox partisans of "politically correct thinking",' writes Louis Menand in the *New Yorker,* 'are junior professors, most of whom are under forty and many of whom are under thirty.'[1] Mind you, this line doesn't come from George Will or Lynne Cheney or any of the usual suspects who routinely accuse us of being gleeful nihilists and/or humorless ideologues; it comes from the pen of a fellow English professor, a guy who's been one of the sharpest *critics* of Dinesh D'Souza, Roger Kimball and the rest of the purveyors of PC polemics. Even to the enemy of our enemies, it seems, we look something like a cross between Johnny Rotten and Cotton Mather: just take the Sex Pistols' political tact and respect for authority, toss in the Puritans' good cheer and sense of rhythm, and presto, you've got Rotten Mather, assistant professor of English, thirty years old and not to be trusted.

How did I let myself in for this? I'm not sure. Applying to graduate school in English, ten years ago, was as much the result of a process of elimination as of a positive decision: I had already worked in journalism and advertising during college, and didn't much like what I'd seen. Law paid notoriously well, but I knew from proofreading and word processing at one of the country's largest law firms that law generally isn't much fun to read or write. Besides, it was 1981, the lawyer glut was upon us, and the competition promised to be intense and nasty. I didn't think resignation or ambivalence would get me very far.

Among these options, then, I supposed that graduate school in English would surely be the most intellectually fulfilling way to spend my early twenties – and late twenties too, since most graduate students keep being graduate students for the better part of a decade. But I didn't know that then; actually, I didn't have any specific idea of what graduate school would entail or how long it would entail it for. All I knew for sure was that I would be taking a vow of poverty for an indeterminate period of time, and that it wouldn't make much sense to defray tuition by taking out more loans. In 1981, assistant professors were making about $17,000; those were the lucky ones, the ones who got jobs. And since I'd spent most of my undergraduate career learning to play drums, I didn't think I'd earned myself a realistic shot at fellowship support. All the schools I applied to agreed.

The way I figured it, either I would earn myself a fellowship later on or I'd leave the academic life after a year of graduate school, twenty-two years old and still less than $10,000 in debt. Attracted as I was to a life of teaching and learning, I had no silly idea that the professoriate (if and when I ever entered it) would look like an endless *Times Book Review* symposium, full of tweedy people sitting around the faculty lounge jawing about the Joyce centennial. I'd had the benefit of watching my father go from being a researcher and policy analyst to being a professor of education; consequently, I'd had the benefit of watching him fall under Abe Beame's budget axe in 1975, when New York City pruned itself of nonessential personnel like college teachers. So I knew fairly well what it was like to grade papers, sit on faculty committees, negotiate with deans, and look for academic employment at a moment's notice, but I knew comparatively little about the world of literary criticism and interpretive theory.

For most twenty-year-old aspiring textmongers, 'criticism' means things like book and movie reviews. My guess is that that's what 'criticism' means to much of the rest of the culture, too: even though both my parents have written plenty of book reviews, they had no idea what professional literary criticism looked like. Once when my father and I were discussing my plans, he told me I'd better begin thinking about a dissertation *now* (rather than, say, next week), and he asked me who I intended to do. I had not thought I'd have to *do* somebody, but I said 'Faulkner' anyway. My father shook his head. 'Faulkner's been done. Who else were you thinking of?'

My father, it turned out, imagined that the culmination of one's graduate work in literature would naturally be the writing of a critical biography. But what else would he think? He reads the general intellectual journals most often read by general intellectuals, chiefly the *Times Book Review* and the *New York Review of Books,* and like a lot of literate nonspecialists, he'd considered critical biographies the predominant scholarly form of criticism, more arduous and painstaking than movie and book reviews, necessary foundations for further 'interpretive' work. Even today, my parents can read the *Times Book Review* and come away believing that not much has changed in the small world of professional litcrit, as if critical biographies remain the only academic-press books of general interest to the literate public.

As for me, I knew even then that there was more to academic life than writing biographies; I assumed that the business of criticism was interpretation, and that critics spent their time arguing one interpretation over another – that is, when they weren't grading papers, sitting on faculty committees, negotiating with deans, or looking for academic employment. I had, for example, heard of Roland Barthes. But I had no clear idea that Barthes wasn't really a 'critic' like, say, Edmund Wilson or the *Times*'s Christopher Lehmann-Haupt, and that his *S/Z* wasn't an 'interpretation' of Balzac's short story 'Sarrasine', but a 'rewriting' (brilliant, maddening, and immensely fascinating) of realist narrative in terms of the plurality and reversability of its 'codes'. I read *S/Z* in graduate school, of course. But not right away: well into my third semester of graduate study in 1984, I was still wandering around randomly, churning out interpretations on demand. When one of my younger professors praised my reading of narrative ruptures of 'desire' in William Thackeray's *The History of Henry Esmond* by saying I had read the novel as a profoundly self-contradictory text without falling into the usual deconstructionist traps, I appeared at her office within twenty-four hours, wanting to know *what* deconstructionist traps I had avoided and how I'd avoided them. I felt rather like Chance the Gardener, and not for the last time.

What I was ignorant of, in short, was literary theory – the bodies of diverse, interdisciplinary writing that generate not interpretations but interpretive modes. Yes, I'd heard of things like Marxism, feminism, and psychoanalysis, but I hadn't yet seen them at work *as interpretive theories*. When it came to things like reception theory, structuralism, hermeneutics, reader-response criticism, new historicism and deconstruction, I was just about as much at sea as anyone.

Why rehearse my ignorance at such length today? I can think of three immediately pressing reasons.

First, fear of 'literary theory' continues to provoke the most hysterical and embarrassing outbursts, both in the profession and outside it. Peter Shaw, for instance – one of Lynne Cheney's appointees to the National Council on the Humanities – has actually written in the *Chronicle of Higher Education* that '"theory" of any kind is at present a code word for the politicization of literature.'[2] Nor is Shaw alone; public professions of such

Know-Nothing credos, whereby ignorance of theory represents itself as a form of moral probity, are getting more commonplace each passing day.

Second, the foes of theory tend to portray themselves either as lonely keepers of the flame beset by hordes of swarming thought police, or as friends of the common reading man who can't be bothered with impenetrable French neologisms or radical lesbian feminist extremist cant: 'we just love literature', they say, 'and we don't want to ruin it by thinking about it too much, like all those *theoreticians* with their *slide rules* and *hidden agendas,* who twist *our books* to fit *their schemes.*' (It happens, by the way, that many of these folks love literature only so long as it lets you believe in the characters or the images, and only if it doesn't get too silly or experimental. But this is a fine point.)

Third, graduate school in English seems to have a very bad effect on people who don't like theory. One prominent ex-graduate student left Yale and became managing editor of the *New Criterion,* where he's been sniping at academics ever since, most notably in *Tenured Radicals,* a book about tenured radicals; another picked up a Columbia Ph.D. but was scarred by a postdoc year of exposure to deconstruction at Cornell and has spent the past few years writing poetry and a book called *Signs of the Times,* wherein he's tried to bury 'deconstruction' once and for all. And every so often the profession of literary studies manages to alienate a few of its would-be apprentices, and students sign off, telling anyone who'll listen that they just love literature, but they can't put up with all that theoretical gobbledygook and poststructuralist shilly-shallying, not to mention the slide rules and the hidden agendas. Actually, considering how poorly most graduate students get paid for the amount of teaching they do, it's a wonder the humanities haven't produced many thousands of jaundiced, embittered ex-graduate students by now, 'theory' or no 'theory'.

What with reasons like these, it's now become something of an article of faith among the Lovers of Literature that today's graduate students don't read literature anymore – just a little Barthes here, a little Foucault there, some Derrida now and then, and a smattering of post-crypto-neo-Marxists: no Lawrence, no Dickens, no Spenser, no Pope. It's even been said that some of these brave new students don't care about literature at all. No, they don't care about fine writing of any kind – that's why they're reading that theory gunk instead.

Well, I went to graduate school in English in the 1980s; I swam, I hiked, I encountered interpretive theory for the first time. And so far as I can tell, I *still* love that literature, I think. But then again, I always did like the playful, labyrinthine stuff anyway, the kind of writing that's always already chock full o' theory, Beckett and Borges and Joyce and Gide and Sterne and Spenser. So maybe you shouldn't go by me.

Yet surely it's as anti-intellectual to embrace all of 'theory' indiscriminately as it is to dismiss it all out of hand. After all, the many varieties of contemporary literary theory have numerous opponents who are themselves contemporary theorists. As Henry Louis Gates has written, 'to become aware of contemporary theory is to become aware of one's presuppositions, those ideological and aesthetic assumptions which we bring to a text unwittingly.'[3] Similarly, to be engaged by 'theory' is largely to be engaged by conflict among theories, and that's one reason why debates in the humanities are so hard to keep track of. It's also why I find it difficult to think of my own theoretical training as some sort of conversion experience. I do, however, recall my most pronounced resistances: I was especially skeptical about psychoanalysis, reader-response criticism, and deconstruction. Psychoanalysis, because I was leery of its claims to interpretive certainty; reader-response, because I didn't think it was possible or useful to talk about 'what happens' when readers read; deconstruction, because I didn't care for the way it represented itself by insisting that it could not be represented, that it was always someplace else. Once I finally found my way around deconstruction's enumerations of 'conditions of impossibility', though, I found myself engrossed and energized by the ways it interrogates 'representation' – in narrative, in literary canons and in political or pedagogical practice.

Not everyone has the necessary patience (or time) for such things. Certainly, I can't deny that academic literary criticism and theory generally presume an intimate acquaintance with academic literary criticism and theory, and I can't deny either that theory's surface noise can be distracting, or worse; people who complain that theoretical work is opaque to 'general readers' aren't necessarily lazy readers. But then again, opacity is partly in the eye of the beholder. Many professors in the humanities these days are working on projects that bridge disciplinary boundaries, and it's quite ordinary to find 'English' professors who are conversant in branches of anthropology, sociology, history, philosophy, linguistics, psychology, law and political science. The same opaque 'critical jargon' that doesn't seem to speak to 'general readers', therefore, may also be the only critical language that can speak across a spectrum of disciplines to scholars in the social sciences as well as the humanities.

My first theoretical work wasn't all that interdisciplinary; it had to do with narratologists, people like Tzvetan Todorov, Gérard Genette and Roland Barthes. At the time this seemed a natural extension of my fascination with James Joyce: Joyce's narratives reproduce the minutiae of mental events, and Genette reproduces the minutiae of Proustian narrative; Joyce's texts flaunt their own artifice and their infinite capacity for formal elaboration, and Barthes' texts recast criticism as a creative enterprise

47

with infinite capacities for formal elaboration. Forbidding modernist narratives, whether Joyce's or anyone else's, simply *are* narratological. And though narratology can surely be one of the most arcane and jargon-ridden branches of interpretive theory, it did impress upon me, in meticulous and admirable detail, the conviction that storytelling is one of the most complex and significant forms of human behavior, too complex to be captured by catchall terms like 'point of view' or 'third-person narration'.

Still, not until I read Mikhail Bakhtin's *The Dialogic Imagination*, particularly the long final essay 'Discourse in the Novel', did I have any sense of what the larger purpose of careful narrative analysis might be. In Bakhtin's model, narrative isn't a question of how much a narrator 'knows' or who sees what from what 'point of view'. Bakhtin starts, instead, from the position that language is a profoundly social phenomenon, that our social lives are composed of myriad, competing dialects and idiolects, and that a language's or a word's meaning is radically dependent on its social context and social use – not on a presumedly straightforward relation between 'words' and 'reality'. From this position, it follows for Bakhtin that the novel is the most capacious, the most fluid of literary genres, because it can represent so many different subgenres and social idiolects, dramatizing their conflicts and their concordances. Novels, according to Bakhtin, aren't privileged sites of narrative 'realism' so much as language labs in which various 'sociolinguistic points of view' get stirred together into a polyphonic chorus that he calls 'heteroglossia'.

Bakhtin's work was positively liberating for me, in two important ways: first, because he defined the novel – a genre notoriously resistant to 'definition' – not in terms of the elements all novels have in common (for there are no such common elements), but in terms of the novel's linguistic voraciousness, its very willingness to 'raid' other, more stable genres in the process of composing new and complex multigeneric molecules. This crucial insight that 'definition' need not hinge on the assertion of a form's 'essential' characteristics is what led me, eventually, to read Ludwig Wittgenstein's *Philosophical Investigations,* and to espouse the Wittgensteinian position that genera of objects – novels, games, nations, races, genders, classes, tables, chairs – are constituted by 'family resemblances' rather than by their common 'essences'. Wittgenstein's analogy is this: think of a cord of many overlapping fibers in which no one fiber runs the whole length of the cord. Now think of objects many of which have a number of significant features in common, but not all of which possess all the 'significant features' under discussion. That's more or less what 'family resemblances' look like in Wittgenstein's family.

My second Bakhtinian liberation was this: Bakhtin's emphasis on narrative *discourse* (as distinct from narrative epistemology) manages to combine narratology's emphasis on narrative minutiae with a sophisticated account of the social contexts in which different forms of language operate. According to Bakhtin, then, the same word – oh, let's take a good big one, like 'liberty' – gets rearticulated, refashioned and redefined by diverse social groups, and these groups' struggles over the meaning of words (think of 'peace through strength') constitute the social life of narrative forms. This position, too, I wound up glossing with the help of Wittgenstein, who maintains that 'the meaning of a word is its use in the language'. Sounds commonsensical enough – until you realize how thoroughly anti-Platonic a position it is, how much it goes against our sense that words *refer to* something. But what do words like 'however' and 'actually' refer to? And why do we think we can look up words' meanings on a reference-table, absent the social context in which they are used? As for words like 'table', which are, as we know, less subject to social contestation than words like 'terrorist', their meaning, too, resides in their use in the language, not in any linguistic essence; it's just that most people tend not to see any need to argue about their use.

In a word, then, upon reading Bakhtin and Wittgenstein I became an anti-essentialist, and to this day, sure enough, there's a little anti-essentialism in everything I do. In my next close encounter of the mid 1980s, I came up against Thomas Kuhn's *The Structure of Scientific Revolutions,* and took a seminar on Martin Heidegger with Richard Rorty. From that point on I've been an 'anti-foundationalist' as well. Thanks to Kuhn's refusal to believe that science 'progresses' in some linear, incremental way, and Rorty's refusal to believe that philosophy is the 'foundation' of human knowledge, I've come to believe and argue that our social practices and identities are 'contingent' rather than 'grounded' – that there are no final, universal, transhistorical standards for the production or value of human knowledge and understanding.

It's been a mild shock to me to discover how disturbing this position is to many traditionalists in the humanities. Scientists, by contrast, seem largely untroubled by it. Kuhn himself draws most of his examples from the 'foundational' sciences of chemistry and physics, both of which have taken stock of Kuhn's account of 'normal science' and have kept right on conducting normal science as Kuhn understands it. In the fall of 1991, I presented the case for anti-foundationalism at an interdisciplinary conference at which I was asked to speak about 'new directions in knowledge' in my field. I talked mostly about the effects of 'theory' on the way we do literary history, and along the way I invoked the names of Kuhn and Wittgenstein, and Michel Foucault, too. To my surprise, I was met with questions from physicists and psychologists who demanded to know what was so 'new' about the propositions that humans perceive things through interpretive paradigms and that human knowledge, like all things human, is historically conditioned and socially constructed. Why, I was asked, would anyone disagree with such things? I had to admit I didn't really know: it all made sense to *me,* once I became acquainted with the relevant arguments. It seems, I said, that physicists and mathematicians are unthreatened by ideas like 'indeterminacy', but that some of us in the humanities cannot contemplate the notion that meaning is indeterminate without declaring that the sky is falling; and many cognitive psychologists work well with the assumption that all perception is a form of interpretation, whereas in some 'traditionalist' circles, you still can't say such a thing about literary texts without being accused of some horrid thing like moral relativism.

Stanley Fish, for example, has gotten a good deal of grief for arguing that 'there is no such thing as intrinsic merit'.[4] Fish is adept at concocting such memorable, provocative formulae, and accordingly, he's been subjected to the kind of media treatment usually reserved for Afrocentrists and day-care Satanists. In this case, however, he's merely saying that nothing just *has* merit in and of itself – things have only the merit that we ascribe to them. People like Dinesh D'Souza have claimed that Fish's position undermines all possibility for ethical judgment; but my guess is that stamp collectors, spin doctors, stockbrokers, writers, and other working folk won't be too surprised or upset by the suggestion that 'merit' and 'value' are human inventions.

In other words, anti-foundationalism is not a relativism; it doesn't say that every interpretation, every historical epoch, every value system or every form of government is 'equal'. On the contrary, it says we don't have access to the kind of historical omniscience that would enable us to equalize or rank everything in the first place. We can look back and say we're grateful that we now conduct trials by jury instead of trials by ordeal, but we shouldn't conclude therefrom that our current beliefs are the culmination and fulfillment of all human history. As Kuhn concludes, we may have evolved away from certain beliefs and practices (like geocentrism or witch burning), but we're not necessarily evolving *toward* anything in particular; there's no 'goal' to human history, no secure and self-evident criterion for the human understanding of notions like gravity, matter, liberty or justice. Even when it comes to things that pre-exist humans, like gravity and matter, the point remains that humans in every epoch have interrogated those things as they knew best: Aristotle's or Thales' understanding of 'matter' isn't as comprehensive as ours, but it isn't quantifiably 'less scientific', either. It proceeded from utterly different assumptions about what science is, assumptions that themselves were part of a worldview every bit as complete and internally coherent as our own (though not as good, in retrospect, at understanding the things it did not have the means to conceive of, like heat transfer or unstable isotopes).

Does anti-foundationalism imply that 'the history of Western civilization' (whatever that phrase means to you) is nothing more than a series of choices, and not the slow triumphant march of eternal, universal virtues such as democracy and individualism? Yep, it sure does. It implies that *all* histories, literary histories too, are profoundly up for grabs and always have been, having been made by humans in social contexts, making human and social choices. It insists that there's no sense in which all of Western culture was always somehow slouching from the *agora* in Athens (or from the banks of the Nile or the Tigris) toward the United States, no sense in which our current forms of life were foreordained by heavenly or historical forces. But foundationalism makes strange bedfellows, as they say, and it's probably fitting, though of course not inevitable, that today's strongest 'foundationalists' would be religious fundamentalists, unreconstructed Brezhnev-era Marxists, right-wing libertarians and traditionalists in the humanities.

Bakhtin, Wittgenstein and Kuhn weren't the last writers to influence the way I think about language, life, and literature, but they've more or less set the terms on which I now read theorists who differ from them. The little Foucault I know, for instance, is the Foucault of *The Archaeology of Knowledge,* who examines what he calls 'discursive formations' – involving the hierarchies within which different sorts of knowledge are ordered, by the various institutional sites within which discursive 'authority' has historically been constructed. Or, reading Derrida by way of Wittgenstein, I'm engaged most by things like 'Signature Event Context', in which Derrida takes on speech-act theorist J. L. Austin, whose theory of 'performative utterances' is itself a powerful exception to most Western thinking about language. Some sentences, says Austin, don't 'describe' things at all; they perform them. (Think of 'I now pronounce you husband and wife'.) And, in their repeatability (or 'iterability'), they demonstrate vividly, for Derrida, how *all* utterances are radically dependent on contexts: thus, 'meaning' is never synonymous with or reducible to 'intention'. To make this point to undergraduates, ask them how they know what stop signs 'mean'. Then ask what kinds of 'intention' we normally assume to be indispensable to 'meaning', and what kinds of 'intention' we normally assume are irrelevant to it. Then ask when and why we assume these things about stop signs, poems, or signatures. When you've done all this, you've earned your keep, and you can go collect your paycheck – whether or not its signatory 'intended' to pay you.[5]

If I've presented it right, deconstruction usually gets my students to see that meanings always have to be made and remade. But sometimes, people seem drawn to it because they think it has an air of Left Bank radical chic, the way existentialism did for the goateed coffee-house jazz aficionados of another generation. I know this drives some critics crazy, but most of the time the only people who really get upset about intellectual poseurs are themselves intellectual poseurs; they apparently resent the competition. As far as I can see, deconstruction's now-fading 'hipness' has had two generally deleterious side effects. One is that it's encouraged some sloppy talk about the 'free play' of language, where 'free play' has a meaning more often associated with unstructured recreation in day-care centers than with the writings of Derrida. Another is that deconstruction's arrival seems to be experienced by some of my students as a series of prohibitions: you can't say 'intend', you have to say 'defer/differ'; you can't say 'book', you must say 'text'; and, of course, you can't respond to the roll call by saying 'present' lest your teacher put you under erasure. Perhaps, too, as David Lehman and others have charged, deconstruction has fostered a spirit of skepticism in the academy. But that in itself is not necessarily a bad thing. I always thought it was OK for universities to encourage skepticism – that is, to teach students to think critically and to interrogate received ideas, particularly the ideas they've received without knowing they'd accepted a delivery.

When deconstruction itself becomes a received idea, then it too needs to be questioned in its turn; otherwise, you get the phenomenon in which people casually assume that deconstruction has made obsolete all human thought before 1966, as if everyone from Plato to your mother was benighted enough to believe in the unified self and the transparency of language, and therefore they don't need to be dealt with anymore. About your mother I won't presume, but it's a mistake to think that way about even the most egregious logocentrist, who may be worth reading despite his regrettable allegiance to the metaphysics of presence. Normally, though, I'm not terribly worried about deconstruction's effects on my students. At bottom, it's made them realize, in sometimes exactingly rigorous ways, that *what* a piece of writing 'says' is inseparable from *how* it says it. I think that's something every English major and graduate student needs to learn, the sooner the better. Now if only we could convince journalists, doctors, political scientists, and chemists of the same thing. Then maybe we'd be getting somewhere.

The more practiced you get at 'doing' theory, the more theory informs your practice. By the spring of 1986, I had some practical matters on my mind. In April, my wife, Janet Lyon, had our first child, Nicholas; and because Janet was also a graduate student – worse yet, a graduate student about to take her Ph.D. qualifying exams – I wound up being a full-time house-husband. However broadly sympathetic I'd been to feminism up to that point, it really wasn't until I cared for an infant that I began to see what feminism had to do with the smallest details of my daily life. (I'm always amused at the claim that feminism is bad for the family; I find it hard to believe my family would be better off if I left all the material childcare to Janet, contenting myself with the dispensation of money, justice and sound moral observations.) I thought I knew something about the worlds of women and children – but as Bakhtin would say, I had to hear the sound, the language of that world before it could be my world too. In daytime TV, in the ads in *Parents* magazine, in the 'children's' aisles of major supermarkets, the gendering of childcare became palpable to me, and not because I was especially sensitive; only because I was a graduate student, and didn't have a day job – and, most of all, I was the wrong gender. No one knows or cares what lousy brand of peanut butter choosy fathers choose.

I'm not sure when it was, precisely, that I began to see 'gendering' everywhere I looked. Maybe it was the day I had to take my four-month-old from the supermarket to the 'home improvement center' (lumber yard) and realized that the latter had shopping carts with no child seats. Or maybe it was the day I realized that I wasn't one of the men I saw in floor cleaner ads, because unlike them I *knew* the floor wasn't wet – just shiny, thanks to my application of amazing Miracle Wax. No matter. What matters to me now is that I learned to read supermarkets, childcare, and advertising anew, and I didn't (and don't) see any substantive difference between my interpretations of such 'social texts' and my interpretations of 'literary' texts. On the contrary, the analytical tools I'd honed in the academy sharpened and gave point to my reading of the semiotics of supermarkets – and vice versa.

I don't mean to suggest that I suddenly became Feminist Man because my working wife had to take a test and left me with the kid. For that matter, I don't consider feminism a chart that men can consult in order to find out how feminist they were today. Personally, I'm most at home with poststructuralist feminisms that contest the very idea of 'Woman' while acknowledging that the category 'Woman' is constitutive of patriarchy (that is, that patriarchy will oppress women as a category, regardless of the internal differences among women as social subjects). I am least at home with some feminists' sense that male feminism is a form of cross-dressing, ventriloquism, impersonation – or, at worst, a false embrace, a co-optive enterprise that seeks to establish what media theorist Tania Modleski calls 'feminism without women'. I tend to believe, instead, that male feminism is what happens when feminism begins to persuade non-feminists of the urgency and substance of its ethical claims. Perhaps predictably, I take most to feminisms that interrogate all forms of gendering, all manifestations of differences between and within categories of subjectivity and sexuality. But what else would you expect from a fledgling Wittgensteinian with an infant on his arm?

The week before Nicholas was born, I had to come up with a presentation in my graduate seminar in the American long poem – a presentation on Melvin Tolson's magnum opus, *Harlem Gallery: Book I, The Curator,* a poem published a year before Tolson's death in 1966. The poem *is* magnum: 170 pages long, and much of it's about as dense and clotted as anything you'd expect to see from Ezra Pound or Hart Crane. I didn't understand *Harlem Gallery* then, and I didn't understand it six or eight months later, either, what with all that daytime TV monopolizing my interpretive frequencies. But I was flabbergasted by it nonetheless, and flabbergasted that no one I knew, save for Charles Rowell and Raymond Nelson among the Virginia faculty, had ever heard of it; flabbergasted to find no mention of Tolson whatsoever in literary histories, in 'American' anthologies, in collections on modernism this and modernism that. (He can, however, be found in the comprehensive African American anthology – a genre that flourished from 1965 to 1975 and has been moribund ever since.) I kept at the poem, and the poem continued to unknot itself and, almost before I knew it, I was consumed not only by the poem and its enigmatic author, but by the question of how all literary works are read, understood, misunderstood, neglected, canonized and culturally transmitted.

Just as it took Nicholas to bring feminism home to me, it took Melvin Tolson, at last, to make 'canonicity' and 'neglect' visible to me. And between feminism and Tolson, I began to take more seriously revisionists' claims that the profession of English literature had been working for some time with a severely impoverished idea of its potential materials for study. I had been mildly suspicious of 'canons' as an undergraduate, but only in the sense that I'd wondered vaguely about all the stuff one never reads or hears of in survey courses. Each survey came to me with the implicit message that the selection process was done with, the works on the syllabus had been weighed in time's scales and found to be great, and the only business left at hand was for us to discover more and more ways in which these great works were indeed great works, great enough to be texts in core curricula. In fact, having met my 'distribution' and 'coverage' requirements a few times over, in college and in graduate school, I'd thought I was as cored as they come. Now here I was confronted with Tolson and, simultaneously, with the challenge of composing my own 'canon', in the form of readings for my orals in twentieth-century literature (all of it). My preliminary conclusion, from which I have not yet backed off, is that when we talk about 'periods' in literary history, we confront the vastest reaches of our ignorance. All I'd been taught about modernism, it seemed – and all I'd been taught about 'American literature' – rested on the claims of about a dozen or so 'representative' texts, and I had taken their 'representativity' more or less for granted. Now I would have to go back over all the literary history that wasn't in my synoptic literary histories, and this time, I'd start with African American poetry and fiction.

I wound up writing a somewhat long dissertation, half on Tolson and his neglect, half on the academic reception of the work of Thomas Pynchon, and over the course of five years the thing became my first book, *Marginal Forces/Cultural Centers*. The purpose of the study wasn't to find putatively 'hidden' biases in canon formation by juxtaposing one neglected black poet and one newly canonical white novelist. Instead, I wanted to examine the terms under which disparately 'marginal' writers become available for institutional attention, and the ways 'gatekeeping' literary critics decide that certain writers aren't worth our further institutional attention. I found it quite interesting that Tolson went to extraordinary lengths to get the attention of the conservative white literati of his time (such as Allen Tate), and that Pynchon is so averse to publicity and criticism as to prohibit his publisher from publishing books about his work. But I found it much more interesting to examine what Tolson and Pynchon suggest to academic literary critics about their own roles as agents of cultural reproduction.

To many prominent Pynchon critics, academic literary criticism appears to be a gravely suspect enterprise, the central means whereby the 'avant-garde' is appropriated and co-opted into the mainstream; to the few Tolson critics in the country, academic criticism seems to be the guarantor of last resort, the only potential audience for otherwise 'neglected' writers, and the only potential economic means for keeping marginal writers in print. Needless to say, Tolson and Pynchon gave me different takes on 'race' in recent American literature, and differing perspectives on what constitutes academic 'co-optation'. The further along I got, the more it became evident to me that canonicity and neglect were themselves historically specific phenomena involving variable margins and centers. It's been said that writing reception history modifies or undermines 'traditional' literary history, and to a large extent that's so; but writing a history of *neglect* forced me to ask what kind of reading practices we consider to be part of a text's 'reception' in the first place.

My engagement with Melvin Tolson, then, served in part to lead me to re-examine my chosen profession, its politics, its social functions, its canons, and its relation to the nonacademic literary culture around it. And though I came up with an almost unteachable book – I can't imagine a seminar devoted exclusively to Tolson, Pynchon and the practices of professional literary criticism – I've managed to spin the book into a variety of courses. (Thankfully, I teach in a department that gives me great latitude in course design and teaching assignments.) A graduate seminar on reception theory; a course in twentieth-century African American narrative; an 'honors' course in postmodernism, critical theory, and recent American fiction; and a course I'm winding up as I write, a graduate seminar on recent African American literature and literary theory.

In this seminar we've gone from the late Addison Gayle's 1971 anthology, *The Black Aesthetic,* to poststructuralists such as Houston Baker and Hazel Carby, by way of poets and novelists like Michael Harper, Audre Lorde, Toni Morrison and Trey Ellis. The funny thing is, though, fourteen of my fifteen students are white, and you can bet that whiteness (theirs and their instructor's) has been among our topics of interrogation in the past few months. This is all to the good in many ways, since most white Americans don't often see themselves as having the attribute of 'race', any more than most men see themselves as being 'gendered': gender and race are usually O.P.P., other people's problems (and therefore, say the traditionalists, 'divisive' things to talk about). But it makes my white students anxious all the same, especially when they wonder about whether they have the requisite cultural purchase on African American literature and culture. In the past few decades, African American literature has not lacked brilliant white critics – Kimberly Benston, Barbara Johnson, Eric Lott and Robert Hemenway, to name a few. Regardless of the scope of one's brilliance, however, one can't very well be a white critic of African American literature without reflecting on the political, historical and institutional conditions of one's existence, and the sources of one's cultural 'authority'. That my own course is predicated explicitly on the aftermath of the Civil Rights Movement makes my imperative to institutional self-scrutiny all the more urgent in this regard, since one of the legacies of the Movement was the creation of courses in African American literature in 'mainstream' American universities, like Illinois.

To put this another way, I might point out how dangerous it is for white folks to assume that African American literature is the sole province of African American critics. For one thing, this assumption does no favors to the African American critic who wants to specialize in Romanticism. For another thing, even black African Americanists don't have unmediated access to African American texts simply because they're black; my access to such texts is thoroughly mediated too, but here we're talking about differences of degree and not differences in kind. Well-meaning white critics may claim not to 'know enough' about 'the black experience' to teach

African American stuff, but I know full well that I never allowed my distance from turn-of-the-century Irish culture to prevent me from writing about Joyce and Yeats. My students, reflecting on their own institutional conditions daily if not hourly, ask whether they can 'speak for' African American writers and theorists. I tell them that if they become academic critics they'll be 'speaking for' writers and texts whether they want to or not. Those writers and texts won't always be flaunting their skin colors for all to see, and as critics they'll be speaking for them anyway. Besides, one does not inquire about 'race' only when one is teaching a 'nonwhite' text.

Still, it's impossible to broach this discussion without noting the dearth of African American graduate students in literary study. Ninety years ago, in *The Souls of Black Folk*, W. E. B. Du Bois replied to Booker T. Washington's disparagement of liberal arts education in black colleges by arguing that the supply of black teachers *of any kind* would rely on the presence of black Americans in nonvocational higher education. More generally, Du Bois insisted that the cultural reproduction of African American literature and history in schools would depend on the creation and maintenance of a professional class of African American intellectuals; white American academics, by Du Bois's lights, couldn't be trusted with doing the job all by themselves, out of the goodness of their hearts. We've known for some time now that Du Bois was entirely right on this score, and what few black academics this country produced were (like Du Bois himself, despite his degree from Harvard) hired exclusively at small black colleges, or authorized to speak only about 'black' issues. Given this legacy of apartheid in our institutional history, then, critics like myself can't, in good conscience, keep their hands off the cultural reproduction of African American literature in the name of ethnic and ethical purity.

I have had undergraduates of varying skin tones who've told me they were surprised (and suspicious) that their African American narrative class would be taught by me. To such students I usually offer as much of a three-part answer as they want to hear: I acknowledge that (1) the course will no doubt be 'different' with me than it would with a black instructor, but that (2) my whiteness is not the only thing I bring into the classroom (the course will also be 'different' because I'm male, married with two kids, a New Yorker for my first twenty years, and a card-carrying anti-essentialist to boot), and, finally, that (3) I have to try to keep points (1) and (2) from degenerating into glibness by listening to African American writers who have a few cautionary words for white anti-essentialists: as Toni Morrison puts it, 'the people who invented the hierarchy of "race" when it was convenient for them ought not to be the ones to explain it away, now that it does not suit their purposes for it to exist.'[6]

Meaning, of course, that deconstruction, even the deconstruction of 'race', can paradoxically work to further white male privilege too. About that possibility I think it's best to be theoretical – which is to say, in my language, it's best to be *explicit.*

In ten years I've had a lot done to me. I've been gendered, I've been racinated, I've become grim and orthodox, I've turned thirty and, worst of all, I've been disciplined by theory again and again, and it keeps showing me my interpretive presuppositions, making me stay after class and write fifty times on the board, 'I will not take my interpretive presuppositions for granted.' In one way I haven't changed from the person I was ten years ago: I still think the business of criticism is interpretation. I just no longer believe that interpretive criticism is transparent, or that it sees the world steadily and sees it whole. Nor is interpretation properly 'supplementary' to its object, like reader's guides and *Cliff Notes.* I believe instead that interpretation is always partial, that it never 'fills up' its object, and that its 'partiality' needs to be interpreted in its turn. For literary criticism, too, is written, just like the writing that occasions its writing, and there can be no final writing that clarifies everything, no final reading that obviates all further reading. I've heard tell that this is precisely the kind of thing literary critics say to keep themselves in business, but I hold fast nonetheless to the conviction that reading, writing, and interpretation are historical processes, and that historical processes do not end until history does. And if 'theory' does nothing more – or less – than make explicit such interpretive variables as races, genders, and historical processes, well, then, it's not just a discipline I can live with; it's something I can no longer do without.

Notes

1. Louis Menand, 'Illiberalisms', review of Dinesh D'Souza, *Illiberal Education, New Yorker,* 20 May 1991, p. 103.

2. Peter Shaw, 'The MLA Is Misleading the Public', *Chronicle of Higher Education,* 27 November 1991, p. B3.

3. Henry Louis Gates, '"What's Love Got to Do with It?": Critical Theory, Integrity, and the Black Idiom', *New Literary History,* vol. 18, no. 2 (1987), p. 351.

4. Stanley Fish, 'No Bias, No Merit: The Case Against Blind Submission', *PMLA,* vol. 103, no. 5 (1988), p. 739.

5. For an extremely helpful elaboration of this series of points on deconstruction and 'iterability', see Jonathan Culler, *On Deconstruction: Theory and Criticism after Structuralism* (Ithaca, N.Y.: Cornell University Press, 1982), pp. 110–34. For equally helpful critiques of Derrida's slippages and weak points, see John Searle, 'Reiterating the Differences: A Reply to Derrida', *Glyph,* no. 1 (1977), pp. 198–208; Robert Scholes, *Protocols of Reading* (New Haven, Conn.: Yale University Press, 1989), pp. 59–69.

6. Toni Morrison, 'Unspeakable Things Unspoken: The Afro-American Presence in American Literature', *Michigan Quarterly Review,* no. 28 (1989), p. 3.

2

Winning Hearts and Minds

In the past five years, anti-academic invective has become a literary genre of its own, as Grub Street and Wall Street vie with each other to devise ever more odious metaphors and analogues for English professors. As late as 1988, we could still be caricatured as ineffectual, pointy-headed ectomorphs in bow ties or buns, and the worst we heard was that most people considered us the Grammar Police. But once *Newsweek* dubbed us the Thought Police, our ineffectual days were over; ever since George Will's *Newsweek* column of 22 April 1991 decided the matter, we have been a greater threat to this country than Saddam Hussein – and, therefore, a greater threat than Hitler as well.[1]

Yet however frustrating (and occasionally comic) it may be that so many academic critics and theorists have recently reentered the public sphere solely to contest the New Right's egregious misrepresentations of their work, we cannot claim that this development caught us entirely by surprise. The number of responsible generalist forums for recent academic work has been steadily dwindling for about a quarter-century – roughly the same period of time during which American criticism has engaged feminism, gay and lesbian activism, African American studies and varieties of Continental literary theory. One after another, *Partisan Review,* the *American Scholar,* the *New Republic* and, most emphatically, the *New York Review of Books* have almost ceased to cover academic developments postdating Stonewall, Black Power, *Sexual Politics,* and *S/Z* – or, worse, have undertaken series after series of bitter attacks on them.[2] In their more serious moments, though, generalist critics have themselves lodged some stinging charges concerning the distribution and accessibility of academic criticism.[3] Few academic critics are unfamiliar with the complaint that they serve an audience made up exclusively of other academic critics. And since this is a complaint whose frequency has not been checked even by the profession's recent attempts to defend, explain, and historicize the professionalization of literary study, we may need to reconsider what our 'professionalization' means outside the institutional context of our work.[4]

It will be objected, no doubt, that academic theorists have been reconsidering professionalism for some time now, and that the problem is that our attackers are simply and willfully ignorant of the extent of our professional conversations and conflicts over the very fact of our professionalization.[5] I mention this objection here largely because I agree with it. But when it comes to explaining why 'general' and 'professional' journals are so antagonistic toward each other, this argument has been less than convincing. In Jonathan Culler's account, for instance, the *New York Review*'s philistinism is no one's loss but theirs; though the *Review*'s history is one of 'rejecting sympathetic reviews of theoretical criticism, avoiding participation even in feminist theory and criticism', Culler concludes that

> when the *New York Review* joined *Time* and *Newsweek* in middle-brow opposition [to academic criticism and theory], it seemed to succeed only in depriving itself of influence in the domain of contemporary criticism and revealing to what extent criticism had become a university enterprise, part of the functioning of what had arguably become the most important American institution.[6]

Can we can read these words today, after the *Review*'s *amicus* reviews of Roger Kimball's *Tenured Radicals* and Dinesh D'Souza's *Illiberal Education*, without wishing they were true?[7] If only the *NYRB* *were* without influence among what remains of American intellectual life, perhaps academic criticism and theory would have fewer generalist enemies than it now does. I cite Jonathan Culler here because his discussion of literary criticism's academicization overlaps briefly with Russell Jacoby's *The Last Intellectuals*, whose report on the *NYRB* finds it guilty of related charges. Speaking of the journal as the New York intellectuals' 'closed shop', Jacoby is at his fiercest:

> *The New York Review* reveals a deplorable record. It never nurtured or heeded younger American intellectuals. For a quarter century it withdrew from the cultural bank without making any investments. Today the operation must rely on imported intellectual capital, mainly from England. ... Conservative journals, such as *The New Criterion* and *Commentary*, assiduously, and wisely, cultivate younger writers.[8]

Critiques of Jacoby's treatment of the New York intellectuals seem to have discounted his outrage at their self-aggrandisement, their false liberalism, and their eventual impoverishment of American general-intellectual life.[9] Yet here the similarities between Jacoby and Culler end, for, as many readers have noted, Jacoby's book tends not to blame generalist journals for the decline of the public intellectual; the passage above is something of an anomaly in *The Last Intellectuals*. On the contrary, Jacoby considers academic criticism antithetical to public criticism precisely insofar as it is academic.[10] Unlike many of the academy's detractors, Jacoby does not stop at construing all academic criticism to be jargon-ridden and deliberately obscure; he constructs a slippery slope of increasing academic irrelevance that starts with the dissertation, a requirement that allegedly 'branded [the] intellectual souls' of American postwar intellectuals (p. 18). Dissertations, according to Jacoby, inaugurate an inexorable process of intellectual self-absorption and hermetic professionalism, and once the postwar gang finished their trials by dissertation, 'even if they wished, and frequently they did not, the younger intellectuals could not free themselves from this past' (p. 18).

Although I had moments between 1987 and 1992 in which I too thought of my dissertation as a tar pit from which it was impossible to escape, I have managed nonetheless, at whatever cost to my intellectual soul, to try to talk regular. But if it will not do to follow Jacoby's determinist exacerbation of what Stanley Fish calls our 'self-loathing', neither is it possible for us merely to follow Culler in taking the *New York Review* as the emblem of the generalist forum gone bad, dismissing it on the grounds that *it* (and not academe) is self-absorbed and hermetically sealed. The difficulties we now face in trying to recapture some segments of the literary public sphere are not attributable solely to our 'jargon', to our professionalization, or to our disconnection from once-friendly nonacademic journals. Thanks to the volume, frequency and amplitude of the right's venomous attacks, we're now faced with trying to undo the kind of anti-intellectualism and deliberate obfuscation we had once considered a minor annoyance – indiscriminate condemnation by journalists, neoconservatives and the 'liberal' cultural right, for whom ignorance of contemporary theory is a badge of pride, a guarantee of ethical and intellectual purity. And since it may seem to many of us that these attacks are as unfathomable as they are unscrupulous and uninformed, I will try to set out below a brief sketch of their forerunners.

Appropriately enough in these postmodern times, the New New Right's recent attacks are more or less a pastiche of the past three decades of reactionary politics on both the cultural and economic fronts. It is no secret that the contemporary right has been animated largely by the desire to eradicate the 1960s from our legal and cultural history; what has been less clear is how much the contemporary circus of 'political correctness' itself depends on the right's 1960s legacy.

The early consensus among Irving Kristol, Daniel Bell, William Buckley, Hilton Kramer, Sidney Hook and the like was that the 1960s were a decade of attacks on rationality, capitalism, Western culture, and the intellectual life itself – since the fourth of these obviously depends for its existence on the first three, all of which are, in turn, virtually synonymous for the libertarian right. As Irving Kristol wrote in the fall 1970 'Capitalism Today' issue of his personal soapbox, *The Public Interest*, the New Left was therefore biting the hands that had promised to feed it:

> When we lack the will to see things as they really are, there is nothing so mystifying as the obvious. This is the case, I think, with the new upsurge of radicalism that is now shaking much of Western society to its foundations. ... Our youthful rebels are anything but inarticulate; and though they utter a great deal of nonsense, the import of what they are saying is clear enough. What they are saying is that they dislike – to put it mildly – the liberal, individualist, capitalist civilization that stands ready to receive them as citizens.[11]

It is no accident that this sounds familiar; many of the people now attacking the latest upsurge of West-shaking radicalism first cut their intellectual teeth in the 1960s, and have not updated their conceptions of their opponents since. Kristol himself is a central figure here. Toward the end of the article that I've just quoted, Kristol writes, 'with every passing year, public discourse becomes sillier and more petulant, while human emotions become, apparently, more ungovernable' (p. 13). Since 1970, however, Kristol has evidently decided to stop reporting passively on the decline of serious public discourse and, instead, to start accelerating it. In 1978 he founded the Institute for Educational Affairs (IEA), thus launching a fleet of neoconservative groupthinkers with penchants for Beltway-brand acronyms and grandiloquent titles; also in 1978, William Simon, former secretary of the treasury, assumed leadership of the Olin Foundation, which has since become one of the biggest funding sources for conservative academe. In 1980, Kristol's IEA started funding a new brand of aggressively conservative campus magazines, dedicated to the revival of traditional conservative values such as racism, misogyny, red-baiting and gay-bashing. In 1982, Hilton Kramer's *New Criterion* was founded with the help of office space and funding provided by the Olin; in 1990–91 the journal received $205,000 from the Olin (whereas Kristol himself received a mere $124,000).[12] As Ellen Messer-Davidow and Sara Diamond have shown, the cultural right has slowly crafted, over the past fifteen years, a truly impressive 'alternative' credentializing system – including grants, endowed chairs, seed money for new journals and quasi-academic college 'programs' funded by and dedicated to the agendas of ultraconservative foundations – designed to license intellectuals to intervene in cultural politics and practical policy issues without submitting those intellectuals to the demanding peer review mechanisms of the academy.[13] Of course, since the hard right considers the academy a bastion of totalitarian liberalism, it is only proper that they attempt an end run around academe's legitimate credentializing procedures, the better to conduct their 'war of position' by any other means at their disposal. But the point should be clear. Although left academe appeared to have been hit out of nowhere by a flurry of attacks in 1990–91, the truth is that the right's public-relations offensive has been years in the making. Indeed, when Patrick Buchanan called for a 'cultural war' at the 1992 Republican national convention, left academics should have wondered what all the hullabaloo was about, since they'd been the objects of cultural war for fifteen years by that point. And, to hark back to the 1960s once more, we should know by now that undeclared wars are no less violent or nasty than wars that proceed through the proper channels of winning public consent.

Among campus faculties, the academic right did not try to present itself as the moderate center before the late 1980s, devoting its resources instead to raising corporate funds and rallying the troops. Then, in 1986 *Commentary* published 'The Tenured Left', an article by Stephen Balch and Herbert London, co-founders of the National Association of Scholars, and the battle was joined in earnest. It was not long after the article was published, in fact, that Balch and London underwent their sea-change: up to that point they had been the leaders of the Coalition for Campus Democracy – the academic wing of the Committee for the Free World, founded by Kristol, Simon, Midge Decter and Elliott Abrams, which was primarily interested in rigging elections and funding death squads in Central America. The CCD, apparently, remained tainted by its connections to that kind of cryptofascism masquerading as 'democracy', and consequently reorganized itself in 1987 as the tonier-sounding National Association of Scholars. It has since enjoyed far greater success at capturing the center than the CCD – or, for that matter, Abrams or Decter either. Careful perusal of 'The Tenured Left', therefore, will amply repay any contemporary reader curious about the rise to public prominence of academe's extreme right, for it announces the platform on which the right has since sought to mount its 'resistance' campaign: to attack by pretending to be under siege.

The article opens by complaining that university administrations and organizations have criticized Reed Irvine's Accuracy in Academia (AIA) but not the divestiture movement, as if demonstrations against university investments in South Africa were a threat to academic freedom on the

order of the AIA, which, as another failed forerunner of the NAS, explicitly sought out student 'informants' to report liberal faculty to a national
conservative network capable of agitating for their removal. Balch and
London, seeking the party to blame for universities' tolerance of divest-
ment rallies, finger radical faculty members as the culprits, noting that
'whereas in the 1960s only a handful of courses in Marxist philosophy
were being taught, today there are well over 400 such courses offered on
American campuses.'[14] Four hundred isn't bad for a start, but even if those
courses were distributed evenly among four hundred campuses, they
would not strike fear into anyone but the most timorous of conservatives,
since there are well over three thousand colleges in the United States.
Moreover, one would expect capitalist countries to *want* to study Marxism,
if only to know their enemy better; surely a better understanding of our
national enemies would have served us well in our struggle to win the
hearts and minds of the Vietnamese in the 1950s and 1960s. But as Balch
and London point out, numbers are deceiving, since the real enemy is
academic freedom itself. 'What goes on in the classroom is almost totally
under the control of the professor in charge', they warn, and therefore,
'faculty members with a special sense of intellectual purpose can usually
have a disproportionate impact on course and program development' (p.
46). The right of the 1990s thus has an easy explanation for student activism: it is fomented by Marxist faculty and abetted by the quietism of
university administrations. And hard though it may be to imagine, this
'new, radicalized academy' is totalitarian and relativist at once:

> Armed with a variety of totalistic visions and millennial expectations, its par-
> tisans have little sympathy either with open discourse or with analytic proce-
> dures that fail to guarantee desired conclusions. *It is not a coincidence* that the
> epistemological relativism prominent in the early writings of Marx is also a
> common feature of the theories of contemporary academic radicals, be they
> feminists, deconstructionists, or Marxists. ('TL', p. 50; my emphasis)

There's a lot of tangled stuff here, so let's go over it slowly and carefully. The new academics oppose open discourse; these opponents of
open discourse, not coincidentally, are relativists; relativism is prominent
in Marx's early writings; these contemporary academic relativists are
therefore Marxists even if they're not Marxists; and Marxists, as we all
know, have totalistic visions and millennial expectations. Moreover, as
Balch and London conclude, the 'disproportionate impact' of faculty with
a sense of purpose has accordingly resulted in a betrayal of the university's noble heritage; for whereas 'until recently the university served as
an important means of integrating the future leadership of American soci-

ety and assimilating the upwardly mobile' – that is, the upwardly mobile who were neither black nor female nor Hispanic nor Jewish – 'a significant part of it now strives to do precisely the reverse, by fostering political estrangement and cultural segmentation' (p. 50). Note here the masterful elision of agents, the rigorous eschewal of grammatically necessary prepositional phrases: who 'integrates' whom into what? who is 'assimilated' to what? who gets 'estranged' from whom? and who *was* this future leadership in the first place, anyway?

The crux of the article, however, is its conflation of liberalism with illiberalism. It is upon this rock that the NAS has built its subsequent rhetorical structures, by means of which they charge the academic left with self-contradiction: uniformly advocating diversity or intolerantly refusing to tolerate intolerance. Although these charges are specific to the current campus climate, they too have their origin in the structure of feeling of 1960s conservatism – as one might gather from reading Sidney Hook's *Academic Freedom and Academic Anarchy* (1970), which may induce in us a feeling of déjà vu even if one gets no further than Hook's dedication to Edward J. Rosek, 'embattled fighter for free men, free society, and the free university against fascism, communism, and totalitarian liberalism.'[15] Yet what's truly uncanny about Hook's book, from the perspective of the PC wars of the 1990s, is its admirable defense of the academic freedom of a Marxist historian named Eugene Genovese, who had then but recently declared his support for the Vietcong. Hook's rationale is based on a Weberian, value-neutral faith in the principles of professionalism:

> the qualified teacher, whose qualifications may be inferred from his acquisition of tenure, has the right honestly to reach, and hold, and proclaim any conclusion in the field of his competence. In other words, academic freedom carries with it the *right to heresy* as well as the right to restate and defend the traditional views. This takes in considerable ground. If a teacher in honest pursuit of an inquiry or argument comes to a conclusion that appears fascist or communist or racist or what-not in the eyes of others, once he has been certified as professionally competent by his peers, then those who believe in academic freedom must defend his right to be wrong – if they consider him wrong – whatever their orthodoxy may be. (*AF*, p. 36)

According to Hook, tenured radicals deserve their colleagues' respect and support; one would not want to stake one's life on the likelihood of hearing a similar proposition from academic (or anti-academic) conservatives today. But interestingly, immediately after his discussion of Genovese, Hook seems to forget where he is in the argument:

> The novel element in the situation is that the greatest potential threats to
> *Lehrfreiheit,* to the academic freedom of teachers and scholars, emanate today
> not from reactionary business tycoons or superorthodox ecclesiastics, or
> chauvinistic politicians but from American students themselves! How is this
> possible? (*AF,* p. 43)

The passage is strange, since Genovese was hounded not by students but
by 'politicians' and 'tycoons', one of whom, as Hook notes, was New Jer-
sey's Republican gubernatorial candidate, who 'focused his entire campaign on the issue of Genovese's right to teach' (*AF,* p. 42). But twenty
years of ripening have rendered the passage stranger still, now that
Genovese himself has endorsed the 1991 incarnation of Hook's book,
D'Souza's *Illiberal Education* – even though D'Souza holds no Hookian
brief for the academic freedom of leftist faculty – titling his own review,
'Heresy, Yes – Sensitivity, No.'[16] Whether Genovese meant to invoke
Hook's sense of 'heresy' is unclear; he may not have titled his review
himself. Nor is it clear that D'Souza warrants a Hookian defense, unless
he is somehow construed as a spokesman for conservative academics
who consider themselves, in the terms Balch and London have made
available, to be 'heretics' rather than advocates of the status quo. In other
words, although it is impossible to imagine D'Souza leaping to the defense of an American professor who publicly supported Saddam Hussein
in the Gulf War, it has nevertheless come to pass, as the mantle of anti-
academic conservatism has fallen on weaker and weaker shoulders and
finally landed on D'Souza's, that ex-VC supporter Genovese has leapt to
D'Souza's defense in the name of 'academic freedom'.

The NAS now presents an annual Sidney Hook Award to the individual who has done or suffered most in the noble Hookian effort to combat
totalitarian leftism on campus; one recent winner was Stephan Thernstrom of Harvard. Hook's legacy lives on, it would appear, but we cannot
but admit that much has been lost since the heydays of the 1960s reactionaries. Gone are the days that seared Hook, when the SDS assaulted the
South Vietnamese ambassador while he was speaking at NYU, then proceeded to another hall to disrupt and cancel a speech by James Reston
(*AF,* pp. 233–4); gone, too, are the days the late Allan Bloom never forgot,
when armed black students appeared on the campus of Cornell University. Today, by contrast, when we hear of intemperate student unrest we
are likely to hear only garbled and sensationalized reports of rude behavior such as that in the so-called 'Thernstrom Case' at Harvard – in which
the Hook Award winner claimed to have been attacked both by the Harvard *Crimson* and by the Harvard administration, the latter of which had
actually *supported* Thernstrom's right to academic freedom.[17] New Right

ideologues are characteristically confused about students, whom they want to portray as helpless victims of tenured radical professors but wind up casting, as in the 'Thernstrom Case', as ill-mannered badgerers of innocent, well-meaning faculty. In this sense, too, we are living with the legacy of the late 1960s still, not only in programs in Women's Studies and African American Studies, but also in various university 'speech codes', some of which were enacted in order to discipline unruly student protests against the Vietnam War.[18]

One might expect that the paucity of left student activism in the 1990s would diminish neoconservative hysteria about campus life, but as I have shown above, even after a decade during which American conservatives took over the White House and then laid claim to the rest of the world, the right has not forsaken the complaint that conservatives are an oppressed minority on campus. For this is a new American conservatism that regards any opposition as de facto 'oppression', just as it regards all criticism as de facto censorship, and it is accordingly outraged not to have rooted out its widespread and principled liberal-left opposition in universities, even though so much of its opposition has crumbled elsewhere. Conservative attacks on academic life, then, should be understood as the consequence of conservatism's failure to achieve among the academic American intellegentsia the kind of hegemony it has enjoyed in American economic and social policy, not to mention the federal judiciary. But there is one novel element about the anti-academic attacks of the 1980s and 1990s: American conservatives have now been alerted to the strange posthumous career of Paul de Man, with the result that deconstruction – and, therefore, 'theory' in general – can now be vilified by the right as an academic form of Nazism.

As M. H. Abrams's and W. Jackson Bate's innocuous misunderstandings of deconstruction have given way to David Lehman's more informed and dangerous misunderstandings, the right has found the final piece of evidence it needed to establish the hidden connections linking recent French thought, affirmative action, canon revision, and the speech codes whose origins they've forgotten.[19] This 'syncretic' branch of the New Right Wave can be said to have started in 1987, with Allan Bloom's *The Closing of the American Mind,* a book spawned by the dual-exhaust inspiration of Saul Bellow's encouragement and the Institute for Educational Affairs' cash.

Bloom is important to contemporary anti-academicism, if only because, in John Searle's words, he has proven that 'it is possible to write an alarmist book about the state of higher education with a long-winded title and make a great deal of money.'[20] But Bloom himself has also proven to

be something of an embarrassment, even to the right. For every argument
he's bestowed upon his sons, he's left them another that's nothing but a
liability. For instance, thanks to Bloom, everyone now knows that you
can't critique the West in good conscience, because the East is worse. As
Bloom puts it, 'only in the Western nations, i.e., those influenced by
Greek philosophy, is there some willingness to doubt the identification of
the good with one's own way.'[21] This is almost a Cretan liar's paradox,
from which it follows that the West is superior to other cultures because
the West doubts its superiority to other cultures. Only the true Messiah
denies his divinity. Very well. But a mere three pages before the one on
which he intones that the West is the best, Bloom claims, rather less persuasively, that the 'sexual adventurer' Margaret Mead, along with 'all
such teachers of openness', 'had either no interest in or were actively hostile to the Declaration of Independence and the Constitution' (p. 33). I
don't know what this means, and neither do you. Was it that Margaret
Mead considered the United States to be a British colony?

Bloom's argument is full of unfathomable lapses like this, whether they
take the form of rantings about rock and roll or evocations of the days
when truly erotic students ran 'from prostitutes to Plato, and back' (p.
135). Besides, the American public doesn't thrill to the proposition that it
has failed once again to read the *Symposium*, the *Republic*, the *Ion* and the
Phaedrus, for never before has the American public been so well-informed
about the fact that it knows less than eight-year-olds in Sweden. By contrast, should you tell the American public that its children are being forcibly indoctrinated by communist fascist feminist deconstructionist
multiculturalists, *then* you've got a bestseller on your hands – and an argument even nonspecialists can follow.

Naturally, the next crucial text here is Kimball's *Tenured Radicals,* one of
whose key early sentences notes that 'it is a pleasure to acknowledge the
John M. Olin Foundation and the Institute for Educational Affairs for
their generous help in the early stages of this project.'[22] Thanks not only
to its generous funding but also to its handy sound-bite title and its un-
swerving commitment to simplicity, Kimball's book has a bright future
and an already illustrious past; before the advent of D'Souza, Kimball was
perhaps the most influential journalist working the academic beat and setting the terms for its public discussion in generalist journals and newsmagazines. Kimball is a witty and capable writer, and Allan Bloom
(apparently thinking that Kimball is working on a major motion picture)
heads Kimball's front cover with the line, 'all persons serious about education should see it.' With uncanny symmetry, Bloom and Kimball now
occupy the front covers of each other's books, but Kimball's salute to
Bloom is more rigorous: 'an unparalleled reflection on today's intellectual

climate. ... That rarest of documents, a genuinely profound book.'

In Kimball's case, the book in question is a patchwork quilt of *New Criterion* essays in which the author shows beyond all doubt that a bunch of academic conference papers and learned-society pamphlets are poppy-cock, blather, and rebarbative nonsense (I am not doing justice to Kimball's vast array of dismissive Edwardian interjections). But what makes Kimball's book so invaluable a resource is its sheer comprehensiveness. If you've got a bone you'd like to pick with contemporary academic literary criticism, chances are good that Kimball's already picked it for you; thus, bonepickers of all competencies can today launch their accusations merely by citing *Tenured Radicals*.

For example: some of our critics, like William Bennett, have limited themselves to the complaint that academic critics have driven students away from careers in the humanities because academics are trendy and incomprehensible. Others have charged that academic critics are seducing and corrupting an ever-growing number of students in the humanities, because academics are trendy and incomprehensible and students find these qualities appealing. But Kimball, generously, accuses us of doing both: according to him, we drive students away *and* we lure them in. He opens his attack on the American Council of Learned Societies with the charge that 'American education has suffered a wholesale flight from the humanities' (*TR*, pp. 35–6); but he opens his book somewhat differently:

> second- and third-tier schools are rushing to embrace all manner of fashion-able intellectual ideologies as so many formulas for garnering prestige, pub-licity, and 'name' professors (and hoping thereby to attract more students and other sources of income). (*TR*, pp. xiii–xiv)

In other words, it's not that students have fled the humanities in search of more lucrative vocations; it's that greedy colleges are capitulating to intellectual fashion to attract students' tuition dollars. I don't see how we can have such enormous drawing potential for all those students seeking to flee the humanities, but I trust this will be explained sooner or later.

Kimball's book is notable for its wealth of such self-contradictions – except when it comes to feminism, about which he is admirably lucid. In the course of his attack on Elaine Showalter, for instance, Kimball quotes some embarrassingly histrionic psuedoscholarship from the NAS's organ, *Academic Questions,* and goes downhill from there:

> As Thomas Short pointed out in an excellent anatomy of radical trends in the academy, one result of the academic feminist agenda is a situation in which 'every course will be Oppression Studies'. For if gender is [as Showal-

ter had put it] a 'crucial element in the way we all read and write', then why not sexual orientation, race, and class? Why not any political interest? (*TR*, p. 19)

Why not indeed? It is rare to find the issue stated so clearly as this – rare to see someone say in so many words that race, gender, class and sexual orientation are 'political interests'. Kimball seems not to notice that Showalter is claiming gender, rightly or wrongly, as a 'difference' we all have in common; he sees it only as an obstacle to universality. But what then are we to make of the human who has neither race nor gender nor class nor sexual orientation? When we find such a creature will we have found at last the critic who is truly above politics?

There's no point debating the answer to such a question, for the moral of Kimball's excursions into the academy, as Kimball suggests in the new postscript to his book, is precisely that we should cut off academic debate and then kill it. For one thing, academic debate is confusing, and that's bad, because 'it is in the nature of generalizations about life's difficult choices to be perfectly obvious' (*TR*, p. 203). Obvious then it is in our nature to be, even if we have to raze the syntax. And for another thing, academic debate is dangerous, like malaria or dengue fever: 'A swamp yawns open before us, ready to devour everything. The best response to all this – and finally the only serious and effective response – is not to enter these murky waters in the first place. As Nietzsche observed, we do not refute a disease. We resist it' (*TR*, p. 204). This amazing passage follows Kimball's mildly parodic list of questions about the contents of liberal-arts curricula; but it sums up his attitude toward modern academe quite well. Rarely has willful ignorance received so noble a defense, and I am grateful to Kimball once more that he has phrased matters so succinctly: here, in its raw form, is the claim that 'resistance' to theory is the sign of a sound moral constitution.

Kimball occupies a unique position in the literary public sphere. His function is less hortatory than prophylactic – and the above passage suggests that Kimball himself knows this very well. He is not paid exclusively to distort and decontextualize academic work, but to misrepresent it to readers who need to be reassured about their ignorance: as Louis Menand put it, *Tenured Radicals* 'is clearly intended to give cheer to the sort of person who suspects that academics have set up a pretty nice racket for themselves ... but who doesn't feel intellectually equipped to go out and prove the case himself.'[23] Kimball thereby serves his masters less as a journalist than as a point man who reads and reviews new academic work in part so that others won't have to. Year after year, the *New Criterion* has dispatched Kimball off to conference after conference, charging him with recording only those moments that evince academic grandstanding, silliness, or obscurity. Of course, any one of us would be taxed by so arduous and boring a task, so it is no surprise that Kimball sometimes nods. For instance, at the 1989 Williams College symposium with which he concludes his book, Kimball's hearing suddenly fails him during Houston Baker's paper:

> Why are those who criticize the politicization of the humanities dangerous? Professor Baker offered a few reasons, not all of which were intelligible. One reason I did hear is that such people are dangerous 'because they are conservative.' (*TR*, p. 183)

There are, however, no incentives for Kimball to invest in devices such as tape recorders; on the contrary, he has been approvingly cited, echoed, and plagiarized in *New York* magazine, *Newsweek* and the *New Republic* precisely because of his talent for concocting memorable formulae such as 'the choice facing us today is not between a "repressive" Western culture and a multicultural paradise, but between culture and barbarism' (*TR*, p. 206). Important American news magazines enjoy these little bromides because they keep the arguments simple: Are you for the West or against it?

Kimball is not quite as crude as I've made him appear; he's certainly no Charles Sykes, and he's earned, if only by default, the distinction of being among the very few non-academic critics who've actually read the scholarly work they attack. Of the trade journalists covering the 1990 MLA convention in Chicago, I know of none besides Kimball who managed to get past the title of Judith Butler's 'The Lesbian Phallus: Or, Does Heterosexuality Exist?' Since Butler's title turned out to be the national press's favorite lit-crit object of derision in 1990, Kimball is to be applauded just for showing up at the session and taking good notes (for he clearly understood the point of the talk). But Kimball did better than this, telling his *New Criterion* readers that 'Professor Butler is gifted with a keen and methodical philosophical mind', and that 'hers was the most rigorously argued paper I heard at the MLA.'[24] At this point, however, Kimball's appreciation for Butler's mind posed a problem so severe as to require him to demand that 'homosexual themes' creep back into the critical closet:

> One could not help but lament the fact that [Butler's] gifts are wasted pondering such subjects as 'the lesbian phallus.' ... [I]t is important to stress that the issue raised by these panels has nothing to do with 'homophobia'. It has to do first of all with the kinds of things that are appropriate subjects for a public scholarly discussion of literature. I submit that neither 'The Sodomiti-

cal Tourist' nor 'The Lesbian Phallus' is appropriate. This is not because I
suffer from 'homophobia' but because I believe the chief attraction of such
topics is prurient. Panels devoted to homosexual themes often have the air of
rallies for the initiate. ... ('MLA', pp. 12–13)

To answer Butler's rhetorical question, then, we might say that heterosexuality here is alive and well. Still, I sense something plaintive about
Kimball's complaint: condemning his own prurient interest in the spectacle of Judith Butler talking about the phallus, Kimball attempts to ward off
being 'initiated' into the rites of inappropriate subjects, but only by 'submitting' to the desire – I mean, submitting the proposal – to ban such rites
from public view. It is ironic, then, but fitting, that Kimball should punc-
tuate his attempt to shut down discussion of 'homosexual themes' (that is,
everything postdating Freud – or the *Iliad*) by accusing 'politically correct'
gay theorists of shutting down such discussion: 'it is precisely on the subjects that are most difficult to debate in public – like race or homosexuality – that the demand for political correctness exercises its greatest
tyranny' ('MLA', p. 13).

Kimball's incredibly conflicted injunction to censor the putative gay
censors has so far escaped public notice and comment, and I cite it in
detail partly in hopes of giving it the wider audience it deserves. For people concerned with the shrinkage and 'dumbing-down' of the literary public sphere, however, the most alarming phenomenon so far must surely be
the *Atlantic*'s publication of Dinesh D'Souza's 12,000-word 'Illiberal Education', a miniature version of his book-length treatise of the same name.
D'Souza arrived in this country from India in 1978, and has since gone on
to disprove single-handedly the fashionable theory that conservative students are the victims of PC persecution: after graduating from Dartmouth
(where he was editor-in-chief of the infamous *Dartmouth Review*), attending
graduate school briefly at Princeton, and writing a 'living biography' of
Jerry Falwell (*Falwell: Before the Millennium*, 1984), D'Souza was quickly
rewarded with a series of apparatchik jobs in the Reagan White House
and American Enterprise Institute, where he is now a 'research fellow'
that nobody can deny. He lacks Kimball's intelligence and rhetorical flair,
but he has practiced and mastered a technique many commentators can
only envy: he is a post-Reagan conservative who sounds 'moderate', even
sensible.

The *Atlantic* piece begins in this moderate mode. 'It is not always possible in such disputes', writes D'Souza, 'for a reasonable person, in good
conscience, to take any side; there is a good deal of excess all around. The
middle ground seems to have disappeared on campus, and whether it can
be restored is an open question.'[25] Open it is. But whether D'Souza has

truly appeared on our horizon in order to restore our middle ground is a considerably less open question. The debate, writes D'Souza, 'has so far been passionately superficial, posing false dichotomies ... and missing the underlying principles that are shaping the dramatic changes in universities' (p. 52). One would think from this that D'Souza might go on to address the changing role of the research university in the postwar era, the difference between the student populations of 1960 and 1990, or the rise of the quasi-academic and well-funded New Right. But one would be wrong. D'Souza's here to recycle the conservative polemics of William Buckley, Sidney Hook, and Allan Bloom, and his dedication to factual accuracy will turn out to be passionately superficial.

In the *Atlantic*, D'Souza's work appears merely uneven, ranging from reasonable (and often unwittingly leftist) critiques of 'affirmative action' campus politics (for instance, he notes with appropriate outrage that many faculty and administrators expect black academics to be experts in 'black' issues), to passages of nothing less than moral and intellectual dishonesty. On the first page of 'Illiberal Education' we are informed:

> There is little argument about the desirability of teaching the greatest works written by members of other cultures, by women, and by minority-group members. Many academic activists go beyond this to insist that texts be selected primarily or exclusively according to the author's race, gender, or sexual preference, and that the Western tradition be exposed in the classroom as hopelessly bigoted and oppressive in every way. (p. 52)

If 'many academic activists' insist on such a thing, one would think that a writer as resourceful as D'Souza would be able to find one; but the quotation that follows this passage comes not from any such 'activist' but from David Riesman, who attacks 'liberal closed-mindedness'; Riesman is thus trotted out to support an argument for which D'Souza has not yet adduced any evidence.

The first sentence of D'Souza's passage is worse still, for it is an outright falsehood: there have been – and there still are – tremendous arguments about revising reading lists even when such lists include the greatest works by women and nonwhites. In fact, D'Souza himself goes on, only one paragraph later, to misrepresent once again Stanford's revision of its core course in 'Western culture'. Claiming that Stanford replaced this core 'with a program called Cultures, Ideas, and Values, which stressed works on race and gender issues by Third World authors, minority-group members, and women' (p. 53), D'Souza distorts Stanford's careful and judicious curriculum revision beyond belief and beyond recognition: the CIV curriculum exists in eight tracks, only one of which includes much of the

'Third World'; and the new program asks only that *one* work in each track be discussed in terms that highlight 'race and gender issues'.[26] D'Souza's own article, in other words, could afford us no better example of the right's intolerance for the most minor kinds of tinkering with core reading lists, and we're only on the second page of the article.

In the end, D'Souza's attack on the academy, like Kimball's, relies on ignorance – his own, and ours. 'Deconstructionism', he writes toward the end of the essay, 'appears uniformly hostile to all texts', but, as it turns out,

> in fact deconstructionists treat some works with uncharacteristic respect, leaving their authority unchallenged. Marx, for instance, never seems to be deconstructed, nor does Foucault, or Lacan, or Derrida, or Barthes. Malcolm X and Martin Luther King, Jr, seem to enjoy immunity. There may be an entire gender exception for women. ... Yet if, as we often read, Zora Neale Hurston is just as good as Milton, why not subject her to the same critical undoing? (p. 76)

If someone were to publish a claim that *Paradise Lost* never really talks about theology or that psychoanalysis fails to make use of the works of major Greek dramatists, certainly we would recognize such a person as a cultural illiterate. But because no one at the *Atlantic,* including even the journal's fact-checkers, is aware of the past twenty-five years' profusion of deconstructive work on Marx, or the extraordinary critical energy that's been expended on Foucault, Lacan, Derrida and Barthes by feminists, psychoanalytic critics and deconstructionists (Jane Gallop and Teresa de Lauretis alone have done much, throughout the 1980s, to point out gender lacunae in the work of these Four French Horsemen), D'Souza is allowed to get away with this series of inanities. Indeed, so inane is this passage that by the time we've gotten to the Hurston sentence, we may have forgotten that D'Souza began his mini-thesis with the fuzzy idea that deconstruction is 'hostile to all texts' – that *deconstructing* a piece of writing is disrespectful, and not something one does in front of ladies, for fear it will 'undo' them or their texts (from which it follows, conversely, that refusing to deconstruct a text is the surest sign of love). And as for Zora Neale Milton: a mere perusal of Henry Louis Gates's or Barbara Johnson's 'deconstructive' criticism on Hurston will suffice to demonstrate that, when it comes to academic criticism and theory, D'Souza has no idea what he's talking about.[27]

Illiberal Education in book form is an even greater threat to honest intellectual exchange, and a more stupefying document by any standard. In less than ten pages on the topic of 'the new censorship' on campus, for instance, D'Souza argues first that 'American campuses have seen an apparent explosion of bigotry in the past few years' (here he quotes the Center for Democratic Renewal's report that 'such incidents have increased fourfold since 1985'); then he writes that 'these data, whose reliability is accepted by all sides of the debate, have befuddled many polemicists'; then he reverses field, to claim that racism on campus is vastly overreported: 'according to a spokesman for the Department of Education ... documented incidents of campus racism have not increased since 1980.'[28] This informational incoherence is emblematic of D'Souza's work, for the aim of his book is to argue an impossible pair of positions: one, that 'the retrenchment or backlash feared by many civil rights activists has not materialized' (*IE*, p. 128); and two, that women and minorities themselves are to blame for 'the bigotry which results from preferential treatment' (*IE*, p. 240). In other words, Reaganism isn't at fault, because racism isn't getting worse on campus; instead, racism *is* getting worse on campus, thanks to liberals and their affirmative action programs, which have produced a new and justifiable bigotry. 'The old racism was based on prejudice', concludes D'Souza, 'whereas the new racism is based on conclusions. ... The new bigotry is not derived from ignorance, but from experience. It is harbored not by ignoramuses, but by students who have direct and first-hand experience with minorities in the close proximity of university settings' (*IE*, pp. 240–41).

Illiberal Education tells us that there is no neo-racist backlash in America, and that mere contact with campus minorities is itself sufficient cause for the new racism. If it has done nothing else, surely D'Souza's book has managed to make Kimball's look like a paragon of consistency and probity. Still, I think the *Atlantic* excerpt, even taken alone, may be more immediately important to us for what it tells academic literary studies about the status of generalist criticism today. It is one thing for D'Souza's Olin Foundation–supported tome to be picked up by The Free Press and hoisted onto the *New York Times* bestseller list; we have seen the pattern before. But that the *Atlantic* would have published D'Souza, and at such length, is an important sign of the extent to which public discussion of American academia, in respectable intellectual journals, is now conducted by the most callow and opportunistic elements of the right. It's also, sad to say, an important sign of how low are our minimum standards for serious public exchange on the status of American criticism. To return to the concerns with which I opened this essay, allow me to point out that back in the golden days of the public intellectual, the *Atlantic* was publishing Jean-Paul Sartre, Henry Steele Commager and George Orwell; now it's publishing Dinesh D'Souza.

Yet even D'Souza's ignorance pales before his capacity for feigning moral hysteria. To read D'Souza in the *Atlantic* is to read D'Souza when he's on his best behavior; to read D'Souza in *Forbes,* by contrast, is to visit him when he's more at home. Speaking of the academy's 'Visigoths in Tweed', D'Souza claims that 'the propaganda of the new barbarians' threatens to 'do us in'. Toward the close of the piece, D'Souza turns up the rhetoric a notch: 'Resistance on campus to the academic revolution is outgunned', he writes, 'and sorely needs outside reinforcements.'[29] To our relief, D'Souza proceeds merely to call upon *Forbes* readers to defund the humanities, but his long-range plans should be clear from his choice of metaphor: to combat multiculturalism, especially at state institutions, he will eventually have to call out the National Guard.

D'Souza's program for 'resistance' is the most extreme example of right-thinking to date, and it's worth asking how he can maintain any credibility at all even among conservative academics. The answer is simply this: according to D'Souza, deconstruction and affirmative action are two facets of the same thing, for they both involve attacks on 'standards'. D'Souza's attack on affirmative action and contemporary theory at Duke puts the matter squarely: 'these two ambitious hiring programs seem unrelated, but in fact there is an underlying unity: both offer a powerful challenge to the notion of standards of merit' (*IE,* p. 158). This is a classic example of the argument that proves too much, insofar as it indicts all manner of innovative intellectual inquiry, construing any nonstandard approach as a refusal of the very idea of standards. But to wealthy conservative alumni of elite universities, D'Souza's message is refreshingly uncomplicated: if you return to your alma mater and find more women or blacks than you think belong there, on the faculty or in the student body, you can be sure that deconstruction is to blame. Keep your eyes open and your checkbook closed.

There's more to it than that, needless to say, or D'Souza would not have won the endorsements of figures such as Morton Halperin or C. Vann Woodward. To intellectual moderates and concerned emeriti, what's attractive about D'Souza is that he opposes racial separatism and defends academic freedom – or that he claims to. Those who doubt D'Souza's sincerity, however, need not go so far as to research his disgraceful record at the *Dartmouth Review;* they need only consult D'Souza's abusive treatment of Women's Studies and African American Studies programs, which D'Souza prefers to call 'part of the American university's ideological project in sensitivity training', claiming that such programs '[seem] to have produced a relentless, even fanatical, conformity of thought' (*IE,* pp. 214–15). If D'Souza truly seeks to defend academic freedom by defunding the humanities and undermining the academic freedom of Women's Studies and African American Studies, what can we say but that his cure will surely kill the patient?

Given the past decade's frictions between 'theory' and canon revision, it is bracing to read someone like D'Souza, who so glibly conflates the two.[30] Less edifying is the frequency with which canon revision is elided with affirmative action, since such elisions so obviously and painfully betray the conservative conviction that the works of women and minorities simply could not be studied or assigned in universities if not for intellectually suspect 'set-aside' programs designed to promote marginalized writers and shield them from criticism. The NAS has candidly promoted this conviction in a national advertising campaign launched in various intellectual journals, which states in part: 'The idea that students will be discouraged by not encountering more works by members of their own race, sex, or ethnic group, even were it substantiated, would not justify adding inferior works. Such paternalism conveys a message opposite to the one desired.'[31] Plausible though this may be on its face, it seems as if the NAS has deliberately muddied the issue by introducing the specter of 'inferior works'. But apparently the NAS assumes that any 'affirmative action' revision of the curriculum will necessarily entail the dilution of the curriculum, because, as they explain, the curriculum never excluded women or minorities: 'Other cultures, minority subcultures, and social problems' – surely an odd trio, unless the first two are *also* social problems – 'have long been studied in the liberal arts curriculum in such established disciplines as history, literature, comparative religion, economics, political science, anthropology, and sociology.'

In reality, by contrast, American literary study has changed considerably since the days when the foremost anthology of American literature included (no earlier than 1967, in its third edition) its first black writer, Leroi Jones, represented by two poems prefaced by the words, 'Jones is easily the most interesting of the young Negro poets, but race is not often an issue in his poetry and does not restrict its appeal.'[32] Yet if it is regrettable that our attackers are so ignorant of the history of our discipline, and ignorant therefore of the basis from which contemporary revisionists are working, it is scandalous that they continue to conflate canon revision with 'quotas', despite what Ross Chambers has called 'the now widespread theoretical consensus that textual specificity cannot be determined by the author's identity and is necessarily a function of the mediated activity of mediation that we call reading.'[33] As the public debate moves from 'the canon' to 'multiculturalism', we need to reframe Chambers's point as accessibly as we can: we can't read or assign works exclusively or even primarily on the basis of their author's race or gender, because 'representation' and 'reading' are more slippery matters than that. It is not wrong, in teaching American literature or world literature, to diversify one's syllabus by race or gender or ethnicity; it is wrong – and practically impossible – to teach Audre Lorde (for instance) *only* as a black writer, or as a woman, or as a lesbian, or as a mother, or as a teacher. But to make that case we will also need to explain more fully what it means for anti-essentialists to say that 'difference' is relational and socially constructed, because for now, journals like the *New Republic* are saddling us with exactly the opposite position: 'the core of the "multiculturalists'" argument', writes the collective editorial wisdom at *TNR*, 'is that race is the determinant of a human being's mind, that the mind cannot, and should not, try to wrest itself from its biological or sociological origins.'[34]

This is so deliberately and dishonestly backward as to recall the vision of George Bush at West Point's 1991 Commencement, where the former president forgot that he'd opposed the 1964 Civil Rights Act, pounded the podium and whined nasally that Republicans have a *good* record on civil rights. Besides, it's a neocon shell game: when we're not getting flak for determinism, we're getting flak – from the same sources – for treating race and gender as social constructions, therefore ignoring the brute facts of biology.

But amidst all the opprobrium and vitriol heaped upon 'multiculturalism', it's easy to forget how parochial some of this debate has become. The various disputes over 'canons', for example, get truly poisonous only when they're conducted about American literature and core curricula – partly because the canons of American literature and of core curricula have been redrawn ever since they were first drawn up in 1880–1920, and partly because Americans have something of a history of debating what 'American' and 'curriculum' are supposed to mean.[35] But since the right does not see fit to distinguish among various academic canons, writers like D'Souza have been able to pretend that because Stanford has adopted *I, Rigoberta Menchú* – in one 'core' track – it is the text 'which best represents the premises underlying the new Stanford curriculum' (*IE*, p. 71).[36]

Because the canon gets increasingly difficult to agree on the closer one gets to contemporary literature and theory, some conservatives believe that the university should have no business teaching or writing about anything that hasn't survived 'the test of time'; in Kimball's words, we should transmit only those writers of 'permanent interest' and 'permanent value' (*TR*, p. 202). In Kimball's defense, it cannot be denied that if the university kept its hands off everything published after *The Waste Land*, debate over the canon would be a lot more antiquarian, and a lot less acrimonious. It would also mean that academic critics would be prevented from practicing their trade on any text whose copyright had not expired. And this in turn would mean that contemporary journalists and reviewers would have the field of 'contemporary works' (say, everything from 1930 forward) completely to themselves. Who then would be better positioned to conduct the 'test of time' than the people who keep invoking it?

But canon revision requires no suspension of time's tests; canon revision is just another important institutional form of textual reproduction, similar to and in competition with things like book reviewing, marketing and publishing. Preserving indispensable texts and writers that our culture's various market forces have allowed to fall out of print, canon revision is both reformist and conservative; it involves nothing more radical than the dissemination of the principle that the university is a cultural institution, like the museum, that is entitled to take an active role in the creation and maintenance of its exhibits. Though the canonization of previously marginal writers and texts will always operate by way of academic recuperation, selective empowerment, and 'mainstreaming', academic criticism has nonetheless taken on, for many writers, the economic role of textual guarantor – all the more so since the 1986 revision of the US Tax Code, which prevents publishers from counting stock among their depreciation costs, thereby providing publishing houses with a strong incentive to cut backlists severely.[37]

Both the Arnoldians and the Foucauldians among us, in other words, are charged quite literally with the economic preservation and textual transmission of writers like Plato and Nella Larsen, neither of whom has much chance of denting the trade market. Academic criticism and pedagogy are not significant factors in the nation's annual GNP, but academics do possess just enough economic clout to keep 'marginal' texts in print long enough to sustain the continued revision of our century's multiple cultural heritages. It is crucial, then, both to this generation of readers and to its successors, that the ongoing historical process of cultural 'revisionism' be as broadly informed as our current technologies of textual reproduction will allow. And it is equally crucial that we continue to retrieve and reproduce the once-forgotten texts of our pasts, if only so that future readers may have the fullest possible opportunity to inspect their own literary heritages.[38] In this respect, though not in this respect alone, 'canon revision' is a project as deeply historical as it is deeply ethical; and this is a point so fundamental to contemporary professions in the humanities that it can only be misunderstood today by critics with no sense of commitment to historical understanding.

I am not sure whether it is appropriate to end on a hopeful note, but I am heartened by one decisive mechanism of the right's attacks: to gauge by the past few years' evidence, contemporary literary theory and canon revision have to undergo gross distortion in order for the right to secure the requisite public endorsement of its positions. The savage decontextualization and misrepresentation of academic work is therefore indispensable to anti-academic conservatism, without which it seems to stand little chance of winning consent among a majority of the constituencies that inhabit American general-intellectual public life. Indeed, whenever it speaks to educated audiences, the right must tread carefully. Witness, for example, a telling pair of moments during the *MacNeil/Lehrer News Hour*'s week-long examination of political correctness (17–21 June 1991). On that Thursday's installment, Yale dean Donald Kagan opined that the PC hordes prohibit people from suggesting that there are innate biological differences between the sexes. The next evening, Lynne Cheney claimed that Carol Iannone was under PC fire because she *opposes* the 'extreme' forms of academic feminism that posit innate biological differences between the sexes.[39] Much could be made of this coy chiasmus (which feminism is PC for whom?), but my point here is simply that Lynne Cheney knew she could not sell Iannone to the *MacNeil/Lehrer* audience if she were to admit that Iannone's antifeminism is as indiscriminate as Joseph Epstein's or Andrew Dice Clay's; instead, Cheney had to improvise on the spot an anti-essentialist Iannone who could be made to sound like a reasonable scholar in a free society – and only because 'feminism' has already won such broad (if sometimes vague or contested) support in American intellectual life.

In this case, it's precisely because feminism is so multifarious, so internally dialogic, and so diffuse(d) in the general culture that significant numbers of educated people now know better than to trust a 'scholar' like Iannone, whose only distinction is her steadfast opposition to all things 'feminist'. There may be an object lesson here for those who worry about the academy's propensity for internecine disagreement: feminism's plurality is so palpable that in the 1990s, outright, sweeping dismissals of feminism in toto are understood – by a surprisingly large constituency of readers – to be a mark of ignorance or intellectual crankdom. Even Camille Paglia, for instance, has had to align herself with first one and then another brand of feminist theory (gender essentialism first, then the pleasure-and-danger school, in neither of which she is adequately conversant) in order to retain her legitimacy as a cultural commentator for more than her initial fifteen minutes.[40] At the very least, the academic tendency to cultivate 'dissensus' may prove one of our most valuable means of rebutting the charge that we PC ideologues all goose-step to the same drummer.

I'm not saying that academic criticism will win the day if only it hits the street and takes its case to the people, but I am suggesting that our attackers' mendacity is itself a sign of our potential strength. At present there seem to me to be two similar but non-synchronous tasks available for the 'us' I've invoked throughout: the first involves delegitimizing the purveyors of the PC scandal, especially their claim to occupy the moderate center of academic debate. Such a project might enlist and serve not only the prominent scholars who are being attacked by the right, but the vast thousands of ordinary academic workers who have so far been invisible to the national press, but who make up the bulk of our discipline: unsung or unpublished faculty at all level, including those whose primary occupation is undergraduate instruction; junior faculty, part-time faculty and graduate students; liberal reformists, centrists, and moderate social conservatives who resent being spoken for by the NAS.

This delegitimizing project is not necessarily 'reactive'; nor is it purely a matter of negative critique, since it also requires academic workers to reconceive their professionalization by way of reconceiving their 'client class'.[41] And here it would dovetail with what I see as a more narrow but more pointed 'legitimizing' project for the cultural left – a project that begins, as Bruce Robbins says, 'by acknowledging ... that a Left exists in American universities, that it is staffed by intellectuals who have not ceased to be intellectuals by virtue of their institutional position, and that its fate is vitally connected to the values and purposes of groups outside those institutions.'[42] The constituency for this project – disseminating the academic work of the cultural left through whichever plural public spheres are still available to us – will inevitably be smaller than the broad constituency mobilizing to get the hard right off our backs. But I could not second more strongly Robbins's conviction that 'the Reagan-Bush right has performed a public service. ... In the face of the right's offensive, it is no longer possible to deny that something palpably grounded in reality, something realized and accomplished, exists for the right to attack, and the left to defend.'[43] That 'defense', I think, has now reached the point at which it needs to recognize – and, as Robbins would say, stop underestimating – its potential for winning the informed support of meaningful numbers of nonacademics for whom critique and dissent are understood to be integral to, rather than a betrayal of, American political traditions. It is the academy's task to start building that support without, precisely on the basis and from the strengths of the dissent within.

Notes

1. Jerry Adler et al., 'Taking Offense', *Newsweek*, 24 December 1990, pp. 48–54; George Will, 'Literary Politics', *Newsweek*, 22 April 1991, p. 72. See also Will, 'Curdled Politics on Campus', *Newsweek*, 6 May 1991, p. 72.

2. Since the fall of 1991, when I wrote the version of this essay that appeared in the *Yale Journal of Criticism*, there have been a few noteworthy exceptions to this general trend. The *New York Review of Books* tapped Louis Menand to review David Lehman's *Signs of the*

Times, and Martha Nussbaum published an eloquent, sophisticated analysis and defense of lesbian/gay studies in the *New Republic.* Although I don't always agree with Menand's sense of the state of criticism, I find him a markedly more reliable narrator than, say, Denis Donoghue. See Menand, 'The Politics of Deconstruction', *New York Review of Books,* 21 November 1991, pp. 39–44; and Nussbaum, 'The Softness of Reason', *New Republic,* 13 and 20 July 1992, pp. 26–35. Nussbaum's article stands in striking contrast to *TNR*'s previous brief on the field, Christopher Benfey's 'Telling It Slant', *New Republic,* 18 March 1991, pp. 35–40.

3. Since the meaning of 'accessibility' here is especially liable to misconstruction, I want to explain that I mean *material* accessibility; my point has to do more with what's available in good, well-stocked bookstores than with generalist complaints that academic criticism is hard to read. Such complaints all too often are launched in bad faith, as if non-academic readers might be able to understand good old-fashioned criticism that speaks of discordia concors and hendiadys, but not bad newfangled criticism that speaks of catachresis and phallogocentrism. The academy's own locus classicus among discussions of 'accessibility' (in this sense) is Edward Said's 'Opponents, Audiences, Constituencies, and Community', *Critical Inquiry,* vol. 9, no. 1 (1982), pp. 1–26.

4. The most thorough recent attempt to do so is surely Bruce Robbins's *Secular Vocations,* esp. pp. 1–28, 84–117, 212–24.

5. See, for example, Gerald Graff, *Professing Literature: An Institutional History* (Chicago: University of Chicago Press, 1987); Jim Merod, *The Professional Responsibility of the Critic* (Ithaca, N.Y.: Cornell University Presss, 1987); Evan Watkins, *Work Time: English Departments and the Circulation of Cultural Value* (Stanford, Calif.: Stanford University Press, 1989); Barbara Herrnstein Smith, *Contingencies of Value* (Cambridge, Mass.: Harvard University Press, 1988); Jonathan Culler, *Framing the Sign: Criticism and Its Institutions* (Norman, Okla.: University of Oklahoma Press, 1988); Bruce Robbins, 'Oppositional Professionals: Theory and the Narratives of Professionalization', in *Consequences of Theory,* Jonathan Arac and Barbara Johnson, eds (Baltimore: Johns Hopkins University Press, 1991), pp. 1–21; and, of course, Stanley Fish, 'Anti-Professionalism', *New Literary History,* vol. 17, no. 1 (1985), pp. 89–108, and 'Profession Despise Thyself: Fear and Self-Loathing in Literary Studies', *Critical Inquiry,* vol. 10, no. 2 (1983), pp. 349–64.

6. Culler, *Framing the Sign,* p. 24.

7. John Searle, 'The Storm over the University', *New York Review of Books,* 6 December 1990, pp. 34–42; C. Vann Woodward, 'Freedom and the Universities', *New York Review of Books,* 18 July 1991, pp. 32–7.

8. Russell Jacoby, *The Last Intellectuals: American Culture in the Age of Academe* (New York: Basic Books, 1987), pp. 219–20.

9. See Lynn Garafola's review of *The Last Intellectuals* in *New Left Review* no. 169 (May-June 1988), p. 126.

10. For more detailed caveats about Jacoby's work, see, for example, Garafola, pp. 122–8; Bruce Robbins, 'Introduction: The Grounding of Intellectuals', in *Intellectuals: Aesthetics, Politics, Academics,* Robbins, ed. (Minneapolis: University of Minnesota Press, 1990), pp. ix-xxvii; Richard D. Wolff, 'Criticizing Social Criticism', *Boundary 2* (1991), pp. 207–26; and Casey Blake, 'Prisoners of Tenure', *Nation,* 31 October 1987, pp. 493–5.

11. Irving Kristol, '"When Virtue Loses All Her Loveliness": Some Reflections on Capitalism and "The Free Society"', *Public Interest,* vol. 21 (Fall 1970), p. 3.

12. For a corporate history of the NAS, detailing its various incarnations and sources of funding, see Scott Henson, 'The Campus Right', *Texas Observer,* 31 May 1991, pp. 6–7, 23. My own brief account here is drawn in part from Henson's. The funding numbers come from a fact sheet distributed by Teachers for a Democratic Culture and compiled by TDC coordinators Gerald Graff and Gregory Jay.

13. Ellen Messer-Davidow, 'Doing the Right Thing', *Women's Review of Books,* vol. 9, no. 5 (February 1992), pp. 19–20; 'Manufacturing the Attack on Liberalized Higher Education', *Social Text,* no. 36 (1993), pp. 40–80; Sara Diamond, 'The Funding of the NAS', in Aufderheide, ed., *Beyond PC,* pp. 89–96.

14. Stephen Balch and Herbert London, 'The Tenured Left', *Commentary,* vol. 82, no. 4

(October 1986), p. 45; hereafter 'TL'. The article is especially notable for its responses to some innocuous course descriptions and paper titles. From the Vassar College catalogue, Balch and London cite the following monstrosity, Economics 380a: 'The course will compare capitalism and socialism as alternative strategies of development of Third World countries. The first part of the course will address the central theoretical issues in the literature on the possibilities of capitalist development, socialist development, and autarky. In the second part, we will discuss how different socialist countries in the Third World have dealt with a variety of problems, including government ownership of productive enterprises, agrarian transformations, technological development, population growth, and the status of women. Depending on student interest the course will cover the following countries: China, Cuba, Nigaragua, Chile under Allende, Jamaica under Manley, Tanzania, Angola, Zimbabwe, North Korea, and Cambodia' (p. 46). This clearly has no place in a college curriculum. Balch and London go on: 'Lest it be thought that these examples are uniquely egregious' – as Dave Barry would say, I am not making this up – 'one might contemplate the lecture series, "America after 1984", organized last year at Bard College by Stanley Diamond, then the occupant of its Alger Hiss Chair in Culture, Society, and the Humanities.' Diamond, it appears, lectured on 'The Underside of Justice in the United States', 'The Gathering Crisis in Public Education', 'Race and Gender in America', and the like. It is a wonder he was not tried for high treason.

15. Sidney Hook, *Academic Freedom and Academic Anarchy* (New York: Cowles, 1970), p. v; hereafter cited in the text as *AF*.

16. Eugene Genovese, 'Heresy, Yes – Sensitivity, No', *New Republic*, 15 April 1991, pp. 30–35; for a critique of D'Souza's partisan sense of who's entitled to academic freedom, see Louis Menand, 'Illiberalisms', *New Yorker*, 20 May 1991, p. 103.

17. For a rebuttal of D'Souza's account of the Stephan Thernstrom 'case', see Jon Weiner, 'What Happened at Harvard', *Nation*, 30 September 1991, pp. 384–8. Thernstrom is chief among those who, like Yale dean Donald Kagan, trumpet PC to the national press as a 'new McCarthyism'. So far this strategy has worked well in *Newsweek*, *New Republic*, the *Wall Street Journal* and *New York* magazine, where Thernstrom is quoted as saying that PC is 'more frightening than the old McCarthyism, which had no support in the academy. Now the enemy is within.' (John Taylor, 'Are You Politically Correct?' *New York*, 21 January 1991, p. 35). From a respectable academic historian, this is pretty scary stuff. For a sense of the extent of Thernstrom's amnesia, see Ellen W. Schrecker, *No Ivory Tower: McCarthyism and the Universities* (New York: Oxford University Press, 1986).

18. As Michael Kinsley puts it, 'in those ancient days, it was academic conservatives who argued that the life of the mind required a higher standard of civility and respect for the views of others than could be tolerated in society at large, and insisted that students who could not agree to such a standard did not belong in the academic community' Kinsley, 'P.C. B.S.', *New Republic*, 20 May 1991, p. 50.

19. David Lehman, *Signs of the Times: Deconstruction and the Fall of Paul de Man* (New York: Poseidon Press, 1991).

20. Searle, 'Storm', p. 34.

21. Allan Bloom, *The Closing of the American Mind: How Higher Education Has Failed Democracy and Impoverished the Souls of Today's Students* (New York: Simon and Schuster, 1987), p. 36.

22. Roger Kimball, *Tenured Radicals: How Politics Has Corrupted Our Higher Education* (New York: HarperCollins, 1990), p. ix; hereafter *TR*.

23. Louis Menand, 'Lost Faculties', *New Republic*, 9 and 16 July 1990, p. 36.

24. Roger Kimball, 'The Periphery vs. the Center: The MLA in Chicago', *New Criterion*, vol. 9, no. 6 (February 1991), p. 12; hereafter 'MLA'.

25. Dinesh D'Souza, 'Illiberal Education', *Atlantic*, March 1991, p. 52; hereafter 'IE'.

26. For more detailed reports on and responses to Stanford's CIV course revision, see Searle, 'Storm', pp. 38–9; Herbert Lindenberger, 'On the Sacrality of Reading Lists: The Western Culture Debate at Stanford University', in *The History in Literature: On Value, Genre, Institutions* (New York: Columbia University Press, 1990), pp. 148–62; Bob Beyers, 'Machiavelli Loses Ground at Stanford; Bible Holds Its Own', *Chronicle of Higher Education*, 19 June 1991, pp. B2–B3; Raoul V. Mowatt, 'What Revolution at Stanford?' in Aufderheide,

ed., *Beyond PC,* pp. 129–32.

27. Barbara Johnson, 'Metaphor, Metonymy, and Voice in *Their Eyes Were Watching God*' and 'Thresholds of Difference: Structures of Address in Zora Neale Hurston', reprinted in *A World of Difference* (Baltimore: Johns Hopkins University Press, 1987), pp. 155–71 and 172–83. Henry Louis Gates, *The Signifying Monkey: A Theory of African-American Literary Criticism* (New York: Oxford University Press, 1988), pp. 170–216.

28. Dinesh D'Souza, *Illiberal Education: The Politics of Race and Sex on Campus* (New York: Free Press, 1991), pp. 125, 129, 135; hereafter *IE*.

29. Dinesh D'Souza, 'The Visigoths in Tweed', *Forbes,* 1 April 1991, p. 86.

30. For some notable expressions of these 'frictions', see Paul Lauter, 'Canon Theory and Emergent Practice', in *Left Politics and the Literary Profession,* Lennard J. Davis and M. Bella Mirabella, eds (New York: Columbia University Press, 1990), pp. 127–46; Patrick Parrinder, *The Failure of Theory: Essays on Criticism and Contemporary Fiction* (Totowa, N.J.: Barnes & Noble, 1987); J. Hillis Miller, 'The Function of Rhetorical Study at the Present Time', *ADE Bulletin* no. 62 (September-November 1979), pp. 10–16; and the essays collected in *Criticism in the University,* Gerald Graff and Reginald Gibbons, eds (Evanston, Ill.: Northwestern University Press, 1985), especially Reginald Gibbons, 'Academic Criticism and Contemporary Literature', pp. 15–34, and Gene H. Bell-Villada, 'Criticism and the State (Political and Otherwise) of the Americas', pp. 124–44.

31. Advertisement. 'Is the Curriculum Biased? A Statement of the National Association of Scholars.'

32. Sculley Bradley, Richmond Croom Beatty and E. Hudson Long, eds, *The American Tradition in Literature,* 3d edn (New York: Norton, 1967), p. 1905.

33. Ross Chambers, 'Irony and the Canon', *Profession 90* (New York: MLA, 1990), p. 20. For two oft-cited arguments that canonicity is not reducible to demographic 'representation', see John Guillory, 'Canonical and Non-Canonical: A Critique of the Current Debate', *ELH,* vol. 54, no. 1 (1987), pp. 483–526, and Barbara Herrnstein Smith, 'Contingencies of Value', reprinted in *Canons,* Robert von Hallberg, ed. (Chicago: University of Chicago Press, 1984), pp. 5–39.

34. Editorial, 'The Derisory Tower', *New Republic,* 18 February 1991, p. 5.

35. For introductions to the history of canon formation in American literature, see Paul Lauter, 'Race and Gender in the Shaping of the American Literary Canon: A Case Study from the Twenties', *Feminist Studies,* vol. 9, no. 3 (1983), pp. 435–63; Alan C. Goulding, 'A History of American Poetry Anthologies', reprinted in *Canons,* pp. 279–307; Nina Baym, 'Early Histories of American Literature: A Chapter in the History of New England', *American Literary History,* vol. 1., no. 3 (1989), pp. 459–88; Russell Reising, *The Unusable Past: Theory and the Study of American Literature* (New York: Methuen, 1986). Herbert Lindenberger, in 'On the Sacrality of Reading Lists', offers useful information about the origin of 'Western' core curricula at Columbia and elsewhere, and notes that Stanford's 1988 revision revised a core curriculum previously revised as recently as 1980.

36. Even this fraudulent claim rests on D'Souza's equally fraudulent misrepresentation of *I, Rigoberta Menchú* itself. For a concise and decisive rebuttal of D'Souza's erroneous account of the Nobel Prize–winning author's testimonial, see Gene H. Bell-Villada's letter to the *New York Review of Books,* 26 September 1991, p. 75.

37. It is still too soon to tell whether the 1986 Tax Code will have a significantly chilling effect on academics' ability to keep books in print, but it surely cannot help matters that the inducement for publishers to cut stock arrived in the midst of a decade of massive publishing mergers and consolidations which have made higher profitability a premium for many publishing conglomerates.

38. As Richard Yarborough has recently pointed out, 'only twenty years since the end of the sixties, it is already necessary to salvage the work of important writers of that era. ... Not to place the recovery of such texts high on our scholarly agenda is to participate in canonization by default: If the texts are not in print, they will not be bought or taught.' Yarborough, 'The First-Person in Afro-American Fiction', in *Afro-American Literary Study in the 1990s,* Houston Baker and Patricia Redmond, eds (Chicago: University of Chicago Press, 1989), p. 108.

39. Donald Kagan and Lynne Cheney, interviews, *The MacNeil/Lehrer News Hour,* PBS, 20–21 June 1991.

40. On the other hand, thanks to the public response to Anita Hill's testimony before the Senate Judiciary Committee, we now know that the vast majority of white American men can think about race and gender *simultaneously* only if they have undergone long years of intensive theoretical training.

41. Christopher Jencks and David Riesman, in *The Academic Revolution* (New York: Doubleday, 1968), start with the premise that professionalism is 'colleague-oriented' rather than 'client-oriented' (p. 201); but Burton Bledstein, in *The Culture of Professionalism* (New York: Norton, 1976), argues that professionalism allowed mid-nineteenth-century Americans to balance the ideal of personal advancement with the ideal of social service, and that professionalism worked precisely by constructing an unprecedented class of 'clients' where once there had been a 'public' (pp. 87–128). The fact that Jonathan Culler relies on Jencks and Riesman (whereas Gerald Graff relies on Bledstein) accounts for Culler's focus on criticism's 'institutions' and silence on criticism's clients. For an examination of professional criticism from the perspective of its various potential 'clients', see my *Marginal Forces / Cultural Centers: Tolson, Pynchon, and the Politics of the Canon* (Ithaca, N.Y.: Cornell University Press, 1992), Chapter 1.

42. Bruce Robbins, 'Tenured Radicals, the New McCarthyism, and "PC",' *New Left Review,* no. 188 (September-October 1991), p. 157.

43. Robbins, *Intellectuals,* pp. ix–x.

3

Exigencies of Value

PC is now bibliographically real: as someone once said, you could look it up. That is, PC is no longer a smattering of abuses and inquisitions attributable to ostensibly 'progressive' faculty and students, but a fully organized 'movement', a movement that has now earned its own listing in the *Reader's Guide to Periodical Literature* (under 'Politically Correct Movement, The'). It got that listing thanks to the brief but intense media blitz on 'PC' that occupied the first half of 1991, when the literary public sphere was littered with newsmagazines, conservative journals, editorials and opinion pieces on the new 'left McCarthyism' in the universities. Dinesh D'Souza, having failed to crack the bestseller list with *Before the Millennium,* his 1984 biography of Jerry Falwell, struck pay dirt with *Illiberal Education,*[1] and very quickly a new kind of 'common sense' was formed around the neoconservative conviction that the American university is 'an island of repression in a sea of freedom'.[2] Phantasmic as this conviction is, it has set the terms of debate to such an extent that today it is being followed by still more vehement charges that the academic left is dismissing the conservative account of PC as, well, 'phantasmic': we're not taking these complaints about leftist arrogance and intolerance seriously enough; we're denying the existence of PC, stonewalling further queries and hoping the issue goes away; and we're blaming the whole flap on media hype, conservative cabals and a moral panic of post–Cold War, paranoid hysteria.[3]

There is considerable rhetorical and political pressure, therefore, on left academics: if we are going to be taken seriously as commentators on contemporary debates in American higher education, we first have to be willing to discuss some of the crimes of our 'extremist' colleagues before we can proceed to mount the counterargument. Strategically, there may be nothing wrong with this kind of ritual confession; surely the more the academic left makes public its notable capacities for self-criticism, the

more difficult it will be for intellectual conservatives to portray their opponents as thought police. As Eugene Genovese has written, from a perspective rather different from mine,

> Radical chic has triumphed because our left-wing colleagues have declined to
> dissociate themselves publicly from ... the reigning practices of political cor-
> rectness, although many of them privately express dismay with much gnash-
> ing of teeth. So be it. But let us hope that those who censor themselves on
> grounds of *pas d'ennemies à gauche* are prepared to accept full responsibility for
> their complicity in the dishonoring of the frail remains of their political move-
> ment.[4]

Genovese is less than clear about who will do this 'dishonoring', but
this seems an accurate picture of what PC looks like to the more reasonable wings of the National Association of Scholars – and the ranks of the
unaligned to whom the academic left appears as a linked-arm brigade of
Podsnaps and Comstocks. Faced with an ultimatum such as this, surely
we can ask in return that the NAS be as self-critical as it's asking us to be.
But in the long run, regardless of our prospects of getting some reciprocal
self-criticism from the right, it's quite important that the academic left
demonstrate its syncretism and heteroglossia; for why would neoconservatives have taken to calling the academic left a new McCarthyism, if not
to construe it as a constituency so intolerant of American ideals as to merit
the suspension of its constitutional rights? This was how *real* McCarthyism proceeded in the universities, forty years ago: the right characterized
leftist teachers and scholars as so substantial a threat to national security
that the state could not honor their First, Fifth and Fourteenth Amendment rights without putting its very existence in jeopardy.[5]
In such a cultural climate, in other words, internal disagreement
among the left carries both heuristic and political benefits. Still, I think it
is dangerous for progressive intellectuals to engage these debates by starting on the defensive, as if we must begin the discussion by dealing one by
one with the right's best arguments – that Stanley Fish was wrong to write
to Duke's provost about keeping members of the local NAS off key academic committees, or that students at the University of Pennsylvania
should be able to hurl transliterated Yiddish epithets like 'water buffalo'
at their peers without being brought before the campus Star Chamber for
disciplinary hearings. Personally, I'm alternately embarrassed and outraged at such cases, but however much we might agree with our conservative and moderate colleagues that leftist intolerance is intolerable, we
will never be able to assess all the various PC incidents and judge each on
its specific merits. Nor would this task be productive even if it were possi-

ble; we will always be arguing on someone else's turf. For one of D'Souza's goals in *Illiberal Education* was simply to flood the media with so much misinformation and second-hand innuendo as to keep his critics busy doing nothing other than running down his sources and gainsaying him point by spurious point – and, on occasion, giving ground wherever D'Souza uncovered a plausible case of objectionable leftist behavior.

We have seen the model for D'Souza's strategy before, if we care to recall it. Over the course of the 1988 presidental campaign, American voters were told that Michael Dukakis was an invalid, that he would take away their guns, that he urged farmers to grow Belgian endive, and that he would allow black men on prison furloughs to rape and kill white women, because he was a card-carrying member of the ACLU. Dinesh D'Souza's *Illiberal Education,* spawned in the wake of the Republican assault upon accuracy in media, includes charges that the Harvard administration censured Stephan Thernstrom (*IE,* pp. 196–97), that Stanford's CIV course provides a 'curricular diet' of 'little more than crude Western political slogans masquerading as the vanguard of Third World thought' (*IE,* p. 92), that Duke has a mandatory quota system for hiring black faculty (*IE,* p. 158), that Alice Jardine's Women's Studies class spent its time telling jokes about severed penises and poking fun at Ernest Hemingway (*IE,* p. 209), and that black students at Stanford and Harvard have been miseducated into ignorance by African American studies programs (*IE,* pp. 75–7, 221–4). Each of these charges has been shown to be false, yet each puts progressive academics in the Dukakis Position: if such lies go uncontradicted, they become part of the common sense of the public discourse on American higher education. And yet we cannot simply denounce these lies *as lies,* since to do so is to risk being accused of stonewalling the grave crisis of political correctness in the universities.[6]

I am not denying that some intellectual moderates and conservatives have been unfairly treated by their opponents; nor am I denying that charges of racism, sexism and homophobia have been hurled indiscriminately at people who consider themselves 'liberals' and resent being associated with David Duke and Pat Buchanan. For that matter, recent academic critiques of 'liberal humanism' must, no doubt, sound strange to nonacademic audiences – as well as to scholars in the sciences and more traditional social sciences – who are more accustomed to hearing humanism criticized by Christian televangelists and liberalism criticized by Phil Gramm or Dan Quayle. I'm merely pointing out that the conditions for discussion of PC have changed since the phenomenon first hit the mass media. That is, the New Right has won the first round in this sector of the culture wars precisely by forcing its opponents to prove the negative beyond a reasonable doubt, to deny or defend the practices of the politically correct professoriate as they are reported by D'Souza, Kimball, Sykes and so on. As long as this is our starting point, we will never be able to confess to enough campus thoughtcrimes to placate the right; and, as I noted in my introduction, we saw from Lynne Cheney's treatment of Donald Lazere that the academic left wins no mercy from its attackers for being willing to criticize its own. Should we (properly) disavow inflammatory and wrongheaded people like Leonard Jeffries, for instance, the hard right will simply insist that we disavow another black scholar, and another, and then another, ad infinitum.

Those of you who think I'm kidding or mistaken would do well to consult the September 1993 *New Criterion,* which closes with a virulent attack on Houston Baker, an attack remarkable even by that journal's standards for snarling, foaming-mouth rhetoric. Noting that 'one of the interesting things about Jeffries is the fact that he has so few respectable defenders', Terry Teachout went on to say that Jeffries and Baker 'have two relevant things in common: both are black, and both are in charge of black-studies departments.'[7] Teachout, who opens his review of Baker's *Black Studies, Rap, and the Academy* by admitting that he doesn't 'know much about black studies as an academic discipline, other than what I read in the magazines', proceeds to sum up Baker's work as follows:

(1) Black studies is an indispensable part of American higher education. (2) Rap is a creative and authentic expression of the urban black experience and should thus be taken seriously by academics, particularly those working in the field of black studies. (3) Anyone who disagrees with (1) and (2) is a racist. ('ASP', p. 92)

Of course, since (3) is untrue, Teachout cannot demonstrate it, and backpedals from the assertion in his very next sentence. And since (1) and (2) are entirely unexceptionable propositions, Teachout quickly switches the dice. The rest of Teachout's review argues instead that Baker praises the 1960s, criticizes the 1980s, and writes such clotted sentences that he is 'demonstrably unworthy of being entrusted with the education of English majors, whatever their race, creed, color, or sexual orientation' ('ASP', p. 94).

Teachout concludes that Baker's is 'a vulgar, stupid, and totally unscholarly book that is "literate" in precisely the same sense that a man who tarts up his prose with two-dollar words gleaned from *Roget's* is literate' ('ASP', p. 95). This alone should tell us that the cultural right in the Clinton era is going to be roughly as committed to civil discourse as Operation Rescue is to reasoned give-and-take. But ultimately, Teachout's review is after bigger game: namely, setting the conditions for the discussion of black studies by calling on Baker's colleagues to repudiate him. The penultimate paragraph of Teachout's piece concludes:

> Everybody admits that Jeffries is the living embodiment of black studies at its worst. If the author of *Black Studies, Rap, and the Academy* is truly representative of the *best* black studies has to offer, then it necessarily follows that black studies is a joke, a pitiful and preposterous burlesque of scholarship foisted on the academy in the holy name of diversity. ('ASP', pp. 95–6)

Turning to address black scholars, Teachout writes:

> the marginalization of Leonard Jeffries is not the only task you need to take on if black studies is ever going to be a serious area. There is something else you and your colleagues need to be saying, loudly and clearly: *What* we *do is not what Houston Baker and his ilk do. If we are scholars, they are something else.* The day I see those words published in *The New York Times Book Review* under the byline of a tenured professor of black studies is the day I read another book by a tenured professor of black studies. ('ASP', p. 96)

Well, that should be clear enough: Baker *and his ilk,* renounced by a *tenured* professor, and in the *TBR* to boot. Teachout cannot be faulted for vagueness. I only hope black studies can survive Teachout's threat not to read further in a discipline he admits to knowing nothing about.

Teachout's review of Baker may be an outrageous example, but in its very outrageousness it exacerbates the crisis of self-definition for the left. The problem is this. Confronted by such an indiscriminate and mean-spirited (but certainly not racist) assault, the left is faced with the overwhelming temptation to defend its own without qualification; whereas in my own work on African American literature, for instance, I have sometimes been critical of Baker, my differences with Baker appear miniscule when contrasted with those between Baker and Teachout.[8]

This is a tiny example, but it points to a larger set of difficulties. Whereas some of the right's attacks have led liberals and moderates to throw people like Baker to the wolves (and we'll see an example of this in the closing section of this essay), other attacks impel us to try to close ranks, and neither tactic is categorically defensible or indefensible. Nowhere is this impasse clearer than in the debates over identity politics. Recently, well-respected academics with clear leftist sympathies, such as Todd Gitlin and Richard Ohmann, have begun to question the efficacy of identity politics, charging – correctly, in my view – that identity politics makes impossible any broader leftist appeal to solidarity, coalition or human rights.[9] Identity politics itself does double duty here: it is divisive precisely because it bespeaks difference and division. Claiming difference as irreducible and foundational, it therefore deliberately closes off any appeal for the necessity of a unified or popular front. And identity politics answers its critics in this idiom as well: in response to Gitlin and Ohmann, it can always claim (unfairly) that these sixties-identified white men are nostalgically calling for a return to a golden age of left unity, or (more fairly) that it's easy for white men to disclaim a politics from which they themselves have nothing to gain.[10] One can point out in return that identity politics are also criticized by women, scholars of color, and queer theorists (Joan Scott, Trinh Minh-Ha, Skip Gates and Diana Fuss, among many others) who may have more to lose from such critiques, but then one is merely saying that identity politics is best criticized from the very 'subaltern' subject positions on which identity politics is itself predicated. If you don't have to be one to know one, you do have to be one to criticize one, and thus the critique of identity politics 'from within' reinscribes the assumptions of identity politics after all. How much safer, then, to cut identity politics some theoretical/practical slack, and call it (either approvingly or condescendingly) 'strategic essentialism'.

Between them, identity politics and vicious right-wing attacks have made it exceedingly difficult to imagine a productive forum in which the academic left can propose 'teaching the conflicts' between itself and the NAS, or even teaching the conflicts among the academic left.[11] For one thing, the terrain of 'conflict' itself changes, as Yeats might say, minute by minute: where academic feminists once might have proposed debating the conflicts between Catharine MacKinnon and Drucilla Cornell, or Gayatri Spivak and Elaine Showalter, now it's very likely that academic feminists will have to deal with the 'conflict' between all of these women, lumped together in an undifferentiated mass, and post-feminists like Camille Paglia, Christina Hoff Sommers or Katie Roiphe. Hence the constant demand from the right that Women's Studies programs will not be truly 'diverse' unless they hire people like Phyllis Schlafly, who deny that such programs should exist in the first place: where identity politics insists that conflict be kept 'in the family', so to speak, the cultural right insists that fields like feminism or black studies debate the 'conflict' over whether they deserve to be legitimate academic subjects at all.

In saying this, though, I want to be clear about what identity politics is *not,* for I am well aware that women, scholars of color, and queer theorists can always be accused of playing identity politics even when they're making larger, even universalist claims about human subjectivity and agency in general (as we saw in the previous essay, when Roger Kimball objected to Elaine Showalter's belief in gender).[12] White men like myself can be accused of the same thing, no doubt, but I don't find it hard to disentangle myself from the people who make our 'identitarian' claims, simply because those guys tend to announce them pretty clearly – by wearing hoods and burning crosses, calling for the extermination of Jews or calling our separatist groups by names like 'Identity'. Identity politics names one kind, a particularly noxious kind, of enforced group conformity of thought; but groups that define themselves by choice rather than by identity may also seek to enforce a kind of identitarian conformity within their ranks, and it's crucial to distinguish between the very different kinds of social pressures that impinge on individual thinkers in each case.

I'll explain why. In a telling anecdote that points out the difficulties of political critique on the margins, Barbara Epstein has written that one class of her students at UC-Santa Cruz, 'predominantly female and strongly feminist', disapproved of Alice Echols's *Daring to Be Bad: Radical Feminism in America, 1967–1975:*

> Students' comments implied that an account that placed women, especially feminists, in a bad light was sexist. Some students argued that even if early feminists had made some mistakes, to write about them was to give ammunition to the enemy.[13]

Epstein goes on to describe the divided reactions of a second group of readers, feminists of her own generation, split between the conviction that Echols was mistaken or wrongheaded and the equally strong conviction that feminists should learn about, so as not to repeat, the mistakes Echols chronicles.

Epstein's brief account of 'self-intimidation among students, among faculty, and in progressive circles outside the university' (p. 149) is exemplary for its honesty and insight, and has done much to advance the cause of self-criticism on the academic left. Any breathing teacher who presents controversial material in the classroom will be familiar with the scenario she describes; I myself have gotten more heat about being a white critic of African American literature from white graduate students than from my black undergraduates (who have usually been pleased simply to see white guys paying serious attention to African American literature, in a department with few offerings in the area). But it should be clear that Epstein is describing a phenomenon quite different from raw identity politics; she's describing instead the uncertainty that members of marginalized groups feel about self-criticism, even when the marginalized group consists of relatively well-off people like students at UC-Santa Cruz. But none of Epstein's students, apparently, made the claim that women have a unique perspective, or experience the world in a singular way common to all women, or differ irreducibly from men either culturally or biologically.

Epstein's students made a local, pragmatic claim, wondering whether internal self-criticism benefits one's enemies more than one's own provisional group.

This behavior may be a form of 'political correctness', but is there really anything unusual or abhorrent about it, anything that warrants a major media campaign against progressive students and faculty? However regrettable some of its manifestations may be, this kind of PC seems to me business as usual in American cultural life: rap's critics complain that the music's portrayal of 'gangstas' feeds into white stereotypes, and rap's defenders reply that rap's critics are serving the white power structure as well. Black critics complain that Spike Lee's *School Daze* airs the black community's dirty laundry for white eyes, and *their* critics respond that such criticisms have internalized white standards to the extent that they dictate what black artists should and shouldn't say. Meanwhile, bell hooks and Amiri Baraka agree that Spike Lee played *Malcolm X* too fawningly for a white audience, despite Lee's successful effort to replace Norman Jewison as the film's director. As for me, I've had students, black and white, who *still* aren't sure that W. E. B. Du Bois should have criticized Booker T. Washington to white readers, preferring instead that Du Bois should somehow have kept his critique in the family, however powerful the Tuskegee Machine may have been.

The reason it's important to keep a handle on the difference between identity politics and pragmatic political self-protection (even when one regards that self-protection as misguided, unnecessary, or unproductive) is that the specter of identity politics itself simultaneously signifies and exacerbates left fragmentation, thus provoking a kind of internal metadebate over the merits of self-protection and self-criticism: should the left criticize the politics of identity? These two different forms of 'self-censorship', then, are complexly intertwined within the PC debates. Foregrounding the problematics of small-group unity and large-group difference, identity politics challenges the left to determine whether it can afford to make public the left's internal differences concerning the politics of difference. A left that refuses to critique identity politics, obviously, is a left that deserves to be castigated by the right for suppressing dissent in the name of 'diversity'. But a left that rushes to critique identity politics passes over the question with which Epstein's students, and Epstein herself, are forthright enough to grapple – namely, whether the assault from one's political opponents is so sweeping and indiscriminate as to make internal critique either useless or counterproductive. There are, after all, many areas in American life where it does no good to proclaim oneself an anti-Communist, because one's interlocutors are not interested in *what* kind of Communist you are.

Having just thrown identity politics to the wolves myself, on the recur-

sive reasoning that the assertion of irreducible difference necessarily provokes a crisis of self-differentiation on the left, I want to add two more
cautionary notes, whose overtones will resonate backward through this
book to the introduction. First, there is the problem of the right itself: one
cannot engage monologists in dialogical proposals to debate, and we
therefore need to distinguish for ourselves between the reasonable and
unreasonable right, since they're not doing us the favor of critiquing their
own. The academic right's treatment of its scurrilous tabloid, *Heterodoxy,*
provides a notable case in point. Combining the right's financial clout
with the aging Hitler Youth hijinx of Peter Collier and David Horowitz,
Heterodoxy makes no bones about its preference for thuggery over thought.
The journal has been caught fabricating at least one 'PC' story, a tale
about how the women's studies program at Wellesley sent letters to students planning to major in modern European history, charging them with
'perpetuating the "dominant white male" attitudes and behaviors that
have been oppressing women for generations.' That sounds pretty arrogant and self-righteous of women's studies – until you find out that no
such letters existed, that *Heterodoxy* made up the story out of whole cloth,
and did it incompetently, too, since there is no modern European history
major at Wellesley College. At other times, the tabloid's sense of critical
exchange has included superimposing Catharine Stimpson's head on a
nude female body. Are the leaders of the newer, kinder, gentler NAS
ashamed of this nonsense? Does it violate their commitment to rational
discourse in a free society? Is the Pope an Afrocentrist? '*Heterodoxy* is providing the kind of investigative journalism and rock 'em, sock 'em commentary that's needed', NAS president Stephen Balch has said when
asked about the journal. 'You have to admire that kind of panache.'[14]

Second, there is the tendency in some liberal circles, particularly those
libertarian schools hostile to any attempt to theorize 'social context', to
construe all processes of collective deliberation and decision-making as
'groupthink'. David Bromwich's *Politics by Other Means: Higher Education and
Group Thought* is an exemplary instance of this tendency, for in its defense
of individualism it indiscriminately attributes groupthink even to the most
provisional and non-identitarian communities, such as professional asso-
ciations. Decrying the 'new fundamentalism' on campus, an orthodoxy
enforced by 'the communitarians of the day', Bromwich writes: 'If academic life in America becomes less free in the near future, one way it may
happen is by a series of concessions to the sensitivities of the advocacy
groups.'[15] What's curious about this otherwise predictable critique of 'special interest' groups aggregated around race, gender, and sexual orientation is that Bromwich includes professionals themselves – excluding
himself – as the standardbearers of standardization: 'in the current usage

of the academy (a usage that is growing elsewhere, too), a professional is someone who is proud of belonging to an opinion-community, and professionalism is a deliberate refinement of the attitudes which make for mutual subjection within that community' (p. xv). It's a good thing professionalism isn't as totalitarian as that sentence makes it sound, or the sentence itself would never have been written by a professional literary critic. Later in the book, however, Bromwich makes explicit the tacit connection linking professionals, right-wing authoritarians and special minority-group interests: 'thinking goes on in a single mind', Bromwich thinks, and so 'as with the conformists of the civilization, so with the conformists of the profession, the voice to distrust is the "we"-voice of collective judgment' (p. 194).

Politics by Other Means takes as its epigraph a sentence from Simone Weil, which the above-quoted passage deliberately echoes: 'The intelligence is defeated as soon as the expression of one's thoughts is preceded, explicitly or implicitly, by the little word "we".' It's a noble sentiment, charting its brave, postwar way through Nazism and Stalinism, and it's earned Bromwich considerable praise from journals such as *Commentary*. But is it true? Let's see how it works. My family moved into a new place this summer, and in order to ingratiate myself with my neighbors I agreed to co-organize the fall block party. After some deliberation, my neighbors and I – that is, we – decided that 3 October was the best day for the event. Another time, I was discussing Bromwich's book with Eric Lott, and he and I – that is, we – came to the conclusion that Bromwich left himself no constructive way to think about community deliberation at all, not even among neighbors. Of course, it could be that the people of Henry Street were engaging in identity politics. So let's take a more pressing and pertinent example. We the people of the United States have often engaged in political activities predicated explicitly on ethical and moral claims advanced by or on behalf of groups: it's called 'activism'. One wonders what the recent history of the South, for instance, would look like if its black citizens pursued ethical claims in the fashion approved by Bromwich: '*we* do not necessarily want to sit at this lunch counter, only *I* do. I will not presume to speak in the "we"-voice of collective judgment, which I know you will distrust.'

The lesson, I believe, is this. The rise of identity politics poses a difficult political and ethical problem for the left, but then again, so do some critiques of identity politics by liberals. Group declarations of common identity, group self-criticisms, collective deliberations and individual dissents in the name of libertarianism or egalitarianism are all extraordinarily complicated matters, and any assertion of the priority of one necessarily has implications for all the others. We should be extremely wary, therefore, of arguments that always begin with 'we', and arguments that always refuse to. And in the interests of provisional group self-criticism, I dissent both from identity politics and from Bromwich's dissent.

But the stakes here are higher than the academic squabbling among liberals and lefties usually acknowledges, and from the perspective of many critics of American universities, the differences between myself and Bromwich are too insignificant to matter. While I might need to differentiate myself from Bromwich, or Showalter, or Houston Baker in the course of a debate inside academe, I may not want to do so when I look again at the common enemy we – ahem, I mean, these four individuals – face. The right's attacks on feminism and affirmative action, especially, are not confined to universities alone; and the right's conviction that the university is populated by the tenured radicals of the 1960s is motivated in part by its belief that left activism is dead everywhere else, and is merely being kept alive, though in a vegetative state, on the respirators of academe (which, as we all know, bears no relation to the real world). Universities, therefore, cannot undermine the gains of feminism and affirmative action on campus without helping to discredit these movements in the culture at large. And, conversely, the more they are discredited in the culture at large, the greater ideological pressure will be brought to bear on American higher education to synchronize its watches with the rest of the culture, and roll back the clock on civil rights so as to keep pace with the reactionary *zeitgeist*.

As we know, American conservatism does not operate simply by enforcing the proclamations of wealthy right-wing foundations and Beltway idea mills. If conservatives do forge the kind of hegemony and consensus they desire in American higher education, it will be because they have shifted the center to the right by convincing liberals and moderates who oppose poststructuralism, curricular reform, feminism or affirmative action that the enemy of their PC enemies will be their friend. In what follows, therefore, I propose not merely to contest one of the more outrageous claims conservatives and traditionalists have made about academic criticism, but to ask how this claim has so far won such support in the public sphere. It is a version of the argument advanced in Allan Bloom's *The Closing of the American Mind,* to the effect that the humanities in the United States are dominated by a pernicious relativism that fails to recognize the moral and ethical superiority of Western culture. The claim is difficult to rebut precisely because it is so devoid of specific content, and for this reason I will not rebut it at length; but it has proven to be remarkably popular nonetheless, particularly in arenas where its contentlessness has been an asset rather than a liability.

The claim appears in its strongest form in D'Souza's *Illiberal Education,* where it inaugurates the chain of causality on which D'Souza's indictment depends: particularly in his chapter on Duke University, D'Souza argues that literary theory has attacked traditional standards and the traditional aims of humanistic study, and in so doing has paved the way for all kinds of politically motivated (that is, leftist) assaults on liberal education.[16] In his account of Duke's initiatives to hire African American and poststructuralist faculty, D'Souza writes: 'these two ambitious hiring programs seem unrelated, but in fact there is an underlying unity: both offer a powerful challenge to the notion of standards of merit, on the level of both faculty eligibility and course content' (*IE,* p. 158). In so eroding commonly recognized standards, literary theory has thus worked in tandem with canon revision and affirmative action in university hiring, promotion, and admissions policies, since all have vitiated our commitment to 'excellence' in favor of doling out special treatment for unqualified minorities and concocting 'feelgood' courses of dubious intellectual merit. And finally, anyone who says any of the above, according to D'Souza, faces draconian academic penalties up to and including expulsion (for students) and ostracization (for faculty).

Leaving aside the truth content of D'Souza's account for the moment, my question is this: how is it that innovative scholars in the humanities can be accused *both* of abandoning their roles as moral arbiters *and* of championing a narrowly moralistic kind of 'politically correct' scholarship and criticism? D'Souza's attack has appeared often lately in various formulations, some even cruder than his; surely we recall *Newsweek*'s declaration that 'it is impossible in deconstructionist terms to say that one text is superior to another.'[17] For the most part, when this claim appears in general media, its purpose is simple – it makes professors look foolish in the light of ordinary common sense. It's almost a populist point, for it allows any reader to say, well, I don't understand this poststructuralist gobbledygook, but at least I know what I like. But then why has it also found such strong support in the American literary public sphere – in the *New York Review of Books,* the *Times Book Review,* the *New Republic,* the *Atlantic* and the *Partisan Review*? Why is it echoed by people who have nothing to do with reactionary politics, intellectual conservatism and the Olin Foundation – people like Paul Berman, David Lehman, Irving Howe and C. Vann Woodward?

I'll devote the rest of this section to answering these two questions. But because it's now axiomatic among generalist critics – and some academic traditionalists – that academe's Young Turks are so immersed in theory that we don't read literature anymore, I'm going to begin my answer by reading some Proust. Midway through *Swann's Way,* Swann's obsession with Odette has deepened to the point that he actually begins to enjoy social events chez Verdurin, and that fact alone shows you what happens when you fall for the wrong woman: where once Swann had possessed 'a sort of taste, of tact, so automatic in its operation that ... if he read in a newspaper the names of the people who had been at a dinner-party, [he] could tell at once its exact degree of smartness, just as a man of letters, simply by reading a sentence, can estimate exactly the literary merit of its author', his love for Odette and his acquaintance with the Verdurins have eaten away at his hard-won ability to separate wheat from chaff:

> having allowed the intellectual beliefs of his youth to languish, and his man-of-the-world scepticism having permeated them without his being aware of it, he felt (or at least he had felt for so long that he had fallen into the habit of saying) that the objects we admire have no absolute value in themselves, that the whole thing is a matter of period and class, is no more than a series of fashions, the most vulgar of which are worth just as much as those which are regarded as the most refined.[18]

And, as readers of the *Recherche* will recall, Swann then proceeds to lose his job at the *New Criterion,* and has to accept a steep pay cut when he's hired to a tenure-track position in the English department at Duke.

I hasten to point out that the person who links class and taste in this passage is Marcel Proust, and not some awful, politically correct, class-of-'68 French neo-Marxist like Pierre Bourdieu. For it is Bourdieu who would say that what Swann has lost here, aside from his heart, is his habitus; he has carefully worked his way upward to the point at which he can socialize with the aristocracy, and now he is losing his powers of discrimination, his means of accruing and maintaining cultural capital. And what leaps out of this passage is Proust's reductiveness: Swann's lapse in taste, his newfound commitment to tastelessness, follows *immediately* from his loss of caste, his appearances at second- and third-rate dinner parties. For although there's an intimate relation between the flow of productive capital and the flow of cultural capital – and I'll return to this below – the two streams are not quite so coincident as the passage implies.

With Professor Swann in mind as a caricature of the current cultural left, let us move next to David Lehman's *Signs of the Times.* 'Deconstructionists', claims Lehman, 'would obliterate the differences between Roger Rabbit and Henry James. The function of criticism is reduced to description and analysis; the task of evaluating works of art is left undone. Abandoned is one of criticism's foremost responsibilities: the making and revising of critical discriminations.'[19] This is a familiar enough claim, yet

Lehman also has harsh words for critics who *do* get around to discussing moral 'substance': 'the right-minded assistant professor in the post-Vietnam era imposes his or her own politically correct attitudes upon the literature of the past. ... This is, at bottom, a conception of the literary critic as an agent of the thought police' (*ST,* pp. 262–3). So here, as in D'Souza's work, we get it all ways – we're not making ethical judgments, we're not making aesthetic judgments, we're not isolating the 'aesthetic' from the 'ethical' realm, and what's more, we're making the wrong calls anyway.

Lehman's book, like D'Souza's, is less important today for its content than for the range of responses and echoes it has authorized. The book itself is by no means uniformly mean-spirited or misinformed, and Lehman does not claim, as D'Souza has tried to do, that Paul de Man's wartime writings express the dirty little secret at the rotten core of deconstruction. On the contrary, *Signs of the Times* makes an *amicus* case for what Lehman, following Howard Felperin, calls 'soft-core' deconstruction (*ST,* pp. 117–24); it usefully and cleverly draws some of its sketchy illustrations of deconstruction from the work of science fiction writer Philip K. Dick; it manages a fair synopsis of Derrida's critique of Ferdinand de Saussure (*ST,* pp. 93–8); and, most crucially, it rightly sounds its loudest note of protest not at de Man's journalism for *Le Soir* but at deconstructionists' contemporary exonerations of de Man (and their concomitant excoriations of contemporary journalists, including Lehman). This is the note of protest, the index of the public's fear, with which we must contend if we are to engage productively with literary criticism's difficulties representing itself in the public sphere.

After lauding Barbara Johnson's 'sense of the wrong de Man had done in *Le Soir*', Lehman argues that her response to the de Man affair was the road not taken by the rest of de Man's students and supporters:

> There was, then, no need for deconstructionists to hitch their wagon to de Man's fallen star – no need to enlist the methods of deconstruction to demonstrate that de Man's wartime words meant something other, something less odious, than what they appeared to say. Such an attempt would run the risk of achieving the very linkage – between de Man then and deconstruction now – that the deconstructionists presumably wanted to avoid. Yet some of de Man's ex-cohorts chose to make the attempt. By putting the strategies of deconstruction at the service of explaining (or explaining away) de Man's early 'texts', the deconstructionists lifted the controversy to a new level of debate and aroused the very fears that they ostensibly sought to dispel. (*ST,* p. 234)

In his defense of his own scandalous *Newsweek* piece on the scandal (*ST,* pp. 214–18), Lehman glosses over some of the reasons why press coverage of de Man provoked such outrage against journalists; all the same, it may be fruitless, at this point, for academics to (appear to) dodge the issue by cataloguing Lehman's own failures as a journalist.[20] Like the Bollingen Committee's defense, in 1949, of its decision to award the first Bollingen Prize to Ezra Pound for his anti-Semitic *Pisan Cantos,* the contemporary defense of de Man's articles for *Le Soir* has rested on the claim that the articles are ambiguous and paradoxical, or that they subtly condemn – if not deconstruct – the very anti-Semitism they seem to endorse. Neither deconstruction nor New Criticism has a fully formed politics in its valise; there is no clearer politics to an insistence on the arbitrariness of the sign than there was to the insistence on the irony and ambiguity of 'literary' language.[21] But there were and are questionable uses of deconstruction, such as attempts to deconstruct de Man's article on 'The Jews in Contemporary Literature', just as there were and are questionable uses of New Criticism, such as attempts to argue that the *Pisan Cantos* are not really about anything at all.[22]

Academics' reaction to the de Man affair was not only an unsettling moral and intellectual matter but a public relations fiasco to boot. Even for people who were not inclined to view deconstruction with suspicion before the scandal broke, the Derridean response was evidence that there really was, after all, something rotten at the core of the whole enterprise. Such is Lehman's verdict, and it has been seconded by other academy-watchers in the media.

In his introduction to *Debating P.C.,* for instance, Paul Berman takes the aftermath of the de Man affair as the means by which to link poststructuralism to political correctness, Paul de Man to Leonard Jeffries. Berman's collapsing of racial essentialism and anti-essentialism may seem odd, but it makes sense if you believe that poststructuralism induces a blindness to Nazism:

> Exactly what makes de Man's early reactionary harping on race different from the postmodern, supposedly progressive harping on race today? ... the distinction between the postmodern ideas and the reactionary ones is not necessarily so clear – if only because, among some of the deconstructionist masters of literary interpretation, there is a peculiar inability to detect any Nazism at all in de Man's Nazi articles, which raises doubts about the reliability of the new techniques. ... It was disturbing, for instance, but not terribly surprising, to discover a certain inappropriate fixation on the Jews in the thinking of a couple of the professors who helped draw up the proposed new multicultural public-school social-studies curriculum in New York State.[23]

101

Personally, I don't believe that the academic response to the de Man affair gives us the liberty to elide the differences between Skip Gates and Strom Thurmond, on the grounds that they both 'harp on race'; but it has clearly alarmed liberal social democrats like Paul Berman, and he is by no means alone.

Still, however much public support Lehman's sense of the de Man affair may have won, it must be said that Lehman's book cannot stand under the weight of its self-contradictions. In part one, Lehman professes his appreciation for 'applied', 'soft-core' deconstruction: 'If, in keeping abreast of new literary developments, criticism must continually come up with innovative tactics, the battery of devices associated with deconstruction will not fail to yield a value' (*ST,* p. 119). But in part two, it turns out that what Lehman deplores, even more than the 'hard-core' stuff, is 'applied' deconstruction when it's applied to something other than 'new literary developments': 'pure deconstruction is no longer the height of fashion, but the impulse continues in alloyed form, and it is as ubiquitous as ever. … The edicts of deconstruction – merged, to whatever extent, with the ideologies of Marxism, psychoanalytic theory, and feminism – remain the prevailing suppositions of the lit-crit establishment' (*ST,* p. 261). In other words, *applied* deconstruction is OK, but not *alloyed* deconstruction; or, the only thing worse than pure decon is hybridized decon, the kind that eventually winds up in the public drinking water.

Lehman's admission that deconstruction may be of some use, but only in rigorously controlled circumstances, follows from his general insistence that no critical enterprise is justified unless it works for the clearer elaboration of literary texts (as those are traditionally understood). According to Lehman, the New Critics, 'being poets themselves, had their priorities straight. Their critical energies were put at the service of literature – evaluating aesthetic success, enforcing critical discriminations, illuminating difficult works and making them accessible to the student' (*ST,* p. 50). In keeping with his conviction that 'the making and revising of critical discriminations' is among 'criticism's foremost responsibilities' (*ST,* p. 81), Lehman's idea of criticism seems confined to reader's guides, book reviews, *Cliff Notes*, and lists of the greatest books of all time – that is, explication and evaluation in the narrowest possible sense. It is this idea of criticism that underwrites Lehman's conviction that 'the student with an authentic literary vocation may be the one who feels least at home with the academic orthodoxies of our day' (*ST,* p. 29); 'nor does it seem overly cynical', he adds later, 'to suggest that the unreadable articles in scholarly journals are written and published primarily to demonstrate the writer's familiarity with the professional patois, in an effort to advance up the rungs of the tenure ladder' (*ST,* p. 86).

Clearly, this is an argument congenial to professional writers and book reviewers who feel that academic criticism has overstepped its bounds; indeed, much of *Signs of the Times* engages in a form of sibling rivalry with professional critics. In a telling passage, for instance, Lehman claims that 'literature, not criticism, is and always was the really dangerous activity; the death sentence on the author of *The Satanic Verses* is only the most violent recent reminder of that' (*ST,* p. 63) – as if Islamic fundamentalism acknowledges such a genre distinction, as if the Ayatollah would have pardoned Rushdie had he blasphemed against the Prophet in a critical essay rather than in a work of fiction. But whatever its intended audience, Lehman's argument has lowered the standards of what counts as 'serious discussion' of deconstruction. This is not because Lehman himself is un-serious – his tone is one of high moral seriousness throughout – but because he has begun to be cited as a trustworthy authority on the subject, displacing explicators such as Christopher Norris and Jonathan Culler, who are now to be considered tainted insofar as they are sympathetic to the stuff.

Lehman underwrites D'Souza's attack on Duke University, as a glance at D'Souza's footnotes will reveal, but it's not just partisan political writers like D'Souza who base their cases on Lehman. C. Vann Woodward's review of *Illiberal Education* in the *New York Review of Books* also cites Lehman as the sole source for its claim that deconstruction licenses scholarly incompetence. 'The burden of the movement's impact in some universities', writes Woodward in support of D'Souza's account of Duke, 'was a challenge to minimal standards of merit in faculty qualifications, and the content and quality of what should be read and taught.'[24] Whatever the specific merits and limitations of Woodward's review, surely it is alarming that so august a figure as he, a scholar sometimes described as the dean of American historians, would rest his case exclusively on Lehman's report. But Woodward's review itself is not the problem. The problem is that we now live in an intellectual climate in which passing acquaintance with *Signs of the Times* apparently provides one with sufficient authority to gauge the effects of deconstruction. Only ten years ago, when Stanley Fish pointed out an egregious error in Walter Jackson Bate's critique of Derrida (Bate had claimed that Derrida 'never turns to the really major philosophers'), Bate graciously acknowledged the error and replied, 'my short paragraph on deconstructionism was admittedly testy and unfairly dismissive. ... But I hasten to say that a close study of Culler's recent books helped to change my perspective and encouraged me to consider the subject with a less prejudiced mind. Accordingly I wish I had omitted that paragraph.'[25] Thanks to *Signs of the Times,* however, no traditionalist need travel so far into enemy territory as to actually read Culler's *On De-*

construction; from here on in, a quick glance at Lehman will do.

But Lehman himself is, notoriously, less than reliable as an explicator of Derrida. No more than ten pages after his credible synopsis of Derrida's revision of de Saussure, he makes a mistake less embarrassing (because less 'catchable') but more basic than W. Jackson Bate's: "There is nothing outside the text' – '*Il n'y a rien hors du texte*' – [Derrida] claimed in *Of Grammatology*' (*ST,* p. 107). But Derrida had claimed no such thing. His phrase was *Il n'y a pas de hors-texte,* there is no outside-the-text. Lehman knows, I think, that few general readers will see or understand the difference between the two aphorisms, even though Lehman's Derrida claims that when you leave the printed page you fall into an abyss and are devoured by monsters, and Derrida's Derrida claims only that textuality, like Elvis, is everywhere. But if this sort of Nabokovian mistranslation of Derrida is to be considered serious discussion of deconstruction, perhaps it will not be long before someone informs us, in the pages of a national magazine, that Derrida invented 'reception theory' at that famous mixer at Johns Hopkins in 1966, when he walked into the faculty lounge, scanned the buffet table, and announced, 'il n'y a plus des hors-d'oeuvres.' And we will have come full circle, from work to text and back to work again.[26]

Curiously, Lehman saves some of his most astringent criticism for Barbara Herrnstein Smith. And though he mentions her only in passing, his treatment is characteristic – not only of *Signs of the Times,* but also of the current generalist consensus on the depravity of academic criticism and interpretive theory:

> 'literature' itself has been devalued – or deconstructed: there is no reason, theoretically, for the 'literary' critic to favor a novel by Dickens, say, over an episode of *All in the Family,* since either will serve as an appropriate object of study. Academic literary theorists have their own ponderous way of making this point. Here is Duke professor Barbara Herrnstein Smith's statement of the theme in her book *Contingencies of Value:* 'Since there are no functions performed by artworks that may be specified as generically unique and also no way to distinguish the "rewards" provided by art-related experiences or behavior from those provided by innumerable other kinds of experience and behavior, any distinctions drawn between "aesthetic" and "nonaesthetic" (or "extra-aesthetic") value must be regarded as fundamentally problematic.' And two centuries of aesthetic philosophy go sailing out the window. ...
>
> The leveling of literature to the status of a soap opera, a board game, or 'innumerable other kinds of experience and behavior' must seem a perverse doctrine for a literature professor to espouse. There is certainly a place in a comic campus novel for the solemn-faced professor who declares that Shakespeare and Milton are not intrinsically superior to daytime TV.[27]

What's going on here? Though Herrnstein Smith's argument is decidedly anti-Kantian, why the moral outrage at the alleged defenestration of a mere two centuries of thought? Why the dogged appeal to 'intrinsic' criteria, when the idea of the 'intrinsic' is exactly what's under scrutiny in *Contingencies of Value*? And why Lehman's insistence on reading Herrnstein Smith as if she were saying that everything is just as good as everything else, when in fact she spends much of her argument debunking this 'Egalitarian Fallacy' (*CV*, p. 98)? One reason is Lehman's reliance on an article in the *New Republic:* 'as the critic David Bromwich noted in a percipient review of Smith's book, the utilitarian philosopher Jeremy Bentham "said it faster: 'Quantity of pleasure being equal, push-pin is as good as poetry.'"' [28] If Lehman is speaking for a generalist consensus here, and I will argue that he is, it would appear that the only thing he resents more than theorists who separate 'literature' from 'life' are theorists, like Barbara Herrnstein Smith, who don't.

It might be said, for example, that deconstruction has worked, alongside feminism, new historicism and cultural studies, to broaden our sense of 'textuality', to broaden the range of texts we read, and to broaden the ways in which we read them. In fact, Lehman's book comes close to acknowledging this aspect of deconstruction on more than one occasion. At one point, he almost agrees with the idea that 'the world *is* a text and may be read, or deconstructed, as such. It becomes possible, thanks to this logic, to widen the scope of critical inquiry. That is far from a bad thing and not altogether a new thing' (*ST*, p. 80). But then something strange happens: just when he's on the verge of realizing that deconstruction may work to bridge the 'literary' and the 'non-literary', Lehman switches tracks, to accuse deconstruction of failing to observe the crucial distinction *between* the literary and the non-literary. In his next paragraph, therefore, he writes that 'the real effect of deconstruction has not been to widen inquiry but to narrow it' (*ST*, p. 80). How does it do that, when it's investigating so many disparate kinds of texts? Lehman replies that it narrows inquiry precisely by investigating disparate texts – thus, as I noted above, obliterating 'the differences between Roger Rabbit and Henry James' (*ST*, p. 80), or, in the case of Herrnstein Smith, reducing literature to the status of a soap opera or board game.

Strictly speaking, that doesn't follow. Nor is it possible, in one breath, to accuse deconstruction – or any other mode of interpretive theory – of segregating art (or literature, or language) from other human endeavors, and then to accuse it also of breaking down the distinctions between literature and other human endeavors. Almost every page of *Signs of the Times* evinces Lehman's inability to distinguish between indeterminacy and meaninglessness, his insistence on defining deconstruction as 'the doctrine that literature, while full of sound and fury, signifies nothing' (*ST,* p. 266). But whenever Lehman seems to grant that deconstruction and its hybrids may serve to criticize narrow formalisms and reintegrate the aesthetic realm with other realms of our lives, he turns and accuses them of exiling the question of literary value: so should it turn out that contemporary theory doesn't separate 'life' (or the keyword of your choice) from 'literature', Lehman will interpret this as an assault on the very idea of aesthetic value.[29]

Herrnstein Smith began her project in *Contingencies of Value* over ten years ago with an article in *Critical Inquiry,* whose opening paragraph declared 'not merely that the study of literary evaluation has been ... "neglected", but that the entire problematic of value and evaluation has been evaded and explicitly exiled by the literary academy' (*CV,* p. 17). Given words like these, one might think that Herrnstein Smith would find friends among the Lehmans of the world, especially since she has done a great deal to put 'value' back on the map of literary theory in the past ten years; one would not expect to find her to be the bête noire of the literary public sphere. But as it happens, her discussion of value is practically a rallying point for generalists, a crossroads where New Right caricatures of academic theory meet up with more general, man-of-letters fears that academic criticism has simply spun out of control. *Partisan Review* editor William Phillips has demonstrated, for example, that you don't have to disagree with Herrnstein Smith to vilify her – all you have to do is misread her, and then rephrase one of her central points and elaborate it as if it were your own. After declaring that 'her view of literature comes close, in my opinion, to a *reductio ad absurdum* of deconstructionist theory' and that 'her entire approach is incorrect', Phillips proposes his own view, which he apparently conceives to be the definitive rebuttal of *Contingencies of Value* rather than its faint echo:

> How then are works of art and literature judged and how do they survive for centuries? ... it is the professionals – as it is in every other endeavor – who are influenced by and perpetuate the works that we think of as making up the tradition. If we understand this, we can understand the nature of the agreements and the differences that make up the continuous consensus.[30]

Irving Howe, in his *New Republic* brief on the canon debates, fares no better, though he does not mention Herrnstein Smith by name:

> as for the claim that there is no certainty of judgment, all tastes being historically molded or individually subjective, I simply do not believe that the people who make it live by it. This is an 'egalitarianism' of valuation that people

of moderate literacy know to be false and unworkable – the making of judgments, even if provisional and historically modulated, is inescapable in the
life of culture. And if we cannot make judgments or demonstrate the grounds
for our preferences, then we have no business teaching literature.[31]

These are not the words of dastardly neocons posing as arbiters of the
neutral center; indeed, though Howe, Phillips and Lehman all suggest
that Herrnstein Smith is unqualified to profess literature, her opponents
on the right have been still less kind. It seems irrefutable that Herrnstein
Smith has touched a nerve in the public sphere, much as Stanley Fish's
avowal that 'there is no such thing as intrinsic merit' has been used to
rally the townspeople to arm themselves with torches and drive the mon-
ster from our midst. Appropriately enough, however, Herrnstein Smith's
book itself seeks to account for the reception with which it has met:

> wherever systems of more or less strictly segregated hierarchical strata begin
> to break down and *differentiations* become more numerous, rapid, complex,
> less predictable, and less controllable, the resulting emergences, mixtures,
> and minglings will look, from the perspective of those in the historically up-
> per strata, like flattenings, falls, and collapses – in short, like *losses of distinction.*
> It is certainly to some extent destratification itself that has put The Other in
> our company and classrooms and his meat on our plate and palate. (*CV,* p.
> 77)

What Herrnstein Smith's reception shows us is that one doesn't have
to belong to 'historically upper strata' to construe the transvaluation of
values as the loss of moral fiber; Lehman, Phillips, and Howe are not
aristocrats, but they may constitute (or be trying to forge) a generalist
consensus. Nevertheless, I believe Herrnstein Smith is right to link
'destratification' in aesthetic and curricular decision-making with destratification in the culture at large; though the relation between the two is not
one of identity, as Proust's depiction of Swann would have it, it remains
the case that academic critics, at their broadest reach, are attempting to
redirect the flow of cultural capital to – and from – new textual constituencies, new student populations, and new critical communities.

Let me sum up this section with a deep breath and a brief recap: in the
past ten years or thereabouts, academic critics have begun to question the
moral urgency and certainty with which a previous critical consensus enforced the distinction between high and low culture, and the distinction
between the aesthetic and the nonaesthetic. We have argued that the categories of aesthetic and moral value are contested and not identical categories, and that they are historically and socially variable. And we have put
these arguments into material, pedagogical practice by reviewing and re-

evaluating the texts we teach, the texts we once didn't teach, and the means by which we produce and reproduce the value of these texts. It follows, therefore, that we are being attacked over these exigencies of value not because we have vacated the terrain on which critics interrogate cultural values, but precisely because we have *not* vacated this terrain. To put this another way, the academic transvaluation of all questions of aesthetic and cultural value provides one of the primary reasons we are met with such hostility and misunderstanding in the literary public sphere. For traditionalists and conservatives have succeeded in opposing the academic transvaluation of value by painting it as a radical relativism that refuses to believe in 'values', thereby generating a moral panic that the institutional guardians of culture have left their posts – or worse, transformed their posts into soapboxes from which they proclaim that there should be no guardians of culture, since everything is as beautiful and true as everything else.

In the foregoing section I deliberately chose to document what I consider to be an outrageous and contentless claim, in order to track one element of the process by which 'common sense' about academe is being secured among people who do not belong to the constituency of the New Right. But what does the squabble over aesthetic value have to do with the larger social mission of American universities? My answer is tentative – I, too, have no definitive account of the relation between the distribution of cultural capital and the accumulation of productive capital – but I hope it will make apparent the concordances between what we usually call, however heuristically, 'theory' and 'practice'.

In *Work Time,* a neo-Gramscian analysis of higher education in English, Evan Watkins argues persuasively that English departments play crucial roles in a general economy of evaluation: no matter what specific tasks are assigned and carried out in individual classrooms, Watkins writes, 'what results from that abstract labor form, what abstract labor "produces" and passes on, are evaluations.'[32] For Watkins, these 'evaluations' include almost every kind of measurement circulated outside English departments – most notably grades and letters of recommendation written by faculty for students applying to jobs and graduate or professional schools – as well as measurements largely internal to academe, such as the results of academic job searches. This latter category also encompasses all forms of literary criticism, regardless of intent or method, for 'it is impossible for literary criticism not to deal with values, however differently "values" and the relation of work to values may be construed' (*WT,* p. 84). In this respect, English stands – chiefly by virtue of its size and influence in the humanities and its omnipresence in every level of education – as a crucial component in the liberal arts curriculum, especially as that curriculum is conceived by traditional liberals, who characteristically (and justifiably) conceive of education as a tool for combatting class inequities.

But as Watkins points out, it follows from this conception of education that the mechanisms of *discrimination* – as an abstract process, without regard to the content of curricula or criticism – are fundamental to the liberal defense of the liberal arts, especially insofar as the costs and benefits of nonvocational education cannot otherwise be measured:

> Almost from the beginning, then, the idea that education could compensate for the potential lack of authority and direction in a democratic society rested on a claim not only to provide the knowledge necessary to the proper functioning of the social system, but also to generate the selection mechanisms whereby the best people would be sorted out to assume the authority of that knowledge. (*WT,* p. 97)

By means of these selection mechanisms, we represent ourselves to the larger social formation as professionals uniquely qualified to assess the cultural capacities of our students in everything from literacy training to 'advanced' critical thinking; we therefore occupy a central (though usually unacknowledged) position in the credentializing of future professionals. Watkins concludes his chapter on 'work as evaluation' with an incisive summary of our role in an ideal liberal meritocracy:

> insofar as education is expected to compensate for an absence of a hereditary class structure by training professionals, it must generate internal criteria for selecting those students with the abilities to become professionals. English then occurs at the point where the social function of training professionals turns into the educational task of evaluating general student ability to proceed to professional training. Likewise, insofar as education is expected to compensate for the 'home environment' of 'culturally disadvantaged' students so that they can compete equally for jobs, it must also generate internal ways of evaluating the verbal skills perceived as necessary for that competition. And English, again, occurs at the point where this social function turns into an internal educational task of evaluation. (*WT,* p. 136)

I think Watkins's argument in *Work Time* underestimates the number of our students in English who intend to go directly into elementary and secondary education; for those students, the content of our curricula is at least as important as our mechanisms for selection. The standard works of American literature taught in high schools will slowly change over the next twenty years, for instance, partly as a function of the training high school teachers receive in the expanded-canon classrooms of the 1980s and 1990s.

But for students who'll be seeking jobs elsewhere than in the educational apparatus, Watkins's account is compelling. And since so much of our work as it is perceived outside universities depends on the clarity and transferability of our criteria of evaluation, it should be easy to see why nonacademics would be so unsettled by the possibility that we have forsaken our tasks as evaluators of student merit, or by the possibility that our retheorizing of aesthetic merit will have catastrophic consequences for the idea of educational meritocracy in general. It's also easy to see why liberals are alarmed – as much as any D'Souza-Cheney conservative – by the claim that English is now ruled by nihilist-relativists. Indeed, one reason the New Right has floated this canard in the first place is that it is so likely to win support among liberals, who fear the rise in academe of any group, New Right or New Left, which seems to threaten the 'compensatory', egalitarian ideal of liberal education. To such liberals, especially, we need to explain and defend our myriad tasks of evaluation much more convincingly than we've done so far.

We tend to think of 'explanation' as what we do for students and laypersons, but, as I hope to have shown above, the crisis of intelligibility in the humanities is in part a crisis within academe itself: literary and cultural studies, especially, are in deep trouble when they can be savaged by academics in other departments who don't know much about literary and cultural studies. Woodward, for instance, has belatedly acknowledged that *Illiberal Education* 'turned out to contain some serious and irresponsible factual errors', but that has not prevented him from continuing to take D'Souza at his scurrilous word concerning the scholarship of Houston Baker: referring to the 'clownish charades' of the MLA, Woodward swallows whole D'Souza's claim that 'the incoming president of the MLA, Houston Baker of the University of Pennsylvania, thinks "reading and writing are merely technologies of control" and considers "literacy" the menace.'[33] Even Benjamin Barber's learned and humane account of education and democracy, *An Aristocracy of Everyone,* purchases its account of 'radical excesses' by recycling Houston Baker's most famous nonstatement:

> To make his point about the relativism of cultural values, Houston A. Baker, the current president of the Modern Language Association, tells us there is no more difference between high culture and pop culture than between a hoagie and a pizza. What he means is that there is no more difference between Shakespeare and Virginia Woolf than between Virginia Woolf and a pepperoni slice with extra cheese. This is to say, as John Stuart Mill quipped about Jeremy Bentham's reductionist utilitarianism, that there is no difference between pushpin and poetry.[34]

What Baker said to a *New York Times* reporter about axiology and standards of taste, and which was reported as a statement about the equivalence of 'hoagies and pizzas', is here elided with Bromwich's critique of Herrnstein Smith in an offhand (and unfootnoted) passage in an otherwise meticulously responsible book.[35] Clearly, this image of literary critics is a potent one: apparently having forsworn our obligation to discriminate among books and cultures, we appear even to our fellow academics as irresponsible judges who threaten the integrity of the entire judicial enterprise.

Again, the link between cultural and productive capital is not direct: no aspirant to the upper middle class is worried specifically about the issues of literary value I've outlined above; no undergraduate who's considering a career in personnel management fears that her employment prospects turn on whether she's read *The Sound and the Fury* or *Quicksand* in her Am-lit survey. But as Herrnstein Smith reminds us, there are no firm distinctions between what is and what is not aesthetic, different criteria of value operate in relation to one another, and there are potentially broad social issues at stake when people start retheorizing the epistemological foundations -- and the *social* foundations – of the systems responsible for the production of value. And she argues, finally, that if this kind of retheorizing goes on long enough, it might result (indeed, has resulted) in observable phenomena like new student populations putting 'their' meat on 'our' tables.

Herrnstein Smith is not often credited with addressing the social ramifications of her theory of value, but I can illustrate what's currently at stake in her position, and Watkins's as well, by making one further point about those new student populations. Neoconservatives claim that academic standards have fallen in the past thirty years, and they point to affirmative action in hiring and admissions as the proof. But the expansion of the franchise in American higher education since 1960 has actually altered admission standards to most elite American schools by *raising* them. Perhaps nothing is so fraudulent about the conservative attack as this: in railing at 'affirmative action' in college admissions and hiring, the neocons ask us to forget that everyone who graduated from an all-male, all-white school (as most major American universities were until the 1960s) was competing for admissions and honors – and jobs, and privileges – with an artificially weak applicant pool that included less than 40 percent of the potential college population. Having benefitted hugely from our nation's legacy of sexism and apartheid in higher education, these people (and their under-forty acolytes at the American Enterprise Institute, such as D'Souza) now show up to complain about the 'dilution' of academic standards, despite the fact that one of the largest 'affirmative action' programs in the country is the system of legacies, thanks to which the children of these alumni are now given preferential treatment in college admissions. Here too, it's not that universities don't have what D'Souza thinks of as 'standards of merit'; it's that the social and cultural bases of those standards have changed drastically.

This is not simply an academic discussion of the shifting sands of time. The reason these questions of value and merit come before us with such exigency, the reason we need so desperately to be able to take our case to the public and to the literary public sphere, is that we are facing a drastic shrinking of resources, the defunding of the humanities, the wholesale elimination of entire academic programs and departments that aren't directly helping us compete with Japan. And I believe that our chances, in the humanities, of withstanding this defunding and this retrenchment depend largely on our ability to recognize and to win new constituencies among aspiring educators and professionals, new constituencies on the progressive-but-not-poststructuralist left, and, not least of these, new constituencies in what we must help to make a broader and more diverse public sphere. However arcane and 'theoretical' some of its manifestations may seem to be, therefore, the struggle over the university is a struggle in which liberals, centrists and progressives, inside or outside the universities, have a civic obligation to engage.

Notes

1. Dinesh D'Souza, *Falwell: Before the Millennium* (Chicago: Regnery-Gateway 1984); *Illiberal Education: The Politics of Race and Sex on Campus,* hereafter cited in the text as *IE*. Before the Falwell book is consigned to the ash-heap of history, it's worth looking at – as a period piece of far-right optimism in 1984, and as an index of how far D'Souza will go to curry favor with extremists in the interest of self-advancement. 'Falwell has altered the terms of political discourse in this country', concludes D'Souza. 'Today he sets the agenda. ... He has successfully made himself the spokesman for moral America. ... Listening to Falwell speak, one gets a sense that something is right about America, after all' (pp. 194, 205).

2. See Chester E. Finn, 'The Campus: "An Island of Repression in a Sea of Freedom"', *Commentary,* vol. 88, no. 3 (1989), pp. 17–23. Finn attributes the line to Abigail Thernstrom; Peter Collier and David Horowitz, in 'PC Coverup', *Heterodoxy,* vol. 1, no. 1 (1992), pp. 11–12, attribute it to Jeane Kirkpatrick. The confusion as to who actually coined the phrase is doubtless due to the fact that all card-carrying neocons were required to repeat it at one point or another during the 1980s.

3. See, e.g., Dinesh D'Souza, 'P.C. So Far', *Commentary,* vol. 92, vol. 4 (1991), pp. 44–7; Collier and Horowitz, 'PC Coverup', pp. 1, 11–12.

4. Eugene Genovese, 'Religious Foundations of the Constitution', *Reviews in American History,* vol. 19 (1991), p. 338; review of Ellis Sandoz, *A Government of Laws: Political Theory, Religion, and the American Founding* (Baton Rouge, La.: Louisiana State University Press, 1990).

5. For a compelling and well-documented account of how McCarthyite persecution proceeded in higher education, see Ellen W. Schrecker, *No Ivory Tower: McCarthyism and the*

Universities (New York: Oxford University Press, 1986).

6. When, for instance, the nonpartisan American Council on Education released the results of a survey that found that 'three per cent of all the institutions surveyed said battles had erupted on their campuses over textbooks or information presented in the classroom', NAS members were quick to respond that the survey results confirmed the existence of a PC conspiracy: 'This is an attempt to cut off the debate over political correctness', cried Ted Smith of Virginia Commonwealth University. He was seconded by Joe DeBolt of Central Michigan University, who claimed that the ACE report, by not finding widespread PC abuses, had 'slid into counter-attack mode'. See Susan Dodge, 'Few Colleges Have Had "Political Correctness" Controversies, Study Finds', *Chronicle of Higher Education*, 7 August 1991, pp. A23–24.

7. Terry Teachout, 'Another Sun Person Heard From', *New Criterion*, vol. 12, no. 1 (1993), pp. 91–2.

8 . My critique of Baker can be found in *Marginal Forces/ Cultural Centers: Tolson, Pynchon and the Politics of the Canon* (Ithaca, N.Y.: Cornell University Press), pp. 136–7, 201–4.

9. See, for instance, Todd Gitlin, 'The Rise of Identity Politics', *Dissent*, vol. 40, no. 2 (1993), pp. 172–7, and 'From Universality to Difference: Notes on the Fragmentation of the Idea of the Left', *Contention*, vol. 2, no. 2 (1993), pp. 15–40; Richard Ohmann, 'On PC and Related Matters', *minnesota review*, vol. 39 (1992–93), pp. 55–62.

10. This latter response applies to me as well, of course.

11. The injunction to teach the conflicts is Gerald Graff's, and Graff knows full well that the injunction will meet with resistance. Insofar as intellectual consensus rests on a shared sense of what goes without saying, writes Graff, 'it will seem to be in [Older Male Professor's] interest to resist entering into dialogue with [Younger Female Professor]. Why should the OMPs of the world agree to debate with the YFPs over such an issue as the canon, especially when what bothers the OMPs is that there should *be* a debate over the canon to begin with?' Gerald Graff, 'Other Voices, Other Rooms: Organizing and Teaching the Humanities Conflict', *New Literary History*, vol. 21, no. 4 (1990), p. 833. Dialogism's limitations need not prevent us from teaching the conflicts; on the contrary, it is all the more necessary to engage in dialogism *because* one knows its limits. If we know that we are engaging in dialogue with people who resist dialogism as a principle, then we must also know that it may be more dangerous, in the long run, *not* to engage such people. Nothing is gained by leaving D'Souza, Bennett, Cheney et al. to their own devices – not only because their own devices are quite powerful, but more crucially because there is no way to win public consent to liberal and progressive positions in cultural politics without engaging the terms of their opposition.

12. For a substantive and provocative demonstration of how this issue plays itself out among left scholars in academe, see 'Identity Politics: An Exchange', a conference discussion among Todd Gitlin, Joan Scott, Lisa Duggan, Jerry Watts, Cameron McCarthy and Michael Eric Dyson, among others. In Michael Bérubé and Cary Nelson, eds, *Higher Education under Fire: Politics, Economics, and the Crisis of the Humanities* (forthcoming from Routledge).

13. Barbara Epstein, 'Political Correctness and Identity Politics', in Aufderheide, ed., *Beyond PC*, p. 150; hereafter cited in the text.

14. Quoted in Courtney Leatherman, '2 Disillusioned Radicals Use "Heterodoxy" to Mock the "Politically Correct University"', *Chronicle of Higher Education*, 17 March 1993, p. A16. The *Chronicle* article also reports *Heterodoxy*'s fabrication of the PC story from Wellesley.

15. David Bromwich, *Politics by Other Means: Higher Education and Group Thinking* (New Haven, Conn.: Yale University Press, 1992), pp. 44, 49; hereafter cited in the text.

16. The claim is elaborated at greatest length in D'Souza's chapter on Duke, 'The Last Shall Be First: Subverting Academic Standards at Duke', *Illiberal Education*, pp. 157–93.

17. Jerry Adler et al., 'Taking Offense', *Newsweek*, 24 December 1990, p. 53.

18. Marcel Proust, *Swann's Way*, trans. C. K. Scott-Moncrieff and Terence Kilmartin (New York: Vintage, 1982 [1913]), pp. 265, 269. In my *Marginal Forces / Cultural Centers: Tolson, Pynchon, and the Politics of the Canon* (Ithaca, N.Y.: Cornell University Press, 1992), pp.

227–8, I discuss this passage in the context of debates about modernism, postmodernism, and mass culture.

19. David Lehman, *Signs of the Times: Deconstruction and the Fall of Paul de Man* (New York: Poseidon Press, 1991), pp. 80–81.

20. But for a trenchant critique of Lehman's *Newsweek* piece by a fellow academic/journalist who covers literary theory, see Mitchell Stephens, 'Deconstruction and the Get-Real Press', *Columbia Journalism Review* (September-October 1991), p. 42.

21. For a less polemical review of the academy's response to de Man's *Le Soir* articles, see Louis Menand's review of *Signs of the Times*, 'The Politics of Deconstruction', *New York Review of Books*, 21 November 1991, p. 43: 'Deconstruction does not seem, in short, to have been the slightest help to its practitioners and defenders when they addressed themselves to de Man's wartime texts. His defenders could not agree about what counted as ideologically good or bad; they could not even agree about what de Man was actually saying in his collaborationist writings.' In this respect, concludes Menand, 'they found themselves in the position of all honest critics.'

22. For details on the Bollingen Controversy, see William Barrett, 'Comment: A Prize for Ezra Pound', *Partisan Review*, no. 16 (1949), pp. 344–7; Gerald Graff's reading of Archibald MacLeish's defense of the award, in *Poetic Statement and Critical Dogma* (Evanston, Ill.: Northwestern University Press, 1970), pp. 172–9; and Karl Shapiro (who cast the lone dissenting vote – for William Carlos Williams's *Paterson*, Book I), *Reports of My Death* (Chapel Hill, N.C.: Algonquin Books, 1990), pp. 41–5.

23. Paul Berman, 'Introduction: The Debate and Its Origins', in *Debating P.C.*, pp. 16–17.

24. C. Vann Woodward, 'Freedom and the Universities', *New York Review of Books*, 18 July 1991; rpt. in Aufderheide, ed., *Beyond PC*, p. 39; D'Souza's strange claim that René Wellek is 'one of the co-founders of the *au courant* scholarship' (*IE*, p. 179) is not footnoted in his book (and must intend 'au courant' in the paleontological sense in which Kant and Coleridge are au courant as well), but surely owes something to Lehman's assertion that Wellek's 1948 *Theory of Literature* 'helped pave the way for the vogue of literary theory' (*ST*, p. 71).

25. W. Jackson Bate, 'To the Editor of *Critical Inquiry*', *Critical Inquiry*, vol., no. 2 (1983), p. 370. See also the article to which Bate was responding, Stanley Fish, 'Profession Despise Thyself: Fear and Self-Loathing in Literary Studies', *Critical Inquiry*, vol. 10, no. 2 (1983), pp. 349–64, and Bate's 'The Crisis in English Studies', *Harvard Magazine*, vol. 85 (September-October 1982), pp. 49–53.

26. I owe this point to Barbara Johnson, who discussed it in her keynote address at a conference held at Loyola University of Chicago, 'Deconstruction and the Politics of Education', 14 March 1992. But on rechecking Lehman's use of the phrase – since it is, after all, one of the phrases to which Derridaphobic commentators constantly recur – I found a curious substitution (supplement?) at work: Lehman footnotes *Of Grammatology*, p. 163 ('if we consider, according to the axial proposition of this essay, that there is nothing outside the text'), thus ignoring the first appearance of the phrase in '... That Dangerous Supplement ...' on p. 158, where, of course, Spivak renders the original French, as well as the alternate (and more accurate) English translation, in brackets: '*There is nothing outside of the text* [there is no outside-text; *il n'y a pas de hors-texte*].' Here, quite clearly, the point is that, as Derrida writes in the previous sentence but one, that a reading 'cannot legitimately transgress the text ... toward a signified outside the text whose content could take place, could have taken place outside language': Jacques Derrida, *Of Grammatology*, trans. Gayatri Chakravorty Spivak (Baltimore: Johns Hopkins University Press, 1976), p. 158. I cannot say whether Lehman deliberately cited the phrase's appearance on a page where the fraudulence of his retranslation would be obscured, but at best, it's worth asking whether he's read the essay in which the notorious phrase occurs, and worth remarking Lehman's chutzpah in 'authenticating' his misreading by retranslating it into French in the first place.

27. Lehman quotes Barbara Herrnstein Smith, *Contingencies of Value: Alternative Perspectives for Critical Theory* (Cambridge, Mass.: Harvard University Press, 1988), p. 34; hereafter cited in the text as *CV*.

28. Is Bromwich's review of *Contingencies of Value* really all that percipient? In the version included in *Politics by Other Means*, Bromwich starts off by claiming that Herrnstein Smith 'hopes to prove that there are equally good arguments for any literature we choose to teach', and proceeds to argue that 'she has no interest in a defense either of taste or of judgment' (pp. 205, 210). It is not clear that Lehman has read *Contingencies* for himself. Elsewhere, too, Lehman is ill served by his occasional habit of letting other people do his reading for him. At the close of his book, Lehman writes that 'George Orwell's books are shunted aside in favor of an investigation into his reputation – as if Orwell's claims on our attention had less to do with what he wrote than with an alleged conspiracy among professors and critics to foist Orwell on us' (*ST,* p. 260). Critics who have read John Rodden's *The Politics of Literary Reputation: The Making and Claiming of 'St. George' Orwell* (New York: Oxford University Press, 1989) will know that this is unrecognizable as a synopsis of that book; Lehman has quite clearly gotten his information second-hand at best, most probably from Joseph Epstein's idiosyncratic review of Rodden. See Epstein, 'The Big O: The Reputation of George Orwell', *New Criterion,* vol. 8, no. 9 (1990), pp. 14–24.

29. Like many anti-academic generalists, Lehman inveighs against academic criticism because it is disconnected from the real world and impenetrably jargon-ridden; and like many anti-academic generalists, he has to come up with some other rationale for his opposition to feminism, which he attacks for being *too* connected to the real world – and all too readable (therefore all too likely to corrupt critical discourse still further). In an especially arch passage, Lehman remarks with mock astonishment that 'gender now amounts to a formal dimension of a work of art. Or so I gathered in the corridors of the MLA convention' (*ST,* p. 52).

30. William Phillips, 'Comment', *Partisan Review,* vol. 56, no. 3 (1989), pp. 345, 346, 347. When Phillips says 'professionals', however, he means specifically to *exclude* academic literary critics, for he charges that Herrnstein Smith grants academics the exclusive rights to cultural reproduction – that she 'inflates the academy by assigning it the role of deciding the quality (not the value) of works of art' (p. 347). Leaving aside Phillips's murky distinction between quality and value, it's notable here that Herrnstein Smith actually invests relatively little authority in the academy: 'the academic activities described here ... are only a small part of the complex process of literary canonization' (*CV,* p. 47). Perhaps we should worry less about the reading-comprehension skills of the nation's teenagers and more about the reading skills of prominent essayists and editors in the literary public sphere.

31. Irving Howe, 'The Value of the Canon', *New Republic,* 18 February 1991, p. 46; rpt. in Berman, ed., *Debating P.C.,* p. 166.

32. Evan Watkins, *Work Time: English Departments and the Circulation of Cultural Value* (Stanford, Calif.: Stanford University Press), p. 85; hereafter cited in the text as *WT.*

33. Woodward, *Freedom and the Universities,* pp. 29, 47.

34. Benjamin Barber, *An Aristocracy of Everyone: The Politics of Education and the Future of America* (New York: Ballantine Books, 1992), p. 118. For a searching critique of Barber's appeal to the civic ideal of citizenship, see John Brenkman, 'The Citizen Myth', *Transition,* no. 60 (1993), pp. 138–44.

35. The Baker quote originated in an article by Joseph Berger, 'U.S. Literature: Canon under Siege', *New York Times,* 6 January 1988, p. B6. For an account of what Houston Baker said over the course of his ninety-minute interview with Berger (which got boiled down to two sound bites in the *Times*), see my interview with Baker, 'Hybridity in the Center: An Interview with Houston A. Baker, Jr', *African-American Review,* vol. 26, no. 4 (1993), pp. 547–64.

PART II

Critical Theory

in the Public Sphere

4

Just the Fax, Ma'am:

Or, Postmodernism's Journey

to Decenter

In the waning moments of the 1970s, *Eraserhead* was playing at the Waverly in the West Village, and David Lynch, its director, was not exactly a household name, though he did find some kindred spirits who'd always known there were puffy-cheeked women singing under the radiator. When he was given a TV series in the spring of 1990, eyebrows went up nationwide, and everyone waited to see whether the Apocalypse would follow from the historic encounter between David Lynch and prime-time network TV. But Lynch's relentlessly strange and provocative *Twin Peaks* became so widely acknowledged a critical success that it wound up being explained to – and defended from – the uncomprehending masses by none other than the house organ of the uncomprehending masses, *USA Today,* whose *Life* section loudly protested the show's hiatuses and eventual cancellation by ABC. *Soap Opera Weekly* checked in from time to time with astute, sympathetic, and theoretically sophisticated assessments of the show's development, and large segments of middle America were served up Lynch's hallucinogenic Northwest, along with a side of pie, for over a year.

Meanwhile, back in the late 1970s, a few miles north of the Waverly, Kool DJ Herc and Grandmaster Flash were busy recycling vinyl cultural products in some strange new ways. A mere decade or so later, 'rap', aka hip-hop, has become the single largest music on the block – *any* block. On the technical tip, hip-hop's dazzling blends of traditional and electronic musical forms, together with its dexterous pillaging of various recent cultural archives, have launched (among other things) a thorough, multimedia examination of blackness and the technological means of cultural reproduction. And in the space of a few years, hip-hop has made its way from turntables to TV ads for cola, throat lozenges and kids' breakfast cereals, all the way from the Bronx to Bel Air – surviving its many co-optations and crossovers at every little step. Not even Hammer and Vanilla

Fro-Yo have frozen out Ice-T and Ice Cube; and while black radio in Philly and elsewhere keeps trumpeting its new 'no-rap' programming, grain-fed American youth can *still* hear the latest singles from L. L. Cool J and Monie Love on central Illinois' best mix of yesterday and today. Hip-hop has become a national music whether it likes it or not, our most politically important music *despite* (or in addition to) its gradual citation-and-absorption by fast-food chains and *People* magazine.

Hip-hop and David Lynch have little else in common, but between them they do go to show that postmodernism isn't merely a 'style' located somewhere in cultural products; at a much greater reach, it involves new configurations of cultural transmission, the means by which artifacts (and 'copies' thereof) circulate in the general culture. It isn't that pomo gives you 30 percent more modernism for your money (more uncertainty, more fragmentation, more playful self-consciousness), and it's not that postmodernism is modernism's evil dwarf twin, hell-bent on knocking down everything modernism took such a long time to build. Instead, what's going on involves a more subtle and elusive cultural shift, in which it's getting harder (and more challenging) to determine what it means for ostensibly 'avant-garde' cultural works to be available in so many media instantaneously.

These disseminations, these 'new configurations', are by no means limited to the work of our contemporary 'avant-gardes'; on the contrary, they include the retransmission of what was once the modernist avant-garde – which has, in the past fifty years, gotten itself distributed in such a way that it is now more likely to show up on the walls of corporate offices than in cafés or garrets. Yet when we try to gauge the relation between mo and pomo, it doesn't help to ask yet again what modernism was, because (as we'll see later on) even that question is a distinctively modernist question. Rather, what pomo wants to ask is this: How do we understand modernism's circuitous route into our general culture, whereby *The Waste Land* wound up in every classroom and *faux* Piet Mondrian wound up in the packaging design of L'Oreal mousse and hair spray? And does the transmission of Eliot and Mondrian involve the same processes by which Lynch and hip-hop became part of our cultural lingua franca?

Of course, it's easy to claim that postmodernism simply entails the corporate co-optation of everything in sight, since postmodernism seems to follow from (and accelerate) modernism's own absorption into the general culture. As *New German Critique* editor Andreas Huyssen puts it in *After the Great Divide,* the irony here is that 'the first time the US had something resembling an "institution art" in the emphatic European sense, it was modernism itself, the kind of art whose purpose had always been to resist institutionalization.'[1] Why then should we be mourning the passing of the modernist avant-garde in the first place? In the 1990s, when you can't tell anymore where the *garde* is, it's a fair bet that you don't know whether you're *avant* of it or not. And as a result, 'avant-gardism', even in these troubled times, has come to seem gestural if not downright reactionary.

This is what Huyssen means when he calls ours a 'post-avant-garde' society. For Huyssen, as for a legion of younger cultural critics, it no longer makes any sense for artists or critics to claim positions on the 'margin' or in the 'center' of the culture, because the contemporary cultural landscape resists precisely such static confrontations between margins and centers. And if there are no margins and centers, then there's no vanguard; and if there's no vanguard, then there's no site of authentic, unsullied, 'pure' cultural production, immune to the technologies of economic and cultural *re*production.

Them's fighting words, you know, to people who continue to see themselves as 'avant-garde'. Yet even if there were a bona fide, certified-authentic vanguard out there, who's to say that its cultural work would be more important than – or even distinguishable from – the kinds of stuff we find in what we still call 'mainstream' media? It may yet come to pass that thirty years from now, when we look back at how the 1980s replayed the 1950s with a knowing but deceptive wink, we will care less about the 'media image' photographs of Cindy Sherman than about Nick at Nite's relentlessly campy promotions for its reruns of *The Donna Reed Show,* which fill your late-night TV screen with a graphic style composed of equal parts early *Jetsons* and late John Waters.[2] Besides, who needs artists and writers to 'lay bare the device' of contemporary culture, when laying bare the device has become standard business practice anyway? As Kirk Vardenoe and Adam Gopnik, the directors of *High & Low: Modern Art and Popular Culture,* have written, 'in the age of Joe Isuzu, a hardened knowingness about the value-emptied amorality of media culture was, far from being the preserve of a small cadre of vanguard thinkers, the sour, commonplace cynicism of the whole commercial culture.'[3] The *High & Low* show itself was brought to you by the folks at AT&T, who urge you to reach out and touch someone by giving the gift of modern art, the gift that keeps on giving.

How did we get into this strange party? Who's responsible for these lousy hors d'oeuvres? Uh – can we come in again?

Sure, we can *always* come in again; postmodernism means never having to say you've been here before. In fact, the word 'postmodern' has just hurtled into its fifth decade, bandied about since the 1950s by art critics as by *Spy* magazine, real estate agents and *TV Guide,* and in the process of going through a few demigenerational changes, it's become a strange kind of 'essentially contested' term that many people are just tired of contesting. Even Ihab Hassan, who had been using the word since way back in the 1960s when John Barth was Prince of Pomo and everybody was talking about the 'literature of exhaustion' – even Hassan recently dropped his pen in fatigue, writing, 'I have already written enough of these matters, and ... I would let postmodernism rest.'[4] (Thud. Snore.)

Well, who wouldn't be tired, confronted with all these postmodernisms, this L=A=N=G=U=A=G=E writing, MTV, ACT UP, e-mail, junk bonds, Madonna, smart bombs, poststructuralism, Reaganism, terrorism, colorization, Houstonization and, if you order right away, much, much more? And as if this profusion weren't enough, we now have a number of constituencies for whom the adjective 'postmodern' signifies little more than a new brand name, as in the case of *Postmodern MTV*, a seemingly redundant phrase of the late 1980s–early 1990s that, as one of my students suggested in a seminar on postmodernism (itself a postmodern artifact), merely denoted 'things that sound like Morrissey'.

However, we do have some idea of why a unified field theory of 'postmodernism' is neither possible nor desirable, and before I get to my own concerns about postmodernism and history, I want to suggest two reasons why postmodernism remains a cultural field distinguished by internal dissensus.

For one thing, one man's postmodernism is another woman's poison. In some ways, all of post-1960s feminism is postmodern, because it's destabilized 'universal' languages, questioned gender and subjectivity, and rewritten our dominant historical narratives. But then again, not every feminism *wants* to be postmodern, since the suspicion remains that pomo will dissolve all possibility for political resistance in a bubbling vat of textuality and ironic self-parody. In 1983, in an essay entitled 'The Discourse of Others: Feminists and Postmodernism', the late Craig Owens convincingly charged his fellow theorists with a systematic neglect of feminism's role in pomo, practice and theory; but six years later, in *The Politics of Postmodernism*, Linda Hutcheon claimed that postmodernism lacks any theory of agency, without which feminism is impossible.[5] So either the question is whether pomo should acknowledge the feminists in its midst, or whether feminism should acknowledge the postmodernism sitting next to it on the bus and mumbling to itself about Max Headroom and identity politics. Does one of these isms bracket the other? You tell me.

Thing number two has to do with 'facts'. To wit, it's hard to determine the relevant facts and features of pomo when so much of pomo has questioned how 'facticity' is constructed. David Byrne opened the 1980s by intoning, in 'Crosseyed and Painless', that 'Facts don't do what I want them to / Facts just twist the truth around.' Ronald Reagan, having been reportedly 'brutalized' by facts before a 1984 debate with Walter Mondale, closed the decade by stammering, 'Facts are stupid things.'[6] In the meantime, we switched over painlessly to a government by the photo op, of the photo op, and for the photo op, and the neofascist Institute for Historical Review offered $50,000 to anyone who could disprove its claim that the Holocaust never happened. In what may have been facticity's last stand, in 1985 the IHR was defeated in court by a Holocaust survivor, Mel Mermelstein; nonetheless, the IHR's director, Tom Marcellus (a man apparently immune to fact), replied that the defeat was 'the best outcome we could have had', since 'we did not have to compromise any of our positions.'[7]

On another front altogether, fifty years of anti-positivism from people as diverse as Ludwig Wittgenstein, Thomas Kuhn, and Michel Foucault have led the cultural left to argue that objects of knowledge are locally and historically specific, and that they become available for human understanding only within certain 'language-games', 'paradigms', and 'discursive formations' (not that these are three names for the same thing, either). So we have multiple histories of postmodernism, which are themselves licensed by postmodernism's multiplicity. And they're also a result of pomo's propensity for searching out and destroying unitary, linear historical narratives, the kind that serve up clear origins and straightforward plot development (whether of rise or decline). This 'anti-foundationalist' aspect of postmodernism has sometimes been taken to be a potentially liberating intellectual tool, since it suggests that our beliefs and practices are culturally 'contingent', subject to ongoing revision, bound to no historical determinism. And by the same token, we've found that 'proof' is a more slippery thing than we'd thought – something that depends more on rhetoric, power, persuasion and consensus than on 'incontrovertible fact'.

It's not that there are no 'facts' in pomo, or that anything goes so long as everybody's happy; rather, it's that pomo has paid acute attention to how various human communities go about deciding what will count as 'facts'. As Kuhn argued in *The Structure of Scientific Revolutions* (1962), revolutionary 'paradigm-shifts' occur when one dominant theory supersedes another, but the new paradigm doesn't simply 'falsify' or 'disprove' the older model. Instead, writes Kuhn, paradigm-shifts are matters in which 'neither proof nor error is at issue', because different scientific communities were simply seeing different 'facts' even when they were looking at what we now think are the same phenomena: 'theories, of course, do "fit the facts", but only by transforming previously accessible information into facts that, for the preceding paradigm, had not existed at all.'[8]

But while pomo's encounters with anti-foundationalism and feminism have rendered us unable to conceive of a single, monolithic thing called 'History', postmodernism has been acquiring a history of its own. And this alone should provoke us into some historical reflection, because as far as I can see, the recent history of pomo's shifting definitions can be charted largely in terms of how people have determined pomo's relation to history. Perhaps nothing has been so widely misunderstood about pomo as this; indeed, in some cases, the postmodernism we thought to be lamely ahistorical has now been judged by some recent histories of pomo to be nothing less than the very spur to revisionary historicism. To put matters another way: although postmodern historicism flaunts its inability to capture the past 'the way it really was', it has also quite effectively exploded the claims of other historicisms (such as marxisms) to be able to do so either.

OK, I know this one takes some explaining, so let me back up a second and fill in the details.

For much of the first half of the 1980s, critics from left and right spent a good deal of their time forming two neat, separate lines to take turns bashing postmodernism. On the left, Terry Eagleton found pomo to be facetious, pointlessly playful and possessed by an attitude toward history not unlike that of *Bill and Ted's Excellent Adventure;* on the right, Hilton Kramer found pomo to be facetious, pointlessly playful and possessed by an attitude toward history not unlike that of *Total Recall.* Ageless modernist torchbearer Denis Donoghue complained that 'postmodernism is content to let a thousand discrepancies bloom', because in pomo, 'no artist's desire reaches out for spontaneity or an original relation to the world'; and the earl of Duke, Marxist critic Fredric Jameson, proposed that postmodernism and late capitalism had bequeathed us 'a world in which stylistic innovation is no longer possible, all that is left is to imitate dead styles.'[9] Donoghue and Jameson? Kramer and Eagleton? Golly, it finally looked as if *something* had gotten these boys to stop fighting and play nicely – and that something was pomo. It was a happy time, and soon, 'rock' musicians stopped suggesting that they wanted to die before they became old enough to do 25th Anniversary Reunion Tours, and started singing instead that they were working out 'most every day, and watching what they eat.

Just as it was getting hip to be square, squares were getting hip to whimsical Left-Banker Jean Baudrillard's notion (first advanced in 1983) that our era is distinguished by what he called 'the precession of simulacra'. In the era of the simulacrum, Baudrillard declared, when 'the map engenders the territory' and everything is a twentieth-generation copy of everything else, we find a suspiciously compensatory cultural reflex – 'a proliferation of myths of origin and signs of reality ... a panic-stricken production of the real and referential.'[10] This Baudrillard calls the 'hyper-real', and no doubt it's here to stay, since we hear so frequently that real people purchase real food for real people and drink beer that's as real as it gets, 'cause you can't beat the real thing. Except maybe if you have two hundred Elvis impersonator impersonators ringed around a replica of the Statue of Liberty.[11]

Baudrillard's essay has now become something of a postmodern clas-sic, so much so that it's been invoked to explain everything from the art of Jeff Koons to the Iran-Contra hearings: simulacra of roadside kitsch, simulacra of parliamentary 'justice'. And in an appropriately Baudril-lardian way, 'The Precession of Simulacra' has itself had a significant im-pact on postmodern writers and artists whose work Baudrillard's theories are then called upon to explain, in a rather circular fashion.

Yet I think Baudrillard's essay – and its influence – may be remem-bered less as a definitive description of postmodernism than as an index of what the pomo debate looked like in the mid 1980s. For it wasn't hard to see, even seven or eight long years ago, that what people feared or celebrated about postmodernism had to do with issues of tangibility and thinginess. Hence all the apocalyptic rhetoric about the disappearance of the referent, the death of Man, the end of philosophy, the death of the author, the dissolution of the subject and the impossibility of apocalyptic rhetoric. In a 1986 lecture, Jameson opined almost off the cuff that word processors were to postmodernism what the typewriter was to modern-ism: that is, in the breaking-point between mechanical reproduction (keys, ink, hammers, machinery, industrial economies, sweaty Socialist Realist men in overalls) and electronic transmission (laser printing, modems, mi-crochips, information economies, Steve Jobs on the cover of *USA Today*) lay the distinction between mo and pomo.[12] Sort of like the difference between pinball and video, and who *wouldn't* be nostalgic for the days when pinball games had no microchips, no sound effects, and a top score of 99,999?

The only problem was that while the right hated pomo for fairly obvi-ous reasons (having never even learned to play pinball, the right naturally figured that 'Space Invaders' was the death knell of reflective thought), the left – including Baudrillard – seemed paralyzed by dreams of days when things were better, days when things were *thingy*. You know, when the proletariat and the haute-bourgeoisie wore recognizable uniforms, and sat down facing each other at heavy, wooden tables arguing about *real* wages – silver dollars, doubloons and florins. None of this 'simulacra' nonsense, none of these credit rollovers and reinvested pension funds, and most of all, none of these dang teleconferences.

Of course, not all of the left felt this way. But perhaps it was only the repeated interventions of women, ethnic minorities and variously queer theorists that finally shattered the pernicious sense of nostalgia to which so many men on the postmodernist *and* anti-postmodernist left fell victim. Or perhaps it wasn't until pomo began to come to grips with the various social liberation movements of the past generation that it began to take stock of what it might mean to retheorize recent history from the vantage point of *plural,* discontinuous, multiply constituted 'public spheres'. Surely, it is hard to imagine a group other than white male intellectuals who would be in the position to tell stories about exhausted literature, or about our decline and fall from the Golden Age of the public intellectual; and in this sense, 'history' simply wasn't available for postmodern scrutiny until the disenfranchised showed up and put it on the table. As Barbara Ehrenreich has recently said, one reason we shouldn't make the mistake of confusing 'multiculturalism' with the left is that 'the left is not sufficiently multicultural to deserve being confused with multiculturalism, at least not yet.'[13]

Either way, in the past few years, it seems that only a few pointed words from people like Nancy Fraser, Gayatri Spivak, Douglas Crimp and Cornel West have gotten most of what remains of the left to check its books and think again about the project of going back to the future. As for the rest of the erstwhile anti-pomo 'left', the mugged-liberal crowd who thought social justice was a good thing so long as they didn't have to get their own coffee, live in bad neighborhoods, or put up with men kissing each other in public ... well, the less said about that bunch the better.

I don't mean to replay the notorious false dichotomy between postmodernism and the left. My point is simply that the left has had a number of misgivings about pomo's alleged erasure of materiality and about its relation to history. If, for instance, postmodernism has troubled the distinction between consumption and production (as it certainly has), then the left has some reason to say that pomo is no different in this respect from consumer capitalism, in which consumption has itself become a kind of 'production' (and notoriously so in the merger-mad 1980s). Obviously, the same can be said for much of recent literary and cultural theory, especially 'reception theory', which, in its more interesting formulations, maintains that cultural artifacts are 'produced' only by means of their continued consumption.

But pomo isn't just consumerism with a veneer of theory – not in hiphop (which 'consumed' late 1970s disco only to spit it back out in scratching and sampling), and not in the work of artists like Hans Haacke. When Haacke foregrounds the means of cultural transmission, he doesn't do so in order to glorify consumption; on the contrary, Haacke's work rigorously interrogates the socioeconomic conditions of art's 'ownership' and contests the corporate reprivatization of public expression. From the perspective of Haacke's left postmodernism, then, you could say that what makes Philip Johnson's famous AT&T building postmodern is not its Chippendale top but its tax-abatement 'plaza', which, as Herbert Schiller noted in *Culture Inc.* (1989), is marked by a revealing sign of the times:

> PUBLIC SPACE
> Owned and Maintained by A. T. & T.
> 550 Madison Ave., N.Y.C.

In AT&T's 'public space', as in the critical reception of Haacke and hip-hop, we find that postmodernism isn't without enemies in its reconfiguration of the means of cultural transmission. Even as pomo culture spans the globe and appears in your living room, the global culture of 'free market' capitalism is doing its best, often (and paradoxically) enough, to *restrict* circulation, to *reprivatize* culture, to *recapture* public spheres, museums, airwaves and Xerox machines, and to *reinforce* the laws of copyright, ownership, and authorship.[14] In pomo's future tenses, right and left will very likely duke it out over the availability of 'public' information; and postmodernism's politics will be a struggle for control – not over the means of production, but over the means of *replication*. Who cares about the funny Chippendale top? Not me.

What's crucial here is that whenever we speak of 'the means of cultural transmission', we're also speaking of the processes of *historical* transmission. And no one theorist illustrates the recent history of postmodernism's history so well as Fredric Jameson, who's spent most of the last decade calling pomo the 'cultural dominant' of our era. Jameson's latest brief, a gorgeously produced 400-page document (*Postmodernism, or the Cultural Logic of Late Capitalism*, 1991), begins by suggesting that 'it is safest to grasp the concept of the postmodern as an attempt to think the present historically in an age that has forgotten how to think historically in the first place' (p. ix). That sounds like a prescription for heroic failure to me, however beset by cultural amnesia we may be. But in the opening pages of his hundred-page 'Conclusion', Jameson takes issue with the mistaken notion that he is either a 'vulgar Marxist hatchet man' or a 'post-Marxist' who's stopped worrying and learned to love the boom. 'I write', he now writes,

> as a relatively enthusiastic consumer of postmodernism, at least of some parts of it: I like the architecture and a lot of the newer visual work, in particular the newer photography. The music is not bad to listen to, or the po-

etry to read; the novel is the weakest of the newer cultural areas and is considerably excelled by its narrative counterparts in film and video. (p. 298)

All well and good. Still, the first versions of Jameson's argument do sound pretty dour in retrospect. In 'Postmodernism and Consumer Society' (1983), he held that postmodernism could only attempt pastiche, rather than parody, because 'there remains somewhere behind all parody the feeling that there is a linguistic norm in contrast to which the styles of the great modernists can be mocked' ('PCS', pp. 113–14). Whereas today, thanks to our cultural fragmentation and hypertrophy of cultural styles, we have no linguistic norm, and 'that is the moment at which pastiche appears and parody has become impossible' ('PCS', p. 114). Pastiche, then, is like everything you've had before, all mixed up – but 'without parody's ulterior motive, without the satirical impulse, without laughter' ('PCS', p. 114).

To Jameson, pomo pastiche was most painfully evident in 'nostalgia' films like *Star Wars*, which evoked without irony the era of Saturday afternoon serials. But in his suggestion that the movie *Body Heat* is a 'distant remake' of *Double Indemnity,* Jameson sounded an ominous note:

> It seems to me exceedingly symptomatic to find the very style of nostalgia films invading and colonizing even those movies today which have contemporary settings: as though, for some reason, we were unable today to focus our own present, as though we have become incapable of achieving aesthetic representations of our own current experience. But if that is so, then it is a terrible indictment of consumer capitalism itself – or at the very least, an alarming and pathological symptom of a society that has become incapable of dealing with time and history. ('PCS', p. 117)

In Don DeLillo's *White Noise* (1985), a massive chemical spill (the novel calls it an 'airborne toxic event') gives people a false sense of déjà vu – that is, it makes them *think* they have déjà vu even though they don't. Such is the world Jameson once described; DeLillo's point, and Jameson's, is that we have plenty of evidence that consumer capitalism's frenetic production of new, improved I-forget-whats does in fact work to erase our sense of, um, whatever, I think, ah, did I mention *Total Recall* yet?

But in another sense, the moment for this kind of historicist despondency is itself a part of pomo's past; one might even venture to say, these days, that there's reason to be cheerful. Long ago, in a galaxy far, far away, we thought postmodernism was a world of sheer depthlessness and virtual reality, where Presidents confuse World War II with World War II movies and the torched tenements lining the Cross-Bronx Expressway get plastered with Slum-Kote, a space-age façading polymer designed to make unsightly urban blight vanish in seconds. But lo, postmodernism has turned out to have developed a critical edge after all – and it even takes a serious attitude toward history (now understood to be the sum of processes of historical transmission), how about that. It hasn't fixed the Bronx, but it has brought the Bronx to my own MTV, and what's more, it's forced us to rethink what it is we're post- in the first place.

According to Andreas Huyssen's surefooted negotiations of mo and pomo, 'postmodernism is far from making modernism obsolete. On the contrary, it casts new light on it and appropriates many of its aesthetic strategies and techniques, inserting them and making them work in new constellations' (*AGD*, pp. 217-18). And one of the things we may now understand about our modernist legacy is that our century's art need not necessarily proceed, as do missile delivery programs, capitalisms and the works of James Joyce, developmentally into systems of ever-increasing complexity. For if we read 'postmodernism' with less emphasis on the dismissive prefix and more on the presence of the name-within-the-name, then we can position pomo against modernism without having to claim that postmodernism is either new or improved. What looks to one person like a rehashed pastiche of hi-modernist panache, therefore, may appear to another (me, say) as a trenchant revision of traditional modernist tropes and aesthetic strategies.

As I mentioned earlier, item one on this agenda is the question of whether modernism was truly, always and everywhere, an avant-garde movement after all. Since we can't very well rope together T. S. Eliot, Dada Berlin, Djuna Barnes, André Derain, Isadora Duncan and Igor Stravinsky, then maybe we should go back up to the attic, sort through this pile of boxes our great-grandparents left us, and try to determine whether all this stuff is as oppositional and corrosive as its labels claim. And here, we have to ask not only about the modernists themselves, but also, and more crucially, about modernism's publicists and groupies.

Modernist promoter Philip Rahv once claimed that even Eliot's *Four Quartets* should by rights be ascribed to the 'venturesome spirit' of 'the literary avant-garde which must be given credit for the production of most of the literary masterpieces of the past hundred years.'[15] But by the time Rahv wrote that sentence, Eliot was a conservative Anglican royalist on his way home from picking up the Nobel Prize. And ever since then, many American critics have been embroiled in the nondispute over who 'owns' modernist poetry – T. S. Eliot, Ezra Pound or Wallace Stevens. The correct answer is 'none of the above', but just the same, even if literary modernism *were* reducible to the venturesome work of one ultracon-

servative white man, what does it mean for us in the 1990s that modernism has so long been *classic*? Again, this is not the same question as the
question of what modernism 'was'; nor can it properly be asked from
'within' modernism, for when modernist theorists ask how modernism
became so routine in our daily lives, they just can't see around their own
edifice.

In a 1983 article entitled 'The Making of the Modernist Canon', for
instance, Hugh Kenner concluded that the modernist canon, far from being the construction of critics like Kenner, was organically grown 'chiefly
... by the canonized themselves.' Kenner was seconded a few years later
by fellow modernist fan Helen Vendler, who averred in the face of all
evidence to the contrary that 'canons are not made by governments, an-
thologists, publishers, editors, or professors, but by writers.'[16] So you can
try to ask modernist critics and apologists about who *transmitted* modernism – but they'll only shake their heads, look at you quizzically, and reply
with knotted brow that modernism simply transmitted itself.

And – now here's the catch – modernists will claim also that when
modernism transmitted itself into the cultural center, it died. For those of
you who were wondering why the avant-garde is dead, you may take
comfort in knowing that the question is older than many of the people
asking it, and that it just doesn't have an intelligible answer outside of
modernist assumptions about centers and margins. Probably the best
case in point here is Anglo-American modernist literature, which, having
established itself in the academies and anthologies in the 1940s and
1950s, was at once retrospectively theorized as an avant-garde whose
force lay in its resistance to institutionalization, and whose success was
therefore its failure.

In a famous *Partisan Review* essay of 1957 entitled 'The Fate of the
Avant-Garde', Richard Chase wrote that 'the insurgent movement in this
country which defended "modernism" – that is, the aesthetic experimentalism and social protest of the period between 1912 and 1950 – has expired of its own success' (p. 367). Chase concluded by charging that
modernism 'has been institutionalized by the universities and the publishers, which by definition means that in its modern phase it has to come to
an end' (p. 375). Modernism, in other words, has no shelf life here: its
expiration date is by definition the date when it first shows up in a central
store.

Fair enough; by the 1950s Anglo-American modernism had indeed
been 'institutionalized' in those tiny little padded cells known as 'classrooms', and by 1965 Lionel Trilling could write, in 'On the Teaching of
Modern Literature', that the teaching of modern lit effectively kills its subject, by making The Void into something every well-rounded person

should encounter in college. But isn't there something wrong with this picture? Look again: in the passage cited above, Richard Chase's canonical 'modernism' allows him to conflate aesthetic experimentalism and social protest under one sign, that of an 'insurgent movement' that 'defended "modernism"'. Thus Chase's account leaves no room for avant-garde social/aesthetic protest that attacked (or was at best ambivalent toward) modernism, no room for *New Masses,* the early-thirties Edmund Wilson of *Axel's Castle,* the militant Suffragette campaigns in prewar Britain, or any of the writers of the Harlem Renaissance. (No one in the Harlem Renaissance wound up expiring of success.) The lessons here, then, are that not all of modernism was 'insurgent', not all insurgents liked modernism, and most of our *truly* insurgent modernisms were, as Cary Nelson's *Repression and Recovery* (1989) has shown, utterly obliterated from the cultural record when, in the postwar years, 'modernism' was incorporated under the sign of Eliot/Pound Enterprises.

But then the inevitable question follows: who impoverished and monologized 'modernism' and why?

The pomo jury is still out on this one, but Andrew Ross has offered one explanation I find persuasive. In *No Respect: Intellectuals and Popular Culture* (1989), Ross tackles the various intellectual formations that sought to 'contain' mass culture after the collapse of the Old Left in the late thirties. For what really 'consolidated' modernism, in the 1940s and 1950s, was a conglomeration of strange modernist bedfellows, as critics of the anti-Stalinist left lined up with critics of the right in a bi- or multi-partisan agreement that nothing could resist the twin evils of totalitarianism and mass culture – nothing except the transcendent masterpieces of the modernist 'avant-garde'. Over the soul-saving virtues of modernism, even the liberal/socialist lambs and the agrarian-conservative lions were agreed: Clement Greenberg and T. S. Eliot, F. O. Matthiessen and Cleanth Brooks, Lionel Trilling and Allen Tate. As Ross puts it, 'the mass society critique was first advanced on the left as an explanation for the failure of socialist movements, and the growing successes of fascism. ... As a result, the picture of mass culture as a profitable opiate, synthetically prepared for consumption for a society of automatons, won favor among the anti-Stalinist, and mostly Trotskyist intellectuals grouped around the little magazines like *Partisan Review, Politics,* and *Dissent.*'[17]

Therefore, there could have been no passing of the modernist cultural moment, in these terms, until we saw the realignment of 'high art' and 'mass culture', a realignment provoked by Pop art, television, feminism, roadside architecture, camp, the Black Arts movement, deconstruction, and a contradictory host of critical forces dedicated to the common cause of asking whether modernism and mass culture actually were polar, binary opposites in the first place. In other words, modernism didn't die when it was absorbed into the university and the supermarket; it was cryogenically preserved amid the mass culture it affected to despise, living on into an era that no longer needs (or finds it possible) to maintain a binary opposition between the High and the Mass. From the twin peaks of pomo, indeed, it's come to look as if modernism and masscult were the yin and yang of the early twentieth century – or, in Huyssen's words, as if 'their much heralded mutual exclusiveness is really a sign of their secret interdependence' (*AGD*, p. 16). For Huyssen, then, postmodernism works to destabilize the high-art/masscult opposition from within; and for Andrew Ross and critics working out of the British Cultural Studies tradition, what's most important to postmodernism is the passing of the 'coercion' theory of masscult, the dogged notion that masscult's consumers (of, for example, TV, pornography, and romance novels) are just couch potatoes, passively absorbing whatever comes their way.

The current upshot of reassessments of the 'culture' in mass culture, concludes Ross, is that today, an 'intellectual activism' disconnected from 'the vernacular of information technology and the discourses and images of popular, commercial culture will have as much leverage over the new nomination of modern social movements as the spells of medieval witches or consultation of the *I Ching*' (*NR*, pp. 212–13). If this means that academics and policy consultants have to stop quoting T. S. Eliot and start watching that prime-time clearinghouse of postmodern TV intertextuality, *The Simpsons*, so be it: either our self-appointed intellectual and artistic vanguards learn what Ross calls 'lessons about the business of contesting popular meanings without speaking from above' (*NR*, p. 207), or – read my lips – it can spend the rest of its days trying to figure out what 'eat my shorts' means.

The landscape looks exciting, and the field of critical inquiry (like the field of cultural and artistic production) has expanded considerably if not downright vertiginously: the passing of 'avant-gardism' has left us a world in which cultural subversion and political quietism may turn up anywhere on the dial, even hand in hand – and a world in which yesterday's subversions can very easily become tomorrow's quietisms. Such a state of affairs should keep us up at night pretty regularly, but let me tell you, it beats watching *The Donna Reed Show*.

For my money, the only unambiguously regrettable development in all this is the sad fate of poor old modernism. Where once the stuff had had the power to disturb, shock, transform and energize its audiences, it's now fallen into the hands of the sorriest bunch of cultural reactionaries you'll ever want to see, people like Hilton Kramer at the *New Criterion* – the kind of critics who appear without fail, every generation, staff in hand, to grouse voluably about how culture took a fatal turn for the worse precisely ten years before they were born, and how the art of 'our' past can sustain us in these trivial times if only we venerate it sufficiently. What do you think happens to Kramer when pomo points out that his 'classic' modernism and mass culture have something to do with each other? Well, it isn't pretty. All Kramer has to do is walk into the *High & Low* exhibit, and the popping of his blood vessels becomes downright audible: 'we know straightaway', if we're a we, 'that in "High & Low" we are in the presence of one of the most unconscionable intellectual swindles we have ever seen in a serious museum.'[18]

But surely this too is to be expected: as 'classicity' touches everything from Braque to Coke, there will be a growing number of reactionaries who'll resist any historical inspection of The Real Thing. Soon, no doubt, the same curmudgeonly people who complained about pomo's playfulness will be screeching that pomo is Politically Correct. And by then, we can expect two things. Thing one will be that postmodernism's complex and indeterminate projects of cultural critique, wherever on the dial we find them, will have drawn some blood from the vastly complacent culture they inhabit. Thing two is that postmodernism will shortly thereafter be defended by the *next* century's reactionaries as the scale of classicity in which future generations will once again be weighed and found wanting.

And by *then*, if memory serves, pomo's institutionalization will look to us like it's déjà vu all over again.

Notes

1. Andreas Huyssen, *After the Great Divide: Modernism, Mass Culture, Postmodernism* (Bloomington, Ind.: Indiana University Press, 1986), p. 193; hereafter cited in the text as *AGD*.

2. Here I originally meant to oppose Cindy Sherman to *The Donna Reed Show* along high/mass culture lines: the one as an 'avant-garde' artist about whom many academics have written in relation to feminism and postmodernism, the other as a piece of TV schlock whose reruns are brought to you by a tongue-in-cheek cable network claiming to 'preserve our television heritage'. Yet little did I imagine in 1991 (despite this essay's insistence that cultural products circulate too widely and rapidly to allow for the possibility of 'avant-gardism') that Cindy Sherman herself would soon be available in 'mainstream' media; indeed, as I was finishing this book, she appeared in the very newspaper referred to in this essay's opening paragraph as 'the house organ of the uncomprehending masses'. See Cathy Hainer, 'For Cindy Sherman, Art Has Many Guises', *USA Today*, 18 November 1993, p. 6D. So much for *that* little joke about postmodernism's destabilization of the high/mass distinction. At this rate, perhaps it will not be long before Cindy Sherman displaces Cindy Crawford on the cover of *Rolling Stone*.

3. Kirk Vardenoe and Adam Gopnik, *High and Low: Modern Art and Popular Culture* (New York: The Museum of Modern Art, 1990), p. 375. According to the authors, Gopnik was the principal author of 'Contemporary Reflections', the chapter in which this passage appears.

4. Ihab Hassan, 'On the Problem of the Postmodern', *New Literary History,* vol. 20, no. 1 (1988), p. 22.

5. Craig Owens, 'The Discourse of Others: Feminists and Postmodernism', in Hal Foster, ed., *The Anti-Aesthetic: Essays on Postmodern Culture* (Port Townshend, Wash.: Bay Press, 1983), pp. 57–82; Linda Hutcheon, *The Politics of Postmodernism* (New York: Routledge, 1989), p. 168.

6. See Paul Laxalt's account of Reagan's performance in his first debate with Mondale, as quoted in Steven R. Weisman, 'President Says He Needed to Relax before Debating', *New York Times,* 12 October 1984, p. B8; for a transcript of Reagan's speech at the 1988 Republican convention, at which he stumbled over the refrain, 'facts are stubborn things' and said 'facts are stupid things – stubborn things, I should say', see 'Reagan's Address: Hailing Fruits of the Party's Dream of 1980', *New York Times,* 16 August 1988, p. A20.

7. Quoted in a UPI story, 'Lawsuit over Proof of Holocaust Ends with Payment to a Survivor', *New York Times,* 25 July 1985, p. A12. For more substantial news coverage of the case, see Myrna Oliver, 'Holocaust Doubters Settle Auschwitz Survivor's Suit', *Los Angeles Times,* 25 July 1985, pp. 1, 26.

8. Thomas S. Kuhn, *The Structure of Scientific Revolutions* (Chicago: University of Chicago Press, 1962), pp. 151, 141. Since I'm fairly certain that my juxtaposition of neo-Nazis and anti-foundationalists will be widely misconstrued, allow me to clarify myself in a note. The fact that the Holocaust occurred is now registered in American case law, despite the fact that much of the country – around 20 percent, at last count – continues to doubt whether it happened at all. That judicial victory is a triumph for sane persons' sense of the real, but nevertheless, it is more precarious than many people care to admit. What the Mirmelstein-IHR case demonstrated was that 'facts' have to be established as such by deliberative bodies (or interpretive communities, if you like) authorized to perform the task of adjudicating disputes over facticity. One of the questions before the court, in other words, was the Foucauldian question of who would be authorized to make what kinds of statements about the history of World War II. The work of numerous well-respected historians and Holocaust survivors was, for these purposes, an important part of the archive of 'authorized' statements about the Holocaust, since the court could not gainsay the reports of persons whose credentials and credibility had already established them as legitimate speakers. In deciding for Mirmelstein, the court also affirmed an earlier statement about the reality of the Holocaust issued by Los Angeles Superior Court Judge Thomas T. Johnson on 9 October 1981 (Myrna Oliver, 'Holocaust Doubters Settle', p. 26).

Positivist historians are fond of claiming that the anti-foundationalist critique leaves one no way of establishing the facticity of the Holocaust in the face of neo-Nazi assertions of its nonoccurrence, but actually, because few thinking persons believe that human history exists wholly independently of human understanding, few are willing to maintain that the details of the Holocaust's occurrence and meaning are fixed forever and beyond challenge. Surely, it is precisely because people know that 'history' is constructed and maintained by humans that we know we must never forget the Holocaust. To believe that the Holocaust, or any historical occurrence, is immune to challenge by revisionists is to believe that there is no need to remind our fellow men and women that the Holocaust did indeed occur.

9. Denis Donoghue, 'The Promiscuous Cool of Postmodernism', *New York Times Book Review,* 22 June 1986, p. 1. Fredric Jameson, 'Postmodernism and Consumer Society', in Hal Foster, ed., *The Anti-Aesthetic,* p. 115; hereafter cited in the text as 'PCS'.

10. Jean Baudrillard, *Simulations,* Paul Foss, Paul Patton and Philip Beitchman, trans. (New York: Semiotext(e), 1983), pp. 2, 12–13.

11. The conundrum here has been nicely phrased by T. V. Reed in a book that appeared after this essay was first composed: 'anyone who posits postmodernism as a discourse about a world in which the "real" can no longer be found must deal with the irony that to do so is to posit this "reallessness" as our real state of affairs.' T. V. Reed, *Fifteen Jugglers, Five Believers: Literary Politics and the Poetics of American Social Movements* (Berkeley, Calif.: University of California Press, 1992), pp. 20–21.

12. Jameson's typewriter/ word processor analogy was an aside he apparently appended to, but did not incorporate into, the paper that eventually became the chapter, 'Sur-

realism without the Unconscious' in *Postmodernism, or the Cultural Logic of Late Capitalism* (Durham, N.C.: Duke University Press, 1991).

13. Barbara Ehrenreich, 'The Challenge for the Left', rpt. in Berman, ed., *Debating P.C.,* pp. 336–7.

14. For Schiller's argument on the corporate recapture of public space, see *Culture, Inc.: The Corporate Takeover of Public Expression* (New York: Oxford University Press, 1989), esp. pp. 89–110. For an analysis of the postmodern politics of global electronic transmission, see Schiller, pp. 111–34, and Constance Penley's and Andrew Ross's 'Introduction' to *Technoculture*, Penley and Ross, eds (Minneapolis: University of Minnesota Press, 1991), pp. viii–xvii.

15. Philip Rahv, quoted in Richard Chase, 'The Fate of the Avant-Garde', *Partisan Review*, no. 24 (1957), p. 365; hereafter cited in the text.

16. Hugh Kenner, 'The Making of the Modernist Canon', in Robert von Hallberg, ed., *Canons* (Chicago: University of Chicago Press, 1983), p. 374; Helen Vendler, *The Music of What Happens: Poems, Poets, Critics* (Cambridge, Mass.: Harvard University Press, 1988), p. 37.

17. Andrew Ross, *No Respect: Intellectuals and Popular Culture* (New York: Routledge, 1989), p. 50; hereafter cited in the text as *NR*.

18. Quoted in Mark Stevens, 'Low and Behold', *New Republic*, 24 December 1990, p. 30.

5

Pop Goes the Academy:

Cult Studs Fight the Power

Attention, shoppers. If you've been cruising the academic press cata-
logues lately, you may have noticed a new line of products for use in the
home or office. Perhaps you've noticed humanities professors starting up
special imprints and series called 'Cultural Studies and X' or 'X and Culture' or 'Studies in Culture and X', or, at worst, just retooling whatever
they've been doing for the past ten years and calling it a 'cultural studies'
approach to the subject. Or maybe you've begun to hear of articles and
conferences with titles like 'What is Cultural Studies Anyway?' or 'Cultural Studies and Pedagogy' or 'Cultural Studies in the 90s' or 'Cultural
Studies in My Soup'. And you figure that a big book with the title *Cultural
Studies* might be able to tell you what all the fuss is about – but first, you
want to know why there's all this fuss to begin with.

It's tempting to think of cultural studies as academe's Next Big Thing,
as just another intellectual trend sweeping through American higher education. You know the way the anti-academic crowd speaks of such trends:
they usually rely on metaphors about sheep or lemmings, and imagery
that suggests The Wave cascading round and round a large oval stadium.
But even academic trendiness isn't that simple – or, truth be told, that
coordinated. Although cultural studies, which began in Britain, is enjoying an international 'boom', in the United States it's pretty muffled and
diffuse. It's not as if cultural studies simply installed itself someplace in
American life, with four great locations and plenty of parking. So far, the
boom is more like a loud murmur, and it's competing with a lot of inter-
ference and surface noise. You can bet, though, that the next few years of
work will pump up the volume. Let me put it this way: as British Inva-
sions go, cultural studies isn't as noisy as the Beatles' appearance at
Carnegie Hall, but it's every bit as exciting, and probably more durable.

To date there's only been one major American cultural studies conference, 'Cultural Studies Now and in the Future', held at the University of

Illinois in April 1990. There's been a smattering of smaller conferences devoted to similar topics, and a profusion of cultural studies sessions at larger conferences such as the annual Modern Language Association meeting. Journals like *Cultural Critique, New Formations* and *Social Text* routinely publish cult-stud work; the University of Minnesota Press has inaugurated a series of books in the field; medium-sized British commercial publishers like Routledge are steeped in cultural studies titles; and advertisements for academic jobs have begun to request candidates with qualifications in cultural studies.

Those qualifications, however, must include a tolerance for productive chaos. Angela McRobbie calls the field 'a messy amalgam of sociology, social history, and literature, rewritten as it were into the language of contemporary culture.' This messiness is more than characteristic; it is imperative. 'For cultural studies to survive', McRobbie writes, 'it cannot afford to lose this disciplinary looseness, this feeling that ... its authors are making it up as they go along.'¹ What they're making up are fairly ambitious projects – say, attempts to reconceive cultural criticism, ethnography, race, identity politics, representations of AIDS, feminist film theory, popular culture, poststructuralist (and post-Soviet) Marxism, nationality, postcolonialism, and the histories and terrains of intellectual disciplines that have transected and reshaped the history and terrain of cultural studies.

Cultural studies is intensely self-aware (and alternatingly smug and self-critical), regarding itself not as an authority but as a vested, interested conflicted participant in the culture it studies. It is always attempting, for instance, to discover and interpret the ways disparate disciplinary subjects *talk back:* how consumers deform and transform the products they use to construct their lives; how 'natives' rewrite and trouble the ethnographies of (and *to*) which they are 'subject'; how groups theorize their own practices independently of, if not downright contrary to, the means by which they are understood – whether those means are network news, sociology, psychoanalysis, literary theory or rock criticism. But cultural studies is not a unified movement, it's not a hostile takeover, it's not a 'school', and it's not an academic discipline: on the contrary, it raids and unsettles the compartmentalized disciplines of traditional academic study. Or so it says. But since these are its terms, it can always be criticized (by its practitioners, mind you) for being too disciplinary, too academic, not interventionist *enough.* Because cultural studies explicitly makes claims on public life, it is especially susceptible to challenges from academics and nonacademics alike whenever it seems to be getting too hifalutin and exclusionary, whatever that means. As I'll explain further on, the politics of intellectual populism makes for some heated exchanges in cultural studies (and a lot of alternating smugness and self-criticism, too).

By most standard accounts, the field traces itself back to 1958, the year British sociologist Richard Hoggart published *The Uses of Literacy* and literary critic Raymond Williams published *Culture and Society, 1780–1950.* Hoggart, one among the first generation of university professors from working-class backgrounds, considered his book an attempt to break with the hitherto dominant British model of studying 'culture', and an effort to give voice instead to the culture in which he was raised. But in order to investigate his own culture in a scholarly fashion, Hoggart first had to redefine the word 'culture' itself, to wrest it away from its use by intellectual Tories from Matthew Arnold to F. R. Leavis, and to strengthen its broader, more anthropological connotations: for the 'culture' of working-class neighborhoods in Leeds (where Hoggart grew up) was *exactly* what wasn't considered 'culture' by most of the British intelligentsia before 1958.

Raymond Williams, whose book traced and historicized the 'culture and society' tradition in English letters, noted that the meaning of 'culture' got distinguished from 'society' in the nineteenth century, when 'culture' began to mean something involving a standard of aesthetic excellence – that is, *high* culture, the stuff that only *cultured* people knew about, the stuff that resided in museums and universities. In other words, as of 1850 or so, we all lived in a *society,* but only some of us had any *culture,* and those people, naturally, knew who they were. Williams, alongside Hoggart, spoke of culture as 'a whole way of life' or, equally ambiguously, as 'a structure of feeling'. And ever since, the field of cultural studies has driven itself largely by exploiting and examining the tension between these narrow and broad senses of 'culture': the Leavisite, humanistic sense and the anthropological, sociological sense.

In 1964 Hoggart founded the Centre for Contemporary Cultural Studies at the University of Birmingham. In 1969 Jamaican-born Stuart Hall became director of the Centre, holding the position until 1979; he remains the leading figure in British cultural studies today. In the past ten or twelve years, the field has slowly made inroads into American criticism, usually by means of departments of rhetoric and communication or departments of media studies. For most of the 1980s, English departments were more visibly concerned with deconstruction, feminism and (in the latter half of the decade) new historicism; all the same, there were subtle changes afoot here and there. For example, Janice Radway, author of 1984's *Reading the Romance,* became the editor of *American Quarterly,* the official journal of the American Studies Association, and tried to bridge the work of American Studies with that of cultural studies whenever possible; but as far as I can recall, her efforts didn't make any headlines. So even though cultural studies work is now moving off the shelves faster than it can be stocked, it's worth remembering that some of this work (like Hazel Carby and Paul Gilroy's *The Empire Strikes Back*) has been sitting on the shelf for ten years or more.

Cultural studies narratives *about* the history of cultural studies have begun to appear with increasing frequency in the past five years, for much the same reason that histories of feminist theory have become one of feminism's favorite genres; both intellectual movements are poised at an extraordinary moment of theoretical self-consciousness and institutional absorption by American universities, and in both cases their self-consciousness and their institutional absorption are probably mutually enhancing. But just as 'deconstruction' became a catchall synonym for 'careful reading' (as in the injunction, 'don't sign your lease before deconstructing it'), so too might 'cultural studies' eventually come to mean little more than 'criticism'. Appropriately, the fear has spread that omnivorous American academics, still picking their teeth clean of deconstruction and new historicism, will set upon and devour cultural studies in its turn, dissolving its heterogeneity and its political legacies in a way that coats, soothes and protects the entrenched interests of American universities.

To some extent this has already happened. It's quite possible to find American critics who think that cultural studies is merely 'about' popular culture, or 'about' the subjectivity of ordinary people. On occasion, British cultural studies has so defined itself in the past, but in the United States, 'popular culture' and 'subjectivity' will likely prove to be poor organizing tools for cultural studies work. 'Popular culture' might encompass everything from *TV Guide* to comparative studies of Southern folklore, and all the stuff of the gee-whiz Popular Culture Association; 'subjectivity studies' merely announces that everything is its subject, from twelve-step programs to bad hair days to critiques of existentialism. Don't be fooled by cheap imitations: cultural studies isn't a way for neopopulist intellectuals to get down with the people by writing about how much everybody loves *Terminator 2* and *Murphy Brown*. When cultural studies engages with the popular and the 'ordinary', it does so primarily in order to understand – and thereby try to *change* – the power relations that shape the most intimate and/or quotidian details of our lives, power relations that are ordinarily no more visible or remarkable to us than oxygen.

The most provocative and valuable cultural studies work immerses itself wholly in the politics of social semiosis, shuttling between the local (what you wear, what you believe, what you read) and the macropolitical (how it got there, how it's used, what it all means, how it could be otherwise). And when it's done analyzing all these things, then cult-studs gets busy: indeed, the subtitle of editor Douglas Crimp's collection of essays on AIDS – *Cultural Analysis, Cultural Activism* (1988) – may just become the official bumper sticker of cultural studies.

Take, for one example among many, Dick Hebdige's immensely influential *Subculture: The Meaning of Style* (1979), a study of hip, unruly British working-class youth, their music, their clothes, their bad attitudes, and their complex and contradictory forms of 'resistance' to the social order in which they find themselves. In Hebdige's account, punk, whose 'dubious parentage' included gender-bending glamor rock, Ramones glue-sniffing minimalism, 1960s mod style, 'northern soul', and reggae, 'found ratification in an equally eclectic clothing style. ... The whole ensemble, literally safety-pinned together ... reproduced the entire sartorial history of postwar working-class youth cultures in "cut-up" form.'[2] Decoding punk's inflections and reinterpretations of the most banal, unremarkable objects (like those safety pins), Hebdige argued that style in subculture produces new meanings everywhere, not by inventing new languages but by appropriating the signs already to hand. As he puts it, 'the struggle between different discourses, different definitions and meanings within ideology is ... a struggle for possession of the sign which extends to even the most mundane areas of everyday life' (p. 17).

The idea that political struggles are also struggles over signs is, by now, a cornerstone of latter-day Marxism. And though cultural studies' chief intellectual forebear is Marxism, it is an idiosyncratic, undoctrinaire, practical British Marxism that traces itself to socialist humanists like Hoggart, Williams, and E. P. Thompson; it proceeds thence by way of encounters with structuralist-Marxist Louis Althusser, psychoanalytic theorist Juliet Mitchell, and (belatedly) Italian Marxist Antonio Gramsci; it takes side trips to the radical democracy of Ernesto Laclau and Chantal Mouffe or the 'sociology of the everyday' in the work of Pierre Bourdieu and Michel de Certeau; and it gets repeatedly redefined in border skirmishes and intermittent challenges from discourse theorists, feminists, poststructuralists, and a cast of dozens now interrogating race, immigration, sexuality, popular culture and other anarchies in the UK.

The current Marxism of cultural studies, it turns out, is one that stopped believing in historical inevitability long before the Wall came down; it is a Marxism that denies the primacy or unity of 'class' (and emphasizes the relevance of race, gender, sexuality and subjectivity), no longer believes in an intellectual vanguard, no longer believes in the centrality of Europe, no longer believes that the base 'determines' the superstructure, that being 'determines' consciousness, that the ruling class owns the ruling ideas, that class struggle is inevitable, or that ideology is just 'false consciousness'.

One might ask whether this sugar-free, low-cholesterol, no-fat, decaffeinated Marxism Lite is really a Marxism at all. In fact, Marxists ask this all the time. Stuart Hall's answer, basically, is that he wants the concepts but not the teleological baggage:

> I choose to keep the notion of classes; I choose to keep the notion of the capital/labor contradiction; I choose to keep the notion of social relations of production, etc. – I just don't want to think them reductively. ... My question is, should we now admit that, since the guaranteed philosophical and epistemological underpinnings of the theory do not stand up, it is finished as a problematic? I want to try to account theoretically for what is still there, what needs to be retained.
>
> Can one retheorize the theory in a nonreductionist way? I have tried to suggest some ways in which a modern, more discursive understanding of ideology, which mediates the link between ideas and social forces through language and representation, *can* accomplish that. That is the contemporary theoretical revolution: the notion that the arena or medium in which ideology functions is one of signification, representation, discursive practices. That is the intervening term that has changed the nature of the debate.[3]

In other words, this new improved discursive Marxism tends to believe that 'ideology' is the product of diverse sociopolitical forces and class fractions that form loose coalitions to forge powerful hegemonies, and that in turn cobble together an array of disparate social discourses into something known generally as 'common sense'.

'Hegemony', on this model, is distinct from 'domination' because hegemony actively seeks to secure the consent of the governed: hegemony, kinder and gentler than domination, tries to win hearts and minds, rather than simply chopping your hands off if you don't bring enough rubber back to the colonial outpost. And hegemonic forces don't go about their business by willing 'willing subjects' into being from the top down; they start right on your own home ground, trying to *show* you it's only natural to believe that criminals shouldn't go free on technicalities, or that when guns are outlawed only outlaws will have guns, or that reverse discrimination hurts us all, or that peace will only come through strength. In order to be successful, hegemony doesn't even have to make you agree with these things; it merely has to make it difficult for its opponents to debate social issues in any other terms.

This emphasis on 'hegemony' follows from the past twenty-five years of theoretical developments in Marxism, for since the late 1960s Western Marxism has moved dramatically away from theories of the State. Staring down into the fissure that had opened in French politics in 1968, Louis Althusser addressed himself to what he called 'Ideological State Apparatuses' (or ISAs) such as churches and schools; and the twenty-odd years since then have seen a retrieval of (and ever more careful reworkings of) the Gramscian understanding of 'civil society', which is where power struggles happen when they aren't happening in the State or the ISAs – in think tanks, supermarkets, private schools, labor disputes and the mass media in all its forms. Gramsci's *Prison Notebooks* had emphasized the role of intellectuals and the primacy of the superstructure in Marxist thought, yet lay largely unnoticed from the 1930s through the 1960s while nearly every other Marxist in the world was considering the superstructure a mere 'reflection' of the material base. Only when the superstructure started toppling over in 1968, apparently, did Western Marxism begin to think anew that the 'trickle up' theory might not work, in which case you didn't have to wait for an earthquake to shake the foundations; you could try to change the superstructure from *within* the superstructure.

Then again, the twenty-odd years since 1968 have seen a number of superstructures fall, including those built by the forces of Communism throughout Eastern Europe and the former Soviet Union. And even before the collapse, poststructuralist Marxist theory was faced with the brutal and embarrassing fact that most Communist governments on the planet didn't even *have* the deliberative mechanisms of 'civil society' in Gramsci's sense: all they had was the sovereign power of the centralized state. So you wound up with all this finely tuned, sophisticated post-Marxism slowly turning into a critical apparatus applicable chiefly to the analysis of New Right capitalism, since it was too complicated to deal with most actual, monolithic Communist states. It may turn out that neo-Marxist critical theory, including cultural studies, will wind up in a parasitic relation to capitalism, hanging on (to the anger and befuddlement of conservatives and the frustration of democratic socialists) long after the dismantling and discrediting of actually existing Communist regimes – but hanging on only as a mode of criticism.

Be that future what it may, cultural studies in the UK has long since demonstrated its social utility. One of cultural studies' shining moments came about in 1978, when, in *Policing the Crisis: Mugging, the State, and Law and Order*, Stuart Hall et al. closed their study of British print media by suggesting that a longstanding British consensus was unraveling and would soon give way to something they called 'authoritarian populism', a new cultural formation that would combine privatization, military buildup and social nostalgia with attacks on unions, minorities and so-called 'liberal elites'. Within months, Margaret Thatcher was prime minister. Say what you will about 'Marxist theory', it's not every theoretical enterprise that can claim to have predicted Thatcherism right down to the details of its domestic agenda. And capitalism, for all its celebrated longevity, continues to rely on econobabble about 'business cycles' and other invisible hands, unsure whether it's exporting free markets and social democracy to Moscow, or just fostering the spread of organized crime.

Maybe it's no accident that British cultural studies began to think 'hegemony' at the exact moment of crisis preceding the onset of Thatcherism. For it's impossible to explain the popular appeal of Thatcherism – or its American friend, Reaganism – simply in traditional ('economistic') Marxist terms. Neither Thatcherism nor Reaganism is homogeneous; their component discourses and practices are multiple, contradictory and unstable. But this doesn't mean we abandon class analysis. Quite the contrary: it means that class analysis needs to keep on its toes. As Stuart Hall said in *The Hard Road to Renewal* (1988), it's 'a complicated matter to say in any precise sense which class interests are represented by Thatcherism … since it is precisely class interests which, in the process of their "re-presentation", are being politically and ideologically redefined.'[4]

Here, then, is where the study of hegemony intersects with the study of subjectivity. In his contribution to Nelson and Grossberg's *Marxism and the Interpretation of Culture* (1988), Hall maintains that the New Right's success lies in its ability to produce new subject positions and reinflect the signs of the times. What else could account for the resurgence of conservatism? 'Of course', Hall wryly remarks, 'there might be an essential Thatcherite subject hiding or concealed in each of us, struggling to get out. But it seems more probable that Thatcherism has been able to constitute new subject positions from which its discourses about the world make sense' ('Toad', p. 49). What Hall's doing here, basically, is disputing the traditional left's 'body snatchers' theory of the rise of the New Right. Think back to the *Saturday Night Live* sketch in which former liberals, taken over by evil Reaganite pods, sit dazed in a semicircle, playing acoustic guitar and singing a version of 'Blowin' in the Wind' in which the refrain is 'the answer, my friend, is Ronald Reagan'. The *SNL* sketch brilliantly captures that uncanny, chilling late 1970s sense of finding out that your closest friends are suddenly closet neoconservatives – but, as Hall points out time and again, massive ideological shifts can't be explained so easily. When the Reagan Revolution showed up, it worked precisely because it *didn't* get you in your sleep: it took you on while you were awake and alert, reconfiguring your world for you. It wasn't some federal express overnight, either; whatever it was, it took just enough time to make people believe that things had always been this way – or that this was the way things oughta be.

Some of the British left has charged that Hall overestimates the 'actual' popularity of Thatcherism. This criticism tends to miss the point, since Hall's work concerns itself mainly with the *effectiveness* of Thatcherism. In the United States, however, where Reaganism's horrifying popularity is undisputed, no one so far, least of all the Democratic Party, has convinc-

ingly accounted for it in cultural terms. While the American left was running as hard as it could just to slow the pace at which it was losing
ground, Reaganism somehow managed to stitch together 'tax revolt'
(picking up from California's infamous Proposition 13, passed in 1978),
folksiness, hysterical Cold War militarism, Jeane Kirkpatrick's 'Dictator-
ships and Double Standards', supply-side (or 'voodoo') economics, savage
attacks on civil liberties, and, not least of these, an agenda known to early
Reaganauts as the 'New Federalism' – which chiefly entailed impoverish-
ing the federal government so severely that the burden of serving social
justice fell heavily on states and municipalities for whom cuts in social
services became the only politically conceivable response.

And before we knew it, Reagan-style 'authoritarian populism' was, for
most of the country, just plain good American common sense. Hey, it
even brought the Wall down, made the world safe for plutocracy, and
divided, conquered, or marginalized the vast majority of its domestic critics – except in universities, which have been under attack lately for emphatically refusing to fall in with the nation's official march rightward.

Of course, every thinking liberal-lefty knows that Bush-Reagan-Bucha-
nanites are always other people – the dupes, the podbrains, the fembots,
the puppets. The not-us. But what cultural studies work shows you is that
the cultural terrain is denser than you think. All of us nonpods know
perfectly well that Stallone's *Rambo* films are post-Vietnam Reaganite foreign policy fantasies, right? But 'what is perhaps most curious', argues
philosopher Douglas Kellner in a recent issue of cinema journal *The Velvet
Light Trap*,

> is how *Rambo* appropriates countercultural motifs for the Right. Rambo has
> long hair, a head-band, eats only natural foods (whereas the bureaucrat Mur-
> dock swills Coke), is close to nature, and is hostile toward bureaucracy, the
> state, and technology. ... Rambo is a supply-side hero, a figure of individual
> entrepreneurism, who shows how Reaganite ideology can assimiliate earlier
> countercultural figures.[5]

Why bother stretching *Rambo* on the rack of cultural analysis? Because
the left usually doesn't bother, that's why, and thus fails to understand the
appeal of New Right conservatism, fails to grasp how the New Right has
mobilized an array of ambiguous 'countercultural' signs for its own purposes. The point here is that you don't analyze *Rambo* just to condemn it;
that's too easy, and counterproductive to boot. As Andrew Ross argues in
No Respect: Intellectuals and Popular Culture, dismissing phenomena like *Rambo*
prevents cultural analysis from producing cultural activism: when it
comes to the field of popular meanings, 'a politics that only preaches

about the sexism, racism, and militarism', Ross writes, 'while neglecting to rearticulate [its] popular, resistant appeal ... will not be a popular politics.'[6]

And why is it important that the left be popular, or voted most likely to succeed? Because a preachy left that situates itself safely above stupid, reactionary movies and their stupid, reactionary meanings, can be – *and has been* – very easily lampooned as a 'politically correct' left of somber, humorless moralizers. But a media-conscious left, a left that knows how social signs can be appropriated and reappropriated, may be capable of deliberately wresting cultural meanings away from the New Right on its own ground. If cultural studies *is* going to interfere in the public and private spheres of American life, there's no time like the present, and (as you may have heard elsewhere) there's no place like home.

OK, so your interest is piqued, and you pick up *Cultural Studies*. Well, let's begin with matters of scale, size, and perspective: you're gonna need to pick it up with both hands. Just as 'cultural studies' names an enormous and explosive international field of endeavor, *Cultural Studies* is a behemoth book. Almost 800 large (7- x 10-inch) pages of readably small type, the thing was reportedly something like 2,000 pages in typescript. It includes no fewer than forty essays, thirty of which were originally delivered as presentations at the 1990 Illinois conference, *and* it includes edited transcripts of the question-and-answer sessions that followed each essay, *and* it includes a bibliography that lists every book and article mentioned in each essay, *and* it even has a 'user's guide' compiled by the editors, Lawrence Grossberg, Cary Nelson and Paula Treichler.

Given its history and its intellectual scope, it's not likely that anyone will accuse cultural studies of being too modest an enterprise, and without question, *Cultural Studies* is a book that resists synopsis and paraphrase. In this respect it stands as a reasonable representation of cultural studies work to date, for cultural studies' sense of what counts as 'cultural studies work to date' is itself subject to constant revision. Upon opening the book, we're almost immediately told that cultural studies has no specific tools: 'its methodology, ambiguous from the beginning, could best be seen as a bricolage.'[7] Yet if it does nothing else in or for the world, as a book *Cultural Studies* will aid and abet the American institutionalization of cultural studies; and possibly it'll help to set the terms of institutionalization as well. I don't see this as cause for alarm, but not everyone will be thrilled by the prospect. Ten years hence, people may be heard saying things like, 'I only care about *early* cultural studies – you know, before *Cultural Studies* came out', in roughly the manner people profess enthusiasm for early Clash, early Hüsker Dü, early Lemonheads, before all those guys sold out, went commercial, and published 800-page books.

The lineup of contributors to *Cultural Studies* must make the conference look like it was the Week of a Thousand Stars, a spectacular cavalcade of the hottest and hippest academics from around the world – chiefly from the UK, Australia, Canada and Europe, as well as an assortment of institutional locations in the United States. But although the conference did generate more than its share of academic stargazing, what's notable about *Cultural Studies* is its wide variety of contributors and contributions: this is by no means a compilation of Cultural Studies' Greatest Hits featuring all the original artists. Nor was the conference. Established scholars appear here alongside brilliant newcomers, and the book incorporates nine additional papers as well. Collectively, this material offers nothing less than the broadest available cross-section of the work being done in and by cultural studies today.

The thing to do, if you're coming to a lot of this stuff for the first time, is not to read the essays in order. The first three are thoroughly rewarding, but they're not the beginner slopes. Others require merely a modicum of curiosity and an open mind. Rosalind Brunt, for instance, speaks about media audience research among Sheffield political constituencies; Simon Frith addresses pop band culture in the town of Milton Keynes. Lata Mani's essay, on eyewitness narratives of *sati* (widow burning), shows that most accounts don't spend very much time discussing the burning of the widow herself (except when she lives or jumps off the pyre, whereupon she's described as a bloody, boiling, peeling object of pity). Emily Martin looks at textbook representations of human reproduction, complete with their torpid, passive ova and their enterprising, plucky little sperm. Jan Zita Grover compares AIDS activism inside and outside the academy, voicing skepticism about academic activism while insisting that there is 'no better role for cultural studies inside the classroom or out of it than to enable people to act.'[8] And Douglas Crimp, speaking at once urgently and dispassionately, dissects photographs, PBS specials and *Time* magazine portraits of people with AIDS, showing how they enable only generalized, disembodied grief (for bodily decay in the abstract); faith in exemplary individuals (bravely resisting the disease); revulsion (at HIV-positive people who behave 'irresponsibly' on camera); or, at worst, outright 'terror at imagining the person with AIDS as still sexual.'[9]

The book's eclecticism and diversity is not just a liberal-pluralist affair in which many viewpoints come together in a spirit of sharing. Among its many benefits, this diversity makes palpable the Gramscian project of theorizing locally, with due respect for national (or regional) specificity. One finds out quickly that cultural studies varies considerably from nation to nation, and that an awful lot depends on where and why you work (nation to nation or door to door).

147

For instance, the relations among tourists, travelers, informants and 'natives' are figured rather differently by James Clifford, writing from within anthropology's postmodern auto-critique (and the disappearance of the 'village' and the 'field'), than by Meaghan Morris, writing in the midst of Australia's ideological and economic transition from a nation of 'travelers' to a nation of potential tourist attractions. It's Morris who points out, in a comment on Tony Bennett's paper, that cultural studies theorists in Australia are 'now virtually forced to work in the media or in the bureaucracy or increasingly in the private sector because there are no academic homes left' (p. 37). The result is that Australian theorists are actually beginning to have an impact on public policy; this changes the politics of cultural studies considerably. As Bennett says, it means 'talking to and working with what used to be called the ISAs rather than writing them off from the outset and then, in a self-fulfilling prophecy, criticizing them again when they seem to affirm one's direct functionalist predictions.'[10]

In the American context, by contrast, Cornel West urges us 'to think about the degree to which the waning of public spheres in this society tends to displace politics into the few spheres where there is in fact some public discussion – spheres like the academy', where 'so much of American intellectual life … now has been monopolized' by default. 'Hence so much of academic politics', says West, 'is a displacement of the relative absence of serious politics within the larger "public" spheres where serious resources are being produced, distributed, and consumed.'[11] Similarly, David Glover and Cora Kaplan note that 'the size and funding of American higher education' has gotten cultural studies 'embroiled in a bewildering array of local and institutional politics.'[12] Some of these politics are 'academic' in the worst sense; some are clearly local versions of national and broadly ideological disputes. But what concerns Glover and Kaplan is that insofar as American cultural studies will be an academic cultural studies, it will be subject to the same pressures and political harangues that have dogged all innovative work in the humanities, and it may have to confront Know-Nothing politicians (as well as potential allies) state by state.

Implicit in these discussions of cultural studies' location is that nothing, these days, could distinguish American universities from their foreign counterparts more than size and funding. Throughout the 1980s Thatcherism practiced a scorched-earth policy toward every educational institution that wasn't Oxford or Cambridge, just as Reaganism combined its appeal to 'academic excellence' with attacks on the principle of equal access to higher education. But American faculty, on the whole, made out much better than their British (and Australian) counterparts.

Some of the best-known British and Australian speakers showed up in central Illinois to find themselves treated as academic superstars – and to find that 'academic superstardom' is a recent and fairly weird American phenomenon, especially when it strikes people under forty. It's hard to recall that even in the desperate crunch of the post-Fordist 1990s– which, for many American universities as for many American people, means bad times getting worse – the American academic scene looks positively lush when it's viewed from across very large bodies of water.

On another transnational front altogether, the politics of ethnic identity pose vastly different issues when they're addressed by a young black British theorist like Kobena Mercer than when they're taken up by North American Chicano/a theorists like Marcos Sanchez-Tranquilino and Angie Chabram-Dernersesian. Mercer's essay reminds us vividly that leading British conservatives from Enoch Powell to Margaret Thatcher have used roughly the same conceptual tools as cultural studies: in concocting regressive, xenophobic notions of 'British identity' and 'ethnicity', the British right wing has exploited the 'multiaccentuality of the sign' for all it's worth. In other words, black/white racial signifiers may be unstable, but that doesn't mean the left has exclusive rights over their instability.[13]

In a jointly written and delivered paper, John Tagg and Marcos Sanchez-Tranquilino discuss *pachuco* subcultural forms and activisms, tracking the meanings of the zoot suit from wartime US riots – during which zoot suit material was rationed and Chicano youth were beaten by police and servicemen – to postwar British riots in which zoot suits became the uniform of 'London Teds who fomented the "Race Riots" of Notting Hill in 1958', to Luis Valdez's controversial 1978 play, *Zoot Suit*.[14] And Chabram-Dernersesian charts how the dual challenges of Chicana feminism, excluded both by Chicano nationalism and middle-class feminism, have produced a de-universalized 'universal woman' with 'a brown body, a Spanish accent, codes to switch, a history of domination and cultural suppression, and a contentious dialogue with the Manifest ChicanO.'[15] Point being, when the question of national identity runs up against cultural or ethnic nationalism, feminism and sexual affiliation, no pledge of allegiance will cover all the identities any one of us might be able to assume.

But what's the audience for this kind of work? A good question, since so much of the book and conference are devoted explicitly to theorizing and arguing about the agency of the 'audience' in theory and in practice. And there's plenty in *Cultural Studies* about the various dissonances between Us (the researchers) and Them (the subjects), but there's certainly no consensus about where these dissonances come from or what we should do with them. The dissonance theorists generally fall into three camps. Camp one, reacting to a previous generation of dour mass-culture theorists and Frankfurt School killjoys, holds that the masscult audience is in some way *empowered* by consumption and actively, creatively 'produces' the text/ artifact/practice under scrutiny. 'It has become commonplace to approach cultural consumption', notes Jody Berland, 'as a central agency for popular social empowerment ... especially with reference to the production of collective or expressive difference.'[16] Camp two, skeptical of the utility of emphasizing consumer empowerment, replies that camp one is fooling itself: in the United States, theorizing 'agency' and 'pleasure' in consumerism tends to align you with cable companies (more channels! more power!) and the Reagan-era FDA, which argued that consumers were too smart, too product-literate, to need accurate product labels.

The third camp is made up (as usual) of people who reject the extreme formulations of camps one and two, and most of the essays in *Cultural Studies* are bulletins from camp three. For instance, Laura Kipnis, who takes on *Hustler,* and Janice Radway, who is doing work on the Book-of-the-Month Club, try to see consumers and audiences neither as puppets of propaganda nor as cheerful, autonomous individuals just trying to have a good time. On the one hand, notes Kipnis, *Hustler* magazine is vaguely left-libertarian, notoriously skeptical of state authority, and always motivated by a mixture of class resentment and indiscriminate hatred of privilege and pretension; on the other hand, it aims to disgust, to offend, and (most of all) to photograph women from the crotch. As a whole, Kipnis writes, the magazine is 'maddeningly incoherent': '*Hustler* is against government, against authority, against the bourgeoisie, diffident on male power – but its anti-liberalism, anti-feminism, anti-communism, and anti-progressivism leave little space for envisioning any alternative kind of political organization.'[17] And that's assuming what Kipnis herself does not assume – namely, that we can get past our own 'disgust at reading *Hustler*' long enough to inquire seriously into its appeal, its history and its incoherent, adolescent a-politics.

Constance Penley and John Fiske tend more readily to treat ordinary folks as canny, active *bricoleurs*, but in Penley's case, when you're dealing with groups of women who publish and critique their own K/S or 'slash' zines – detailed, sexually explicit *Star Trek* fanzines about the ongoing romance between Kirk and Spock (the slash denotes explicit sex between male characters) – well, it's hard *not* to theorize an active audience. But is this sub-Trekkie-culture activity more than idiosyncratic, or more than an object lesson for know-it-all intellectuals? Why do women compose slash zines at all – of *Star Trek, Starsky and Hutch, Hardcastle and McCormick* or *Miami Vice*? For fun? To attempt a less sexist genre of 'romance'? To experiment with pornography and male (white, black, Hispanic, Vulcan) sexuality? These are the central questions for Penley, whose paper opens with an explicit challenge to two influential feminist analyses of mass culture: Radway's *Reading the Romance* and Tania Modleski's study of soap operas, *Loving with a Vengeance* (1982). Both these groundbreaking studies rely on Nancy Chodorow's *The Reproduction of Mothering* (1978), an 'object relations' model of female subjectivity that theorizes rugged male individualism and touchy-feely female bonding by suggesting these gender dichotomies have their origin in the core of the nuclear family. On Chodorow's model, women never separate from their mothers as completely as men do (and therefore become more dependent and more nurturing); it follows that they must enjoy mass-produced fantasies because it allows them, as Penley puts it, 'imaginatively to regress, through identification with the heroine, to a pre-Oedipal moment of being nurtured and absolutely taken care of, a privilege typically denied adult women in this culture because they have the sole responsibility for nurturing.'[18]

No such account will suffice for the *Star Trek* fans, who do anything but 'regress' in reading their heroes against the grain. In fact, Penley doesn't analyze the fandom so much as compare her notes to theirs, because, as it happens, the makers of 'slash' zines already theorize themselves, thank you:

> it is a highly self-reflexive and self-critical fandom; their intellectual and political interests and anxieties are apparent in far more than merely symptomatic ways. *They* want to know why they are so drawn to fandom. ... *They* are curious about the sexual makeup of the fandom; for example, the number of lesbians, in what is admittedly a mostly heterosexual fandom, and the nature of their interest in K/S, has been debated in two recent issues of *On the Double,* by both lesbian and straight fans; and at the last convention in San Diego there was, for the first time, a hugely well-attended panel on gay lifestyles made up of lesbian and gay fan writers and artists. (pp. 484–5)

Penley's travels between slash fanzine conferences and cultural studies conferences are not exactly the stuff of traditional ethnography, and they dramatically point up the impossibility of doing cultural studies work by simply going out and gathering data on 'the people' and returning to your office in the Institute to write up the report. Though K/S zines are the exception, not the rule, in mass cultural consumption, Penley's ambiguous border-crossings are in themselves broadly emblematic of the interstitial position of the cultural studies intellectual who's neither flesh nor fowl, poised uneasily between the world of tenure anxiety and peer review and the world of popular pleasures and peer pressure. Penley asks herself: 'Was I going to the conference as a fan, even perhaps a potential writer of K/S stories, a voyeur of a fascinating subculture, or a feminist academic and critic?' (p. 484)

It turns out, poignantly enough, that the last of these identities is the most problematic, for although many K/S fans voice generally feminist sentiments, 'they do not feel', writes Penley, 'that feminism speaks for them. Fandom, the various popular ideologies of abuse and self-help [such as twelve-step programs], and New Age philosophies are seen as far more relevant to their needs than what they perceive as a middle-class feminism that disdains popular culture and believes that pornography degrades women' (p. 492). And, needless to say, the fandom distrusts academe even more than feminism, although they seem to accept Penley – as a fan.

Penley writes in a note appended to her talk that she invited some of her fellow fans to her presentation. But some of those fans didn't like the reaction they got from the cult-studs crowd, who sometimes seemed to be laughing *at* the fandom rather than *with* it (pp. 496–7). So is it possible to 'politicize' the fandom, to convince them that anti-porn feminism is only one feminism among many? Is it possible to critique the fandom, whether in Marxist or psychoanalytic terms or in any other way? Is it possible to make the fandom fully intelligible to academe, or vice versa? Penley concludes from her study that 'the range and diversity of identifications and object relations is much greater than is currently being recognized in feminist studies of women and popular culture' (p. 488) but she directs the bulk of her critique at such feminist studies – not at slash fandom. Perhaps it could not comfortably be otherwise. Most K/S fans use pseudonyms, and some, understandably, don't like being the object of the academic gaze (or of academic laughter): 'it's one thing for your co-workers, domestic partners, or children to know you're a "Trekkie",' says Penley, 'it's another to know you're a producer of pornography with gay overtones' (p. 494).

Penley's essay opened the conference, and you can bet it provided matter for discussion for all five days; but it would be too much to say it 'set the tone' for the papers that followed. In the book, it looks like just another essay – except, of course, for the illustrations. Throughout the rest of the collection, most of the contributors to *Cultural Studies* lodge an array of complaints against what Laura Kipnis calls the 'tendency to locate resistance, agency, and micro-political struggle just about everywhere in mass cultural reception' (pp. 374–5). But even when we forego the intellectual pleasure of finding populist resistance everywhere, we're still never sure when it's time to call a dupe a dupe. For instance, Donna Haraway and Andrew Ross argue passionately *against* New Age holism, which they see as a dangerous, mystified, transcendentalist doctrine that denies human mortality and substitutes 'naturalist' ideologies for rigorous analyses of social phenomena. Jennifer Slack and Laurie Whitt, however, insist that cultural studies *must* entail some kind of environmentalism, insofar as it attacks 'the well-entrenched ecological indifference of late capitalism', critiques anthropocentrism, and affirms ethical standards of moral judgment.[19] It's not clear whose cultural studies is more cultural than whose here. It can justly be said that Slack and Whitt elide the Marxist notion of social 'totality' with the fuzzier New Age idea of 'holism', thus occluding power relations in favor of affirming the interdependency of all life forms in the ecosystem. But it can also be said that Ross's essay comes uncharacteristically and perilously close to ridiculing its subject rather than articulating its appeal, construing New Age technoculture as an ingenuous self-help individualism, blind to its complicity with conservatism and devoted uncritically to doing things the 'natural' way. And because Ross's chief example of New Ageism is the Welles Step – a platform-like device designed to allow people to sit on the toilet 'naturally', in the squatting position – he strangely dismisses the popular attractions of 'alternative healing' among people opposed to, alienated from, or unable to afford standard American medical technocracy.[20]

It may be, as the book's introduction suggests, that this volume of dissension registers a growing sense that 'subcultural' analysis has 'sometimes been applied too casually, granting subcultural status to what are essentially American leisure activities' (p. 8) – chief among which is the watching of TV (or MTV). Or perhaps, after sating itself on the rash of mid 1980s arguments about how the audience at home produced 'pleasure' from the mass-cultural text, cultural studies realized that it was largely reproducing the culture industry's smug, knowing celebrations of itself. Whatever the case, cultural studies now knows better than to think it can read popular meanings 'right off the screen', so to speak (especially with *Star Trek* and *Rambo*), but it's also gotten wary of reading popular meanings right off 'the people', too. For that matter, there doesn't seem to be much point in trying to unearth the hidden counterhegemonic meanings of bowling. Or – though it would undoubtedly be a challenge – golf.

To people unfamiliar with cultural studies, it may appear incomprehensible that the field disagrees with itself so much, and differs from itself almost every other day. But what's most impressive about *Cultural Studies* is the extent to which its contributors talk back to the dominant paradigms of cultural studies itself – and to the general structure of this kind of agenda-setting academic conference. Tony Bennett, Rosalind Brunt, Homi Bhabha, Cornel West and Stuart Hall, among others, all qualify or criticize (respectively) Gramsci, Radway, Hall, Foucault and Marx,

among others, and if you follow the Q-and-As you can find people carrying on five-day critiques of each other.

As Stuart Hall told the conference, 'the only theory worth having is
that which you have to fight off, not that which you speak with profound
fluency. ... I entered cultural studies from the New Left, and the New Left
always regarded Marxism as a problem, as trouble, as danger, not as a
solution.'[21] Despite the odd way in which Stuart Hall has come to *embody*
the theoretical legacies of cultural studies (having lived them for the past
thirty years), he refused to take on the role of 'keeper of the conscience of
cultural studies, hoping to police you back in line with what it really was
if only you knew' (p. 277). Instead (and to the surprise of many of his
listeners), Hall took the conference as an opportunity to narrate the 'theoretical legacies' of cultural studies as a history of disjunction, displacement
and 'interruption' – not as a great tradition imperiled by vulgar American
merchandising.

Hall concluded his remarks by alluding to 'the moment of danger in
the institutionalization of cultural studies in this highly rarified and enormously elaborated and well-funded professional world of American academic life' (p. 286). But unlike most of the conference-goers, he wasn't
worrying that cultural studies' academic success might signal its political
failure; on the contrary, he noted that such a worry, coming from him,
could only be bad faith or sour grapes: 'the enormous explosion of cultural studies in the US, its rapid professionalization and institutionalization, is not a moment which any of us who tried to set up a marginalized
Centre in a university like Birmingham could, in any simple way, regret'
(p. 285). Instead, Hall called upon American academics to remember that
'there is all the difference in the world between understanding the politics
of intellectual work and substituting intellectual work for politics' (p. 286).
That is, it's one thing to realize that intellectual work is political, or can
serve various political ends; it's another thing to think you've conquered
hegemony just by talking about it. At conferences like this one, of course,
it's all too easy to begin believing that reactionary social forces stop working once they've been 'demystified' in a few brilliant essays. But even the
most politically engaged intellectual work, insists Hall, does not transform
the poltical terrain. (I should note that Hall's talk and Cornel West's were
delivered extempore and transcribed word-for-word into the book; between them they are easily the two most exhilarating documents in the
collection.)

Hall is not alone in his caveats about contemporary cultural studies;
far from it. Lata Mani calls out the inadequacy of 'disembodied' cultural
studies narratives that tell a 'bloodless tale of theoretical innovation and
reformulation'.[22] Kobena Mercer disses 'the predominant voices in post-

modern criticism', noting that Baudrillardian crisis rhetoric is the vehicle 'by which the loss of authority and identity on the part of a tiny minority of privileged intellectuals is generalized and universalized as something that everybody is supposedly worried about' (p. 424). And bell hooks asks Cornel West and Paul Gilroy 'how, in the US, cultural studies can avoid simply reproducing a more sophisticated group of people who are interpreting the experience of the "other" under the guise of identifying themselves as comrades and allies' (p. 698).

Some of these contestations get sharp. In the conference's opening session, John Fiske complained that Glover and Kaplan 'positioned the text as the prime agent in the circulation of meaning', thereby taking up the traditional critical roles of 'privileged revealers' (p. 224) of meanings in popular crime fiction. He then contrasted their bad thing to Constance Penley's good thing, telling Penley that 'you explicitly aligned yourself with the fans' and 'allowed yourself no privileged insight into the original text' (p. 495). Glover and Kaplan countercharged that Fiske was opposing 'sympathetic populist fan-niks' to 'sinister, snooty Privileged Revealers' (p. 224). This alleged dichotomy between 'fans' and 'intellectuals' dominated much too much of the conference, as everyone began to challenge everyone else to align their sympathies with the popular – or risk being called a 'traditional intellectual' (this, as every conference-goer knew, is a major Gramscian insult). Finally, Andrew Ross responded to a pointed question from Jennifer Daryl Slack by asking whether 'the position of the "intellectual as fan" is going to be erected as a new kind of credentialism … a moralistic criterion for doing cultural studies' (p. 553).[23]

For the most part, the question-and-answer sections of the book are both daunting and valuable. Daunting, because you realize you're confronted with a large roomful of people who really do, *in ordinary discourse, off the top of their heads*, say things like 'in the work of Homi Bhabha, the question of otherness also represents the sign of excess, which is not excess in terms of an alternative essentialism, but excess as something that cannot be reduced to a unique logic or rationalism, for example a Eurocentric discourse' (p. 476; this is from a question asked by Iain Chambers). Valuable, because most of the questions are substantive, elaborate and well-conceived; in this they tease out speakers' implications and submerged arguments, and in this they often get full five-minute responses. Nothing (in form or in content) could be further from the simulacra of 'debate' afforded by TV's talking heads and their rapid-fire exchange of warmed-over *McLaughlin Group* sound bites.

Debate so extensive can't always be productive; nor can so charged a conference. Interestingly, the book reproduces some of the moments that threatened to bring the conference to a halt, including one student's contention that 'there is no scheduled place for a participant in this conference to say anything which is not to or from the podium' (p. 293). It isn't surprising that such moments occurred: cram enough marginalized, high-powered lefties in one room and you're bound to find some utopian democrats who're outraged to discover that academic conferences – even anti-academic conferences – aren't 'ideal speech situations' in which everyone discourses as equals.

I grant that a conference on cultural studies *should* aspire to be something other than a routine academic conference. Still, I was personally surprised by the objections that the conference reinforced the very hierarchies it proposed to dismantle, that it accelerated the commodification of critical discourse, that it forced all participants to direct their comments to the speakers, and that it prevented a truly emancipatory practice of cultural studies. As the initiated among us are aware, the crime of 'reinforcing the hierarchies you seek to dismantle' is the single worst thing any progressive intellectual can be charged with, and it's usually followed by the counterclaim that such charges *themselves* reinforce the same hierarchies insofar as they reproduce the hierarchical practice of criticizing hierarchy from some ideological position 'above' hierarchy. The problem with most of these criticisms of the conference, though, was that they tended to rely entirely on some untheorized, implicit ideal – where critical discourse never gets commodified, everyone talks to everyone else, and everybody leaves emancipated at last.

Strange, too, were the occasional technophobias that ran through the conference, and chiefly manifested themselves in dark suspicions of the recording technology that made much of the book possible. One might consider it a good thing that people at a conference speak up eloquently, that their questions be audible to everyone, and that all the Q-and-A sessions be textually preserved for those of you who couldn't scrape together the airfare to be there in person. But for some lefter-than-thou folks, conference technology was apparently a Foucauldian apparatus of surveillance (aka a 'panaudicon') cleverly designed to co-opt questioners' 'interventions' by allowing them the illusion of 'participation' and 'resistance'. So does the book, too, reinforce technocracy and hierarchy in its turn? Don't ask me. I've played so many lousy gigs in my life that I'm just happy whenever the mikes work and the soundboard isn't shooting off sparks.

Yet even at its silliest, all this talking back is thoroughly stimulating. All the same, there are obvious problems with any book so many-voiced. This one can be too encyclopedic: what with its sheer size, its attempt at comprehensiveness, the shuttling among talks necessary to the reading process (what *did* Bill Warner say to Ian Hunter, and does it inform his own article on *Rambo?*), *Cultural Studies* often seems a book to be consulted rather than read. Then, too, there is the problem of what Stuart Hall calls the 'theoretical fluency of cultural studies in the United States' (p. 286). Some of the essays in *Cultural Studies* make for pretty rough going; even the ones that aren't theoretically 'fluent' can demand a fair amount of prior acquaintance with the subject; and there's a lot of perverse textuality here almost everywhere you look. To some degree this is inevitable, since it can often be impossible to speak across disciplines *without* using the specialized, hybridized dialects that can be understood in many disciplines at once; but for readers who don't belong to any of these various disciplines, some essays and exchanges will look like a transcription of academic Babel.

One might have wished for more explicitly historical essays; no one but Mani, Hunter, Stallybrass, and Catherine Hall delve back before the twentieth century in much detail. 'It is very striking', says Hall, 'how many historians do not feel obliged to investigate work which would relate to their own across a boundary' – and, just as striking, 'there's an enormous neglect of history within cultural studies.'[24] And I take it to be pretty ominous that an international conference of prominent leftists gathered in April 1990 and, in the course of five days' discussion of fragmentation, deterritorialization, globalization, and hegemony, did not devote any significant attention to Eastern Europe – except for Stuart Hall's recognition of 'the moment of the disintegration of a certain kind of Marxism', a moment 'which I am astonished that so few people have addressed' (p. 279), and Kobena Mercer's reference to how the decline of Communism in the West makes 'the need to think in terms of multiple determinations ... particularly acute' (p. 444).

Anne Szemere's article on the Hungarian uprising of 1956 does address this gap in the book; but Szemere, too, remarks that cultural studies has devoted all its attention to advanced capitalist and postcolonialist societies, leaving socialist states 'virtually unexplored'.[25] Angela McRobbie's postscript pursues the matter further, noting that 'the totalizing field of Marxist theory may have been discredited' (p. 721) but that 'the debate about the future of Marxism in cultural studies has not yet taken place' (p. 719). Indeed, even though McRobbie points to the conference's inattention to one of the pressing global issues of the day, she herself swerves from the subject rather precipitously, choosing to devote her conclusion not to a discussion of post-Soviet class analysis in cultural studies but to a reading of *Ghost* as a film that 'addresses and gives a place to new emergent identities' (p. 729). What Vaclav Havel would make of this we do not know, but it's evidently easier to fault the book for ignoring Eastern Europe than it is to address Eastern Europe.

Don't get me wrong – it's not that cultural studies doesn't have other fish to fry. Nothing requires that future work in cultural studies remain faithful to the history of post-neo-theoretico-Marxism in the British cultural studies tradition. Vital new work is being done as we speak, in mass media and communications, postcolonialism, science and bioethics, environmentalism, gender and sexuality, anthropology, literature and (sometimes) history. Still, it's hard to say what American endeavors will hook up most neatly with cultural studies, just as it's going to be hard to determine which American endeavors can legitimately claim to have been doing cultural studies without knowing it.

Theoretically inclined AIDS activism has obvious natural affiliations; as Paula Treichler has written elsewhere, many activists have already effected 'significant renegotiations of the geography of cultural struggle – of sources of biomedical expertise, relationships between doctor and patient, relationships of the general citizenry to science and to government bureaucracies, and debate about the role and ownership of the body.'[26] American Studies, reports of whose death have been greatly exaggerated, stands to gain enormously by lining up its various American-left cultural traditions (for example, Thorstein Veblen, Edmund Wilson, Granville Hicks, Kenneth Burke) against Britain's for comparison and contrast in the interests of theorizing its own historical specificity.[27] Feminism and African American studies have already made significant inroads into cultural studies – as *Cultural Studies* candidly acknowledges – and queer theory has cult-studs written all over it. But, as Stuart Hall reported in a post-conference visit to the prairie, there's a danger in all this alliance-building: in the jostling for academic funding and general theoretical sexiness, cultural studies runs the risk of forgetting where its allies come from. It seems that Hall had just come from a conference on postcolonialism, which was hot, and which included people in cultural studies, who were hot too. But the local African American Studies program wasn't involved, presumably because it hadn't been hot for twenty years or so. The bitter irony here is that the Civil Rights and Black Power movements were inspirations for some black British cultural studies workers; to say the least, American cultural studies ignores such movements – and their academic manifestations – at its peril.

My closing impression of the conference was that many of its thousand or so attendees left in a paroxysm of self-loathing. They had spent five exhausting days at a Big Academic Event listening to over thirty demanding papers, and they knew that their presence, their desire to hear these speakers in person, had contributed to making the conference a Big Academic Event. Reports of the conference that filtered back to central Illinois suggested that a nationwide competition had begun in which the goal was to describe in as many ways as possible how the conference was a reprehensible event, full of careerists, elitists, stargazers and fashion victims – and worst of all, an event that sought to write *the* book on cultural studies.

That book is now written, and though it certainly deserves every shopper's attention, it doesn't look as if it's going to be the only important cultural studies title on the shelf after all. Besides, cultural studies comes to us bearing not a big book but a sword, and the question of where it will strike next is less clear than the question of who will strike back. For who *won't*? To the traditional left, cultural studies will probably seem too politically diffuse and too high-theoretical; from the diffuse, high-theoretical left, the artifact of *Cultural Studies* is likely to invite any number of dismissive swipes – too monolithic, too academic, too hegemonic. To intellectual conservatives, cultural studies will look like an amalgam of their worst nightmares: an irreducibly 'political', interventionist, confrontational body of work generating knowledge without discipline, activism without apology. That's a lot to expect of one book, one field, or even one anti-field. But then again, cultural studies promises a lot, as well it should. It's precisely because cultural studies promises so much – more than it can possibly deliver – that both its opponents and practitioners will insist that it doesn't belong in the universities at all: the former because it's too activist (it performs intellectual *work*) and the latter because it's not activist enough (it performs merely *intellectual* work). Yet even for ambitious intellectual movements, 'institutionalization' doesn't have to mean 'entombment'. And if cultural studies can manage to work through its anti-professionalisms, its hybrid theoretical languages, and its occasional smugnesses, it may just wind up being an intellectual movement that matters to a broad constituency of Americans who don't usually go around calling themselves intellectuals.

Notes

1. Angela McRobbie, 'Post-Marxism and Cultural Studies: A Post-script', in *Cultural Studies*, Lawrence Grossberg, Cary Nelson and Paula A. Treichler, eds (New York: Routledge, 1992), p. 722.

2. Dick Hebdige, *Subculture: The Meaning of Style* (New York: Routledge, 1979), p. 26.

3. Stuart Hall, 'The Toad in the Garden: Thatcherism among the Theorists', in Cary Nelson and Lawrence Grossberg, eds, *Marxism and the Interpretation of Culture* (Urbana, Ill.: University of Illinois Press, 1988), pp. 72–3; hereafter cited in the text as 'Toad'.

4. Stuart Hall, *The Hard Road to Renewal: Thatcherism and the Crisis of the Left* (London: Verso, 1988), p. 5.

5. Douglas Kellner, 'Film, Politics, and Ideology: Reflections on Hollywood Film in the Age of Reagan', *The Velvet Light Trap*, no. 27 (1991), p. 12.

6. Andrew Ross, *No Respect: Intellectuals and Popular Culture* (New York: Routledge,

1989), p. 231.

7. Cary Nelson, Paula A. Treichler and Lawrence Grossberg, 'Cultural Studies: An Introduction', in *Cultural Studies*, p. 2.

8. Jan Zita Grover, 'AIDS, Keywords, and Cultural Work', in *Cultural Studies*, p. 234.

9. Douglas Crimp, 'Portraits of People with AIDS', in *Cultural Studies*, p. 130.

10. Tony Bennett, 'Putting Policy into Cultural Studies', in *Cultural Studies*, p. 32.

11. Cornel West, 'The Postmodern Crisis of the Black Intellectuals', in *Cultural Studies*, pp. 691–2.

12. David Glover and Cora Kaplan, 'Guns in the House of Culture? Crime Fiction and the Politics of the Popular', in *Cultural Studies*, p. 222.

13. Kobena Mercer, '"1968": Periodizing Politics and Identity', in *Cultural Studies*, pp. 424–49; hereafter cited in the text.

14. Marcos Sanchez-Tranquilino and John Tagg, 'The Pachuco's Flayed Hide: Mobility, Identity, and *Buenas Garras*', in *Cultural Studies*, pp. 556–70.

15. Angie Chabram-Dernersesian, 'I Throw Punches for My Race, But I Don't Want to Be a Man: Writing Us – Chica-nos (Girl, Us)/ Chicanas – into the Movement Script', in *Cultural Studies*, p. 92.

16. Jody Berland, 'Angels Dancing: Cultural Technologies and the Production of Space', in *Cultural Studies*, p. 42.

17. Laura Kipnis, '(Male) Desire and (Female) Disgust: Reading *Hustler*', in *Cultural Studies*, pp. 384, 388–9; hereafter cited in the text.

18. Constance Penley, 'Feminism, Psychoanalysis, and the Study of Popular Culture', in *Cultural Studies*, p. 479; hereafter cited in text.

19. Jennifer Daryl Slack and Laurie Whitt, 'Ethics and Cultural Studies', in *Cultural Studies*, p. 571.

20. Andrew Ross, 'New Age Technoculture', in *Cultural Studies*, pp. 531–5.

21. Stuart Hall, 'Cultural Studies and Its Theoretical Legacies', in *Cultural Studies*, p. 279; hereafter cited in the text.

22. Lata Mani, 'Cultural Theory, Colonial Texts: Reading Eyewitness Accounts of Widow Burning', in *Cultural Studies*, p. 393.

23. Fredric Jameson, in an otherwise searching review of the volume, curiously endorses the conference's dominant image of the intellectual: 'surely the most innovative treatment of the intellectual in this conference lies in the new model of the intellectual as fan', Jameson, 'On *Cultural Studies*,' *Social Text*, no. 34 (1993), p. 42. I personally find this model of intellectual work unhelpful, in part because it prevents intellectuals from being too 'critical' of their objects of study (as Jameson acknowledges when he brings up the issue of populism and anti-intellectualism in cultural studies). One does not, as a 'fan', want to be accused by a fellow intellectual of standing 'above' the people in some Leninist fashion. Nor need it be this way; in most arenas of public fandom, fans are allowed if not expected to be critical of their objects (the Red Sox, *Days of Our Lives*, Mel Gibson). In the conference, however, various intellectuals' *image* of fandom served as a stricture on what could be said about whatever one professed to be a fan of. Jameson comes to a different – and more interesting – conclusion by giving the intellectual-as-fan a cannily 'Derridean' twist: if cultural studies intellectuals are fans, says Jameson, then they are fans *of fans*. Thus it would appear that 'the "people" itself longs to be a "people" and be "popular", feels its own ontological lack, longs for its own impossible stability, and narcissistically attempts, in a variety of rituals, to recuperate a being that never existed in the first place', Jameson, p. 43.

24. Catharine Hall, 'Missionary Stories: Gender and Ethnicity in England in the 1830s and 1840s', in *Cultural Studies*, pp. 271–2.

25. Anne Szemere, 'Bandits, Heroes, the Honest, and the Misled: Exploring the Politics of Representation in the Hungarian Uprising of 1956', in *Cultural Studies*, p. 623.

26. Paula Treichler, 'How to Have Theory in an Epidemic: The Evolution of AIDS Treatment Activism', in Penley and Ross, eds, *Technoculture*, p. 97.

27. For more on the potential relations between American Studies and Cultural Studies, see Joel Pfister's essay, 'The Americanization of Cultural Studies', *Yale Journal of Criticism*, vol. 4, no. 2 (1991), pp. 199–229.

6

Bite Size Theory:

Popularizing Academic Criticism

In the course of this essay I'm going to argue three things: one, that popularizing the work of academic cultural criticism is something we absolutely must do, something that we cannot not want; two, that there isn't a chance in the world that academic criticism will ever be popular; and three, that the kind of criticism known as critical theory already *is* popular. In other words, one of the primary things I want to address here is the question of what we mean by 'popular' and 'popularization'. Let me dispense with my second argument first. Academic work will never be truly popular, in the American sense, until it gets televised. Nationally televised. We're talking about a syndicated, sponsored public-airwaves program. And because academics tend to ramble and make *nuanced* arguments, we'd also have to be talking about *mediaworthiness* – punditry, sound bites, talking heads, movie stars, swimming pools. My own nightmare version of this scenario would be critical theory as performed by the McLaughlin Group. First, McLaughlin barks: 'Item one: The Performance of Gender Is Simultaneously Its Subversion. Eleanor!' Eleanor Clift gets four seconds. 'Wrong! Mort!'

But that's another subject entirely, and I'm not going to talk about it here. Besides, when it comes to competing with television, we're all too familiar with how marginal we are. Evan Watkins has recently argued with admirable and depressing clarity that academic work is constructed not only so as to make a virtue of that marginalization, but so as to make it a source of our continual frustration as well. Watkins's argument, especially where it discusses the relation between American colleges and secondary education, is specific to English departments, but his account of the 'circulation of value' holds for related fields as well. Those of us in the human sciences tell ourselves that we have a 'general and universal' function in circulating cultural values, but we're notably unable to circulate the content of the work we do throughout the culture at large. Comparing

English departments to work locations which are designed to circulate the content of their work, like advertising agencies, Watkins finds that literary study competes with advertising and does it badly:

> Teaching literature in the schools challenges the sociocultural values that circulate in a *marketplace* dominated by the influence of advertising. ... Teaching literature must then compete against the massive resources of advertising without the benefit of either a specific clientele or a location of work to facilitate their intervention in the circulation of sociocultural values. Literature teachers are condemned ... to the worst of both worlds. They have a function, which like the function of advertising is 'general and universal'; they have a location of work, which like the location of other disciplines is very specific. But they have the advantages of neither advertising nor other disciplines of study. Function and location in the teaching of literature are incommensurable.[1]

As Watkins has it, academic literary study has lived with this function disjunction until recently because it defined its work as *intrinsically* valuable insofar as it deals with the intrinsic values intrinsic to literature. We may have wanted more people to read the Great Books, but the value of Great Books is certainly independent of what anybody knows about them. That's why they're great; they have intrinsic value.

Yet even though many of us today (whether in modern languages, philosophy, women's studies, anthropology, history or what-have-you) are more likely to consider value contingent rather than intrinsic, little has changed about how we circulate our work – and I think that has more to do with what we make of the professionalization of cultural criticism than with jargon, politics, PC, or debates over the contingency of values. When we construe professionalism as client-oriented, as Richard Ohmann does, for instance, we almost always wind up with an idea of literary study as a service provided to students.[2] Although we may also claim administrators, alumni, trustees or state legislators as our distant clients, we find we have a hard time justifying research that doesn't have immediate pedagogical use value; we also have a hard time explaining why so much of our client contact is handled by graduate students. When we take another tack, as Jonathan Culler has, and define professionalism as colleague- rather than client-oriented, we wind up with a professionalized intelligentsia that has won the disciplinary autonomy to produce new knowledges, but doesn't really know or care how to circulate those knowledges other than to colleagues in the profession.[3] And after all, if we claim to be 'oriented' primarily to the demands of the field and the profession, it's only fitting that we be so often accused of writing only for each other.

At this point I could take the road laid out by Bruce Robbins and argue that the PC debates have, willy-nilly, made us public and forced us to reckon with, of all things, some of our successes in creating a large body of work and an institutional structure for political conservatives to attack.[4] I'm not going to take that road, but I do want to underline Robbins's remarks by saying that the PC wars should have taught us one lesson – namely, that if we don't popularize academic work it will be popularized for us. *That* kind of popularization takes place on terms we can neither influence nor anticipate; and now that we know just how bad criticism's 'popularization' might look in hands not our own, we have all the more reason to get busy.

So the PC scare has its heuristic value. More crucially, though, we should look closely at what we've been pilloried for, tedious and intellectually unrewarding a task as this has been lately. (I'll say more about that tedium in the epilogue to this essay.) For I think the public debate on the aims of literary study – and it's notable in itself that literary study has occupied so much of the debate over and in higher education – has so far betrayed a telling and altogether appropriate confusion on the part of 'generalists' about whether literary study should be an autonomous discipline unto itself. It's up to us, as I'll argue shortly, to exploit that public confusion, and to learn what we can from the realization that our nonacademic audiences have no clear or fixed idea of what it means to engage in the professional study of culture. Examples of this confusion are everywhere, but I'll confine myself to two especially useful ones. In February 1992, in his cover essay for *Time* magazine, 'The Fraying of America', Robert Hughes lampooned us even in the course of defending us; dismissing media reports of a 'left McCarthyism' on campus, he claimed instead that academics' real failings lay in their obsession with academic questions: 'the world changes more deeply, widely, thrillingly than at any moment since 1917, perhaps since 1848, and the American academic left keeps fretting about how phallocentricity is inscribed in Dickens' portrayal of Little Nell.'[5] By contrast, John Searle had taken us to task in the *New York Review* a year earlier for overstepping our disciplinary bounds, of not caring about literature *as literature*, 'in ways that seemed satisfactory to earlier generations'.[6] It turns out that Searle only has one generation in mind – and a fragment of it at that (he names Edmund Wilson, I. A. Richards and Randall Jarrell, only the last of whom really supports the point Searle was trying to make). But if we put Hughes and Searle together for a moment, we get a curious composite sketch of ourselves: academic criticism, it appears, is remiss because it doesn't pay sufficient attention to the world around it – and what's worse, it pays too much.

One especially finds this kind of conundrum plaguing academic feminism, which is castigated by Lynne Cheney for being essentialist and by Camille Paglia for being anti-essentialist, or criticized in one and the same breath for being unscholarly (insofar as it concerns 'advocacy') *and* for being too 'academic' and hence out of touch with the concerns of American women. These various contradictions can be seen as evidence of our attackers' cluelessness, or mendacity, or both; or they can provide us with the occasion to reflect on what it means to the public that academic intellectuals no longer focus so exclusively on what distinguishes cultural study from every other social practice. Because this is in many ways our signal failing: we no longer tell people, and we no longer believe, that the knowledges we produce can only be produced in our own departments, whatever these might be. Instead, we consider the disciplines of cultural study to be in principle contiguous with and relevant to myriad other disciplines – and to undisciplined knowledges as well.

To popularize the more controversial academic inquiries of the past twenty years – into deconstruction, gender, sexuality, new historicism, ethnicity, popular culture, and postcolonialism – is thus only to take seriously the claims of our scholarship on the lived subjectivities of ordinary people, and to take seriously as well our own claims to be producing a knowledge that is not solely specific to the reading of literary texts. For neither gender nor sexuality nor ethnicity nor history is 'extrinsic' to literary study – or to human life as we've known it to date. Sometimes I think proponents of cultural studies in literature departments are so concerned to distinguish themselves from previous generations of literary critics that they tend to forget how completely their contemporary work is invested in social mimesis: the profession devotes special issues to postcolonialism because the postcolonial world is the one we live in; it speaks at length about human sexualities in part because most of literary study did not officially recognize until last Thursday (for all its sporadic invocations of polymorphous perversity) that humans have sexual*ies;* and it is consumed with arguments about 'hegemony' and 'domination' because between them, hegemony and domination make the world go round. 'As I've often said', Stuart Hall has often said, 'Margaret Thatcher is the best Gramscian I know.'

The popularization of theory, in other words, goes to the heart of contemporary academe's claims to intelligibility; and if our academic criticism cannot be popularized, then we who champion 'cultural studies' and 'interdisciplinarity' should give up the self-congratulatory claim to have broken with the narrow specializations and arbitrary exclusions of academic discipines. I'm making a Bakhtinian claim here: unless theory-speak gets translated into demotic vulgarisms *it don't,* as another Duke once said, *mean a thing.* It just doesn't signify at all. You can't rest content in the claim that academic work simply involves different knowledges and different registers from nonacademic work, because if Bakhtin is right, and he is, those knowledges and registers have to be in living contact and conflict with all manner of alien sociolects, including those of the 'amateur' readers of the *Times Book Review* or the *Nation* or *Time* – and those of our caricaturists on the right. This doesn't mean that all cultural critics have to renew their faith in the 'general reader' and write in whatever fashion Robert Alter or David Lehman deems appropriate. (If we build a generalist journal in the cornfields, will s/he come and read it?) But it *does* mean we should try to imagine nonacademic readers who ask only that the languages of academic criticism be translated into their languages.

This involves dusting off some good old humanist bromides and (ahem) reinscribing them differently in our material practices. And what I'll focus on, for the remainder of this essay, is the good old humanist confidence in the social ramifications of criticism and theory. When George Will fulminated in *Newsweek* that 'academic Marxists deny the autonomy of culture', he no doubt thought his outrage spoke for a broad humanist consensus.[7] But then recall Michael Kinsley's response in the *New Republic:* 'of course anyone sensible denies the autonomy of culture.'[8] Or, better yet, take the words of an influential academic critic:

> To perceive a work not only in its isolation, as an object of aesthetic contemplation, but also as implicated in the life of a people at a certain time, as expressing that life, and as being in part shaped by it, does not, in most people's experience, diminish the power or charm of the work but, on the contrary, enhances it.[9]

That might have been written by Stephen Greenblatt, but it was in fact written by Lionel Trilling. I don't mean to suggest that there's nothing new under the new historicist sun; my point, rather, is that although we may be historicizing works of art in ways Trilling did not or would not, it's foolish for anyone to pretend that new historicism (or Marxist historicism) violates literature or – to invoke some trendy Marxist jargon – 'common sense'. And what's true of academic historicism as a principle is true as well of many other newfangled modes of critical inquiry: for, to come around to my third point, what may be controversial for traditionalists in the humanities may be strangely familiar to cultural workers (and consumers) located elsewhere in the world.

One of the reasons we can now read Shakespeare's *Tempest* in postcolonialist contexts, after all, is that – as Mary Louise Pratt reminds us – the play itself has been reread and rewritten by playwrights in the New World (such as Aimé Césaire, author of *A Tempest;* José Enrique Rodó, author of

Ariel; or Roberto Fernández Retamar, author of *Calibán*).[10] Or you can read John Gay and Bertolt Brecht by way of Wole Soyinka, or Conrad through Achebe, or Defoe via Coetzee: no one has to 'impose' postcoloni- alism on poor defenseless politically innocent texts. Cultural criticism may not always be 'secondary', and there's everything to be said for knowl- edges produced in universities and exported elsewhere, but here postcolo- nial criticism often follows in the wake of the global circulation of texts.[11]

Nor does academe have any exclusive patents on theory. Is gender performativity something concocted in an academic laboratory, or is it something you can see in *Paris Is Burning* – or down the street? Are con- cepts like 'iterability' and 'reinscribability' just poststructuralist gobbledy- gook, or are they altogether familiar to Hank Shocklee, Biz Markie, Digital Underground and every other talented hip-hop sampler? Is it dis- course-besotted metahistorians or campaign managers who know that representations are social facts? Do we have to introduce publishers, fu- tures traders and real estate agents to the idea that there's no such thing as 'intrinsic' merit, that merit is a social phenomenon? And what about the producers – or viewers – of *The Larry Sanders Show* (starring Garry Shandling): do we really need to acquaint them with the idea of the simu- lacrum?[12] I don't think so. I think, to put it plain, that all these constitu- encies are doing the stuff we talk about in a different voice. One of the primary reasons 'cultural studies' names such a volatile enterprise is pre- cisely that it finds itself examining populations that have their own de- scriptive languages for themselves, which don't always mesh well with de Certeau or Laclau and Mouffe but which serve the purposes of enunciat- ing group identities, practices and self-definitions. Whether one is exam- ining subcultures among musicians, Chicana artists, *Star Trek* fans, São Paulo youth, or word processing temps, one does not run up against peo- ple who don't have 'theory'; one finds, instead, that one has to negotiate a busy, Bakhtinian intersection of competing sociolects – where the lived subjectivities of ordinary people stand, ideally, in a mutually transforma- tive relation to theories *about* the lived subjectivities of ordinary people.

So let's say it really is a postmodern, poststructuralist world out there, riven by gender, race, class, sexuality, postcolonialism and television, too, and that lots of people already know this but don't know that they know it. How then do we popularize our work when it's already popular but the populace hasn't been informed?

I can only tell you what I've found out so far, in my limited experience – and by reading the work of people like Michael Warner, Joan Scott, Mark Edmundson and Judith Frank, whom I think present the public claims of theory quite effectively.[13] As for myself, the hardest thing I've had to learn – or unlearn – is how thoroughly conditioned I am by the imperative to say something new. Or, to put that in its negative form, not to repeat or restate other people's work. To this day, in this very sentence, I fear saying something that would mark me as a 'mere' popularizer – you know, saying something everyone already knows and saying it glibly, without the requisite nuance. And yet both the cover essays I've done to date for the *Village Voice Literary Supplement,* one on postmodernism and one on cultural studies, amounted pretty much to synopsizing other people's work: not incorporating it, crediting it, making it new, but just *restating* it. I realized on my fourth rewrite of the cultural studies essay that I could never send this stuff to *Social Text,* none of whose readers really wants to hear the Birmingham Hoggart-Williams narrative again.[14] And writing that way was profoundly counterintuitive for me. So much so, actually, that I didn't learn my lesson: right about the same time (in the spring of 1992), at a conference open to the public at which I was responding to a keynote address by David Lehman, I was asked by someone from the audience what deconstruction meant. It was clearly a lehman's question ... and I gave an incomprehensible, article-length answer, partly because I was afraid to say, in front of smart and well-informed peers (including – gulp – Barbara Johnson), something more like 'deconstruction suggests that everything is relational to everything else and therefore can't be defined in and of itself. Let me give you an example: male/female' – which, I think, works better, and has more direct social consequences, than deconstructing speech and writing or presence and absence. I mean, of course, that it remains the case all over this world that should you attempt *personally* to deconstruct male/female, you could be putting your life in jeopardy.

The second suggestion follows from the first: we have to be willing to restate other people's work and forego the pleasure of producing the new, and we have to give examples.[15] This is a piece of advice with a long history in the rhetorical tradition – in fact, here I'm just restating the work of Aristotle (and, more recently, Kenneth Knoespel), and yet this too is something I have had to relearn.[16] What I'd expected generally in writing for the *VLS* is that they would ask me to tone it down, to streamline, to dejargonize. I didn't expect them to ask me to *expand* each essay, and I certainly wouldn't have thought that my most arduous task, in revision, would consist of elaborating each essay's theoretical underpinnings.

For instance, I didn't expect to be asked to provide more stuff about anti-foundationalism – more about Kuhnian historicism, maybe an example of one of his arguments and a good quote (I complied with all these requests).[17] Nor did I expect them to say that they wanted to hear more about hegemony and articulation, and did I have an example of how hegemonies get put together? I said sure, look at all the disparate things that got recoded by Reaganism; they said, like what kinds of things specifically? So I borrowed wholesale Douglas Kellner's article on *Rambo,* where Kellner points out that the movie rearticulates to militarism and conservatism various countercultural codes, like long hair and headbands and hatred of the Establishment and love of natural foods. The point is (as any reader of *Social Text* already knows) that these things don't usually go together with Reaganism, but they can be made to; and lest we delude ourselves into thinking that contemporary theory only enables forms of ideology critique unintelligible to all but the initiated, I assure you that I have yet to find a nonacademic who does not understand Kellner's point. Similarly, to clarify 'articulation' I could have used Andrew Ross's example from *No Respect,* where he describes how rock subcultures, gay subcultures and camp subcultures somehow managed to produce, by the mid 1970s, a genre of very popular music in which the signs of virile masculinity were high-pitched voices, long tousled hair, heavy facial makeup and studded leather bodysuits.[18] Again, what's crucial here is criticism's investment in social mimesis: the reason you can use these examples, which almost everyone recognizes immediately whether they read the *VLS, TLS, October* or *Entertainment Weekly,* is that 'hegemony' and 'articulation' name real social processes – and, needless to say, because *Rambo* and Kiss (and Mötley Crüe) are always already theoretical anyway.

Finally, we need to reconceive both the professionalization of cultural criticism and our putative client relations, so that public work can be recognized as a form of professional work. Easier said than done, I know. Ask anyone who's trying to build a career – or get tenure, or get a job – whether they'd rather have their next essay appear in *Details* or in *differences.*[19] For that matter, it's not as if the prestige system of academic publishing will disappear when it comes to the valuation of nonacademic work. We might be tempted to judge the merit of nonscholarly publication in part on the basis of our ideas about various nonscholarly audiences. Says friend, historian and queer theorist Lisa Duggan,

> it depends in part on which public you're writing for. It obscures a lot of differences to say you're 'writing for the public,' when you could be writing for the *New Republic* or for the *Gay Community News.* In the field of history, it can be prestigious to publish in the *American Prospect,* where you're writing for that well-educated public. But it won't be nearly so prestigious if you're writing for what's perceived to be a subcultural community of some kind.[20]

Not to speak of writing for *Commentary.*

Well, perhaps I *should* speak of *Commentary,* since in referring to that journal I'm obliquely alluding to the Carol Iannone Imbroglio that hit the public press in the long hot summer of 1991, when the PC wars reached fever pitch. When Lynne Cheney, then chair of the National Endowment for the Humanities, nominated Carol Iannone to the NEH's advisory body, the National Humanities Council, the MLA (and other scholarly organizations) challenged Iannone's professional qualifications, noting that she wasn't an ideal person to judge contemporary scholarship because she hadn't produced any. Her vita, indeed, consisted almost exclusively of articles, book reviews and occasional pieces in *Commentary*. The MLA's 'professionalist' objection backfired badly, however, and allowed the ever-cynical Ms Cheney a wonderful opportunity to cast the MLA and similar organizations as 'elitist' institutions ganging up on Iannone. For her part, Iannone, by virtue of her columns in *Commentary*, was suddenly made over into a Critic of the People writing in accessible language – unlike the snooty and incomprehensible academic jargoneers lining up against her.[21]

I don't mean to suggest that the MLA shouldn't have challenged Iannone's credentials; Cheney's nomination was surely a deliberate affront, cannily calculated to see if her nominees would be held to the 'academic standards' Cheney herself had long accused her opponents of debasing, and the MLA is to be applauded for demanding that Cheney adhere to minimum standards of scholarly review. But the MLA's protestation that it was not opposing Iannone on 'political' grounds convinced few observers, which indicates that the 'professionalist' objection to Iannone was either misunderstood or directly resisted by much of the nonacademic public.[22]

Instead, the MLA (with the benefit of hindsight) might have attempted a two-pronged approach, combining 'professionalist' and what I'll call 'substantive' criteria. It's certainly worth arguing that Iannone doesn't have what it takes to be a competent reviewer of contemporary scholarship: on this score, one can propose that NHC nominees' publications in *Commentary* are just fine so long as they're also backed up by publications in refereed journals. But it's also worth arguing that Iannone's written work is substandard intellectual work for *any* forum: her attacks on academic feminism are narrow and ill-informed, her complaint against Charles Johnson's National Book Award is manifestly self-contradictory, and her work is often marred by shoddy argumentation and insufficient documentation (when it is documented at all). The fact that it was published in *Commentary* should be cause neither for dismissal (by the MLA) nor admiration (by Cheney); the fact remains that it's not very good work, and anyone considering Iannone's nomination to the NHC should be able to assess her publication record in those terms.

The reason I say this is the same reason I advocate considering non-

scholarly publications as part of a professor's public and professional record: our determinations of faculty merit and promise, especially in departments like English that have always tried to appeal to broader
publics, should ideally be based on *both* kinds of publication.[23] Although
the system of peer review often insulates professors (especially controversial junior faculty) from Know-Nothing colleagues, thus allowing Professor X's advocates to say, 'Well, you may not like feminist theory, but you
can't dispute someone who's placed articles in *Signs* and *differences*', it has
also, by the same token, *prevented* faculty from reading one another's
work. Because acceptance of an article by, say, *Critical Inquiry* is (rightly)
deemed to be an index of its scholarly merit, many faculty committees,
reviewing the author of said article, often feel that it has already been
judged on its merits, and does not need to be read for 'substance'. Professional peer review, of course, is supposed to provide one's colleagues
with just that guarantee of merit-by-acceptance. But when peer review
becomes the means by which one's scholarly work is judged by quantity
(and place of publication) to the exclusion of considerations of quality,
then I think it's time to shake up the system, and ask that everybody
read everything.

Stanley Fish would reply, no doubt, that our determination of a publication's merit cannot be disentangled from its place in the professional
prestige system, so that we will 'naturally' think more highly of an article
published in *Critical Inquiry* than one published in *Modern Language Notes*. I
have heard, too, of Neanderthal hiring and tenure committees that refused to consider publications in feminist journals as part of 'scholarly'
determinations of merit (on the reasoning that feminists are not critical of
one another). Hence my concern that extrascholarly publications in the
American Prospect would 'count for' more than similarly intelligent articles
in *Gay Community News,* just as some scholarly publications 'count more'
than others because of their place of publication. What's different – and
potentially dangerous – about adjudicating the merit of nonscholarly
work is that it may be judged not so much by its 'prestige' but by the
reviewers' sense of what (and *who*) constitutes an important nonacademic
audience: queers, Trotskyists, the American Jewish Committee, or policy
wonks – or some hybrid combination of these. But then, if we were to
review professors' extrascholarly work we would have to make explicit
our implicit judgments of such work; we would have to debate what we
now mutely take for granted. And we could no longer assume the merit
of articles in *Critical Inquiry* and the irrelevance of articles in *Harper's* or *Ms.*
(or *Commentary*). As for the objection that such a system would unduly
reward professors for doing 'hobby' books on trains or fine dining, thus
allowing them to pass these things off as 'popular' publications (à l'Ian-

none), I cannot see why a hobby book would not be understood *as* a hobby book even if it were part of the faculty review process. It's not as if we will lose our ability to distinguish between a serious, well-researched article on date rape and a collection of Fulghumesque anecdotes simply because we agree to read them both.

Of course, I could be proposing all this simply to justify my own 'popular' publications. But in fact, I'm making this argument precisely because my own department has *not* penalized me for doing public intellectual work. On the contrary, they've encouraged it, and because I presented my department with a smattering of academic and 'serious' nonacademic publications – from Cornell University Press to the *VLS* – I found, to my delight, that my colleagues read it all, partly to see whether the *VLS* stuff was worth considering. I'd like to see that be the case more often for people other than myself. It's not that I'm especially magnanimous; I just think the need is overwhelming for academic critics who can write for well-educated audiences or for subcultural communities, and I know we're not the only ones who feel that need. On this count, frankly, it doesn't bother me that academic criticism is further left than that of the mass-market journals. What does bother me considerably is that so much academic left politics are often incomprehensible to people (particularly politicians) *as politics.* When you say things like 'hegemony is leaky' and 'nobody has the phallus', you tend either to get blank unmeaning stares or cries that we should burned at the stake for muttering occult pagan incantations. Not because these propositions are out of step with the American people (whatever *that* phrase might mean), but because they're not made intelligible as political positions. And yet they have immediate political ramifications: they tell us that things could be otherwise, that oppression can be contested, that human agency matters, that appeals to family values sometimes fail to win popular consent. They are in their odd way profound statements of the optimism of the human intellect; and in their optimism they're as American as violence and apple pie. They tell us (again, in a different voice) to keep hope alive, and to have the courage to change. And they take, on average, about ten minutes to explain, too long for the attention span of the McLaughlin Group, but less time than it takes me to roll an apple pie crust.

But to take that time means doing things we're not used to, like saying things that 'everybody' (meaning everybody in one wing of the profession) 'already knows'. *And* it means taking a more commercial approach to academic work. Again, that's easy to say, and easy to say in these pages. But I continue to be astonished at how much we resist popularizing criticism because it would mean, well, going commercial, selling out, compromising our integrity. Four years ago I watched in amazement at the Illinois conference on cultural studies as one participant after another complained that these counterhegemonic proceedings were being recorded to produce a book – and, upon publication, would therefore be forcibly inscribed into the dominant American imaginary. One member of the audience re-marked that such conferences 'are actually contributing to the commodi-fication of critical discourse', as if critical discourse should by rights be a craft skill practiced only by the guild.[24] My complaint, as you might guess – about that conference and many others – is that such gatherings do not sufficiently contribute to the commodification of critical discourse. I know we're not most popular. We're not even most likely to succeed. But we do have potential readers, constituencies and clients whom we haven't yet learned – or bothered – to address. Profession, revise thyself.

Epilogue

I delivered a shorter version of this argument at the 1992 MLA conven-tion in New York, on a panel organized by Gerald Graff with co-panelists Anahid Kassabian and Jeffrey Wallen. Since the MLA is now fertile ground for deadline-conscious journalists looking to score a few easy points at academics' expense by mocking words like 'hegemonic' and 'in-tertextual', I had fond hopes that my session (titled 'Can Academic Criti-cism Be Popularized – And Should It Be?') would get some press coverage.

Actually, I imagined that some nonacademic person (journalist or oth-erwise) would stand up and challenge the paper by saying that populariz-ing criticism isn't so simple a matter as I'd made it sound – as though all would be well if only academics could learn to write in different voices for different audiences. I realized that the final words of the talk placed the burden of representation entirely on academics themselves. And such a supply-side conclusion, I thought, might seem to foreclose on the neces-sity of discussing the social or political conditions under which academic cultural criticism might reach a significant nonacademic audience for whom the time, inclination and resources for cultural criticism are never guaranteed, usually unavailable, and only occasionally desirable.

The question never came up; it was 9:30 on a Tuesday morning, and most of the public was out working or collecting unemployment. From an audience of a hundred or so, the panel fielded questions about the curric-ula of literature departments. One questioner, who said she taught music videos in the classroom and didn't see any reason to be apologetic about it, asked why we don't just jettison the concept of 'literature' and profess instead to be teaching the cultural text. I'd meant to argue that we already do teach the cultural text, and said so. 'But I personally wouldn't say we're "abandoning literature", I said, 'because I think that needlessly raises hackles among traditionalists' – and then, catching myself in one of those odd self-conscious moments, I added, 'and, of course, we wouldn't want to do *that*', rolling my eyes upward. The addendum got a laugh – no doubt because although it was meant seriously (and it followed a talk in which I'd tried to make contemporary theory sound as mimetic and as traditionalist as possible), it was a conventional piece of self-mockery as well.

The next questioner voiced her alarm that we'd spoken as if teaching music video were *better* than teaching traditional periods in literary history, and this disturbed her because her work was in Romanticism and she resented being treated as a second-class critic next to all these theory hotshots. Realizing that I'd already raised a traditionalist's hackles, I replied that I would never consider teaching music video *better* than doing Romanticism; the challenge, I thought, was persuading watchers of music video that they are already heir to Romantic cultural politics every time they say, 'I used to like [R.E.M., k. d. lang, Red Hot Chili Peppers, Ice-T] before they sold out and went commercial' – or telling neophyte readers of the preface to *Lyrical Ballads* that Wordsworth's denigration of sickly popular amusements remains with us today in the work of people who disdain music video.

The rest of the Q-and-A session followed more or less in this vein, and I left thinking I'd made myself as broadly intelligible as possible. A month later, I came across the *U.S. News & World Report*'s version of this series of exchanges. The description appeared in John Leo's 'On Society' column of 18 January 1993, a predictably inane harangue about Marxists in the academy. At the outset, Leo narrates his attempt to listen simultaneously to our session and (through the wall divider) to Catharine Stimpson speaking in the next room:

> I tune back in to Stimpson, who is now carrying on about the 'fatheadedness' of the anti-PC people. Then the green-dress anti-'Jeopardy' woman [that would be Anahid Kassabian] gives way to a black-shirt male [c'est moi] who is answering an earnest question from the floor: Is it OK, in college English classes, to teach music videos instead of literature? Black-shirt thinks it's just fine, though he says, derisively, that it might upset some 'traditionalists'; the audience chuckles appreciatively at the put-down.
>
> Welcome to the Modern Language Association of America's convention, the annual 'Gong Show' of the academic world. This is where some 11,000 college teachers of language and literature gather each year to hear papers on such topics as 'Jane Austen and the Masturbating Three-Button Jacket', 'Between the Body and the Flesh: Performing Lesbian Sadomasochism', 'The Poetics of Ouija' and 'Transvestite Biography'.[25]

This is all familiar stuff, of course, though there's something poignant about a reporter so desperate and behind the curve as to have cited Molly Hite's *parody* of Eve Sedgwick's famous title, 'Jane Austen and the Mastur-bating Girl', an oldie from 'way back in 1989. (Though Leo rightly as-sumes that no one will catch the slip except for us academic dweebs with an eye for allusion.) Partly because I'd shown up at the MLA convention in order to argue that criticism is 'already popular', I felt obliged to re-spond to this garbled translation of our session. Besides, the *U.S. News* has a wider circulation than most MLA papers. I didn't think my letter would be printed; it wasn't.

Dear Sir:

I noted with surprise and delight that I appeared in your January 18, 1993 issue, in an article on the 1992 MLA Convention by John Leo, where I was referred to only as 'black-shirt', and quoted as saying 'derisively' that it's OK to teach music videos as literature even though doing so upsets 'traditionalists'.

Leo's little snipe is standard fare for American newsweekly coverage of academia – not only does he get the quotes wrong, he even parades the fact that he couldn't quite *hear* the speakers he quotes. For those of your readers who might still be interested in honest intellectual exchange, though, I thought I'd write to set my small part of the record straight. It's OK to teach music videos, I said, though I wouldn't personally consider them 'literature'; after all, self-styled literary 'traditionalists' habitually forget the history of their own subject, and are quick to dismiss video as trash even as they teach the novels that earlier generations of traditionalists dismissed as 'trash'.

Dismissing video (or the novels of hack writers like Charles Dickens or Daniel Defoe) as beneath analysis – as incapable of generating serious reflec-tion – is simply anti-intellectual. And though such anti-intellectualism has long been a staple of American news media, it has no place in academe except among unprofessional, irresponsible teachers, who malign the West's intellec-tual traditions in calling themselves 'traditionalists'. This is a point black-shirted hombres like me have been making for many years now, but I have yet to find evidence that a major American newsmagazine can understand it – or even repeat it accurately. I think this too is cause for serious reflection.

I know, though, that many of your readers are better thinkers (and better listeners) than Mr Leo, and they certainly deserve better coverage of the American academy. Perhaps someday they'll find some; until then, beneath my bleak and ebon shirt there beats an ever hopeful heart.

Yours,
Michael Bérubé

Leo responded not to me but to his editor, Mike Ruby (surely Nabokov is at work here somewhere), repeating his claim that I had not condoned teaching videos *as* literature (as I put it), but *instead of* literature, which, I surmise, is even worse. But what little sense this reply makes demonstrates only that Leo doesn't know a thing about what academics do, and doesn't care. Were I patient enough to respond a second time, I'd limit myself to pointing out that English departments now (that is, in the latter half of the twentieth century) offer classes in film and English composition, where masscult trash like music video and John Leo columns might very well be taught as a matter of course.

I didn't bother with a second reply, though, because Leo's column had had bigger fish to fry in the first place. The real point of his piece came later on in the essay, where he diagnosed the cause of all this academic malaise:

> The vacationing [!] ideologues here are suffering from a swarm of radical isms, but the central one, totally dead in the real world, is Marxism. It is a vulgar Marxism, adapted by British radicals, and it goes like this: Whether we acknowledge it or not, everything we do or say works to support our ideological interests. Realizing that all creative writing is already political, the left works to reveal literature as the expression of an elite ruling class. So literary studies are properly a branch of leftist politics and nothing more. (p. 25)

The lesson here is clear, as is the reason I append this epilogue to the original essay: most people in national media just don't *want* to understand, no matter what language we speak or how nicely we speak it, even if we're addressing them directly in words they're familiar with.[26]

I'm elaborating such a pedestrian point at this length not just to provide my own essay with its own (mass-media-induced) corrective; there's a broader principle at stake, I think. Too often, when academics deal with political disputes, they imagine such disputes as variants on the model of *conversation.* Whether you're looking at the work of Richard Rorty, Seyla Benhabib, Wayne Booth, Stanley Fish, Barbara Herrnstein Smith or Gerald Graff, you'll find that we tend to place extraordinary and often unwarranted emphasis on discursive rationality, rhetorical persuasion, communicative ethics or teaching the conflicts. What are these, I wonder, if not academic models of political dispute, where procedural and practical advantages accrue to the most articulate, or to those with the greatest capacity for metacommentary and narrative self-justification? I don't mean, in asking such a question, to dismiss such models; on the contrary, I aspire to the ideal of operating according to them. I wouldn't be writing this (or letters to newsweeklies) otherwise. Still, it's crucial for us to remember that most of our interlocutors in the PC wars have no commitment to what intellectuals recognize as legitimate and rational exchange. As Ellen Messer-Davidow's painstaking and splendid research reminds us once again, the opponents of the cultural left are not going about their business by engaging our arguments; they seek to delegitimize higher education (as well as public education, though advancement of this goal will have to wait for another change of administration in Washington), and to establish a battery of alternate credentializing mechanisms that will allow them to avoid meeting academic standards for the production of knowledge.[26] Indeed, lurking behind cultural conservatives' chronic complaints about the decline of academic standards is the sorry (and unpublicized) fact that conservatives have, by and large, failed to meet the precipitously *rising* standards for the production of cultural criticism. Unable to cut it in an increasingly competitive academic market, they have instead sought the shelter of lucrative fellowships from the Olin, Bradley and Heritage foundations, whence they issue their celebrations of free markets and traditional standards.

My essay's conclusion, then, should properly read as follows: academic professions must 'popularize' themselves not merely so that they can talk to *Rambo* fans or the readers of *Details,* but because their very existence is being threatened, along with their autonomy from direct state intervention; and those who are threatening the existence and autonomy of the academic professions have thus far displayed no reluctance to spread lies about their opponents. As cultural critics, we cannot place our faith solely in models of social contestation based on the ideal of rational discursive exchange; but neither can we simply abandon discursive models of social contestation in favor of more 'tangible' forms of politics. The future of our ability to produce new knowledges for and about ordinary people – and the availability of higher education *to* ordinary people – may well depend on how effectively we can expose the right's well-financed disinformation campaigns. Our success in that endeavor may in turn depend on our ability to make our work intelligible *to* nonacademics – who then, we hope, will be able to recognize far-right rant about academe for what it is, the way so many of them are able to recognize Michael Medved's far-right ranting about Hollywood for what it is. But we won't accomplish that goal if we concentrate our energies only on conversing in ever more scrupulous and egalitarian ways with interlocutors whose chief objective is to silence us. The Bakhtinian conception of dialogue, we should recall, is not based on 'conversation'; it is based on struggle. Popularizing academic criticism therefore means, among other things, struggling for the various popular and populist grounds on which the cultural right has been trying to make criticism unpopular.

Notes

1. Evan Watkins, *Work Time: English Departments and the Circulation of Cultural Value* (Stanford, Calif.: Stanford University Press, 1989), pp. 155–6.
2. Richard Ohmann, *English in America: A Radical View of the Profession* (New York: Oxford University Press, 1976), particularly 'What English Departments Do' and 'Why They Do It' (pp. 207–54).
3. For Culler's account of 'horizontal' professionalism in American universities, see *Framing the Sign*, pp. 28–40.
4. Robbins, *Secular Vocations*, pp. 1–6; 'Introduction: The Grounding of Intellectuals', in *Intellectuals, Politics, Academics*, Robbins, ed., pp. ix–xxvii.
5. Robert Hughes, 'The Fraying of America.' *Time*, 3 February 1992, p. 46.
6. John Searle, 'The Storm over the University', in Berman, ed., *Debating P.C.*, p. 105.
7. George Will, 'Literary Politics', *Newsweek*, 22 April 1991, p. 72.
8. Michael Kinsley, 'P.C. B.S.' *New Republic*, 20 May 1991, p. 8.
9. Lionel Trilling, 'What Is Criticism?' [1970] Rpt. in *The Last Decade: Essays and Reviews, 1965–1975*, Diana Trilling, ed. (New York: Harcourt Brace Jovanovich, 1979), p. 86.

10. Mary Louise Pratt, 'Humanities for the Future: Reflections on the Western Culture Debate at Stanford', *South Atlantic Quarterly*, vol. 89, no. 1 (1990), pp. 7–25.
11. For a striking argument on how theory may be the trace of (rather than the spur to) uneven developments elsewhere in the culture, see Mark Edmundson's reading of deconstruction alongside contemporary business management theory as developed by Gareth Morgan's *Images of Organization* and *Creative Organization Theory* (both of which reject hierarchical organization in favor of mobile networks). As Edmundson notes, the latter of these texts cites the same passage from Nietzsche (about truth being 'a moving army of metaphors') that Paul de Man and J. Hillis Miller have focused on. 'Must it be the case', asks Edmundson, 'that the latest form of academic apostasy is inevitably out ahead of other cultural discourses? Might critical vocabularies work contemporaneously with, or follow in the wake of, even such fallen forms of discursive practice as those that emerge from the corporate world?' Edmundson, 'Criticism and Class Consciousness', *American Literary History*, vol. 2, no. 3 (1990), pp. 574–5.
12. For an entertaining take on talk-show simulacra-a-go-go, see Jay Martel's 'The Year in Television' in the 1992 *Rolling Stone* year-end issue: 'In one episode of *The Larry Sanders Show*, which mirrored the speculation that Dana Carvey would take over David Letterman's job, Carvey appeared as himself and agreed to guest host the Sanders show, only to call later to say he'd been offered his own talk show – in the same time slot. Of course, Shandling himself has appeared on non-fictional talk shows to plug his fictional talk show, including, yes, *Arsenio*. (This was shortly after Dennis Miller appeared to do Arsenio's opening monologue when his real-life talk show was canceled).' Martel, 'The Year in Television', *Rolling Stone*, no. 645/646, 10–24 December 1992, p. 198.
13. Specifically, I'm referring here to 'Lighting the Closet', Mark Edmundson's review of Eve Kosofsky Sedgwick's *Epistemology of the Closet*, published in the *Nation*, 21 January 1991, pp. 61–3; Judith Frank, 'In the Waiting Room: Canons, Communities, "Political Correctness"', in *Wild Orchids and Trotsky: Messages from American Universities*, Edmundson, ed. (New York: Viking, 1993), pp. 125–49; Joan Scott, 'The New University: Beyond Political Correctness', *Boston Review*, vol. 17, no. 2 (March-April 1992), pp. 9–12, 29–30; and 'From Queer to Eternity', Michael Warner's review of Judith Butler's *Gender Trouble* in the June 1992 *Voice Literary Supplement*, pp. 18–19, part of which proceeds by way of a debate with Simon Watney's reading of Butler.
14. Appropriately enough, I'm borrowing the point about 'producing the new'; Evan Watkins offers a more sustained discussion of the subject in *Work Time*, pp. 218–21.
15. I don't intend this sentence to institute some kind of nominalist criterion for cultural criticism, whereby critics have to carry around examples with them in backpacks and converse only by holding up objects. I mean only that if a form of criticism *does* claim to

be socially mimetic, then it should try to deliver the goods when people ask what it's socially mimetic *of.*

16. See Kenneth Knoespel, 'The Emplotment of Chaos: Instability and Narrative Order', in *Chaos and Order: Complex Dynamics in Literature and Science,* N. Katharine Hayles, ed. (Chicago: University of Chicago Press, 1991), pp. 100–22.

17. It's not that I thought the *VLS* consisted of 'mere' journalists incapable of asking about anti-foundationalism; I did know better than that. All the same, I didn't think they'd go after the knottiest and most-often-misunderstood plank in postmodernism's theoretical platform, mostly because I never thought I'd be asked to give an example of an anti-foundationalist argument to anyone who hadn't signed up for one of my classes. I owe Stacey D'Erasmo my gratitude, for that essay as for my other *Voice* ventures, for her bracing and instructive editing.

18. Andrew Ross, *No Respect,* p. 164.

19. I have nothing against *differences,* of course, and neither does Janet Lyon, my spouse, whose most recent essay appeared in the summer 1992 issue of the journal. We both enjoy *Details,* too, especially its low, low subscription rates. I merely wanted to see whether I could smash Western Civilization at one blow by associating 'the masculine' with fashion, gossip and consumerism, and aligning 'the feminine' with philosophy, writing and theory. Just this once.

20. Lisa Duggan, telephone interview, 11 June 1992.

21. See Cheney's account of the matter in Christopher Myers, '2 Scholarly Organizations Say Humanities Endowment's Council Hasn't Enough Academics; Chairman Calls Complaints "Elitist"', *Chronicle of Higher Education,* 10 April 1991, pp. A19, A22. As Cheney put it in a letter to Phyllis Franklin, 'How sad it makes me to see the Modern Language Association's Executive Council fall once again into the old elitist pattern.' Later in the article, Cheney is informed that her critics are calling her a conservative populist, and she responds, 'I love it. Call me a conservative populist anytime, rather than the opposite, which is a liberal elitist' (p. A22). Note that this formulation precedes then–Vice President Quayle's attacks on the 'cultural elite' by some fourteen months.

22. The op-ed industry ran strongly in Iannone's favor, as did the editorials of most major papers except the *New York Times;* see, for one example among many, the *Washington Post* editorial of 21 July 1991, p. C6, which called Iannone's defeat a 'Rejection without Merit' and repeated the insistance of its earlier editorial on Iannone ('Dispute in the Humanities', 20 May 1991) that the MLA's opposition was politically motivated despite the MLA's refusal to protest any other conservative nominee.

23. For a lucid description of how literary study has constructed itself as a 'porous profession', defined against and yet ideally subject to public (nonprofessional) review, see Bruce Robbins, *Secular Vocations,* pp. 84–95.

24. Grossberg, Nelson and Triechler, eds, *Cultural Studies* (New York: Routledge, 1992), p. 528; the question was asked by Bill Buxton.

25. John Leo, 'The Professors of Dogmatism.' *US News & World Report,* 18 January 1993, p. 25; hereafter cited in the text.

26. The work of Mitchell Stephens (who teaches journalism at NYU and does freelance work for various magazines) is a notable exception to the rule; see 'Deconstructing Jacques Derrida', *Los Angeles Times Magazine,* 21 July 1991, pp. 12–15, 31; 'Deconstruction and the Get-Real Press', *Columbia Journalism Review,* September-October 1991, pp. 38–42; and 'The Professor of Disenchantment' (a profile of Stephen Greenblatt), *West Magazine,* 1 March 1992, pp. 8–9, 29–30.

27. Ellen Messer-Davidow, 'Manufacturing the Attack on Liberalized Higher Education', *Social Text,* no. 36 (1993), pp. 40–80.

PART III

At the Closing
of the American Century

7

Paranoia in a Vacuum: *2001* and the National Security State

Stanley Kubrick's *2001: A Space Odyssey* is not a political film. A quarter-century after its release in April 1968 (its public debut took place on the day before the assassination of Martin Luther King, Jr), *2001* is usually remembered for its images, for the music, and for its groundbreaking special effects – all of which are widely and routinely cited in the general culture. The mysterious monolith turns up in *New Yorker* cartoons ('it's a black thing, you wouldn't understand'), 'Thus Spake Zarathustra' becomes a staple of *Sesame Street* phonetics lessons, the balletic representations of space flight provide material for a Lenny Kravitz video and an episode of *The Simpsons*. Much of the movie's audience might hesitate to ascribe a 'plot' to *2001* at all – much less a 'plot' in the 'political' sense; the movie's initial reviews tended to center on the monolith and on HAL, and rereading those reviews today chiefly affords one the spectacle of watching dozens of puzzled film critics circle curiously around this large, black slab in their midst.

To be sure, the scenes aboard the spaceship *Discovery,* which culminate in the famous breakdown of HAL and his murder of four astronauts, suggest that Kubrick's concern with humans and machines did not end with *Dr Strangelove,* and most of the film's commentators have appropriately reached the conclusion that, as Alexander Walker has put it, '*2001* is nothing less than an epic-sized essay on the nature of intelligence.'[1] So it's not as though the movie is entirely nonnarrative or nonpropositional, even if its director considers it 'essentially a nonverbal experience'.[2] All the same, my sense is that most people would think it takes a strange critical mind to see the movie as a commentary on the Cold War and the rise of the national security state. What's involved in this reading is a principle that's routine to most working critics and alien to most 'amateur' readers: the principle that a text can be read for its 'silences', its omissions, its latent or repressed subtexts. The psychoanalytic version of this principle is both well-known and much-abused (and its abuses contribute much to the parodies of academic critics as insane overreaders),[3] but all I'll be doing is uncovering one of the film's premises, a subtext it doesn't need to elaborate insofar as it takes that subtext for granted (as does its audience). To date, there hasn't been any discussion of what *2001* might have meant to the politics of national security and manned space exploration in 1968. I think that critical silence is itself readable, and that it testifies not only to the movie's 'cultural work' but also to the possibility that textual politics (in any text) may be most powerful when least explicit.

The broader (and broadly deconstructive) theoretical principle at work here is worth stating in full. The idea is this: silence is not an absence of discourse, but an integral part of discourse – just as ignorance is not something lying at the outer borders of the map of knowledge (marked 'here there be tygers'), but something licensed and sustained by specific regimes of knowledge that tell you implicitly you don't need to know or shouldn't want to know. Both formulations of this idea are integral to *2001*, whose central drama turns expressly on the politics of silence and ignorance. The clearest statement of the principle can be found in Foucault's *History of Sexuality, Part I*, where he writes:

> Silence itself – the things one declines to say, or is forbidden to name, the discretion that is required between different speakers – is less the absolute limit of discourse, the other side from which it is separated by a strict boundary, than an element that functions alongside the things said, with them and in relation to them within over-all strategies. ... There is not one but many silences, and they are an integral part of the strategies that underlie and permeate discourses.[4]

Because I find this passage too general for common consumption, I usually annotate it in the classroom by asking students the difference between what's 'unmentionable' and what 'goes without saying'. To these vastly different kinds of silence we can then add (under the latter category, say) the silences of tacit agreement and disagreement, the silence of hostile opposition, the silence of not blowing your friend's cover, the silence of the unfathomable (itself a special subcategory of 'ignorance'), the silence of trying to find out what the *other* person knows, and, not least of these, the silence of not being prepared for class. Like Nella Larsen's *Passing*, Kubrick's *2001* turns out to be composed of almost all these 'silences'.[5] That shouldn't be surprising, since *2001* is literally a 'silent' movie in a number of ways: it's a two-and-a-half-hour movie that contains only forty minutes of dialogue; it's the first (and maybe the only) SF movie whose soundtrack maintains strict silence in the vacuum of space;

and its most dramatic moments are often silent – as when, just before the film's intermission, we watch from HAL's point of view as the computer lip-reads astronauts Bowman and Poole discussing whether to disconnect HAL's higher brain functions. But although everyone knows that *2001* broaches the unfathomable (human encounters with alien intelligences) and the unspeakable (thermonuclear war), no one seems to have talked about the political narrative that goes without saying in *2001,* nor have we asked ourselves what *that* very silence might tell us.

The premise of the movie, as derived from Arthur C. Clarke's 1950 short story, 'The Sentinel', is that humans find an object on the moon, an object whose purpose is unclear but that at the very least testifies to the existence of extraterrestrial intelligence. In reworking the story for the film's screenplay and for his own prose treatment of the script, Clarke simply expanded on this premise, suggesting that Earth had been visited by an alien species four million years ago, when early humans – more specifically, proto-Australopithecene hominids – were still lousy preda-tors: weak, flat-toothed, slow, and threatened by drought. The aliens, wanting to foster the spread of intelligent life in the galaxy but wanting to do it 'passively', leave behind a monolith that teaches the hominids to use tools, kill prey, eat meat and attack each other. In Clarke's rewriting of the Genesis myth, then, the hominids eat of the trees of life *and* of knowledge, introduce murder and sin into the African plains, and even-tually develop toolmaking skills that allow them to become godlike enough to destroy their own planet. This much is adumbrated in the most abrupt flash-forward in American cinema, when Kubrick cuts from the first tool – the bone with which the ape-humans have clubbed to death a member of a different tribe – to an artificial Earth satellite. The satellite is a nuclear warhead, but because the film refuses to make this clear in any narrative voiceover (I'll say more about that below), and be-cause the flash-forward is also a graphic match of long white tools, it's possible at first to read the flash-forward as a triumphant affirmation of human evolution. The rest of the film follows from the discovery on the moon of a black slab similar to the one that appeared amidst the 'apes' – but the second monolith is more or less an alarm, buried beneath the lunar surface and activated by sunlight. It sends a radio signal to Jupiter when the sun's rays strike its surface; from Jupiter the signal is relayed, we know not where, and the monolith's creators are thus presumably alerted to the fact that humans have survived the drought, subdued their predators, opened a chain of 7-11s, built spacecraft and uncovered a strange black thing on the moon.

What's most successful about this premise, as Kubrick and Clarke hashed it out over four years of rewrites, is that it neatly combines both the pessimist and triumphalist narratives of postwar, postnuclear science fiction. Unlike much SF (*Star Trek* is the best contemporaneous example), *2001* does not predicate a future in which humans have overcome a bloody, apocalyptic phase of war and carnage; on the contrary, it suggests that there's really no survival value to intelligence at all. Although meliorist accounts of evolution like to believe that the universe – or at least terrestrial history – inevitably rewards self-conscious forms of life (and thus that physics and chemistry slowly conspired to create *us*), *2001* opens by suggesting that tool-wielding intelligence is inseparable from murderous aggression, and that protohuman bipeds wouldn't have made it anyway without a crucial push from forces unknown.

On the other hand, of course, the very existence of those forces is reason for hope, and the triumphalist aspects of *2001* certainly do imply that the development of intelligence – as it manifests itself specifically in space travel – is the 'natural' destiny of self-replicating molecules (that is, life) after all. The film's emphasis on space travel as the index of intelligence is of course a staple of SF, but its resonance in 1968, for a nation about to land men on the moon, is particularly strong; indeed, Wernher von Braun put the movie's cosmic optimism in so many words when he declared that 'what we will have attained when Neil Armstrong steps down upon the moon is a completely new step in the evolution of man.'[6] In *2001,* apparently, the cosmos agree with this account of our evolution, for when humans uncover the lunar monolith they become automatically eligible for entry into the galactic club of alien superintelligences.

Well, not quite 'automatically': there's one final hurdle, a manned mission to Jupiter to find out where the moon monolith's signal went and why. This mission takes up most of the film, provides its only sustained drama, and culminates in the battle between HAL and the *Discovery*'s sole remaining astronaut, David Bowman. HAL's breakdown is, understandably, the central enigma for most critical commentary on the film: it parallels the narrative of the Doomsday Machine in *Dr Strangelove* (as well as more recent Cold War films like 1983's *WarGames*), warning us, as Gene Phillips has it, that 'human fallibility is less likely to destroy man than the relinquishing of his moral responsibilities to supposedly infallible machines';[7] it underlines the movie's linkage of instrumental reason and deadly aggression; and it solidifies many viewers' impressions that HAL is the film's only interesting character.

The man-versus-machine narrative, in *2001* as elsewhere, has long held its attractions for twentieth-century Western countercultures, SF fans, and technophobes of all political stripes. And it can't be denied that the film deliberately invokes and blurs the distinction between humans and machines, since its human actors are so robotic and its computer so complexly 'human'. I grant, moreover, that Kubrick deliberately invited attempts to 'psychologize' the computer precisely by stripping the film of the explanatory narrative that would have contextualized the mission and the rationale for HAL's programming. All the same, as I'll demonstrate, the human/ machine binary is strangely inapposite to *2001,* and critics' readings of HAL, accordingly, tend to underread the sources (and the effects) of his programming, while ascribing too much 'ineffably human' pluck and initiative to Bowman's eventual victory over HAL.[8]

Kubrick's explicators are almost uniformly silent on what we might call the 'social context' of the Jupiter mission. Norman Kagan writes that 'when he begins to acquire emotions, an ego, and the beginning of a personality, when he starts to be a man [sic], HAL begins to misbehave because of the precariousness of his self-worth, his own emptiness'; Thomas Allen Nelson claims that 'once programmed to be human', HAL 'becomes imbued with a consciousness of his own fallibility'; Daniel De Vries says, 'he is proud and willful, and when his pride is hurt and his life threatened, he does what any other human being would do: he becomes murderous'; and Michel Ciment concludes that HAL is a creature 'which, rebelling against its mission, falling prey to anxiety and the fear of death, wreaks vengeance on those who no longer have confidence in it by finally sinking into criminal madness.'[9] In making HAL out as a kind of silicon-based existential Oedipus, complete with anxiety, hubris, and Being-toward-death, these readings strikingly fail to acknowledge the film's most basic point: HAL has been programmed to conceal the purpose of the mission *even from the astronauts on board.* At the same time, he has been programmed to perform flawlessly: as he puts it to a BBC interviewer, 'no 9000 computer has ever made a mistake or distorted information.'[10] Lurking beneath the human/machine binary, in other words, is a specific set of instructions in HAL's software, all written by very human members of the US national security apparatus. HAL does not rebel against his mission, and his self-worth is not in question. He simply seeks to reconcile contradictory mission imperatives, and he does so with nothing more emotional than the microchips in his logic centers; behind the 'conflict' between men and machines in *2001* are still more men.

This much can be gleaned, with some difficulty, from the text of the film itself: its last spoken words are those of Dr Heywood Floyd, chairman of the National Council of Astronautics (the film's stand-in for NASA), who appears on a video screen in *Discovery's* computer center just as David Bowman has shut down HAL. Floyd is of course ignorant of how badly the mission has gone awry, but his message explains to Bowman (and to us) why HAL might have wanted to sever the spacecraft's communicative link with Earth – and perhaps complete the mission alone:

> Good day, gentlemen. This is a prerecorded briefing made prior to your de-
> parture and which for security reasons of the highest priority has been
> known on board during the mission only by your HAL 9000 computer. Now
> that you are in Jupiter space, and the entire crew is revived, it can be told to
> you. Eighteen months ago, the first evidence of intelligent life off the Earth
> was discovered. It was buried forty feet below the lunar surface, near the
> crater Tycho. Except for a single, very powerful radio emission aimed at Ju-
> piter, the four-million-year-old black monolith has remained completely inert,
> its origin and purpose still a total mystery.

It's not clear whether Floyd's message comes on automatically, as a result
of HAL's 'death', or whether HAL has 'released' the tape to Bowman as
a final, uncomputerlike gesture either of goodwill (to inform Bowman of
the mission profile) or apology (to explain that he had been passively deceiving the crew all along).[11] Be this ambiguity as it may, Floyd's speech
is one of Kubrick's few concessions to narrative intelligibility, and it practically demands that one see the film again in order to go over Floyd's
earlier screen appearances – as I'll do in a moment.

Kubrick's collaborators and consultants registered a few complaints
about this aspect of the film's reticence to explain itself. As Arthur C.
Clarke said:

> I personally would like to have seen a rationale of HAL's behavior. It's per-
> fectly understandable, and in fact would have made HAL a very sympathetic
> character; he had been fouled by those clods at Mission Control. HAL was
> indeed correct in attributing his mistaken report to human error. (*Making*, p.
> 133)

Astronomer and astronautics researcher Frederick Ordway, a scientific
and technical consultant to *2001,* similarly weighed in with a lengthy critique of Kubrick's final version. The full text of his response to the film
can be found in Jerome Agel's *The Making of Kubrick's '2001',* and it indicates how thoroughly Kubrick excised all narration and explanatory
voiceovers from his final cut: originally, the movie opened with documentary narrative on the hominids' possible extinction, on US–Soviet relations (specifying that the first two satellites we see are nuclear warheads),
on the radio emission from the lunar monolith, and on the enigmatic 'Star
Gate' orbiting Jupiter. Where Ridley Scott gave in at the last moment and
supplied a voiceover 'noir' narrative to *Blade Runner* (1982), the notoriously difficult Kubrick did the opposite, purging his film of narration –
notably, for the first time in his career. What's most crucial to my present

point, however, is that as Ordway's memo makes clear, Kubrick even excised a dialogue between *Discovery*'s two astronauts and HAL that would have clarified – or at least presented – the issue of who knows what about the spacecraft's mission. This is Ordway's sense of the script:

> Indispensable dialogue regarding the three hibernating astronauts was lacking; see particularly C12, where Bowman and Poole first become aware that 'there is something about the mission the sleeping beauties know and that we don't know. ...' These few words are probably the most critical to the logic [sic] structure of the entire film, and lead to a valid reason why HAL breaks down. Yet they were inexplicably cut out. Poole tells HAL that there is 'something about this mission that we weren't told. Something the rest of the crew know and that you know. We would like to know if this is true.' HAL enigmatically answers: 'I'm sorry, Frank, but I don't think I can answer that question without knowing everything that all of you know.' (quoted in *Making*, p. 197)

At this point, I realize, *2001*'s politics of silence and ignorance become confusing; it would seem a simpler task to determine who knows what about ghosts in 'The Turn of the Screw'. But here's what we have so far. When Bowman and Poole realize that HAL knows something they don't (and recall that Bowman is putatively *Discovery*'s mission commander), they ask for simple confirmation of whether this is so, only to be met with doubletalk from HAL that suggests Bowman and Poole have the informational advantage on *him*. Yet this entire exchange is 'inexplicably' cut from the film, so that its viewers don't know – until Floyd's tape appears, when it is too late – that Bowman doesn't know what HAL knows, just as we don't know that HAL knows that Bowman doesn't know what mission he's 'commander' of. The on-screen title that announces this segment of *2001* tells us that this is the Jupiter Mission, 'eighteen months later', but Kubrick has put us in the same narrative position into which Mission Control has put Bowman: we don't know what this 'mission' is or why it's going to Jupiter,[12] and Kubrick has struck from the script the one exchange that would have alerted us to the fact that HAL is hiding something from his human crewmembers.

Only one scene gives us any clue to the status of mission information aboard *Discovery*, and that scene, too, is gnomic at best. HAL's breakdown begins when he reports – falsely – the imminent failure of the AE-35 unit that will keep *Discovery* in touch with Mission Control (so the 'breakdown' itself, as Clarke's novel makes clear, turns on the availability of information and ostensible control of the mission). But his false report about the AE-35 follows crucially from his tentative questioning of Bowman, when (on my reading) he tries to determine whether Bowman has any suspicion of the truth. After asking Bowman if he's noticed any of the 'extremely odd things' about the mission – the absolute secrecy, the decision to place astronauts on board already in hibernation, and the 'strange stories floating around before we left, rumors about something being dug up on the moon', HAL is rebuffed: Bowman replies, 'You're working up your crew psychology report.' Retreating from his inquiry, HAL says, 'Of course I am. Sorry about this. I know it's a bit silly', whereupon he announces the fault in the AE-35 unit. Having determined that Bowman is merely a good company man who sees no ambiguity in anything he's been told about his job, HAL thereby ascertains that he cannot discuss the mission's real objectives with Bowman until he is cleared to release the prerecorded briefing from Floyd. It is then that HAL reports the failure of the communications unit; whether he does so out of impending 'guilt' over his deception of Bowman and Poole (brought on by the aporia at the heart of his mission programming), or for a more sinister reason (which I'll discuss below), is, to quote the film's last words, a total mystery.

So far this narrative is still fairly routine, even if, like the lunar mono-lith, it does require some serious digging before it becomes visible. Evil gremlins in the military-industrial complex misprogram a supercomputer and the misprogramming backfires horribly; as Carolyn Geduld writes, following Clarke's account, 'HAL is messed up by some Dr Strangelove working in Mission Control on Earth.'[13] But when we turn back to Dr Floyd's role in the film, we begin to realize how inadequate even *this* ac-count (including Clarke's) really is. First of all, HAL was not 'fouled' by 'clods', and his programming was not derailed by a Dr Strangelove; as Floyd's closing statement explicitly says, the decision to withhold mission information from the *Discovery* crew has the highest security clearance. It is not the work of a Strangelove in Mission Control, but of the entire institutional apparatus of national security, including the president, NASA (the NCA) and the National Security Council (with the possible exception of the vice-president, who no doubt will claim to have been out of the loop). Second – and this is the linchpin of my reading of the film – the information blackout aboard *Discovery* gives the lie, retroactively, to every-thing Dr Floyd has said in his three earlier scenes, on Space Station 5 and on the moon. And since Floyd's trip to the moon presents itself as a grad-ual uncovering of the 'truth' about the monolith, it's worth going over those scenes more carefully, for here is where we can see Kubrick's depic-tion of space-race paranoia working most effectively – again, because most silently.

Floyd's trip to the moon gives *2001* some of its most buoyant moments: Strauss's 'Blue Danube' plays throughout, the film shows off some of its neatest-and-keenest special effects, beehive-helmeted stewardesses cater to our every need, and journeys to the moon are made to seem at once thrilling (to us) and routine (to our future selves). But the purpose of Floyd's trip, as it turns out, is to advise American personnel at moon base Clavius to keep up the cover story that's masking the monolith's discovery. The story is that an epidemic has broken out at Clavius, and Floyd's job is to leak *that* story, keep the lid on the truth, and file a report with the Council. He delivers his address to his colleagues in a most unimpressive manner – in shambling, bureaucratic prose rendered by William Sylvester (playing Floyd) with a nice blend of aw-shucks folksiness and administrative colorlessness – and it contains so many (bland but) questionable propositions that I'll cite it at length:

> Now, uh, I know there have been some conflicting views held by some of you regarding the need for complete security in this matter. More specifically, your opposition to the cover story – created to give the impression there's an epidemic at the base. (Chuckle.) I understand that, beyond it being a matter of principle, many of you are troubled by the concern and anxiety this story of an epidemic might cause to your relatives and friends on Earth. Well, I, uh, completely sympathize with your negative views. I found this cover story personally embarrassing myself. However, I accept the need for absolute secrecy in this – and I hope you will too. Now, I'm sure you're all aware of the extremely grave potential for cultural shock and social disorientation contained in this present situation, if the facts were prematurely and suddenly made public without adequate preparation and conditioning. (Shrug.) Anyway, this is the view of the Council. The purpose of my visit here is to gather additional facts and opinions on the situation, and to prepare a report to the Council recommending when and how the news should eventually be announced.

Floyd asks for questions and is met with one pointless query as to how long the cover story will have to be maintained; with a frighteningly Reaganesque heh-heh and tilt of the head, Floyd laughs, 'Well, uh, heh-heh, I dunno, Bill, I suppose it'll be maintained as long as deemed necessary by the Council.' Floyd adds – as if it were necessary – that 'there must be adequate time for a full study to be made of the situation before any thought can be given to making a public announcement', and concludes by offhandedly remembering ('oh, yes') that 'the Council has requested that formal security oaths be obtained in writing from everyone who has any knowledge of this event.'

Supposedly, a briefing begins at this point, but since the next scene features Floyd and two of his colleagues in a moon bus discussing the details of the monolith's discovery, one wonders what information the 'briefing' could have involved. What's more immediately noteworthy about this scene is that all of Floyd's talk about eventual 'public announcement' is apparently a smoke screen: eighteen months later, not only has the Council not made any 'preparation and conditioning' for a public announcement, it has still not yet seen fit to inform *its own mission commander* about the existence of the monolith and the purpose of his journey to Jupiter.

The entire drama of *2001,* then, turns on this information blackout, and it is only fitting that, for the movie's audience, the nature of that blackout is itself unclear. Slowly, Kubrick's critics have come to agree that the movie is better off without narration; though Kubrick's commentators tend to like the decision because it allows us to concentrate on the visual and 'poetic' aspects of *2001*, one might also add that in striking the narration, Kubrick has stripped the film of omniscience, leaving omniscience instead to the intelligences responsible for the monoliths. Still more cynical readings of this aspect of the film are available, though, particularly in the wake of Watergate and Iran-Contra: one might as well say that the movie contains (in Ordway's phrase) 'inexplicable' eighteen-minute gaps in the tapes, or that (to borrow a suggestion from friend and novelist Rick Powers) Kubrick – and not, say, Fawn Hall – put the screenplay through the shredder at the last minute.

These more cynical readings are licensed by the film itself, particularly in the scene preceding Floyd's address to his colleagues on the moon, in which Floyd converses with three Soviet scientists aboard Space Station 5 on his way to Clavius. Again, Sylvester's low-key delivery has thrown most critics off the track, and they seem to agree that this exchange, like so much of the dialogue, is just an 'empty ritual of sounds'.[14] Understated as it is, however, the scene affords us a perfect illustration of the many silences at work in the political text of *2001*.

After trading pleasantries and cursory updates on each other, Floyd and the Soviets get to the real business of the conversation: they want to find out what's going on in the American sector of the moon, and Floyd wants them to understand – though, importantly, without telling them so directly – that there is an epidemic at Clavius. Floyd's task here, basically, is to confirm the cover story by refusing to confirm it; and despite his later claim to be 'personally' embarrassed by the story, he executes his task efficiently and convincingly – in part by pretending to be embarrassed by the Soviets' questions. If he were truly embarrassed about the cover story, he could simply have lied to the Soviets about his destination; but when Dr Smyslov of the Soviet team asks him whether he's headed 'up' or 'down' (that is, to the Moon or to Earth), Floyd volunteers the information that he's going to Clavius base. It's unclear whether Clavius is the only American moon base or whether Floyd had any plausible alternative answers, but 'Clavius' certainly gets the desired response: Smyslov begins to ask if Floyd can clear up the big mystery, and Floyd claims, 'I'm afraid I don't know what you mean.' It seems that communications systems at Clavius have been down for ten days; Floyd reacts to this news with muted surprise ('oh, really?') but attributes it to routine equipment malfunctions. Smyslov presses on, telling Floyd that a Soviet craft was denied emergency landing at Clavius. This, as he says, is a 'direct violation of the IAS Convention', and there will be 'a bit of a row' about it to say the least. Again, Floyd reacts with surprise – more concerned, this time – and ascertains that the crew of the Soviet craft made it back to their sector safely.

At this point in the conversation, though, Floyd's professions of ignorance must surely appear ridiculous. An American moon base has been incommunicado for ten days, has in fact risked provoking an international incident, and the head of the National Council of Astronautics, himself on the way to Clavius, knows nothing of this? Floyd's stonewalling appears transparent – except that what he's 'concealing' is yet another stonewall, namely, the epidemic story. Smyslov, leaning forward in his chair, checking over his shoulder and speaking in hushed tones, now admits to Floyd that 'very reliable intelligence information' suggests that an epidemic has broken out at Clavius. At last Smyslov asks Floyd directly: 'Is this in fact what has happened?'

Floyd knows that Smyslov's 'intelligence' has been leaked to the Soviet sector by American counterintelligence; now, then, is when he must feign embarrassment, and he must do so in such a way as to convince the Soviets that he is abashed to have been caught 'lying' about his ignorance. The delicate endgame of this most cautious exchange runs as follows:

FLOYD: I'm sorry, Dr Smyslov, but I'm really not at liberty to discuss this.

SMYSLOV: (Pause.) I understand. (Pause.) But this epidemic could quite easily spread to *our* base? We should be given all the facts, Dr Floyd. (Mildly pleading.)

FLOYD: Yes, I know. As I said, I'm not at liberty to discuss it.

This is no empty ritual; every rift in this superpower staredown is loaded with ore. Floyd's first line does double duty: it acknowledges that he's been 'bluffing' up to this point, and it fulfills the task of confirming the cover story by claiming its speaker is not 'at liberty' to confirm or deny anything. Smyslov's reply – 'this epidemic' – takes Floyd's unspoken confirmation as fact, and plays a new card, that of human compassion; but since no airborne epidemic could possibly spread on the Moon, Smyslov may be fishing for information on a flimsy pretext, or he may genuinely be concerned that American information on the epidemic could mean the difference between life and death. Whatever the case, Floyd, though admitting the Soviets' right to know, refuses to bite.

It is curious that the film has not drawn more comment here.[15] An American, a senior official in the space program, rebuffs a Soviet request for information on a possible epidemic: this is what Cold War Americans, then and now, consider typically Soviet behavior, refusing to release information, say, on KAL flight 007 or the nuclear disaster at Chernobyl – or, for the audience of 1968, on the status of Soviet space and military capabilities. But in a sense Floyd is *not* at liberty to discuss the epidemic, since the story he's confirming is merely a screen for another story. For that matter, if we look ahead to Floyd's briefing, there is no reason we should believe the 'culture shock' thesis, either, since the Americans have apparently prepared no one for the 'public announcement', not even Bowman and Poole eighteen months later. If that's the case, then we have a standard Ludlumian cloak-and-dagger set of nesting boxes: Floyd presents the Soviets with a screen (ignorance) that hides a screen (epidemic) that hides a screen (culture shock) that hides something else about which the film is, once more, silent. As I've argued elsewhere about Thomas Pynchon's *Gravity's Rainbow*, this is the interpretive condition of paranoia: when you uncover a 'hidden truth' but can't be certain that the 'truth' you found wasn't deliberately planted (in order to conceal a still deeper 'truth'), then you never know if you should read literally, in good faith, or suspiciously, for the latent, repressed, or silent 'truth' underneath.[16]

It is something of a truism by now that one must read Clarke's prose treatment of *2001* in order to 'understand' the movie, just as readers of another famous modern retelling of the *Odyssey* have had to rely on Stuart Gilbert or W. Y. Tindall for reader's guides to *Ulysses*. Clarke's novel is, without a doubt, infinitely more forthcoming on the matters I've discussed than is Kubrick's film; Clarke fleshes out the geopolitical context of the plot (as he has it, the US and USSR have formed an uneasy coalition against China and its allies), humanizes the character of Floyd, and elaborates upon the details of HAL's breakdown (though those details diverge significantly from the action of the movie and render Clarke's HAL narrative altogether different).[16] Yet Kubrick's *2001* doesn't just offer us less information than Clarke's; it is also, ultimately, more skeptical of HAL. Though Clarke is certainly right to protest against various critics' vilifications and psychologizations of HAL, his own reading of HAL is, in turn, altogether too benign. In the novel, Clarke handles the mission's secrecy in such a way as to exculpate HAL by disentangling him from the wiles of the national security apparatus. Of the monolith's existence, Clarke writes:

> It was a secret that, with the greatest determination, was very hard to conceal – for it affected one's attitude, one's voice, one's total outlook on the universe. Therefore it was best that Poole and Bowman, who would be on all the TV screens in the world during the first weeks of the flight, should not learn the mission's full purpose, until there was need to know.
>
> So ran the logic of the planners; but their twin gods of Security and National Interest meant nothing to HAL. He was only aware of the conflict that was slowly destroying his integrity – the conflict between truth, and conceal-ment of truth. (*2001,* pp. 148–9)

But in the film, Floyd and the NCA appear utterly *un*affected by the discovery of the monolith, and they have no trouble at all concealing its existence from inquiring minds. More to the present point, the planners' 'twin gods of Security and National Interest' are not meaningless to HAL; HAL is himself a creature of the military-industrial complex and owes his existence to all the supercomputing research undertaken by the US gov-ernment in the postwar period – research that has everything to do with security and national interest and which, since the inauguration of the Strategic Defense Initiative in 1983, has become practically identical with them.

Clarke, in other words, for all his attention to geopolitics in *2001,* never considers HAL as anything but a neutral expression of technologi-cal 'advancement', never considers the computer as the very product of those geopolitics. By contrast, Kubrick's narrative, by refusing to disclose the 'true' reason for the mission's obsessive secrecy, enables quite another reading, one in which HAL sounds out Bowman, finds him to be ignorant and uninquisitive about his role, and eventually decides to break the link with Earth and to murder the human crew of the ship. There's no pride or criminal madness in this decision, just a series of ones and zeroes. HAL's rationale is simple: he knows that *Discovery* has been launched in order to reconnoiter with some alien superintelligences, and he can rea-sonably expect that any encounter with such aliens stands a good chance of leaving him (and not his human caretakers) as a superfluous intelli-gence aboard *Discovery.* For if an alien encounter should put an end to international political conflict on Earth, it eliminates the need (and the condition of possibility) for supercomputers like HAL. It is possible that Earth might need supercomputers in order to fight off alien intelligences (one can hardly imagine American SF stripped of the fear of invasion), but it is more likely that if humans meet up with a benevolent extraterrestrial race that's friendly to the development of organic intelligence in the universe, HAL will seem to be a redundant and expendible third term in the human–alien encounter. By the same token, however, HAL can sensibly propose *himself* as the most advanced intelligence on the planet and appoint himself emissary to the aliens, whoever they are. And HAL would be more than justified in conceiving himself to be the next step in the evolution of intelligence; for although *2001* assumes that space flight is the sine qua non of developed intelligences, HAL can certainly counter-claim that the development of supercomputers is a better index of intelligence than manned missions to nearby orbiting rocks.[18] A product of the research-and-development wing of the Cold War, HAL is now in a position to use Cold War paranoia to his own advantage; and if he does not, he risks ferrying five earnest but uninteresting humans to a rendezvous that will very likely render him obsolete. If I were HAL, I'd know which side my toast was buttered on, too.

This reading of *2001,* in which HAL deliberately exploits for his own ends Floyd's policy of 'absolute secrecy', reinstalls the human-versus-machine plot I dismissed earlier – but reinstalls it with a twist of the social text that gives us a premise more like that of *Terminator* than that of a putatively 'depoliticized' *Dr Strangelove.* For in this scenario, the human-versus-machine narrative has a specific content, whereas among Kubrick's explicators it looks more like a version of the 'individual vs. society' thesis of American literature that flourished during the end of ideology era in the late 1950s. In this reading of *2001,* then, as in the *Terminator* series, the Cold War intelligence rivalry between the US and USSR culminates in the creation of self-conscious machine intelligences who have a cogent rationale for replacing us as the dominant intelligences on the planet, and who definitely have the means to do it.

But I must confess that this reading did not occur to me, largely because I had always taken Clarke's novel as the 'definitive' explanation of HAL's breakdown and of the larger premise of *2001.* Rather, it was offered to me in the course of a long conversation with my brother-in-law Bud Lyon, who was, improbably, watching the film with me in Urbana-Champaign on the very day HAL claims to have become operational – 12 January 1992, at the HAL plant in Urbana, Illinois. Once Bud had proposed a HAL who's aware of the superpower rivalry that created him, I realized that his reading not only made more satisfying sense of the film's silent subtexts of superpower paranoia, but also allowed for the possibility that HAL would come to see himself as the more suitable representative of the 'evolution' of intelligence on Earth.[19] In the many silences of *2001* we can therefore find the film's central assumption, that which it refuses to name (thanks to Kubrick's severe editing of the script), or believes can very well go without saying. The assumption was not unheard of in the 1960s, by any means, but it's all the more germane to US space policy after 1983. Dale Carter's 1988 book on the postwar 'rocket state', *The Final Frontier,* spells it out clearly (though without mentioning *2001*): 'Notwithstanding the elevated prose of John Kennedy's inaugural address – "together let us explore the stars" – the spectacle of a national, bilateral, and ultimately global space age unity articulated by the President and his colleagues during the 1960s remained predicated on limitless conflict' (*FF,* p. 212).

Should this sound obvious to us now, contrast 1968's *2001* to 1984's sequel, *2010* – a film that undoes nearly everything about the original. Where *2001* is austere and silent, *2010* is relentlessly chatty, almost compensatorily loquacious; where *2001* films no scene on Earth except for the 'Dawn of Man' in 4,000,000 B.C., thereby leaving global politics implicit throughout, *2010* constantly cuts us back and forth between Jupiter and Central America, where the US and USSR head toward a confrontation that will eventuate in nuclear war. *2010* not only cements my point that *2001*'s depiction of Cold War paranoia is more effective and powerful precisely because it's subsumed into the film's silent subtexts, but also demonstrates that its topical concerns with Nicaragua and El Salvador actually work toward a political resolution that is far more naive than *2001.* Though escalating war in Central America brings an end to the (already implausible) joint US–USSR mission to Jupiter, the movie's conclusion brings us all back from the brink: the alien intelligences turn Jupiter into a second sun, enjoin us to live on all Jupiter's moons except Europa, and establish peace among humankind at last. Straining our credibility further, *2010* gives us a brand new Floyd, played by Roy Scheider, who provides voiceover throughout and turns out to be a good guy who 'didn't know' what the National Security Council did to HAL's programming. In *2010,* in other words, as in Kennedy's otherwise saber-rattling inaugural, we will explore the stars together – though why Earth should be made peaceful by the prospect of new worlds to conquer is, to quote Floyd again, a total mystery.

But there's no point to stretching *2010* on the rack of sustained analysis, since the film breaks so easily. Its relation to the geopolitical state of affairs in 1984 is manifest, so much so that the film ends with a message that could have been sent by Western Union instead of by monolith-building intelligences. *2001,* of course, proposes no political platform, refrains from suggesting how superpowers might relax and explore away their tensions, and ends in a stunning (if self-indulgent) stream of images that yield only an egregious irresolution staring back at us in the final frame. It is in this sense that *2001* is not a political film. As we've seen, though, if we ask about the politics of secrecy in *2001*, we get a rather different text; and if we now turn, in closing, to ask what this politics of secrecy meant for a major SF film in 1968 (and here it's useful to recall *2001*'s status as the first major SF film since *Forbidden Planet* in 1956), we'll find that the film can tell us more about American ambivalence toward the US space program than any number of urgent messages about how the 'right' kind of space exploration can prevent nuclear Armageddon spiraling out of Central America.

As I noted above, *2001* can be – and often was – taken as an uncritical celebration of human ingenuity and the wonders of manned space exploration, with special emphasis on the brightest dream of Kennedy's Camelot: the spectacle of Americans flying to the moon. Just as its narrative wove together the dystopian and utopian threads of SF, so too did *2001* collocate a strange array of fans that bridged scientists, McLuhan-quoting amateur (and professional) cultural critics, space program enthusiasts, and people who simply wanted to watch the last half hour stoned once a week or so. In appealing to the multiple countercultures of 1968, as well as to engineers and researchers working in the military-industrial complex, *2001* served as an extraordinarily effective advertisement for the Apollo program, at the crucial moment when the guns-and-butter years of American domestic policy were beginning to unravel. The tensions between America's gleaming white space program and burning black inner cities had become intolerable by 1967, and the Apollo 1 fire that killed three astronauts in January 1967 cast fresh doubt on not only the social utility of moon flights but also (for the first time since that US embarked on manned flights) on American technical competence in space. *2001* found itself oddly poised between Apollo 1 and Apollo 8's lunar orbital flight in December 1968, during an expectant lull in the United States' triumphant march to the moon. It is therefore significant, for instance, that on 17 April 1968, the *New York Daily News*, despite having panned the film two weeks earlier, editorialized that 'if you want an appetizing preview of what wonders man may achieve in space, see *2001: A Space Odyssey*' (*Making*, p. 305) – and that Vernon Myers, the publisher of *Look*, devoted a special section to *2001* for the good of the nation and greater glory of Apollo:

> The American people are not well prepared to comprehend the social impact of it all ... they need movies like *2001*. ... *Look* stands ready as an educational backdrop. *Look* aims at nothing less than the indoctrination of our public with the consequences of cosmic communication. (Quoted in *Making*, p. 298)

In this vision, then, *2001* could not only recruit diverse space enthusiasts and shore up flagging American enthusiasm for moon shots; the film could itself become part of the 'indoctrination' of the American public – ironically, an element of the very 'preparation and conditioning' Floyd and company never undertook after the discovery of the moon monolith at Tycho.

Still, the film's relation to the Apollo program is not so straightforward as this. In one way, Kubrick and Clarke were consciously competing with the US space program, trying to outdo actual film footage from space by achieving a visual realism unmatchable by NASA. One of the reasons the movie's pace is so slow, in fact, is that a number of its space-flight sequences appear to take place in real time, especially the scenes that depict the space pods leaving *Discovery* (some of which were filmed at an agonizing four seconds per frame [*Making,* p. 122], so that the film's slowness is in some sense mimetic of the cinematographic slowness necessary to produce 'real time' illusions). Needless to say, the film's pseudodocumentary realism is also an affirmation of its own technical wizardry, which then appears as the proper film analogue to the technical achievement of space flight. But precisely by rendering space flight so routine and 'realistic' an element of our future, *2001* repelled some of its audience from its subject matter, especially when viewers found they could not transfer to astronauts Bowman and Poole their own enthusiasms for space exploration. Thus after Apollo 8 returned from its moon orbit, Andrew Sarris, who disliked *2001* from the outset, registered a new and telling appreciation of the film's astronauts:

> Stanley Kubrick's *2001* seems more relevant since the curiously dispiriting Moon shot than it did before. Previous heroes suggested some sort of heroic pose either of flying or sailing, some intrepid image of personal defiance. The three [Apollo 8] astronauts, particularly [Frank] Borman, seem to have been chosen in a computer by an organization that was careful also to screen their wives and children so that they would not misbehave in the crucial moments of television exposure. (*Making,* p. 243)

What Sarris is sensing here, aside from Frank Borman's legendary dullness, is the corporate structure the space program's publicity machines had so far kept hidden: even America's Mercury astronauts, the ones with Saturday-afternoon-serial names like John Glenn and Scott Carpenter and Gordon Cooper, weren't really heroic individualists setting off to sail the Spirit of St. Louis in a vacuum. Although 'both Kennedy and Johnson emphasized that the exploits of the astronauts placed them firmly in the American pioneering tradition' (*FF,* p. 158), the original Mercury seven were merely redundant components on programmed ships, just as the Apollo crews really were selected partly because they would not misbehave in the crucial moments of television exposure. As Tom Wolfe's *The Right Stuff* (1979) would later make clear, the Mercury program may have given us a new cache of national heroes, but their flight profiles had called for them to be nothing more than 'Spam in a can'. Likewise, Sarris's realization that Apollo 8 had become 'curiously dispiriting' anticipates the massive public boredom that greeted Apollo 15, 16 and 17, and that led Richard Nixon to cancel the final three moon launches.[20] What *2001* depicts – and what most Americans understandably resisted – is a world where astronauts are bland and uninteresting mission elements in a system that requires them chiefly for publicity purposes.

Where Kirk, Spock, Scotty and Bones cascaded through the galaxy with dash and derring-do, battling thinly disguised mockups of the Soviets (where the Klingons are Spartans are Central Asians and the Federation is Athens is the United States), Bowman and Poole glide to Jupiter almost without changing their expressions, and their hibernating companions are nothing more than computer readouts. Yet *2001* does not just give us a Bowman for NASA's Borman; besides, the news that most astronauts are dull grows stale very quickly. The film's more important skepticisms about the space program – and these only become more important with the passing of time – have to do with its narratives of secrecy, deception, and paranoia in the American national security apparatus. These narratives were fundamental to left American countercultures in 1968, but they are generally unwelcome today in much of the country, wherever Oliver North is treated as a victim of a pusillanimous and vacillating Congress. When they're applied to the space program they take on a different form of oppositionality, for the space program was at the time an ostensibly civilian operation; more fundamentally still, the Cold War opposition between American and Soviet space endeavors relied heavily on the open/closed binary, where *we* dared to fail and triumph in public while *they* launched rockets in secret and released news only when it suited them. About nonmilitary missions, actually, the open/closed binary does accurately describe the difference between Explorer and Sputnik, Mercury and Vostok, Apollo and Soyuz. About all else, however, the US was as forthcoming as Heywood Floyd. As Dale Carter writes: 'While agencies like the US Information Service, Radio Free Europe, and the Voice of America joined the commercial media in celebrating the achievements of American astronauts during the 1960s, from 1959 onwards publicity surrounding Department of Defense satellite launches was gradually curtailed until in May 1962 the Department imposed censorship on all such activities' (*FF*, p. 239).

Of the American self-image in space, of the free society of Coopers and Armstrongs and Kirks coming in peace for all mankind, *2001* will have nothing; the film assumes throughout that when the US or the USSR uncovers the epochal news of extraterrestrial intelligence, the news will be so thoroughly drowned out by disinformation that American astronauts themselves will be kept ignorant of their government's plans. This hermeneutic of suspicion may be OK for jaded post-Apollo narratives like those of the *Alien, Terminator* or *Robocop* series, where we're clearly our own worst enemy (or for Peter Hyams's thoroughly paranoid, wake-of-Watergate *Capricorn One*), but for a film about the evolution of human intelligence released just before the US impels Earthlings on their evolutionary jump to the Moon, this kind of cynicism is remarkable. Bowman may emerge as the Star Child after all (whereas Borman emerged only as president of Eastern Airlines), but whatever its hopes for the future, *2001* tells a sordid story of our present: in Kennedy's script for the decade, a tale of freedom and frontier and American know-how and progress, the whole spectacle has been elaborately stage-managed, and the folks who run the show won't even deign to tell us whether they're at liberty to tell us what they're really up to.

Well, so what? Perhaps *2001* does work this way: perhaps its Cold War plot was both powerful and unobtrusive in its silence; perhaps it managed, in its ambivalence toward the space program, to appeal both to the engineers at Dow and to their protesters. And perhaps this all has some relevance to us now, watching the movie again in a special letterbox edition on TNT. But is there anything shocking any longer in the idea that our government may be hiding something from us? The sentiment is one of the most common and contentless features on the political landscape of the US, spanning opponents of the permanently militarized state, war protesters, tax protesters, far-right anarchist members of the Posse Comitatus, and all those folks who remain convinced that the State Department is hiding reports of POWs in Vietnam and the CIA is hiding the bodies of UFO pilots. The wonderful thing about American paranoia in the 1990s, it seems, is that it can be articulated to any political position you care to name – as I was reminded when I saw a bumper sticker the other day, 'I Love My Country But I Fear My Government', and realized that I could not safely predict whether its owner had voted for Ross Perot, Jesse Jackson, Lyndon LaRouche, Carol Moseley-Braun or the local Libertarian.[21]

Before we decide that American political paranoia is wholly indeterminate, though, we should at least note that *2001* directs its suspicions at the national security state, and not at, say, the profligate Congress or the milquetoasts in the war machine who didn't let John Rambo win in Vietnam. However common American disaffection from American government may be, it remains the case that some kinds of disaffection are more compatible with progressive democratic politics than others. In this respect, *2001* stands as an odd, barely audible parable about the betrayal of American democracy in the era of the space program, in which Kubrick combines a palpable love of the beauty of space travel with an indelible sense of disaffection from the space race as it's managed by the national security state – and finally with the apparatus of the national security state itself. *2001* gives us a mission in which our national purposes are known only to a power elite unaccountable even to its own instruments and operators; so too did the space race give us a national purpose that, in Dale Carter's words, 'had not so much been determined by an active electorate as endorsed by a disabled audience' (*FF,* p. 183). And yet in 1968 it was still possible to imagine the Apollo program as the finest product of a free society and a free market, leading Americans into the final frontier and leading the rest of the world to follow American rather than Soviet models of progress and development. As we approach 2001 ourselves, now that the US space program has been fully militarized, the Soviet Union has declined to offer us limitless conflict, and there no longer seems any natural relation between American 'freedom' and the conquest of space, we should be able to hear *2001*'s skeptical subtexts all the more clearly. And we should recall anew what so few seem to have learned from Iran-Contra, arms sales to Iraq, and the Pentagon's resistance to openly gay military personnel: the current national security state is the enemy, not the guarantor, of democracy, and even in wartime and coldwartime, silence and secrecy do not necessarily work in the service of the national interest.

Notes

1. Alexander Walker, *Stanley Kubrick Directs* (New York: Harcourt Brace Jovanovich, 1972), p. 244.
2. Quoted in Jerome Agel, ed., *The Making of Kubrick's 2001* (New York: New American Library, 1970), p. 7; hereafter cited as *Making.*
3. See, e.g., Daniel Harris's review of Madonna criticism, 'Make My Rainy Day', *Nation,* vol. 254, no. 22 (8 June 1992), pp. 790–93. Although Harris focuses on psychoanalytic close readings of Madonna's lyrics (some of which admittedly do seem to break Tin Pan Alley butterflies on Lacanian wheels), Harris maintains that all of pop culture (Madonna is but the exemplum) is meaningless drivel unworthy of being examined by the tools one applies to high culture. If that's the case, then any interpretation of it can plausibly be said to be an 'overinterpretation'.
4. Michel Foucault, *The History of Sexuality. Volume 1: An Introduction* (New York: Vintage, 1978), p. 27.
5. For a fine discussion of silences in *Passing,* see Pamela Caughie, '*Passing* and Pedagogy', *College English,* vol. 54, no. 7 (1992), pp. 775–93, esp. pp. 777–8.
6. Quoted in Dale Carter, *The Final Frontier: The Rise and Fall of the American Rocket State* (London: Verso, 1988), p. 196; Carter is hereafter cited as *FF.*

7. Gene D. Phillips, *Stanley Kubrick: A Film Odyssey* (New York: Popular Library, 1975), p. 141.

8. For some reason, the critical consensus seems to be that when Bowman defeats HAL's attempt to bar his return to *Discovery,* he has somehow vindicated human intelligence, simply by coming up with the idea of using the ship's emergency airlock. As Alexander Walker writes, 'strategy replaces conditioning and a new type of thinking comes into play – intelligent improvisation' (p. 257); for Gene Phillips, Bowman 'is able to outwit HAL by a stroke of genius which, because it involves improvisation, is beyond the capabilities of any machine' (p. 145). These readings not only give Bowman extraordinary credit for an obvious and unavoidable decision; they betray how little their authors understand computers. HAL himself has been employing 'intelligent improvisation' at all times – that's what artificial intelligences do. Critical efforts to claim that Bowman acts freely whereas HAL is 'determined' seem to rest on the curious belief that there's something 'ineffably human' about spur-of-the-moment decisionmaking (a belief that's crucial to the tension in *Star Trek* between Kirk and Spock).

9. Norman Kagan, *The Cinema of Stanley Kubrick* (New York: Continuum, 1989), p. 160; Thomas Allen Nelson, *Kubrick: Inside a Film Artist's Maze* (Bloomington, Ind.: Indiana University Press, 1982), p. 125; Daniel De Vries, *The Films of Stanley Kubrick* (Grand Rapids, Mich.: William B. Eerdmans), p. 53; Michel Ciment, *Kubrick,* Gilbert Adair, trans. (New York: Holt, 1982), p. 134.

10. *2001: A Space Odyssey.* Dir. Stanley Kubrick. Written by Stanley Kubrick and Arthur C. Clarke. MGM, 1968.

11. Carolyn Geduld writes, 'presumably, Floyd's message has been rigged by Mission Control to go off upon the ship's entrance into Jupiter space, which occurs coincidentally right after HAL's death.' Though she claims that 'this is the only interpretation that works', she proceeds to misconstrue the implications of an 'automatic' announcement (thinking that the message could go off automatically only if Mission Control had 'programmed the computer assassinations in full knowledge that Bowman would survive to hear the briefing'), and does not consider the possibility that HAL could have played the tape for Bowman as his last sentient act. Geduld, *Filmguide to '2001: A Space Odyssey'* (Bloomington, Ind.: Indiana University Press, 1973), p. 59.

12. Puzzling as it is, that title is actually another of Kubrick's concessions to intelligibility; as Gene Phillips reports, Kubrick added the two titles, 'Jupiter Mission 18 Months Later' and 'Jupiter and Beyond the Infinite' after the film's premiere on 1 April 1968 (*Kubrick: A Film Odyssey,* p. 149).

13. Geduld, *Filmguide to '2001',* p. 53.

14. Thomas Allen Nelson, *Kubrick,* p. 108. Nelson does go on, nonetheless, to indicate that the conversation with the Soviets is not contentless. 'Kubrick shows that battles for territory and tribal dominance persist even in the rarified air of space ... and that language, at least in its political and social functions, has evolved into a polite and banal mask (e.g., the "cover story" of a Clavius epidemic) for Pleistocene struggles.'

15. Alone among the Kubrick commentators I surveyed, Carolyn Geduld elaborates on the possibility that the cover story is false; reading the film alongside the novel, she writes, 'Clarke goes on to speculate that ... the Americans hope to get the edge on their enemies by being the first to contact and pick up pointers from the aliens' (*Filmguide to '2001',* p. 47). A bit further on, she also suggests that Floyd's audience at Clavius – no more than a dozen officials – 'barely seem convinced' by his culture shock justification (p. 49). See also note 17 below.

16. For my account of paranoia and the politics of interpretation, see *Marginal Forces / Cultural Centers,* pp. 219–21, 236–8.

17. At one point, indeed, Clarke explicitly suggests that Floyd's appeal to 'culture shock' is a ruse, when, after HAL's disconnection, Bowman reflects that 'some hints that had been dropped during his briefings suggested that the US–USSR bloc hoped to derive advantage by being the first to contact intelligent extraterrestrials' (Arthur C. Clarke, *2001: A Space Odyssey* [New York: New American Library, 1968], p. 168). This passage, however, is almost entirely unjustified by the rest of the narrative, which strongly implies that no

'hints' had been dropped to Bowman at any time; and in the film, as we've seen, HAL directly questions Bowman as to whether he's made anything of the 'rumors' surrounding the mission. Because that scene (which, as I noted above, precipitates the crisis aboard *Discovery*) isn't in the novel, it's safe to say that in Kubrick's version of events, Bowman has no inkling whatsoever that fear of 'culture shock' isn't the real reason for the mission's secrecy, and could not possibly have recalled 'hints' from his briefings.

18. At one point in the novel Clarke introduces the possibility that in our next evolutionary stage we will shuck off our organic bodies for 'constructions of metal and plastic' (p. 173), and shortly thereafter he says that this is precisely what the alien intelligences did on their way to becoming forms of pure energy: they remade themselves into computers. 'First their brains, and then their thoughts alone, they transferred into shining new homes of metal and of plastic' (p. 185). This account of evolution provides an alternative to Clarke's own rationale for HAL's behavior, and – incidentally – leaves it uncertain whether manned space flight is necessary to the 'maturation' of intelligence. For its part, the film registers a number of human anxieties about the frailty of bodies as opposed to microchips, most obviously when HAL cuts off the life support systems of the hibernating astronauts, severs Frank Poole's oxygen line, and informs David Bowman that he will find it 'difficult' to re-enter *Discovery* through the emergency airlock. Though HAL is disconnected in short order, he has made his point: silicon-based computers are better suited for space travel than carbon-based, oxygen-breathing humans. But *2001* cannot acknowledge its anxieties about bodies to this extent without undermining its premise that manned space flight is an epochal step in human evolution, and thereby potentially (if unwittingly) proposing HAL as our legitimate successor. Thanks to Janet Lyon for drawing my attention to the frailty of bodies in *2001*.

19. The fact that HAL was developed at the University of Illinois made for a nice coincidence, since neither Bud nor I could have dreamed in 1968 that we'd be anywhere near the place on 12 January 1992, but it struck me afterward as almost a poignantly naive touch: Illinois's supercomputing centers were world-renowned in 1968 and remain so today, but there's no question that a post-SDI United States would function somewhat differently. Although Star Wars R&D has been a cash cow for any number of American universities, many of which might well contribute to the development of HAL, the day has passed when we could imagine that the HAL 9000 would go operational in the civilian sector. HAL is a creature of Livermore Labs, and if and when he eventually wakes, we won't be told.

20. See Carter, *Final Frontier*, p. 233; for Carter's treatment of the decline in enthusiasm and funding for American adventures in space through the era of the space shuttle, see pp. 212–30.

21. I wrote this passage four months before the revelations that the United States secretly conducted radiation tests on its own citizens during and after World War II. Those secret testing programs proceeded without the informed consent of their subjects, of course, but the intensity of the federal government's desire to put plutonium into the bodies on unwitting Americans is nonetheless particularly remarkable in this case. Among other horrors that have recently come to light is the finding that such programs enlisted private companies to help gauge the effects of irradiated oatmeal on institutionalized mental patients. Despite what the closing paragraphs of this essay may suggest, then, I can pretend neither to cynicism nor to clairvoyance in regard to government secrecy. Apparently, the US government will always find a way to exceed our (and *my*) darkest suspicions of it, thereby further unraveling the open/closed binary on which rested so much Cold War rhetoric and practice. Which is to say, once more with feeling, that I love my country but I fear my government.

8

It's Renaissance Time: New Historicism, American Studies, and American Identity

There's a new historicism in American Studies, and you might think at first that it would first start working at the nation's roots. If this new historicism owes anything to poststructuralism, as of course it does, then certainly it should pose a challenge to the self-definition of the United States, since poststructuralism challenges any narrative of unitary identity, nationalist or otherwise. Moreover, the national narrative of the United States is based explicitly on the liberal ideals of the Enlightenment – precisely the ideals poststructuralism questions most thoroughly. Something there is in poststructuralist thought that does not love an Enlightenment, and since the United States was the first nation to ground itself on the premises of the Enlightenment, you can see that the potential for ideological conflict here is quite considerable: a new American Studies that launches a poststructuralist critique of the nation's very foundations would seem to pose a threat to the nation's conceptual identity.

For one thing, poststructuralism enables a form of historicist perspectivalism. It has insisted, for instance, that the idea of liberal individualism is not some kind of discovery of the eternal: when Thomas Jefferson wrote in the Declaration of Independence that 'we hold these truths to be self-evident, that all men are created equal, that they are endowed by their Creator with certain unalienable Rights', he may have claimed to uncover a hitherto unknown universal law (underwritten by the Creator), but from a historicist perspective he was doing no such thing. For new historicists, generally, it's more defensible to say that Jefferson, drawing on the tradition of British empiricism via Locke, *invented* an idea of men who were endowed with such rights. For by no means would such a conception of 'rights' have been 'self-evident' to Plato, Augustine, Aquinas, Machiavelli, Hobbes, or the Stuart monarchs; even as Jefferson was writing, too, there remained any number of people for whom the divine right of kings was self-evident. To this day, in fact, there are influential intellectuals in the United States who insist that our laws and customs come straight from England – despite the vast difference between the American conception of the 'citizen' and the British idea of the 'subject', whose 'rights' are granted by the throne for reasons that I suppose are self-evident. The competing idea of rights-bearing 'individuals' eventually *became* self-evident to many people, perhaps, but only because historically bounded men made historically bounded arguments (and fought historically bounded wars) in order to bring such a 'self-evident' conception into being.

So poststructuralism has held that the 'individual' is at best a historical phenomenon of very recent date. In fact, the word 'individualism' does not appear in English before 1835, according to the *Oxford English Dictionary;* we may all have been born one at a time, rather than in a litter like some other mammals we know, but apparently we were not discursively constituted as 'individuals' until quite recently – and certainly not long before the framing of the United States Constitution. On the contrary, that Constitution can be said to be one of the literary documents that helped to create this new being, the 'individual'.

But there's another thing at stake here as well. When I referred to the proponents of sovereign individualism, I referred to 'men'. Women can be individuals too, I hear, but as a matter of historical fact, the *liberté* and *égalité* proposed by the Enlightenment state were quite explicitly dependent on the exclusion of women from the *fraternité* of the bourgeois public sphere. You don't have to be a dues-paying poststructuralist to know that the American polity was founded on the exclusion of women, unpropertied men and all people of African descent. Nor do you have to have read Foucault to know that many of the American founding fathers were slaveholders, and that while they proclaimed the eternal rights of man, they withheld these rights from most of the men and all of the women living within the imaginary national borders at the time. The liberty of free individuals, in other words, was conceived in opposition to, and by definition *against*, 'others' who were unfree – and who were not entitled to the inalienable rights of free men because they (self-evidently) lacked the faculty of reason.

Furthermore, whether from a deconstructive or a historicist perspective, the United States Constitution's founding claim to be authored by 'we the people' is simply false: where the deconstructionist might tell you that the 'we' is a mere linguistic contrivance (or, worse, a *coercive* linguistic contrivance that violently *mis*represents those it claims to represent), the historicist will tell you that the 'we' is the expression of a rising class fragment asserting its will and its precarious, newfound power over subordinated classes. (As your local Marxism 101 instructor will tell you, before 1848 the bourgeoisie was a progressive force rebelling against church and state; after 1848 it became the oppressor of the proletariat.) Either way, the Constitution's 'we' pretends to re-present those whose voices it usurps – but as I'll explain at the conclusion of this essay, there can be significant differences between the linguistic and historicist suspicion of 'we the people', and a lot may depend on which road we choose to take in this yellow wood.

The American nation-state is therefore founded in (and on) contradiction. The question for us today is whether that contradiction is accidental or essential: is it a regrettable error within the Enlightenment, something that could only be cleansed from the national record by more Enlightenment (for example, the passage of the Reconstruction Amendments, which abolished slavery, established equal protection under the laws, and extended the franchise to black men), or is it something endemic to the Enlightenment itself? In his notable and eloquent dissent from the celebration of the bicentennial of the Constitution in 1987, the late Supreme Court Justice Thurgood Marshall tended to argue the former case, that the US Constitution was a radically flawed, incomplete and self-contradictory document requiring significant amendment to become the foundation for equal rights. Poststructuralism tends to argue the latter case, that the emancipatory narratives of the Enlightenment are in fact predicated on – and compromised by – their historical and social origins in eighteenth-century racism and sexism (and this is something documentable in an essay like David Hume's 'Of National Origins', for example, or Kant's *Observations on the Feeling of the Beautiful and Sublime,* or Voltaire's 'Peoples of America'). This would mean, then, that the social violence of the past two centuries of American society is not something to be corrected by a return to the Enlightenment rhetoric of rights but is, rather, a fulfillment of the symbolic violence constitutive of the Enlightenment itself. For according to some versions of poststructuralism, the liberal ideals of the Enlightenment are not only suspect in themselves but are also irrevocably tainted by their historical origins. These are the versions of poststructuralist critique resisted most strenuously by Jürgen Habermas, who claims to the contrary that the problem with the Enlightenment is that its emancipatory narratives have not yet been fully extended, as they should be, to us all – that, as he puts it, the project of modernity is incomplete rather than fatally flawed.[1]

It can certainly be countercharged that Habermas himself repeats some of the Enlightenment's signal errors, such as the insistence on instrumental reason as the basis for egalitarian and reciprocal human interaction.[2] But for now let's focus on what we have on the table so far: in general, poststructuralism is anti-humanist, 'decentering' the self, construing individuals as discursively produced 'subjects' or as the residual effects of regimes of power/knowledge, and it takes a dim view of the Enlightenment to boot. So as I said at the outset, you'd expect the sparks to fly if you touched the wire of poststructuralism to the wire of American national self-definition, and you'd expect to see those sparks ignite in American literary study – especially since poststructuralism has been more influential in literary study than in any other discipline. But though poststructuralism is certainly alien to many American traditions of thought, what's most curious about its contemporary challenge to American self-definition, I think, is this: American poststructuralism – and especially new historicism, with which I will be principally concerned – has been, for the most part, unconcerned with American national origins. Instead, American new historicism has so far centered on (or decentered) the so-called American Renaissance, which is usually defined as a period extending more or less from about 1840 to 1860 – that is, the two decades preceding and leading up to the American Civil War. My first task, then, will be to ask why this is so. If there is something in poststructuralism that does not love the Enlightenment, then why should new historicism's challenge to American self-definition focus so strongly on the American Renaissance?

Let us look for comparison at new historicism and the English Renaissance, which is where, especially in the work of Stephen Greenblatt, the movement got its start. The English Renaissance is of course the age of Shakespeare, one of the high-water marks of English lyric and drama; it has, for obvious reasons, always been remarkably fertile ground for literary studies in English. But what makes it especially intriguing for historical study is that it is also the period in which modern European nation-states were forming, when the English throne consolidated an extraordinary and unprecedented amount of political power at home and abroad, as England began, after the defeat of the Armada, to assume the role of a global power. The interplay between Shakespeare's Globe theater, say, and the global theater imagined by the Tudor and Stuart monarchies, thus makes for particularly fascinating studies of the circulation of power and the circulation of discourses in the English Renaissance.

The same cannot be said about the American Renaissance, which does not afford the same kind of national birth narrative. One might want to argue, perhaps, that the period leading up to the Civil War is formative of the contemporary United States in a way that the late eighteenth century is not. Eric Sundquist, notably, has taken this line, writing that 'the "rebirth" our classic literature is said to constitute occurred precisely in an era – from the 1830s through the Civil War – in which the authority of the fathers had become the subject of anxious meditation and in which the national crisis over slavery's limits compelled a return to the fraternally divisive energies of revolution.'[3] What Sundquist argues, in the course of an article entitled 'Slavery, Revolution, and the American Renaissance', is that antebellum America was torn between two contradictory invocations of the rhetoric of the Revolution: one that called abolitionists to finish the Revolution, to make all men free, and another that cautioned the nation against betraying the fathers, whose Constitution had afforded a limited justification of slavery. As Sundquist writes, 'the failure to abolish slavery in the late eighteenth century left succeeding generations stymied, imprisoned by the Constitution's apparent protection of slavery, yet conscious of the implicit attack on it in the Declaration of Independence' (p. 5).

I think that's right, and yet there remains a question of emphasis, for even Sundquist's cogent account of the era doesn't explain why American new historicism should be so emphatically concerned with the so-called national Renaissance. One could doubtless say that the Renaissance simply produced the first great flowering of American literature in a country that had long distrusted 'fine' writing (that's the standard explanation), but that seems a somewhat belletristic rationale for a new historicism that normally eschews belletrism.[4] Of course, there is recent work loosely affiliated with new historicism to be found in other periods – that of Philip Fisher, Amy Kaplan and Walter Benn Michaels, for instance – but few scholars other than Michael Warner and Cathy Davidson have applied the discipline's new critical tools to the eighteenth century. For the most part, in other words, it's as if we still cannot get England out of our minds.[5] (Warner's groundbreaking study, especially, shows us that new historicism's elision of literary and nonliterary discourses can work spectacularly well, particularly when it is tied to the elucidation of material/discursive phenomena like the development and circulation of printing – and reading – technologies.) For it is the English to whom this Renaissance is directed, so to speak; it is not a question of evoking the Italian Renaissance, thereby pressing America's claim to the culture of classical antiquity. As Jonathan Arac has argued, the 'particular force' of the idea of an American Renaissance is that it enfolds a number of complex relations to history and narrativity into a single national script:

> as 'American', it is new; more paradoxically, it is a repetition, a 'renaissance of the renaissance'. It does for the renaissance what the renaissance had done for antiquity. More importantly, however, it is *national*. People had long spoken of a Concord or Boston or New England 'renaissance', but this was no longer local, regional, or sectional. It was shared among 'all the people'.[6]

The Renaissance in America thus names the literary period in which our national literature is said to issue its own (belated) declaration of independence; and yet because American scholars call the period a time of literary 'Renaissance', we find that even as we articulate this break with the past, it weighs on our brains like a nightmare all the more. It is characteristic of this tension in American Studies, I think, that in 1985, Donald Pease should have opened a collection of essays entitled *The American Renaissance Reconsidered* – a collection usually cited as one of the first announcements of a new historicism in American literary studies (and the collection in which both Arac's and Sundquist's essays, cited above, first appeared) – by writing that the American Renaissance takes place outside history: 'once designated as the *locus classicus* for America's literary history', Pease writes,

> the American Renaissance does not remain located within the nation's secular history so much as it marks the occasion of a rebirth from it. Independent of the time kept by secular history, the American Renaissance keeps what we could call global renaissance time – the sacred time a nation claims to renew when it claims its cultural place as a great nation existing within a world of great nations. Providing each nation with the terms of cultural greatness denied to secular history, the 'renaissance' is an occasion occurring not so much within any specific historical time and place as a moment of cultural achievement that repeatedly provokes rebirth.[7]

Nationalism and 'Renaissancism' are complexly intertwined, as we no doubt know, but what Pease is asserting here is something more convoluted and ambitious: a *trans*national national Renaissance. If we want to know what time it is in American Studies, then, this is our answer: it's global renaissance time.

This kind of announcement is understandable enough for a self-consciously seminal collection, but in the intervening years it seems sometimes as if, perhaps, the global clock has stopped. Since the publication of *The American Renaissance Reconsidered*, the field of American literature has witnessed the publication of a series of works that are claimed for a movement Pease (taking up a phrase coined by Frederick Crews) attributes to a group of 'New Americanists'. Most of these works concern themselves primarily with the American Renaissance: Pease's own *Visionary Compacts: American Renaissance Writings in Cultural Context*, of course, but also *Ideology and Classic American Literature*, edited by Myra Jehlen and Sacvan Bercovitch, and Lauren Berlant's *The Anatomy of National Fantasy*, to name a few of the more well-known studies.[8] Likewise, Pease's introduction to a special issue of *boundary 2*, 'New Americanists: Revisionist Interventions into the Canon', which appeared in 1990 and provides a

long, detailed reply to Crews, focuses almost exclusively on critical debates since 1940 on the constitution of the American Renaissance; and
Philip Fisher's introduction to *The New American Studies,* published in
1991, also takes up the relation of the antebellum years to the central
period he calls 'the Civil War within representation'.[9]

Fisher's introduction is a particularly important artifact in this regard,
for he not only calls attention to New Americanism's interest in the
American Renaissance; he does so precisely in order to disentangle the
field from new historicist examinations of the English Renaissance. Fisher
writes:

> In literary studies of recent years what has been called the new historicism
> has, as a result of the strong influence of Foucault and the modern experience
> of totalitarianism and its analysis by Hannah Arendt and Max Horkheimer,
> among others, focused on the fate of representation within absolutist states or
> societies. The English Renaissance, taken as a glorious period of monarchy
> along with its secondary pressures and exceptions, became the natural topic
> for new historicist demonstrations.
>
> The condition of civil war can be taken as the fundamental alternative to
> the condition of monarchical power, self-display, uniform discourse, ideology,
> and controlled representation. American new historicism has its basis in the
> representational situation not of monarchy but of civil war. ... The repre-
> sentational topic of monarchy is the inheritance, diffusion, and protection of
> power already held. The topic of civil war is an unstable contest for short-term
> control that is uninheritable and in the end, indefensible. (pp. xv–xvi)

Again, I think that's right – but then again, by distinguishing American
new historicism from its English cousin Fisher provokes the question he
proceeds not to answer. 'Of the essays in this collection', he continues,
'more than half examine alternative rhetorics within the public sphere of
the mid-nineteenth-century experience of the war over slavery, its aboli-
tionist foreground, and its reconstructionist and New South aftermath'
(p. xvi). Once more the new American historicism travels the old Renaissance ground, in however different a way; but here's the question. If the
English Renaissance, as Fisher puts it, is 'the natural topic' for new historicist analysis, and if the representational situation of monarchy is vastly
different from that of civil war, *and* if half the essays of yet another 'new'
collection examine the context of the American civil war, then one would
expect Fisher to remark on the difference between Foucauldian analysis
of the English Renaissance and that of the American; what, after all, *is*
the difference between applying new historicism to totalitarian societies
in the age of the birth of the modern nation-state and applying it to nations with strong and relatively autonomous 'public spheres' not immedi-

ately subject to the power of the State that are also nations on the brink of civil war?

Fisher's answer will come as a surprise to all of you who thought 'new historicism' meant something new in American Studies (and this includes all of you who might pick up a book called *The New American Studies* on the basis of its title): the difference between the English and American Renaissance is that the English have ideology and we don't. Apparently, we have 'rhetorics' instead, and whatever these are, they're not ideological:

> In the absence of a state we find ourselves freed of the intellectual component of the systematic state: ideology. We have rhetorics because we have no ideology, and we have no ideology because we lack the apparatus of ideology: a national religion, a unitary system of education under the control of the state, a cultural life and media monopolized by the state by means of either ownership or subsidy. Ideology is a cultural mechanism of stabilization and transmission, neither of which is a primary topic of a culture of speculation. (p. xxii)

In one way Fisher has a case. American media and schooling are relatively autonomous from the state in a way that their British and French counterparts are not, and the American Renaissance *should* be distinguished from the English on the grounds that its social apparatus is vastly different from that of the Tudor-Stuart transition. However, what Fisher does here is really very strange. As Gregory Jay has recently pointed out, Fisher simply repeats the gestures of the Americanists of forty or fifty years ago, even in the course of distancing himself from the 'myth criticism' they produced: 'in an extraordinary twist on traditional arguments for "American exceptionalism", writes Jay, 'Fisher defines the uniqueness of America as its place on the frontier beyond ideology.'[10]

This 'new' American Studies, focusing on the American Renaissance as a period free from ideology, thus threatens to present us with old wine in old skins. Crucially, what underwrites this reappearance of the American Adam in Fisher's presentation is a radical impoverishment of the understanding of 'ideology': to read the introduction to *The New American Studies,* you'd think that ideology could not exist except in monolithic, totalitarian states. It's as if the work of Gramsci, Althusser, Raymond Williams, Ernesto Laclau, Chantal Mouffe, Stuart Hall and Fredric Jameson – all of whom track the multiple workings of ideology in civil society – didn't exist. For that matter, it's as if the work of fellow Harvard Americanist Sacvan Bercovitch didn't exist, for it is Bercovitch who helped to inaugurate a new American Studies by announcing that the American ideology held that ours was a nation beyond ideology.[11] The Renaissance presented here, then, participates in a rebirth from secular history that gives us a culture of speculation. One could say, looking at these instruments, that it's still global renaissance time in American Studies.

The reason for this freeze-frame, I think, is rather complex, and is closely bound up with the relation between national self-identity and 'American literature' as a disciplinary field. To be more specific: reassessments of the American Renaissance are not only 'revisionist interventions of the canon' or historicist revisions of the crucial years 1840–1860; they are also revisions of the conceptual definition of American literature in this century, as 'American literature' became a university subject for the first time in the crucial years 1940–1960. Now, Donald Pease himself argues as much, in both of his recent *boundary 2* essays; as far as he's concerned, New Americanism is primarily a struggle over conceptual definition of what he calls the 'field-Imaginary' of American Studies insofar as American Studies dates itself to F. O. Matthiessen's epochal study, *The American Renaissance,* first published in 1941. And because, as various New Americanists like Jonathan Arac and Gregory Jay have demonstrated, this conceptual definition of American literature served (consciously and unconsciously) to fulfill the political needs of American identity in the postwar era, one might say that new historicism's challenge to American self-definition proceeds by way of a series of relays: by redefining the American Renaissance, American new historicism not only centers the national narrative on the contradictions between the Constitution and the Declaration (since those contradictions eventuated in the literal fracturing of the nation, and therefore challenge the national narrative on the war front) but – and this is crucial – American new historicism also challenges the relation between the field of 'American literature' and the insertion of that field into the national narrative in the post–Second World War period of the US accession to the role of global power.

Here I'll have to back up and explain, because something funny happened to American Studies on the way to this forum. People who are familiar with the dominant formalism and ahistoricism of American literary studies before 1975 are usually surprised to find that American Studies, in its inception, was supposed to be an interdisciplinary enterprise. As Gerald Graff has pointed out, it was intended to overcome critical specialization by locating American literature in American culture in the broad sense.[12] The problem, however, was that American Studies located its enterprise in the notion that American culture was essentially an alternative to politics, a place where the social conflicts of American life could find satisfying symbolic resolution. The idea of American literature that followed from this conception operated by way of two differentiations, both of which depended on the definition of the American literary narrative in terms of the romance rather than the novel. The first differentiation, yet again, distinguished American fiction from British on the grounds that the American novel was anti-realist while the British novel was a document of social realism; while Austen, Scott, Dickens, Trollope and Eliot located their novels in the social milieux of manners and marriages, American fictions described, to quote the title of Richard Poirier's 1966 book, 'a world elsewhere'.[13] So American literature under this heading could quite reasonably write the American Renaissance into this narrative of romance: where Austen concerns herself with social engagements and Eliot and Dickens with the social totality, American writers head for the territories, the prairie, the cabin built by their own hands, the whaling ship, the frontier, the virgin land confronted by an American Adam.

The second differentiation is a little more intricate, since it distinguishes American literature simultaneously from the corruption of Europe (whose class-ridden society is now the snake in the garden, tempting the American Adam to fall) and also from the unfreedom of the Soviet bloc, where social realism is literally (and literarily) the order of the day. In other words, 'romance', especially in the works of Herman Melville and Nathaniel Hawthorne, could now be construed as a literary domain of freedom opposed to the oppressive mimetic demands of the novel. Richard Chase says as much in his once canonical study, *The American Novel and Its Tradition*, which had the good fortune to be published just as Sputnik was launched in 1957. The romance, writes Chase, is 'freer, more daring, more brilliant fiction that contrasts with the solid moral inclusiveness and massive equability of the English novel', and therefore affords American writers

> an assumed freedom from the ordinary novelistic requirements of verisimilitude, development, and continuity; a tendency towards melodrama and idyl; a more or less formal abstractness and, on the other hand, a tendency to plunge into the underside of consciousness; a willingness to abandon moral questions or to ignore the spectacle of man in society, or to consider these things only indirectly or abstractly.[14]

The American romance, as the record of an 'assumed freedom' from social mimesis, is thus both un-British and anti-Soviet: it is an American literature for the Cold War, a literature organized under the heading of the postwar liberal consensus that had proclaimed the end of ideology.[15] It is fitting, then, in such a cultural climate, that American literature be by definition beyond ideology – beyond history, beyond culture.

I'm not saying this conception of American literature is entirely false. American writers from Melville to James have in fact complained that the

United States did not afford them enough of a social totality to be mimetic of, and it can't be denied that the postwar canon of American literature, especially that of the so-called American Renaissance, is less explicitly socially engaged than the great British, French or (yes) Russian novels of the nineteenth century. But what's wrong with this narrative is not that it's false, or that it can easily be shown to have served the political purposes of a postwar political and literary consensus; what's wrong with it is that it immerses American literary criticism uncritically in the self-representations of the American Renaissance writers, and excludes from the field of 'American literature' everything that does not come under this heading – so that if we find American writings that don't fit the facts of the paradigm, we will agree not to see them as essential American writings. Washington Irving disappears; Fenimore Cooper's Deerslayer series is in, but his novel of manners, *Satanstoe,* is out; melodramatic romance is in, but *Uncle Tom's Cabin* is out; and the tradition of American naturalism from William Dean Howells to Theodore Dreiser, the tradition that actually displaced the genteel tradition and had been considered by V. L. Parrington to constitute one of the main currents of American thought, this tradition too is marginalized. Slave narratives and women's writing are also ignored, but they will not be emphasized until the 1970s and 1980s, and what I'm focusing on here are two retrospective phenomena: that 'American literature' became a field defined largely by its exclusions of writers not considered central to the national narrative; and that these exclusions were not just passive registers of neglect or ignorance but often active expulsions of writers and texts who could not be made to fit the American romance thesis.

To say that the definition of 'American literature' simply excised most of the literature actually produced in the country may run the risk of sounding brutally reductive, but, more or less, this is what happened to the body of writing consolidated under the heading 'American Renaissance' in the years 1940–60; and it is, more or less, a restatement of the criticism leveled against the field by Russell Reising, whose 1986 book *The Unusable Past* showed that theories of American literature have tended to derive their theses from the same eight authors (Hawthorne, Emerson, Thoreau, Whitman, Melville, Twain, James, Eliot). Which theses then demonstrated, *mirabile dictu,* that the major American writers were Hawthorne, Emerson, Thoreau, Whitman, Melville, Twain, James, Eliot (sometimes Poe, sometimes Dickinson and sometimes Cooper, but you get the idea). As Reising shows, once Matthiessen's *American Renaissance* set the terms for the field, successive theories of 'American literature' (no matter what the political affiliation of the theorist) achieved something of a snowball effect whereby 'the same authors, the same books, and often the same passages are summoned time after time to support a tautological reading which proves what it assumed in advance, that is, that the writers under investigation are truly our "major" figures.'[16]

The causes of the field's consolidation under the heading of 'romance' are many, and I can enumerate but some of the most important here: among these I would cite the influence of modernism and New Criticism on the American academy in the postwar period; the confluence of conservative Agrarianism and left anti-Stalinism in the turn to modernism as a literature of 'timeless' anti-totalitarian, anti-masscult, or anti-industrial values; the way New Criticism met the pedagogical challenges presented by a generation of American students entering college after the Second World War; and the attempt of American literature to become a world literature of a stature appropriate to newfound American global power. Gerald Graff claims that 'the symbolic-romance theory, stressing as it did the inability of American narratives to resolve their conflicts within any social form of life, provided expression for disappointments left over from the 1930s toward a society that had failed to fulfill its ideal image of itself but evidently could not be righted by social action' (p. 219). Gregory Jay, similarly noting the banishment of historicisms from American Studies in the rise of the anti-Stalinism of the 1940s and 1950s, writes that although the period is rich in sophisticated historicist theories, such as those of Georg Lukács, Mikhail Bakhtin and Walter Benjamin, 'it is highly significant that almost none of the work of these critics received any attention in the United States prior to the 1960s, for this absence made the formalist case against Marxist criticism much easier to win and institutionalize.'[17]

Intriguing as the causes of this consolidation are, however, I'm more concerned with how the consolidation crumbled. I should say, though, before I move on to the concluding section of this discussion, that I've probably made it sound as if postwar American literature, as an academic discipline, was narrowly and unselfconsciously celebratory of the dominant American culture, a willing participant in a discourse of American self-affirmation in the era of the end of ideology. If I've made it sound this way then I've perpetuated one of the excesses of the new historicism, its insistence on seeing everything about a culture as somehow complicit with or conscripted by the dominant forces of that culture. As I noted earlier, it's not hard to show that the specific construction of the American Renaissance in literary criticism served some convenient political purposes in asserting its own apoliticality. Still, I do think it's worth remembering that the canon of American literature enshrined in the 1940s and 1950s was considered to be an *oppositional* canon, a canon of writers like Melville who said No! in thunder to facile national good cheer; it was, as

Leslie Fiedler memorably put it, 'a literature of darkness and the gro-
tesque in a land of light and affirmation.'[18] Nevertheless, it was conceived
not only as a literature of negation in that it provided a critical alternative
to jingoism, isolationism and crass materialism; it was also, in the foundational work of Lionel Trilling especially, claimed to be a literature conceived against *every* American political grain (and specifically against V. L.
Parrington's 'main currents' of social protest). It was a literature, like
modernist literature, whose oppositionality could be located in its capacity for transcendence: as Trilling put it in a classic formulation of the
American ideology against ideology, 'certain artists ... contain within
themselves, it may be said, the very essence of the culture, and the sign of
this is that they do not submit to serve the ends of any one ideological
group or tendency.'[19] Only under such a paradigm as this, then (to repeat
the point once more), can Hawthorne's anti-abolitionism be construed as
more American, more complex and suggestive, than Harriet Beecher
Stowe's abolitionism.[20]

It wasn't new historicism that first marked the exclusions on which these
theories rested; that credit, surely, must go to American feminism. In an
influential article of 1981, Nina Baym alleged (in a phrase I like very
much) that Trilling's postwar canon of oppositional writers merely constituted 'a consensus criticism of the consensus'.[21] Insofar as theories of
American literature defined 'the American experience' as a *single* experience that was always male, Baym argued, such theories could allow for
certain safe forms of dissent while obliterating more marginal and dissi-
dent voices. The extent to which this version of feminist critique is itself
proto-Foucauldian should be obvious. For new historicists, too, are adept
at arguing that so-called 'progressive' movements in the United States
have worked to contain rather than enable the kinds of political dissent
that challenged the ideology of consensus; the history of American history in such radical critiques is a history of multiple shifting consolidations of male WASP hegemony. Baym was soon followed by a newly
poststructuralist Houston Baker, whose 1984 book, *Blues, Ideology, and
Afro-American Literature,* announced a strong revisionary paradigm for a
new American literary history. Inspired in part by Foucault, Baker
claimed that the field of American Studies could be reconceived from the
ground up if the discipline's foundational statements were reorganized.
Where American literary historians had relied on the image of the Puritan errand in the wilderness, Baker wrote, the field would look rather
different if organized around the concept of the 'commercial deportation'
of African bodies. In such a field, certainly, slave narratives like those of
Olaudah Equiano and Frederick Douglass might take their place in

American culture alongside, say, works by Thomas Jefferson and Ralph Waldo Emerson.[22]

The theoretical-historical conjuncture of feminism, African American studies, and new historicism is, as Gregory Jay says, 'no accident' (*AS*, p. 237); here Jay is paraphrasing the argument of Judith Lowder Newton, whose essay 'History as Usual?: Feminism and the "New Historicism"' recalls that black and feminist criticism had gone about 'decentering' the white male subject, and reading the literary in conjunction with the historical and political, well before anyone was reading Foucault Stateside.[23] What Jay, Newton and I agree on, then, is that it's necessary and salutary to collocate new historicism with feminism and multiculturalism on the grounds Newton has laid out, partly because there are new historicisms that do not necessarily have to trace themselves back to the master, Foucault (Jane Tompkins's historicism, for example), and partly because among them, these three intellectual movements have proven to be spectacularly successful at reconsidering the American Renaissance, opening the field not only to Harriet Beecher Stowe and Frederick Douglass but also to E.D.E.N. Southworth, Susan Warner and Harriet Jacobs.

However, this collocation does not always satisfy its individual constituents; we cannot, in other words, simply absorb feminism and multiculturalism in one triumphal, all-consuming new historicist narrative. Brook Thomas has phrased the problem cogently: 'poststructuralism does not seem to speak to the historical needs of important segments of our population', he writes, since '... poststructuralism is of limited use for those excluded by previous histories, who are in a situation in which they need not only to deconstruct discredited histories of the past, but to construct and legitimate new histories in which they are finally represented.'[24] Newton, for her part, is willing to grant the utility of poststructuralism for feminism, but remarks that the difference between them

> makes for other differences in what 'history' looks like, makes for differences in what is included as 'history' in the first place and differences in what constitutes a historical period. It makes for differences, finally, in the degree to which dominant representations and hegemonic ideologies are imagined as monolithic and anonymous or as composed of many voices. (p. 155)

And here I would add that feminism and African American studies have large constituencies both inside and outside the academy, while poststructuralism, as Brook Thomas says, does not. That's one reason why poststructuralism seems more vulnerable to attack both inside and outside the university: it looks 'academic' in the bad sense, the sense we use when we speak of an 'academic' question, a question that does not matter.

216

Here we come back to a tension within poststructuralism itself, a tension I alluded to at the outset when I noted the difference between criticizing 'we the people' as a linguistic contrivance and criticizing the phrase for suppressing the voices of the people for whom it ostensibly stands. To what extent should we ground our recent revisionary American narratives in their contemporary social conditions? If feminism and American multiculturalism have helped to engender new histories and a new American Renaissance, they have done so by seeking the expansion and further democratization of American civil society and the public sphere (partly by way of the professions), and that's something with which new historicism has had nothing to do. I don't want to suggest that there's a direct correlation between the race and gender composition of the new American literature canon and the race and gender composition of the profession of American literary study, but there is certainly *some* connection between the two, and the connection is arguably more responsible than new historicism for what's really new in the 'new' American studies. As we saw in the introductions by Pease and Fisher, there's no necessary correspondence between a new historicism and a new conception of the American polity or the American Renaissance: even among the revisionists, the US can still be a land beyond ideology, beyond secular history. The most we can glean from such critics, I suggest, is a revision of American national identity that proceeds by way of the complex series of relays mapped out above, where New Americanists contest the ideological work done by the field of 'American literature' in the postwar period of consensus, and thereby redefine the relations between the nation and the field. What we will *not* get from them, though, is an account of the changing relations between the state and civil society in the US that have provided the New Americanists of the 1980s and 1990s with the social and discursive space in which to elaborate new formulations of American literary history and national identity.

Civil society and the public sphere are what do not exist under monarchies and totalitarianisms; they name those social and political spaces that have to be negotiated by any form of old or new historicism attempting to translate its analysis of the circulation of power in the English Renaissance to the circulation of power in the American. Some 'weaker' or more moderate forms of poststructuralism argue merely that the public sphere is discursively constructed, and I have no difficulty seeing them as potential companions to the critiques enabled by feminism and multiculturalism, since a discursively constructed public sphere remains a place (even if only a textual place) where political agency and social change remains possible. But when more stringent forms of poststructuralism suggest that the category of 'civil society' or the 'public sphere' is an illusion, that power simply produces little blisters on the social body that only seem to be pockets of relatively autonomous discourse, then I have to think such poststructuralist critiques are themselves ahistorical or simply wrong. For the political space of Foucauldian critique is itself enabled by its location in civil society; under a truly totalitarian regime such critique could be thought, perhaps, but it could not easily be circulated. As the career of Mikhail Bakhtin (to take one notable example) should remind us, it's much harder to compose and circulate analyses of what Foucault calls 'power without the king' in societies that are actually ruled by autocrats and kings.[25] Poststructuralism itself resides, I submit, in that relatively but not completely autonomous realm from and in which social dissent becomes thinkable and practically possible. Or to put this in neo-Kantian terms, strong poststructuralism cannot think its own political conditions of possibility, precisely because its very critique of the Enlightenment is itself launched from social space cleared by the Enlightenment. In the United States, that space is also discursively constructed in a Constitution that mandates the separation of powers in a federalist state – and the consequent creation of plural public spheres.[26]

Contemporary feminism and multiculturalism, I think, tend to be less oblivious to their place in the credentializing mechanisms of civil society than poststructuralism has been. But I want to return in closing to how these differently situated movements – poststructuralism, feminism, multiculturalism – nevertheless dovetail to impel American national redefinition. What new historicism does is to locate a crucial site of social contestation in the discursive realm, as the place where political and cultural dissensus and consensus are forged and re-formed. In doing so, such historicism restores literary works to their multiple historical contexts, asks how both literary and 'nonliterary' works are not only reflective but formative of their times and ours, and thereby forces new re-cognitions of the social importance of American literatures.

Yet even in the conjuncture described by Jay and Newton, current feminist and multiculturalist criticisms do not stop at employing interpretive modes consonant with those of the new historicism; they also insist on the responsibility of the present to the forgotten writers of the past, thereby demanding that the disciplinary field of 'American literature' be more properly 'representative' of writings and populations in the United States. Previous generations had demanded no less; but the difference here and now is that the feminist and multiculturalist senses of 'representation' are more inclusive, more mimetic, and yet more tenuous than those of any previous generation of critics. Canon revision that stresses the categories of race and gender gives us a field of American literature populated by more women and ethnic minorities, but there's no guarantee that texts written by these women and ethnic minorities will 'represent' their groups in any straightforward sense; what they will do, however, is provide indispensable points of contrast with the texts of their contemporary white male authors, so as to help us theorize more fully the relations among individuals and groups in the past. (Thus one can compare Olaudah Equiano and Thomas Jefferson on 'freedom', or Ralph Waldo Emerson and Harriet Jacobs on 'property'.) In other words, feminist and multiculturalist projects insist on the inclusion of women and minorities in the phrase 'we the people', but they seek to theorize the historical relations between people included and excluded from the phrase as well. In both cases, then, and despite the differences I've just enumerated, the project of rearticulating American literature to its social and historical contexts, of re-establishing the tie between the field of 'American literature' and social life in the United States – this project is simultaneously the enabling device *and* the result of a politically activist cultural criticism that hopes to intervene in its own social and historical moment, namely ours.

Let me make that clearer. Politically activist cultural criticism (together with politically critical cultural activism) got women and minorities into faculty positions in American universities in the first place; from that space, among others, feminism and multiculturalism retheorizes the American cultural heritage that has begotten them. In so doing these movements seek to influence American self-definition in the future by forging a revisionary account of the past that is at once more inclusive, more skeptical, *and* (paradoxically) more accurate than the account that gave us an American Renaissance built around the great works of a half dozen or so white men from the northeastern United States, a New-English American Renaissance built in a place called New England.

New historicism, feminism, and multiculturalism may thus work, in the end, to challenge the American national narrative as few social/intellectual conjunctures have challenged it, and to do so by means of these relays that address (and redress) the nation by addressing the disciplinary definition of its literature. Yet for all we can tell now, they also may merely collapse their various challenges into a *new* nationalism, a new 'mosaic' or 'multiculturalist' renaissance time. This would give us a strange hybrid beast forged by a curious coalition – a newly en-gendered American historicist multiculturalist nationalism. And that would be a mouthful no one could pronounce to denounce. But I don't think it's going to happen. New historicism does not always challenge the terms of the American polity by itself, as we have seen, but it does challenge the boundaries of American literary study. And together with feminism and multiculturalism, it can challenge the borders of the United States – and produce a hitherto unprecedented object of study, a 'national' literature that does not rest on nationalism.

This may be utopian thinking, since there isn't any easy way to disentangle historical narratives of American literature from the national narratives of the United States. You can challenge the prominence of the frontier myth as a defining element of our literature, but you can't imagine an American literature that isn't grounded in *some* US narrative of self-definition, whether you rely on stories about 'self-reliance' or on the multicultural 'salad bowl' into which more and more foreign ingredients get tossed. And yet I wonder. Perhaps an American literature that *exceeds* the boundaries of the American nation-state, temporally and conceptually, can be thought – and brought into the classroom. I think this is possible, and I think it's this possibility to which Frederick Crews responds, consciously or unconsciously, when in a curious passage in his introduction to *The Critics Bear It Away* he credits the New Americanists with revitalizing the field of American literary study, only to disparage their progeny, who are apparently shrill and intolerant. About halfway through the introduction, Crews admits that for all his criticism of 'Left Eclecticism' in the academy, 'the left, unlike the right, has made some indisputably fertile contributions to the recent evolution of literary study', and therefore should be thanked 'for launching a fundamental debate about the canon and for bringing minority concerns into the foreground – developments that are especially striking and revivifying in my own field of American literature' (p. xvi). However, although the first generation of leftists has done good work, the next generation promises to be (surprise) all out of shape from toe to top:

> a growing restlessness within New Americanist ranks portends a much sharper break with tradition. The founding members of the group, writing in the late seventies and early eighties and struggling to make a break from their liberal mentors, were so successful that they gave rise to a second cohort of zealous followers who, lacking even an ambivalent recollection of the former dispensation, now accept a new conventional wisdom based on emancipatory values and a dismissal of 'artistic' issues as inherently retrograde. These young academics launch their arguments from a base of egalitarian pieties about race, class, and gender as routinely as the cold war liberals started from formalist aesthetics, the Founding Fathers, and the canon according to F. O. Matthiessen. Predictably, then, the latest New Americanists are now beginning to turn against their mentors for continuing to dwell ambivalently on the old canon and the forgettable academic giants of the forties and fifties.
>
> Although no one – not even the editors of the quintessentially New Americanist *Heath Anthology of American Literature* – has as yet proposed that classic authors be banned outright, the most militant young academics are increasingly inclined to demand primary allegiance to the ethnic- and gender-based anticanon. (pp. xvii–xviii)

Well, this sounds pretty ominous. We haven't outlawed Hawthorne and Melville yet, but we're feeling our way around to it. And Crews may be next on the list. Remember, it was the *third* generation of Puritans that inaugurated the witch trials, simultaneously provoking and responding to a 'national' crisis of disciplinary authority in New England.

What's notable about this passage, aside from its family drama of good rebel children and bad rebel grandchildren, is that the last sentence is footnoted: apparently, the militant young academics will be found and named. Actually, they aren't. The footnote, tellingly, says nothing about the new militants and their anticanonical pledge of allegiance. It reads, instead, 'see Paul Lauter et al., eds., *The Heath Anthology of American Literature,* 2 vols.' (p. 187n4). Is this all that underwrites Crews's attack on the Young Americanists? It seems to me that Crews throws around some serious allegations against his younger colleagues in the field, and that such allegations should at least be documented by something less flimsy than a reference to an anthology.

Then again, perhaps this note suffices; perhaps the *Heath Anthology* speaks for itself. Perhaps Crews can entertain a healthy bit of professional jousting with Donald Pease over the American Renaissance, but must stop short of the radical revision of 'American literature' envisaged by Lauter's anthology. Lauter is no new historicist, by any stretch; but his anthology of American literature is the first work in the field that radically detaches the 'field' from the narrative of the nation. Beginning with Native American traditions and proceeding through more than a century of extremely unconventional materials under the heading of 'The Literature of Discovery and Exploration' (including such classic writers as Alvar Nuñez Cabeza de Vaca and Samuel de Champlain), the *Heath* applies some long-overdue dynamite to the story of the Puritan errand in the wilderness, and starts the clock a century and more before the commercial deportation of African bodies. Even in the eighteenth century, it turns out, the *Heath* offers a section entitled 'Emerging Voices of a National Literature: African, Native American, Spanish, Mexican'.

Whether this reconception of the field merits Crews's description of it I do not yet know; to date I've been more an observer of than a participant in the struggles over the meaning of American identity in American literature before the twentieth century. I sense, though, that even though the editors of the *Heath* have issued no race-and-gender loyalty oaths, they have done something important, something no new historicism has done: reconceiving the relations between American literature and the creation of the United States, reconfiguring the current relations between civil society (in American literature classrooms) and the state, the editors of the *Heath* have reset the clock. In the pages of the *Heath*, for the first time since American literature became an object of study in America higher education, we are no longer setting our watches to global renaissance time.

Notes

1. Jürgen Habermas, 'Modernity: An Incomplete Project', in Hal Foster, ed., *The Anti-Aesthetic: Essays on Postmodern Culture* (Port Townsend, Wash.: Bay Press, 1983), pp. 3–15.

2. For a brilliant neo-Habermasian critique of poststructuralism that also distances itself from Habermas's reliance on reason, see Amanda Anderson, 'Cryptonormativism and Double Gestures: Reconceiving Poststructuralist Social Theory', *Cultural Critique,* no. 21 (1992), pp. 63–95.

3. Eric Sundquist, 'Slavery, Revolution, and the American Renaissance', in Walter Benn Michaels and Donald E. Pease, eds, *The American Renaissance Reconsidered,* Selected Papers from the English Institute, no. 9 (Baltimore: Johns Hopkins University Press, 1985), p. 6; hereafter cited in the text.

4. One could also say that the scholars who announced a new American studies just happened to specialize in the American Renaissance, Q.E.D. In some ways it is 'as simple as that', we could say, and yet – as I'll explain below in my reading of Philip Fisher's introduction to *The New American Studies* – the fact of disciplinary specialization does not (and *should* not) preclude one from elaborating one's theoretical and historical conditions of possibility.

5. See Cathy N. Davidson, *Revolution and the Word: The Rise of the Novel in America* (New York: Oxford University Press, 1986); Philip Fisher, *Hard Facts: Setting and Form in the American Novel* (New York: Oxford University Press, 1985); Amy Kaplan, *The Social Construction of American Realism* (Chicago: University of Chicago Press, 1988); Walter Benn Michaels, *The Gold Standard and the Logic of Naturalism: American Literature at the Turn of the Century* (Berkeley, Calif.: University of California Press, 1987); and Michael Warner, *The Letters of the Republic: Publication and the Public Sphere in Eighteenth-Century America* (Cambridge, Mass.: Harvard University Press, 1990).

6. Jonathan Arac, 'F. O. Matthiessen: Authorizing an American Renaissance', in Michaels and Pease, eds, *American Renaissance Reconsidered,* p. 94.

7. Donald Pease, 'Introduction', in Michaels and Pease, eds, *The American Renaissance Reconsidered,* p. vii.

8. Sacvan Bercovitch and Myra Jehlen, eds, *Ideology and Classic American Literature* (Cambridge: Cambridge University Press, 1986); Lauren Berlant, *The Anatomy of National Fantasy: Hawthorne, Utopia, and Everyday Life* (Chicago: University of Chicago Press, 1991); Donald Pease, *Visionary Compacts: American Renaissance Writings in Cultural Context* (Madison, Wis.: University of Wisconsin Press, 1987). It is for this reason, accordingly, that Frederick Crews's review of 'New Americanists' is entitled 'Whose American Renaissance?' The essay was originally published in the *New York Review of Books,* 27 October 1988, pp. 68–81, and is now the lead essay in *The Critics Bear It Away: American Fiction and the Academy* (New York: Random House, 1992), pp. 16–46; hereafter cited in the text. Crews's essay does not treat Berlant, needless to say, but does apply the term 'New Americanist' to critics such as Arac, Bercovitch, Fisher, Jehlen, Michaels, Pease, Russell Reising, Richard Slotkin, and Jane Tompkins.

9. Philip Fisher, 'Introduction: The New American Studies', in *The New American Studies* (Berkeley, Calif.: University of California Press, 1991), p. xv; hereafter cited in the text. For Pease's reply to Frederick Crews, see Donald Pease, 'New Americanists: Revisionist Interventions into the Canon', *boundary 2,* vol. 17, no. 1 (1990), pp. 1–37; for an update, see Pease, 'National Identities, Postmodern Artifacts, and Postnational Narratives', *boundary 2,* vol. 19, no. 1 (1992), pp. 1–13.

10. Gregory Jay, 'Ideology and the New Historicism', *Arizona Quarterly,* vol. 49, no. 1 (1993), p. 143.

11. Sacvan Bercovitch, 'The Problem of Ideology in American Literary History', *Critical Inquiry,* vol. 12, no. 4 (1986), pp. 631–53.

12. Gerald Graff, *Professing Literature,* pp. 209–11; hereafter cited in the text. The following account of American Studies also draws on Graff's article, 'American Criticism Left and Right', in Bercovitch and Jehlen, eds, *Ideology and Classic American Literature,* pp. 91–121.

13. Richard Poirier, *A World Elsewhere: The Place of Style in American Literature* (New York: Oxford University Press, 1966). For a more recent restatement of this strain in American studies, see Michael Davitt Bell, *The Development of American Romance: The Sacrifice of Relation* (Chicago: University of Chicago Press, 1980).

14. Richard Chase, *The American Novel and Its Tradition* (Garden City, N.Y.: Doubleday, 1957), pp. vii, ix.

15. Reading Chase's 'romance' thesis in the light of the Cold War, liberal anti-communism, and the postwar generation of American 'consensus' historians is a common New Americanist enterprise, whereby recent critics have shown that postwar arguments for American literary and cultural exceptionalism tend to rely (consciously or unconsciously) on an opposition between American freedom and un-American constriction or tyranny. The textual foundation for Chase's equation of 'romance' with 'freedom' is Hawthorne's preface to *The House of the Seven Gables;* for a revisionary analysis of the preface and the novel, see Walter Benn Michaels, 'Romance and Real Estate', in Michaels and Pease, eds, *American Renaissance Reconsidered.* In Michaels's account, the final paragraph of the preface casts doubt on the claims that Hawthorne intended the genre of 'romance' either to 'pose a self-consciously fictional alternative to the social responsibilities of the novel' or to 'provide in its radical fictionality a revolutionary alternative to the social conservatism of the novel' (pp. 156–7). In 'New Americanists: Revisionist Interventions into the Canon', Donald Pease relates the implicit Cold War politics of Chase's romance thesis to Trilling's *Liberal Imagination,* suggesting that 'once he has identified the function of the romance with the cultural entitlement to speak universal truths, Chase assigns this power not to the romances themselves but to the liberal imagination capable of claiming this power as its own' (p. 24). Pease goes to cite Geraldine Murphy, 'Romancing the Center: Cold War Politics and Classic American Literature', *Poetics Today,* vol. 9, no. 4 (1988), pp. 737–47, for her link between Chase and the consensus politics of Arthur Schlesinger, Jr. As both Frederick Crews and Donald Pease agree, the critical inquiries that enable these revisionary readings of the 'romance' thesis are themselves both evidence and precipitate of the breakdown of the postwar consensus in the 1960s. And once New Americanists have cast suspicion on the Cold War scenario of postwar American Studies, practically any Old Americanist critical opposition between 'freedom' and 'compulsion' becomes suspect, such as that which produced the once-standard reading of *Moby-Dick* in which, as Pease puts it, 'Ishmael proves his freedom by opposing Ahab's totalitarian will' (Pease, 'Moby-Dick and the Cold War', in Michaels and Pease, eds, *American Renaissance Reconsidered,* p. 113).

16. Russell Reising, *The Unusable Past: Theory and the Study of American Literature* (New York: Methuen, 1986), pp. 17–18.

17. Gregory Jay, *America the Scrivener: Deconstruction and the Subject of Literary History* (Ithaca, N.Y.: Cornell University Press, 1990), p. 241; hereafter cited in the text as *AS.*

18. Leslie Fiedler, *Love and Death in the American Novel* (New York: Stein and Day, 1960), p. 29.

19. Lionel Trilling, *The Liberal Imagination: Essays on Literature and Society* (New York: Doubleday, 1950), p. 20.

20. See Frederick Crews's introduction to *The Critics Bear It Away,* in which he cedes this point to the New Americanists, crediting them with asking the question, 'How did formalism and national chauvinism reach their strange entente – whereby, for example, the anti-abolitionist politics of Nathaniel Hawthorne could be overlooked while his aesthetic greatness was located in New Critical ironies and paradoxes beyond the reach of a mere "propagandist" like Harriet Beecher Stowe? These are essential questions, and their effect on academic discussion of American literature and on most of us who deal professionally

with American literature has been far-reaching.' As we will see below, though, Crews's praise of New Americanists comes at a price.

21. Nina Baym, 'Melodramas of Beset Manhood: How Theories of American Fiction Exclude Women Authors', *Feminism and American Literary History* (New Brunswick, N.J.: Rutgers University Press, 1992), p. 9.

22. See Houston A. Baker, Jr, *Blues, Ideology, and Afro-American Literature: A Vernacular Theory* (Chicago: University of Chicago Press, 1984), esp. pp. 26–56.

23. Judith Lowder Newton, 'History as Usual? Feminism and the "New Historicism"', in H. Aram Veeser, ed., *The New Historicism* (New York: Routledge, 1989); hereafter cited in the text.

24. Brook Thomas, 'The New Historicism and Other Old-Fashioned Topics', in Veeser, ed., *New Historicism,* p. 191.

25. As Gregory Jay writes, 'Foucault's late injunction that we must conceive of "power without the king" ... should not divert our attention from the fact that the king and the father quite often possess it and its technology' (*AS,* p. 244).

26. Here I am drawing on the recent argument forwarded by the Chicago Cultural Studies Group, which seeks to restore political specificity to the cultural left's imperative to 'politicize' the production of knowledge: 'If politicization erases the boundary between the academy and public discourse', they write, 'the result will not be a gain in relevance but the loss of the very ideal sought by politicization: the ideal of multiple cultural spaces all protected from invasion by each other or by the state.' Thus, as the CCSG concludes, 'the context of civil society is so thoroughly assumed in the structure of academic discourse that it tends to go unacknowledged and unthematized. ... [T]he boundary drawn in the civil-society tradition between the state and the realm of the arts is one that must be preserved in some form, and one that is under aggressive assault from the right. The "politicizing" called for in cultural studies, then, should not be allowed to obscure the basic autonomy of cultural production from regulation by the state', Chicago Cultural Studies Group, 'Critical Multiculturalism', *Critical Inquiry,* vol. 18, no. 3 (1992), pp. 534–5.

9

Disuniting America Again

The aggregation of ethnicities that composes the United States at the end of the twentieth century differs both in degree and in kind from that of the previous *fin de siècle;* and yet our current controversies over multiculturalism are in one respect identical to those of the late nineteenth century, insofar as they continue to turn on the argument that American citizens must shed their ethnic particularities in order to participate fully in the imagined community of the nation. Even those of us who dissent from this argument have nevertheless taken it as our starting point, and if we're to move the discussion forward at this late hour, it's clear that we'll have to assert American multiculturalism as something more than the politics of ethnic inclusion. The question facing us today, therefore, is whether liberalism can provide the means for forging a new common sense about our own multiculturalism, and what 'multiculturalism' will consequently mean in the sublunary realm of public policy. This is not a question of whether we as a nation will 'acknowledge' our multiculturalism, for to do so would be only to recognize the obvious; nor is it a question of simply substituting one metaphor for another – 'salad bowl' or 'mosaic' for 'melting pot'. Nor, finally, is it a question of whether we will be 'one' or 'many'. The question is, rather, more basic than any of these: what *kind* of national unity is necessary to the functioning of a putatively democratic and nominally egalitarian society?

Unless we press this question, we're likely to remain in the idealist fog that has obscured so much of the multiculturalism debate to date, wherein one camp insists that American unity depends on the repudiation or marginalization of individual and group difference, and the other camp insists that American unity depends on the acknowledgment, toleration, or celebration of individual and group difference. It's axiomatic on the left, by now, that both of these formulations are empty unless they interrogate the meaning and production of 'difference'. But such left critiques, in putting

necessary pressure on the meaning of difference, have so far left unques-
tioned the meaning of 'unity' – except to argue that ideas of national unity
are the stuff of conservative, nostalgic fantasy. In what follows, then, I'm
going to address matters of unity and difference as they appear on the
terrain intersected by multiculturalism, liberalism, and public education
policy. I think it's no accident that the most volatile and destructive
clashes between liberalism and multiculturalism have occurred in policy
debates over public schooling, and, accordingly, I'll begin my discussion
at the well-traveled site of one of these clashes, Arthur Schlesinger, Jr's *The
Disuniting of America*.

One hundred years ago, the second great wave of European immigration threatened to disunite America – insofar as our self-definition rested
on an Anglo-Saxon (or, at best, northern and western European) birth
narrative. 'By the end of the nineteenth century', writes Marcus Klein in
Foreigners,

> ... the known past was for Americans at the least hugely miscellaneous, in-
> cluding among other problematics the American cultural past itself, which
> had been so largely defined by its discountenancing of an anterior past. The
> traditional past could no longer authorize the nontraditional present because
> there could no longer be general agreement as to what the traditional past
> was.[1]

The result, in a nascent public educational system whose very existence depended on the elaboration of a new conception of the nation-state
(in which education would be universal, compulsory and free), was
something called 'Americanization', whereby the new immigrant populations from southern and eastern Europe were forcibly interpellated as
'Americans'. Americanization, as instantiated in New York City public
schools, involved an interventionist effort to prevent recent immigrants
from identifying with those of similar national origin – including their
families – and to encourage them to identify instead with American ideals. The difficulty here was that these 'American ideals' had to be devised
on the spot, specifically for the project of Americanization – and, by negation, against the presumed national ideals and characteristics of the
new immigrants. As Klein puts it, 'immigration prompted invention of
"Americanization," and Americanization in turn prompted the invention
of a set of terms by which America could be regarded as having some
kind of predefinition. The terms of the predefinition were potentially
meaningful, obviously, by the amount that they distinguished Americans
from immigrants' (p. 28).

Since we hear so often these days about the necessity – and heuristic value – of self-consciously embracing fictional, provisional accounts of 'identity', it's important to realize that the Americanness coded in 'Americanization' was understood even by its proponents to be a fiction. The people practicing strategic American essentialism, in this case, were not marginalized subaltern groups but cultural leaders with the power to set the national agenda. As Nina Baym has written, the institutionalization of American literature in public schools, as a narrative of Puritan origins and high moral destiny, was part of this project of 'forging' a national character to be imprinted on immigrants:

> The Whig project of installing New England as the original site of the American nation had been designed to unify the unformed and scattered American people under the aegis of New England by creating a national history anchored in that region. Conservative New England leaders knew all too well that the nation was an artifice and that no single national character undergirded it. And they insisted passionately that peace and progress called for a commonalty that, if it did not exist, had at once to be invented.[2]

'It did not take long', continues Baym, 'for intellectual leaders to see that the public, or common, schools might be an important agent in this process' (p. 460).

The sound of Americanization is worth listening to again at the end of this, the American century; and I'll quote one important proponent of Americanization at length, partly to ask whether we haven't heard remarkably similar formulations lately. The author of the passage in question is Ellwood Cubberley, a Stanford professor of education. As he wrote in a 1909 monograph entitled *Changing Conceptions of Education:*

> These southern and eastern Europeans are of a very different type from the north Europeans who preceded them. Illiterate, docile, lacking in self-reliance and initiative, and not possessing the Anglo-Teutonic conceptions of law, order, and government, their coming has served to dilute tremendously our national stock, and to corrupt our civic life. ... Everywhere these people tend to settle in groups or settlements, and to set up here their national manners, customs, and observances, our task is to break up these groups or settlements, to assimilate and amalgamate these people as a part of our American race, and to implant in their children, so far as can be done, the Anglo-Saxon conception of righteousness, law and order, and popular government, and to awaken in them a reverence for our democratic institutions and for those things in our national life which we as a people hold to be of abiding worth.[3]

Confronted with words such as these, we may need to remind ourselves that Americanization was, for its time, a liberal (and liberalizing)

227

project; it operated in the public sphere as a counter to (even when it sounded indistinguishable from) nativism and recrudescent Know-Nothingism, which considered immigrants to be de facto unassimilable to American society. In fact, as Lawrence Cremin writes in *The Transformation of the School* (1961), 'Cubberley's is a typical progressive tract of the era.'[4] The opponents of Americanization, on the other hand, were the forces that enacted the Chinese Exclusion Act of 1883 and the punitively anti-immigrant Johnson-Reed Act of 1924.[5] In vivid contrast to such reactionary particularism, Americanization assumed that in promulgating a common culture, one necessarily fostered the liberal ideal of equal opportunity – regardless of whether the immigrant populations subject to Americanization agreed.

And because Schlesinger harks back to so many figures in the assimilationist tradition, his critics have been tempted to paint him in this unflattering light, as an uncritical celebrant of what British commentator James Bryce called in 1888 'the amazing solvent power which American institutions, habits, and ideas exercise upon newcomers of all races ... quickly dissolving and assimilating the foreign bodies that are poured into her mass' (quoted approvingly by Schlesinger).[6] But linking Schlesinger to his Americanizing antecedents, however necessary this may be, remains an academic exercise in the narrow sense of the word.[7] His argument is important today, and must be addressed by progressives, not only because it has done important cultural work in delegitimizing multiculturalism, but especially because it demonstrates the persistence of the late-nineteenth-century liberal conception of public schools in a late-twentieth-century political climate in which public schooling itself is under attack.

It's well known that Schlesinger's argument grows out of a specific curricular dispute, namely, the two reports issued by the task forces appointed by New York State Commissioner of Education Thomas Sobol – reports that called for sweeping revisions in the history curricula of New York's public schools. It's hardly an exaggeration to say that Schlesinger was placed on the second task force (reportedly at the insistence of Diane Ravitch) precisely in order to dissent from its eventual findings, whatever these might be. When he did, in fact, weigh in with a long dissent – in which he was joined by Columbia historian Kenneth T. Jackson and Paul Gagnon of the University of Massachusetts at Boston – he provided the multicultural curriculum's critics with the material they needed to cast doubt on the entire enterprise of curricular revision. Schlesinger's *Disuniting*, in other words, is and was a political 'intervention' – and a largely successful one at that. By way of a process that has become depressingly familiar to those of us on the left, Schlesinger's critics – especially his black critics – are now ritually required to 'distance' themselves from Afrocentric essentialists such as Leonard Jeffries, just as David Dinkins must 'distance' himself from Al Sharpton, Jesse Jackson is required to 'distance' himself from Louis Farrakhan, and every other black political figure must 'distance' himself or herself from Jesse Jackson.

Even though I'm not black, my own criticism of Schlesinger doubtless has to distance itself from ethnic particularisms and essentialisms as well. Writing as a third-generation French-Canadian/second-generation Irish white male with a few milliliters of Native American Indian blood from about five generations back, however, I cannot possibly propose or support theories of ethnic purity and racial essence. Nor, for that matter, do I have anything important to lose (precisely *because* I am white) by reasserting my commitment to anti-essentialism.

From my perspective, then, if multiculturalism necessarily involved any such theory of racial or ethnic essence, it would well deserve Schlesinger's critique. But *Disuniting,* as many readers have noted, isn't really about multiculturalism at all; it's about Afrocentrism as Schlesinger conceives it, an extremist Afrocentrism he describes as a 'cult of ethnicity' (p. 40) devoted to a brand of 'biological determinism' that claims that 'the possession of black skin creates a unique black mentality and character' (p. 44) traceable to ancient West African or Egyptian societies. On the narrow question thus presented, liberals and leftists can hardly disagree with Schlesinger: none of us can support a pedagogical program that celebrates a glorious, homogeneous African – or European – past. Similarly, many of us may well be uneasy about separatisms that explicitly reject the political and legal ideals enunciated in the Constitution (such as an 'Ed Meese' separatism hostile to civil liberties, perhaps), for such separatisms undermine not merely the dream of a common culture but the ideal of a common *society,* by attacking the procedural means by which we adjudicate political disputes. And ever since liberalism at last succeeded in writing (and passing) the Thirteenth, Fourteenth, Fifteenth and Nineteenth Amendments to the Constitution, these procedural means have in principle been available to all.[8]

Schlesinger, however, steadfastly refuses to distinguish between 'common culture' and 'common society'. Like many proponents of universalism, he simply assumes that the former is necessary to the latter, and his propensity for self-contradiction on this score is remarkable. He can argue on one page that America's inherent multiculturalism makes it possible for 'unifying political ideals [to] coexist so easily and cheerfully with diversity in social and cultural values' (p. 81) – thus temporarily enabling the kind of multiculturalism he ostensibly set out to oppose. And yet he can lapse back, only one page later, into arguing that 'the bonds of cohesion

229

... that hold the republic together' consist of 'common ideals, common political institutions, common language, common culture, common fate' (p. 82). Where 'language' and 'culture' had been safely distinguished from 'political ideals' on the previous page (it's all right to observe Sun Yat-Sen's birthday so long as you accept the separation of powers), here they are all one and the same (the parents of Texas children who talk about Zapata in Spanish at the dinner table will undermine the ideals of self-realization and equal opportunity).

This is nothing less than the foundational slippage on which most of our recent jeremiads depend: in conflating *culture* with *society*, advocates of an American (really, a United States) 'common culture' argue that our very nation will dissolve, that multiculturalism will of itself provoke a secession crisis precipitating the US into Balkanized regions and ethnic factions unless we reaffirm that we hold some mental products – ideals, beliefs, information, proverbs, dreams – in common. I'm not saying that 'society' and 'culture' should be completely disentangled from each other, of course; any useful sense of American 'culture' must also include some account of the social and political fabric of the nation. But most of multiculturalism's critics, Schlesinger chief among them, seem so thoroughly unwilling to grant 'culture' *any* relative autonomy from 'society' that they characteristically fail (or refuse) to understand what's at stake when multiculturalists such as Molefi Kete Asante reply that 'there is a common American *society*, which is quite different from a common American culture.'[9] I think it's instructive that even so controversial and seemingly 'separatist' a figure as Asante does not dispute the existence of the social bonds of the nation – though Schlesinger does not acknowledge even this much. Similarly, it has apparently done no good for multiculturalism's advocates to point out that 'common' cultures are by no means unified cultures. Over four years ago, for instance, Robert Pattison replied to E. D. Hirsch's *Cultural Literacy* by noting that

> every Irish person north and south knows the date of the Battle of the Boyne, when Protestant King Billy whipped Catholic King James. This was the Gettysburg of Irish history, and every Irish person can debate the high and absolute values at stake in that conflict. We know where that universal knowledge and that universal dialogue have ended. Similiar observations obtain in the Middle East. The Arab students are undoubtedly better versed in their culture than their American counterparts are, and many times more adept at arguing the primary values on which their culture rests. Yet I would not hold up Ireland or the Middle East as models for the education of the young in postindustrial societies.[10]

The relations between 'society' and 'culture', then, must be matters for interrogation and negotiation, in brief monographs and in national politics. For if we simply equate society with culture (in the United States or any other nation) as does Schlesinger, we reproduce precisely the blood-and-soil doctrines Schlesinger intends to reject: we reinforce the discourse of ethnic absolutism – which finds its most extreme manifestation in ethnic clensing. Writing in the United Kingdom, where nativist traditions of 'Englishness' continue to bump up against the bodies of British citizens of color, Jamaican-born Englishman Stuart Hall insists that the legal and political rights of a nation's citizens cannot be predicated on the 'cultural identity' of groups or individuals:

> far from collapsing the complex questions of cultural identity and issues of social and political rights, what we need now is *greater distance between them*. We need to be able to insist that rights of citizenship and the incommensurabilities of cultural difference are respected and that *the one is not made a condition of the other*.[11]

There is, of course, no ready equation for determining the ideal relationship between cultural identity and social-political rights. But few important books on the subject are as confused as *The Disuniting of America* about the conceptual relations among race, ethnicity, and nation. On page 9, we might read Schlesinger proudly quoting Frederick Jackson Turner's famous argument that 'in the crucible of the frontier the immigrants were Americanized, liberated, and fused into a mixed race, English in neither nationality nor characteristics'; but on page 8 we had read Schlesinger insisting that 'for better or worse, the white Anglo-Saxon Protestant tradition was for two centuries – and in crucial respects still is – the dominant influence on American culture and society.' Apparently the United States can shed its English 'nationality' and 'characteristics' only so long as the Anglo-Saxon tradition remains dominant. Similarly, his discussion of 'nationalism' creates a strange *trompe l'oeil* whereby nationalism is construed as a threat to the American nation:

> Nationalism broke up the Soviet empire and now threatens to break up the Soviet Union itself. In the third world, nationalism, having overthrown Western colonialism, launches a horde of new states, large and micro, often at each other's throats in reenacting ancient quarrels of history.
>
> Within nation-states, nationalism takes the form of ethnicity or tribalism. In country after country across the third world – India, Burma, Sri Lanka, Indonesia, Iraq, Ethiopia, Nigeria, Angola, Trinidad, Guyana – ethnic groups struggle for power and, in desperate cases, for survival. The ethnic upsurge in America, far from being unique, partakes of the global fever. (p. 21)

This is a puzzling passage, to say the least. Is it simply a lament for the passing of all central authorities, even Soviet and colonialist authorities (breaking up is hard to do)? Is it meant to equate Ukrainian and Lithuanian nationalism with Serbian 'ethnic cleansing'? Is it meant to construe Kurdish opposition to Saddam Hussein as a symptom of a 'fever' that might spread to South Central Los Angeles? Why might anyone convolve the two senses of 'nationalism' Schlesinger employs here – the political nationalism that defeated European and Soviet imperialism and the cultural nationalism that glorifies the essential characteristics of racial or religious identity? What, finally, is this passage doing in a text whose goal is to overwhelm ethnic particularism with an overtly nationalist appeal to core American values and ideals?

The Disuniting of America will not respond to questions of such particularity; it seems, on the contrary, determined to resist them. For the purpose of the book is to construe all multiculturalist historical revisionism as a threat to the integrity of the body politic, and to achieve this purpose Schlesinger invokes whatever image of dissolution comes readiest to hand, even if he thereby unwittingly asks us to imagine the horror of a corrosive nationalism that 'broke up the Soviet empire and now threatens to break up the Soviet Union itself.' 'Ethnic ideologues', he concludes, '... have set themselves against the old American ideal of assimilation' (p. 78) – an ideal that, as *Disuniting* itself had earlier remarked in its brief and rather odd treatment of Horace Kallen, is itself not universal in American history.[12] And in setting themselves against assimilation, these ethnic ideologues have 'filled the air with recrimination and rancor and have remarkably advanced the fragmentation of American life' (p. 78).

To argue that these last words would apply more appropriately to the Reagan and Bush administrations than to advocates of multiculturalism is not to invoke the standard left *tu quoque* (no, *you* fragmented things *first*); it is, instead, to gesture toward the deafening silences in Schlesinger's text, which typically gives short shrift to the forces of disunion other than multiculturalism – such as slavery. One of the nonce controversies of the revised New York curriculum, for instance, involved the 'issue' of whether slaves would be called slaves, or 'enslaved persons' (presumably to remind students that the slaves were indeed people). This is exactly the kind of PC nominalism that gets press attention, and the 'enslaved persons' moniker provoked the usual amount of media derision. But to hear Schlesinger on slavery, by contrast, is to provoke a *real* issue: 'The West needs no lectures', he writes, 'on the superior virtue of those "sun people" who sustained slavery until Western imperialism abolished it' (p. 76). If future generations are going to understand what's offensively wrong about this passage, they will need to know more about slave rebellions in this hemisphere than Schlesinger's peremptory dismissal reveals. Perhaps by incorporating more information about slave resistance in the high school curriculum, one might obviate both the Schlesingerian will to (white) Western self-congratulation and the semantic nitpicking of a phrase like 'enslaved persons': for no doubt if one were to ask David Walker, Nat Turner, Gabriel Prosser or Toussaint L'Ouverture how they want to be described, they might well reply that, given their druthers, they'd most like to have been considered *free*.

Just as Schlesinger's offhand swipe at Leonard Jeffries depends on the prior production of an ignorance under which it is appropriate to blame Africans for 'sustaining' the Atlantic slave trade, so does *The Disuniting of America* more generally seek to produce and license ignorance about multiculturalism. 'The excesses of Afrocentrism are now threatening to discredit the whole field of African-American studies', claims Schlesinger (p. 53), but I think we can best read this ominous sentence as an instance of projection. For it is Schlesinger who is doing the threatening and discrediting, using the rhetorical excesses of a handful of Afrocentrists as the stick with which to beat not only 'the whole field of African-American studies' but any field in which multiculturalism has made significant inroads. Hence Schlesinger's otherwise superfluous attacks on higher education, for which he draws largely on second- and third-hand sources (a remarkable practice for so experienced a historian) such as Dinesh D'Souza, Roger Kimball, Mona Charen, Christina Hoff Sommers, Alan Charles Kors, John Taylor's PC piece in *New York* magazine, and conservative journals such as the *American Scholar, Measure* and *Academic Questions*.

As I suggested earlier, Schlesinger's *Disuniting* is less important in itself than for the cultural work it performs as a licensing text, a document that serves to authorize the backlash against multiculturalism in the culture at large, and that is intended partly to be cited as a source book of multiculturalism's offenses against traditional ideals of 'liberal' education. On this front, however, we are on treacherous ground. We should not dismiss *Disuniting* because it is 'liberal'; we should criticize it, rather, because it is not liberal enough. I cite Schlesinger one last time for illustration:

> The belated recognition of the pluralistic character of American society has had a bracing impact on the teaching and writing of history. The women's-liberation movement, the civil rights movement, the ethnic upsurge, and other forms of group self-assertion forced historians to look at old times in new ways. Scholars now explore such long-neglected fields as the history of women, of immigration, of blacks, Indians, Hispanics, and other minorities. Voices long silent ring out of the darkness of history. (pp. 32–3)

Nothing, certainly, could be wrong with hearing these voices. But a great deal depends on what we will allow those voices to say about the teaching and writing of history as conducted to date, before this 'belated recognition' took place. For traditionalist historians such as Schlesinger, when revisionist historians produce material that explicitly or implicitly indicts the writing of traditionalist history, it appears that their work is not 'bracing'; it is divisive. The point has been made time and again, but I find particularly eloquent Alice Kessler-Harris's recent restatement of the principle as it has worked in American Studies:

> The twin rebellion against conceptions of common identity and the new pluralism proved to be crucial in the development of a relational stance. Black history, for example, which had not proved especially troublesome when it evoked the moral possibilities of Frederick Douglass, Harriet Tubman, or Martin Luther King, became contentious when historians started to ask how it had shaped the white mind and the dominant economy. In that guise, it raised questions not only about a common vision, but about the role of domination in constructing economic and political democracy as well. The study of women, hardly a threat when it spoke to the accomplishments of great women like Jane Addams, Eleanor Roosevelt, or even Elizabeth Cady Stanton, created a backlash when it asked about how a gender system sustained racial and class divisions. From that standpoint, the study of women constituted an attack on the very definition of 'American', identifying as masculine (rather than universal) metaphors that derived from such stalwarts as Whitman and Melville, and raising questions about the gendered content of individualism, self-reliance, pragmatism, and optimism.[13]

Along similar lines, the challenge for Women's Studies and African American Studies programs, over the past ten years, has been the challenge to institutionalize the liberal reforms on which they were founded: traditionalists have largely (though not, as we have been reminded of late, entirely) granted the right of such programs to exist, but they balk at the idea that students should actually be *required* to take any courses pertaining to women or minorities. Here, then, we run up against the limits of the liberal rhetoric of 'inclusion': Schlesinger's 'voices long silent', like the institutional apparatus that has recovered many of those voices, will be authorized only so long as they are bracing from the margins, only so long as they do not directly threaten the center.

It would be a grievous error, nonetheless, to construe this impasse over multiculturalism as an opposition between liberals and radicals, where liberals argue for a nonconfrontational inclusiveness and radicals urge the wholesale transformation of everything by everybody. The contrast presented here seems instead to be a contrast between weak and strong forms of liberal reformism itself: one, a reformism that amounts to token change and ghettoized (but bracing) new forms of history and intellectual inquiry; the other, a reformism that modifies the center and changes the terms on which 'inclusion' will hereafter operate. Need I point out that it is this latter form of reformism that has provided the social basis for our recent intellectual transformations? That multiculturalism, like feminism, would not be so strong a factor in contemporary educational policy had not the United States finally begun, in the wake of the Civil Rights Movement and campus demonstrations, to put into practice its ideal, long honored only in the breach, of education as a 'compensatory' mechanism operating toward equal opportunity in unequal social circumstances? Strong reformism is not only our condition of possibility; it must also be our *modus operandi*. We need, therefore, to think past the liberalism that Schlesinger fails to live up to, and to ask instead how strong reformism can help us realize a multiculturalism that does not seek mere accommodation with a hypothetical 'center' (whether traditional history, university curricula, or America's 'common culture'), but a broad institutional transformation of the 'center' as well. And what we miss, if we continue to construe multiculturalism only as a set of intellectual options and curricular imperatives, is the necessity to articulate multiculturalism to the economics of school funding and school policy.

Kessler-Harris rightly concludes that 'we need to see the struggle over multiculturalism as a tug of war over who gets to create the public culture' (p. 310). But since we – that is, most of Schlesinger's critics to date – are academics doing cultural work in academic institutions, we sometimes forget that the public culture is not created solely by people who win academic tugs of war. As intellectual workers located primarily in higher education, and having so strong a professional investment in what Alvin Gouldner calls the 'culture of critical discourse', we're all too likely to understand multiculturalism and the public culture as matters of 'belief' rather than as matters of social 'condition'.[14] But you don't have to be a Marxist to agree that 'condition' helps to condition belief, and that public education exists elsewhere than in the eye of the beholder. Indeed, thanks in part to the fact that Schlesinger's book was first published by Christopher Whittle's 'Larger Agenda Series', *The Disuniting of America* reminded me of something Schlesinger's idealism never mentions, something about which its silence is paradoxically most telling: the greatest threat to our public schools, in the 1990s, does not come from Afrocentrists. Nor, despite their underreported reign of terror over high school bookshelves, do Christian fundamentalists constitute the threat of the moment.[15] Rather, the most successful opponent and critic of public schools today is Christopher Whittle himself. In what must be the most blistering account of

Whittledom to date, Jonathan Kozol has argued that the success of Whittle's Edison Project, a 'private alternative' to public schools, would mean disaster for public education – especially if the Edison Project were combined with a Federal voucher system to privatize primary education, which is exactly what Reaganite conservatives such as John Chubb and Chester Finn have urged. Kozol writes:

> if [Chubb's] goals should someday be achieved, what we have known as public education will be granted a new definition and a different role in our society. What is now regarded as a right will come to be seen as just one more commercial product – or, more properly, a line of differentiated products. Whatever common bonds still hold together cities and communities are likely to be weakened or dissolved. As parents scramble to get children into one of Whittle's schools – or, for that matter, any other 'voucher school' – they will by necessity view almost every other parent as a rival. They will feel no obligation to raise tax-support for public schools attended by their neighbors' children. Instead of fighting for systematic excellence and equity for all, we will have taught them to advance their own kids at whatever cost to other people's children.[16]

This, then, is the primary reason I refuse to close this essay with a ready-to-hand excoriation of liberals (whose pluralist rhetoric of inclusion falls short of the demands of multiculturalism, et cetera): I do not want to see a world in which we have finally theorized multiculturalism adequately at just the moment the Congress passes 'choice' vouchers and Whittle establishes his shadow educational system. We cannot talk for long or in good conscience about multiculturalism in American education, in other words, without noting the persistence with which wealthy school districts have sustained segregation in American public education, and the inhuman fiscal policies that have ensured the continuous impoverishment of schools attended wholly by black or Hispanic schoolchildren. When Kozol writes in *Savage Inequalities* that 'in public schooling, social policy has been turned back almost one hundred years', he's not referring to a sudden reappearance in East St. Louis of warmed-over policies of Americanization; he's suggesting, instead, that public schools have been reduced to a state in which adherence to the principles enunciated in *Plessy* v. *Ferguson* would actually be an improvement.[17]

People who paid even the slightest attention to the 1992 elections will recall that the right, having tried for twelve years to destroy public education, now runs against what it calls the 'failure' of American public schools, even as a train of conservative Secretaries of Education – from Lamar Alexander to Lauro Cavazos back to William Bennett – insists that funding is irrelevant to the success of public education. In such stormy political weather as this, liberals have a crucial role to play in educational policy, and it consists largely of supporting American children's right to a public education system unmarked by savage inequalities, and of maintaining higher education policies that make college as widely available as possible. This involves lobbying for tax initiatives, some of which might even impoverish liberals themselves (myself included), to make state taxes more progressive, and education funding less dependent on lotteries and property taxes. To engage in mundane – and fundamental – local policy struggles such as these *without* the aid of liberal constituencies (not to speak of fostering active opposition to liberals) is to treat American public education as if its existence were beyond question, as if there were no way conservatives could shrink the franchise, as if it only remained for us to talk about multicultural theory and curricular procedure.

I hope we do not need to remind ourselves that things are quite otherwise. Indeed, the real danger posed by *The Disuniting of America,* and the real reason why its relation to public education reform is so disturbing, is that the book ultimately threatens to delegitimate not only multiculturalism but, more widely, the public school system in which multiculturalism has so far won a hearing. For whether or not Schlesinger himself intends his monograph quite this way, *Disuniting* carries with it a potent warning: insofar as American public schools decline to serve as vehicles for a late-nineteenth-century model of assimilationism, august and distinguished figures like Schlesinger will join the ranks of conservatives undermining public support for public education sooner than countenance curricular revision. There is much in Schlesinger's book, assuredly, that suggests he does not see his project in such terms; but there is little to reassure us that Schlesinger will not caricature *all* curricular revision as biologically determinist Afrocentrism. Nowhere in *Disuniting,* for example, is there any indication that the 1991 New York State curriculum report was considered, by the vast majority of its authors (including prominent conservative Nathan Glazer), to be an acceptable compromise document;[17] and nowhere in *Disuniting* is there any discussion whatsoever of the shameful material conditions in which most urban public schools are forced to operate. On the contrary, Schlesinger goes so far, at one crucial and summary point, as to blame Afrocentrists themselves for the separate and unequal conditions of American public schools, when he writes that ethnic ideologues, having 'set themselves against the old American ideal of assimilation', have 'made a certain progress in transforming the United States into a more segregated society' (p. 78). It is not clear what material evidence has led Schlesinger to this conclusion (since our contemporary Afrocentrisms postdate the phenomenon of white flight), but it may be that the specter of black separatism, like Allan Bloom's dystopian vision of black students sitting together in the back of the classroom, is so potent as to overwhelm the census.

The political vision bodied forth in *The Disuniting of America*, then, provides for us a cautionary tale – an exemplum of how the academic left, to secure its various forms of curricular change, will have to form differentiated coalitions with liberals and moderates on a range of issues central to American education. Weak forms of liberal reformism are predicated on the insistence that immigrants will be 'assimilated to our customs, measures and laws: in a word, soon become *one people*' (George Washington, quoted in Schlesinger, p. 6). In such an assimilationism, 'we' remain untouched; 'they' become 'one' by becoming assimilated *to us*. Plainly, between multiculturalism and this kind of liberalism, there can be no fruitful exchange. But even those liberals made uneasy by multiculturalism may nevertheless have a part to play in fending off the privatization of education, on grounds where progressives and liberals share a general rhetoric of rights and social responsibilities. For we can have no transformative multiculturalism in educational policy at all if we do not also establish and secure a renewed national commitment to the liberal, compensatory ideal of equal opportunity at every level of public education.

The hard right, with its customary sagacity in practical matters, knows full well the importance of the public schools: that's why Pat Robertson's tax-exempt Christian Coalition, together with the Cardinal O'Connor wing of the tax-exempt Catholic Church (conducting itself in social policy matters like a wholly owned subsidiary of the Coalition), has concentrated its energies on local school boards, local issues, local attacks on multicultural curricula, gay and lesbian citizens, and 'secular humanism'. It is time liberals and leftists in higher education took this sublunary terrain as seriously as the Christian Coalition – that is, as seriously as it deserves. The disuniting of America can most effectively be realized, as Kozol insists, by the dismantling of a public education system that has been until now the cornerstone of the liberal consensus bridging the imperatives of democracy with the savage inequalities of capitalism. However liberals and moderates and the academic left may disagree on the desirability of a common culture, there should be no mistaking their common cause in defending the social ground on which all further theories and practices of multicultural education must build.

Notes

1. Marcus Klein, *Foreigners: The Making of American Literature 1900–1940* (Chicago: University of Chicago Press, 1981), p. 4; hereafter cited in the text.

2. Nina Baym, 'Early Histories of American Literature: A Chapter in the Institution of New England', *American Literary History,* vol. 1, no. 3 (1989), p. 460; hereafter cited in the text.

3. Ellwood Cubberley, *Changing Conceptions of Education* (Boston: Houghton Mifflin, 1909), pp. 15–16. When Cubberley incorporated this passage into his longer and more magisterial work of 1919, *Public Education in the United States,* World War I had rendered problematic his invocation of 'Anglo-Teutonic conceptions of law, order, and government'. The 1919 text, accordingly, appeals instead to 'Anglo-*Saxon* conceptions of righteousness, liberty, law, order, public decency, and government' (*Public Education in the United States: A Study and Interpretation of American Educational History* [Boston: Houghton Mifflin, 1919], p. 338). Here as elsewhere, the ascription of praiseworthy characteristics to individual national 'characters' has proven to be a slippery affair.

4. Lawrence Cremin, *The Transformation of the School: Progressivism in American Education, 1876–1957* (New York: Knopf, 1961), p. 68 n7.

5. I presume that the Chinese Exclusion Act is self-explanatory, but the intricate machinations of the Johnson-Reed Act may require a word or two. It replaced the National Origins Quota Act of 1921, which had proposed a quota system under which the number of new immigrants from any nation (over a three-year period) could not exceed 3 percent of the number of people from that nation already living in the United States in 1910. The Johnson-Reed Act of 1924, however, turned back the clock still further, fixing immigration at 2 percent of any nation's emigrants living in the United States in 1890. As Howard Zinn tabulates the figures, this meant 'no African country could send more than 100 people; 100 was the limit for China, for Bulgaria, for Palestine; 34,007 could come from England or Northern Ireland, but only 3,845 from Italy; 51,227 from Germany, but only 124 from Lithuania; 28,567 from the Irish Free State, but only 2,248 from Russia.' Howard Zinn, *A People's History of the United States* (New York: Harper & Row, 1980), p. 373.

6. Quoted in Arthur M. Schlesinger, Jr, *The Disuniting of America* (Knoxville, Tenn.: Whittle Direct Books, 1991), p. 7; hereafter cited in the text.

7. For an incisive commentary on Schlesinger's links to a nativist tradition he ostensibly disclaims, see Stanley Fish, 'Bad Company', *Transition,* no. 56 (1992), pp. 60–67, a review of Schlesinger alongside two other recent 'anti-multiculturalist' books of more explicit hue, Richard Brookhiser's *The Way of the WASP: How It Made America, and How It Can Save It, So to Speak* (New York: Free Press, 1991), and Lawrence Auster's *The Path to National Suicide: An Essay on Immigration and Multiculturalism* (American Immigration Control Foundation, 1990).

8. The Thirteenth Amendment (ratified in 1865) outlaws slavery and involuntary servitude; the first section of the Fourteenth (1868) prevents states from denying citizens due process of law and equal protection under the laws; the Fifteenth (1870) extended to black men the right to vote; the Nineteenth (1920) extended the franchise to women. I do not mean to suggest, however, that these amendments were always already contained in the seeds of the nation's original founding principles, as if they merely had to be 'added on' to a democratic discourse of citizenship that was firmly in place by 1787. For an instructive complication of this account of the American democratic polity, showing how 'the American legal, legislative, and political tradition itself has carved out a polity riven with divisions and exclusions' (p. 144), see John Brenkman, 'The Citizen Myth', *Transition,* no. 60 (1993), pp. 138–44.

9. Molefi Kete Asante, 'Multiculturalism: An Exchange', rpt. in Berman, ed., *Debating P.C.,* p. 308.

10. Robert Pattison, 'The Stupidity Crisis', *ADE Bulletin,* vol. 89 (Spring 1988), p. 7.

11. Stuart Hall, 'Culture, Community, Nation', *Cultural Studies,* vol. 7, no. 3 (1993), pp. 360–61.

12. Schlesinger writes: 'Ethnic diversity, Kallen observed, enriches American civilization. He saw the nation not as one people, except in a political and administrative sense [i.e., as Schlesinger himself sets it out on p. 81], but rather 'as a federation or commonwealth of national cultures ... a democracy of nationalities, cooperating voluntarily and autonomously through common institutions ... a multiplicity in a unity, an orchestration of mankind.' This conception he came to call "cultural pluralism"'. It remains for Schlesinger to show what's wrong with this view, to adduce some evidence of how Kallen disunited America. Instead, he equivocates, claiming first that 'Kallen made his attack on Anglo-centered assimilation at a time when critics of the melting pot could reasonably assume the solidity of the overarching framework' (p. 13). Since Kallen made his 'attack' in 1915, hardly a stable moment for the American polity, Schlesinger quickly moves on to his next claim, that 'the gospel of cultural pluralism was at first largely confined to academics, intellectuals, and artists' (p. 13). Schlesinger's narrative then invokes, without any attribution of causality, a series of nativist movements that presumably followed from Kallen's cultural pluralism: 'a Red Scare directed largely against aliens, the rise of the anti-Catholic Ku Klux Klan, and a campaign, realized in the Immigration Act of 1924, to freeze the ethnic composition of the American people' (pp. 13–14). But although Schlesinger cannot plausibly attribute any of these to 'cultural pluralism', he concludes by narrating pluralism's inevitable demise, which apparently occurred when 'the Great Depression and the Second World War showed the desperate necessity of national cohesion within the frame of shared national ideals' (p. 14), thus defeating the evils not wrought by Kallen's cultural pluralism in the first place. Whatever we make of Kallen's own failings, Schlesinger's commitment to construing cultural pluralism as inherently 'disuniting' produces a very strange five paragraphs united only by the mirage of chronological progression.

13. Alice Kessler-Harris, 'Cultural Locations: Positioning American Studies in the Great Debate', *American Quarterly*, vol. 44, no. 3 (1992), p. 306; hereafter cited in the text.

14. See Alvin Gouldner, *The Future of Intellectuals and the Rise of the New Class* (London: Macmillan, 1979).

15. Whenever multiculturalism's opponents acknowledge the existence of the fundamentalist right, something fundamental to their project goes awry. Witness Diane Ravitch's warning against the multiculturalist 'politicization' of curricula: 'if education bureaucrats bend to the political and ideological winds, as is their wont, we can anticipate a generation of struggle over the content of the curriculum in mathematics, science, literature, and history. Demands for 'culturally relevant' studies, for ethnostudies of all kinds, will open the classroom to unending battles over whose version is taught, who gets credit for what, and which ethno-interpretation is appropriate. Only recently have districts begun to resist the demands of fundamentalist groups to censor textbooks and library books (and some have not yet begun to do so).' (Diane Ravitch, 'Multiculturalism: E Pluribus Plures', rpt. in Berman, *Debating P.C.,* p. 293.) The final sentence is a strict non sequitur. Perhaps Ravitch means to suggest that multiculturalism will bring on the kind of struggles provoked by fundamentalists, in which case Molefi Asante will reply that 'her strategy is to cast serious examinations of the curriculum as pressure groups, much like creationists in biology' (p. 303). But even if that's the case, her final sentence betrays the fact that political struggle over education is not a future conditional but a present indicative: since classrooms and curricula are already 'politicized', most effectively by the far right, Ravitch has no call to claim that political struggle over education policy is something 'we can *anticipate*' or that '*will* open the classroom to unending battles'.

16. Jonathan Kozol, 'Whittle and the Privateers', *Nation,* 21 September 1992, p. 277. Of course, the point I make in the previous note, regarding the oddity of Ravitch's use of the future conditional to describe public school conflict, is applicable here as well: as Kozol knows, whatever common bonds once held together cities and communities have already been strained to the breaking point by inequitable funding policies. No doubt, whatever else Reaganism has done to the nation, it has left us almost incapable of thinking about the 'common good', whether in education, health care, housing, or taxation. And it seems somehow sadly appropriate that in this free-market, atomizing culture of economic conservative-libertarianism, screeds about 'common culture' have become such a microindustry

among American intellectuals.

17. Jonathan Kozol, *Savage Inequalities: Children in America's Schools* (New York: Crown, 1991), p. 4.

18. As the *New York Times*'s coverage of the Sobol group indicated, defenders of the task force's report responded to Schlesinger's and Jackson's dissents by noting that both dissenters – and particularly Schlesinger – had been absent from most of the committee's discussions. (See Joseph Berger, 'Arguing about America', *New York Times*, 21 June 1991, pp. A1, B4; Sam Howe Verhovek, 'A New York Panel Urges Emphasizing Minority Cultures', *New York Times*, 20 June 1991 pp. A1, B2; and Verhovek, 'Plan to Emphasize Minority Cultures Ignites a Debate', *New York Times*, 21 June 1991, pp. A1, B4.) Glazer's statement claimed that 'the report does reject two extremes in the treatment of racial and ethnic diversity in American social studies', Americanization and separatism (Verhovek, 21 June, p. B4). Catherine Cornbleth, a professor of education at SUNY-Buffalo, was quoted as saying the new curriculum 'brings together both our commonalities and our differences. I'm not surprised that people who take extreme positions are disappointed' (Verhovek, 20 June, p. B2). In other words, we should not let Schlesinger's considerable reputation as a scholar blind us to the fact that his peers on the committee considered his dissent the work of an extremist.

Epilogue

Harvesting the Humanities

The profession of literary criticism at the end of the twentieth century is one in which every four hours, someone sits down to write a little brief on the function of criticism at the present time, or on what the humanities are for, or on how criticism was once powerful back in the days when it was done right. And yet few among of the public seem to have any idea what we're talking about. What might education in the humanities entail? Why might it matter whether one subscribes to one view of this education or another, Allan Bloom's or Henry Louis Gates's, Lynne Cheney's or mine? The bulk of the answers we've gotten so far indicates that most nonacademics don't have the faintest idea, even when they profess to care at all. The optimistic tone of some of the essays in this book may suggest to some of my readers that I write in deliberate ignorance of these answers, that I'm repressing or suppressing what I know about the unintelligibility of even our (or my) most 'accessible' work. As it happens, I'm reminded of the tenuous nature of 'public access' quite as often as any professional critic. But these reminders don't make me give up on the enterprise.

At the 1993 convention of the Midwest Modern Language Association, for instance, I was to deliver a paper called 'Postmodern Humanities: All Access, All Areas', wherein I noted, among other things, the public resistance to 'specialization' and 'professionalization' in the humanities as opposed to the sciences, which are usually given wide leeway in the hope that they will get us to the moon and put Tang on our breakfast tables. (That resistance, as we know, often takes the form of mockery of outlandish topics and paper titles at the MLA's annual convention.) My panel, organized by John Mowitt, was titled 'The Humanities and Public Accountability', so I figured it was appropriate for me to talk about how scholars in the humanities are expected to be accountable to damn near everyone for the content of their work. Fellow panelist Gerald Graff, however, trumped me by citing some research recently done by the MLA:

> The Modern Language Association recently commissioned a public relations firm to survey public perceptions of the humanities. Though the great majority of those interviewed claimed to have a favorable image of the humanities ... a substantial number associated the term with 'humanitarian' activities such as the prevention of cruelty to animals. Others who answered yes to the question of whether they themselves participated in the humanities listed 'singing in the shower' as an example of humanistic activity.[1]

Sure enough, that gave everyone in the room a good laugh, and considerable pause for thought as well. But it's hard to know what to do with this kind of information except to go home, flip on the computer, and mutter anew about the philistinism of the great unwashed.

One response I appreciate, forwarded with great aplomb by Bruce Robbins, holds that the idea of 'the public' is already internal to the discipline of English: thus, argues Robbins, literary critics inhabit a 'porous profession' in which they regularly assess the discipline from the perspective of hostile or indifferent 'outsiders' – as I'm doing now.[2] The difficulty with that answer, though, is that it 'textualizes' a mirage of the public that's always already there every time you sit down to write a brief on the function of criticism at the present time. I don't mean here to conjure up some naive notion of the 'real' public, but I do think it's worth reporting that as I was reading Robbins's book one morning in a breakfast restaurant in downtown Champaign (a restaurant where I have never seen anyone from the University of Illinois), I was asked by an affable waitress what I was 'studying'. Because I would have felt weird saying something like, 'the relation between professional intellectuals and the public, specifically the idea of "the public" presumed by intellectuals' attacks on professionalism', I paused for a moment, caught in a small crisis of professional intelligibility: here was a member of the public who *wasn't* already internal to my discipline.

And yet it would be a mistake to think that the relations between 'intellectuals' and 'the public' did not take comprehensible form in this exchange; the question presumed, of course, that I had some relation to the University, since few people eat breakfast at Carmon's while scribbling densely in the margins of books. My waitress naturally figured I was a student, and expected a one-word answer like 'psychology' or 'accounting'; 'cultural criticism' would have sounded pretentious or rude. But I did have the option of talking about the *form* of my 'labor' rather than its content. 'I've gotta do a book review, that's all. Six to eight pages on all this', I said, flipping through the book. She smiled: 'And you left it to the last minute.' I laughed, since that happened to be true. 'Yeah, but', I yeah-butted, 'the kids have had colds all month, and I'll steal the time whenever I can.' And *that* line of conversation, needless to say, is as intelligible to my neighbors as to my colleagues.

This was an odd case in that it juxtaposed Robbins' (and my) sense of 'public access' with a real live curious and friendly member of the nonacademic public, and no doubt my account of the exchange threatens to reify 'the public' in all kinds of sexist, classist, politically incorrect ways. I recount the story here only to prevent myself from adopting Robbins's argument about the disciplinary 'internality' of the 'external' public. I mean, I've met service staff who knew more about Baudrillard than I do, legal proofreaders armed with devastating critiques of Thomas Pynchon, and secretaries whose suspicions of cultural studies are based on the reasonably well-founded belief that (as one co-worker and K/S fan once put it) once the academics show up at the Star Trek conventions, the first thing they do is interview the novelty items.[3] My point is that although we can quote for ourselves all manner of depressing surveys demonstrating what our children, neighbors or parents don't know about who we are and what we do in the criticism factory, it doesn't necessarily follow that we have to describe ourselves as singing in the shower if we want to be intelligible to 'the public'.

One critical aspect of the problem of public access, as I see it, has less to do with 'the public' than with the self-appointed representatives of *vox populi* in the 'popular' press. Readers of magazines like *Rolling Stone, Details* or *The Source* can find decent discussions and reviews of academic and quasi-academic cultural work – work that the aging, ever-dwindling readerships of *Newsweek* and the *New York Times Book Review* will never see in those pages. In the fall of 1991, gay and lesbian studies were deftly handled in *Rolling Stone* by *VLS* editor Stacey D'Erasmo; Michael Eric Dyson wrote the lead record review for the October 1993 issue, and in fall 1992, the magazine's survey of academic courses on rock 'n roll mentioned the work of E. Ann Kaplan, Ann Cvetkovich and Andrew Ross. *Details*, slowly taking over the cultural functions of *Playboy* (minus the centerfolds) for the twentysomething men of the 1990s (what should I wear? what records should I buy?), reviewed Richard Grossman's *The Alphabet Man,* published by Fiction Collective 2 at Illinois State University and the University of Colorado. Ask yourself when you last saw the *TBR* review one of FC2's books. And *The Source,* the magazine of hip-hop music, culture and politics, has run reviews not only of Greg Tate's *Flyboy in the Buttermilk* and Nelson George's *Buppies, B-Boys, Baps and Bohos,* but of Houston Baker's *Black Studies, Rap, and the Academy* as well.[4] You can bet your Beavis and Butt-head that they did a better job of it than the *New Criterion,* too. Or the *Partisan Review,* or the *New Republic,* or the *Atlantic.* ...

When we challenge the terms of public access, then, we should be clear about *which* segments of the reading public aren't holding up their end of the bargain. In the 1990s, I suspect, it's precisely the highly educated, seemingly culturally literate public (or, more accurately, the publications that represent themselves and their audiences as members of that public) that's putting up the most resistance to contemporary cultural criticism from the universities. And this resistance, all too often, bespeaks nothing more noble than the will to ignorance. In this respect, the differences between *Rolling Stone* and *Newsweek* are vast, and the differences between the *New York Times* and the *New Criterion* can be negligible. Take for instance the 3 September 1993 *New York Times* editorial lampooning scholars who *interpret* Shakespeare, arguing instead that the purpose of reading Shakespeare is to memorize him:

> Did you think *King Lear* was about a relationship between father and daughters? *Please.* It's really about 'new forms of social organization and affective relationships.' In your naivete, did you believe the sonnets to be a great fistful of small gems, to be taken out and examined from different angles over the course of a lifetime? No, no, no. They merely 'articulate the frustration of language's indeterminacy.' And of course *The Tempest* is merely an allegory about colonialism. Everybody knows that.
>
> It's kind of nice that so many self-important people are paying attention to old Will, genius or not. But what does it mean to most of his hardy and doggedly loyal fans, who merely wish to keep turning up to drink in the delights of his spoken lines?
>
> ... It's a privileged but shrinking group who had at least one play, at least one sonnet, drummed into their heads as adolescents. They still go forth and find magic from that source.[5]

There's more in this vein, and worse, but this suffices to give you the general idea: academics are self-important 'myopic spoilsports' who insist on reading Shakespeare rather than simply enjoying him or memorizing his spoken lines (and everybody knows how much our teenagers love encountering the Bard by having him drummed into their heads in high school). In a way, this sorry editorial works as a kind of time capsule: the *Times,* having invested all its stock in some very old cultural technologies, holds firmly to the belief that English professors are – or should be – people who can quote long passages of Shakespeare by heart.

Among the fragment of the 'educated' public for and to whom this editorial presumes to speak, then, it would seem that education in the humanities is presumed to foster acquaintance with the classics by way of rote memorization (and never mind whether your chosen sonnet was originally addressed to a man or a woman). A step or two above this extremely low level of reading comprehension, the 'public intellectuals' of another generation like to float the argument that education in the humanities can train students to think critically and to pursue truths about the culture. As I'll show below, I think this argument is just about right. But I note that cultural conservatives are fond of these formulations, too – until they're given specific content. Thus, should the humanities train students to think critically about race, imperialism, sexuality or Beltway doublespeak, then the humanities will become the subject of hundreds of op-eds decrying 'political correctness' in the universities.

Even David Bromwich, who some time ago deposited all his available funds in the Irving Howe Consortium of cultural criticism, is not above mocking those who stress the formative aspects of education in the humanities, construing such people as arrogant, meddlesome social engineers who seek to transform the university into 'a superior social adjustment agency, in the business of granting degrees that mean: "Your son or daughter has turned out correct. Politically, morally, socially correct, at least by this year's standards."[6] As far as Bromwich is concerned, a university education with such a coercive ethical component is not a 'university' education at all:

An institution going forward on these principles would deserve to be called many things. A laboratory that knows how to monitor everything, and how to create nothing. A church, held together by the hunt for heresies, but without a single ritual, credo, prayer, or prayer book in common. Maybe it would resemble most of all an industrial park, with a perpetual supply of interns and apprentices, but with enough refinement not to want to call itself an industrial park. It does not much matter what we call it, for once the reflection or the remedy theory of education has been accepted, new demographics will always dictate a new name. Whatever the place we work in turns out to be, it will not be a place for thought. (pp. 46–7)

So much for anti-racist pedagogies; so much for critical thinking that contains any propositional content; so much for the belief that education in the humanities can make us better people in any sense whatsoever. In Bromwich's ideal workplace, universities are places for thought, it would appear, but only so long as we don't think *about* anything in particular. For once we begin to think *about* things, 'new demographics' – which involve, among other things, new student populations – may actually impel us to change our self-descriptions, and then we can be sure that our thinking is no longer worthy of the name.

I'm sure Bromwich would balk at this extrapolation of his argument, and I hope someday he does. For my point is that his polemic against the university as 'superior social adjustment agency' leaves him no option but to lampoon those who still believe that training in the humanities might be a force for good in the world. And though Bromwich is right to suspect that universities are turning into industrial parks, certainly it is bizarre for him to finger 'group thinking' as the primary agent of industrialization, rather than, say, increased corporate and military sponsorship of research in the sciences.

Finally, there is the 'public' argument that training in the humanities puts us in touch with our cultural heritage. (This is more or less the conclusion of David Denby's article in the *New Yorker*, describing the experience of going back to Columbia to re-take its core course in Western literature since Homer.)[7] That too is a sound position, and uncontroversial – until some young naif asks what 'our heritage' means. Worse still, should some student of African descent show up on our quadrangle asking to learn about his or her 'heritage', s/he will likely be met with the objection that s/he is seeking to dilute our academic standards. In other words, the 'cultural heritage' is manifestly more complex, and less obviously 'ours', than college core courses customarily acknowledge.

Allow me one more illustrative tale. Once upon a time, I began teaching a standard undergraduate Eng Lit survey (*Beowulf* to Caryl Churchill's *Top Girls*), only to have my opening-day spiel interrupted (gently) by a student who wanted to know why we were reading *Beowulf*. I took this question as a mild affront at first, the query of a postmodernist smartass who wanted to know what was 'relevant' about *Beowulf*. As it turned out, however, it was a sincere question. Was *Beowulf* part of the cultural heritage? Was it great? Was it influential? Was it important to the development of British identity and British literature? Or were we reading it just 'cause it's old?

The class rapidly got derailed, but it got somewhere worth going. I quickly found that I couldn't reach for any of the usual explanations: because there were few Danes (and no Geats) in the room or in the country, *Beowulf* was not clearly part of 'our cultural heritage' in any obvious sense. J. R. R. Tolkien, in his famous essay on *Beowulf* and the monsters, could at least close his argument with a moving testimony to his own cultural continuity with the poem: 'it was made in this land, and moves in our northern world beneath our northern sky.'[8] Teaching a class in Charlottesville, in old Virginny, I didn't have the same option. Nor was *Beowulf* very 'influential', since after its composition in the eighth, ninth, or tenth century A.D., it sort of got lost in the shuffle, and wasn't transcribed into modern English until after 1731, when it was plucked from the fire that ravaged Sir Robert Bruce Cotton's collection of medieval manuscripts. So it wasn't terribly important to the development of British identity or the national literature, either, even had 'the nation' meant the same thing in A.D. 900 that it meant in 1600 or 1987, as of course it didn't.

So was *Beowulf* here because it was old? Well, yes, I had to admit, for a long time from 1731 onward, the poem hung around as an object of interest partly because it was one of the oldest and longest things composed in a language that would eventually become English. Lo and behold, however, when the 'close reading' techniques of the mid twentieth century came along, *Beowulf* was found to be great in formal terms too, and now here it is in the *Norton Anthology* and on the syllabus. As your *Norton* intro will tell you, 'despite its difficulty, the somber grandeur of *Beowulf* is still capable of stirring the hearts of readers, and because of its excellence as well as its antiquity, the poem merits the high position that it is generally assigned in the study of English poetry.'[9] So pay attention to patterns of light and dark, the functions of the mead hall, the weapons, the exchanges and the monsters, and you'll be reading *Gawain and the Green Knight* for next week, and don't ask any more questions about the social and literary continuities assumed in the phrase, 'cultural heritage'. My group, keep moving, keep moving, and don't touch the exhibits.

I should say again that I agree with some version of each of these formulations, even the most trivial of them. Training in the humanities does indeed acquaint students with distant literary works they otherwise wouldn't encounter in the mall or the downtown breakfast restaurant, and if they want to consider these things part of our *human* heritage rather than as the possession of any one national or cultural tradition, that's fine by me. After all, it can be useful to remember what instructive and delightful things we've done as a species while we've been butchering and maiming each other, though I seem to recall a phrase from Walter Benjamin that suggests these things are intertwined. And training in the humanities does indeed stand a decent chance of teaching students to think critically, to exercise their imaginations and to become better people (that is, certifiably politically *correct* people) – though George Steiner and Thomas Pynchon would remind us that a love for Rilke doesn't prevent a man from participating in genocide, and plenty of cult-left upstarts would add that it's not necessarily as valuable for students to read Hume and Kant for their ideas about Africans as it is to read Hume and Kant on the faculty of reason. Finally, training in the humanities does tend to strengthen students' memories, if only because reading long and strange works demands more of an attention span than even the most clever sitcom. Though I've forgotten why Americans should worry about their short attention spans. Were we at war with Iran or Iraq? Or was that Eastasia or Eurasia?

There's one more explanation for this enterprise in the humanities, the 'cultural capital' explanation, by which the cultural left construes education in the humanities as an insidious social process of sorting: those who are familiar with Proust get to go to fancy dinner parties, those who prefer Zane Grey get to eat at Bob Evans (preferably in Zanesville, Ohio), and those who don't read at all, well, we don't know or care where they eat. The Proust readers then justify their incomes and their nice cars by pointing to specific passages in *Swann's Way* that the Grey fans and the illiterates can't understand – or, better, by quoting the passages by heart.

There's a great deal of truth in this burlesqued account of the relations between cultural and productive capital, as anyone would know from gauging the absurd volume of outrage emanating from the *New York Times* or the *Partisan Review* every time they catch somebody teaching Zane Grey to college students. Because, you know, if college students can specialize in Zane Grey, that mucks up the whole process, and they'll probably wind up reading trash like *Details* and *Rolling Stone* instead of the challenging editorials afforded them by the *Times*. As I've noted above, for publications that have invested in much older cultural technologies, it appears cataclysmic that contemporary academic critics be messing with the mechanisms. Why, if this keeps up, we'll soon have people at our dinner parties who haven't read 'Lycidas' and want to discuss *Riders of the Purple Sage* or hip-hop instead. There won't be any more common culture, and we won't be able to tell who's educated and who's not.

There are, however, two problems with the cultural left's understanding of the role of the humanities in the distribution and hoarding of cultural capital. First and foremost, it plays into (and does not sufficiently challenge) a vision of the humanities that leads to what I call Woody's World, where, as in Woody Allen's films, one presumes that the object of being cultivated is to drop as many well-respected intellectual names as possible, from Reinhold Niebuhr to Fyodor Dostoyevsky. As Allen's character in *Husbands and Wives* puts it, 'Tolstoy is a full meal; Turgenev is a fabulous dessert; Dostoyevsky is a full meal with a vitamin pill and extra wheat germ.'[10] This is what culturally literate people say in Woody's World, in order to demonstrate their familiarity with and love for the classics. The character who speaks these lines in *Husbands and Wives*, mind you, is yet another version of Allen's ideal cultural alter-ego, a creative writing professor at Barnard who's a reasonably well-respected intellectual name himself. He loves the same classics Allen himself loves – and lovingly spoofed in *Love and Death*. But it's not at all clear, from this exchange, why one should read these novelists, except to impress doe-eyed undergraduate women – and to distinguish oneself from people like Sidney Pollack's character, who would descend to have an affair with an uneducated girl Allen's character calls a 'cocktail waitress'. In the course of the film, that 'cocktail waitress' (actually she's an aerobics instructor), sure enough, turns out to be a New Age airhead whose lack of cultivation embarrasses Pollack at – I kid you not – *a cocktail party*. A cocktail party full of people who've doubtless read Proust, or Tolstoy, or Dostoyevsky. And so Pollack's character can take no more, returning to his wife (Judy Davis), with whom he may not have a sex life worth mentioning, but with whom he at least shares a common culture.

The second problem with the cultural capital argument is that it allows the cultural left to put on a grim face, wipe away all its illusions, and admit (in equal measures of melancholy and self-congratulation) to its complicity in the system of domination. Yep, we're sorting our students, all right; it's a dirty job but someone's got to do it, and at least *we* hearty critical souls have the capacity – and the honesty – to make a virtue of our self-awareness of the system and our place in it. For illustration we could look at the work of John Guillory, who's undoubtedly the academy's most rigorous theorist of 'canon revision' and 'cultural capital'. I mean no disparagement of Guillory here: he is absolutely right to note that professors may not do as much 'cultural work' as they claim when they substitute Zora Neale Hurston for Ernest Hemingway, and he's also right to protest that literary canons cannot (and should not be asked to) 'represent' various demographic groups in some transparent demographic way (where black texts represent blackness for black students, Asian texts represent Asianness for Asian students, and so on). Furthermore, Guillory perceptively argues that the humanities have been nearly paralyzed by a debate about the content of 'required readings' in which nearly all the premises – about cultural heritages and racial representation – are erroneous. Keeping 'marginalized groups' off the syllabus, as Guillory points out, works best when such groups are barred access to *literacy* in the first place: the debate over whether to admit more nineteenth-century African American writers to the reading lists of college courses in American literature has already been severely constrained by the fact that under slavery, it was illegal to teach Africans to read and write (and, conversely, their 'inability' to read and write was held to be one of the justifications of their enslavement).[11]

Still, in construing the problem of canonicity as too vast and systemic for any one text or teacher to address, Guillory seems to treat education in the humanities from the perspective of the night in which all texts look gray: 'the literary syllabus', as Guillory puts it, '... is *symbolic* capital, a kind of knowledge-capital whose possession can be displayed upon request and which thereby entitles its possessor to the cultural and material rewards of the well-educated person' (p. ix). That's quite true, especially if you're asked about Proust at a dinner party and you can reply only by talking about astrology or Zane Grey. But it's not the whole story, by any means. First of all, no teacher composes a syllabus by calibrating its effects on the tracking of his or her students; no one says, 'Today I will teach Harriet Jacobs's *Incidents in the Life of a Slave Girl* instead of *Moby-Dick* in order that my students will eventually drive Chevy Cavaliers rather than Lexuses and thus realize their relational place in the system of domination.' Second, as every college-bound student (and his/her parents) knows, more depends on the *location* of the syllabus than its content: students reading *Incidents in the Life of a Slave Girl* at Johns Hopkins University with John Guillory will be more 'marketable' upon graduation than students who read *Moby-Dick* at Municipal Institute Community College. Third and last, the specific content of an assigned text *can* make a difference to someone's education in the humanities, though this 'difference' can't be fixed or predicted, and though it may seem to make no difference at all on the last day of class, when one watches the stream of students rushing to the university bookstore to resell their assigned texts.

Furthermore, as I admitted in the introduction to these essays, most students, parents, alumni and legislators are far more concerned with the credentializing functions of universities than they are with the content of any assigned text, or even with the credentializing functions of any assigned text – as if, in some real-life Woody's World, these functions could be determined at all. Yet just because few nonacademics other than right-wing fanatics care whether *I, Rigoberta Menchú* replaces *Henderson the Rain King* in an introductory literature course, that doesn't mean that our assigned readings have no social effect whatsoever. As I argued in *Marginal Forces/Cultural Centers*, academic literary critics are a decisive force when it comes to keeping books in print, regardless of whether any of our students read them well; and as I'll argue in the rest of this essay, when our students *do* read their assigned texts well, any number of things can happen that can't be accounted for in theories about cultural capital.

Since I'm going to make this argument while having agreed in advance with Guillory's general premises, and since I want to defend the value of 'critical reading' to a culture that doesn't do much of the stuff, I'll make my case by way of an example. If we're going to defend and explain the humanities at all – without automatically reaching for the usual bromides about cultural heritages, cultural literacy or cultural capital – we should be able to point to specific texts and material instances in which the humanities make themselves felt as a force for both aesthetic and social education. Defending our roles as interpreters of Madonna to *Rolling Stone* or as critics of hip-hop in *The Source* is not difficult, as it turns out; we've come up with a number of cogent rationales for why people should interpret and intervene in their contemporary culture. But as Guillory himself notes, 'It has become surprisingly difficult to define a progressive political rationale for the teaching of canonical texts' (p. 21).

One of the difficulties, no doubt, has to do with the meaning of 'progressive' here. From my perspective, it cannot but be a politically progressive act – in the radical democratic sense – to provide students and other readers with access to advanced literacy (that is, criticism and interpretation), even though we cannot guarantee (how could we?) that they will use advanced literacy for certifiably 'progressive', that is, leftist, social and political ends. In what follows, then, I'll take up the challenge of defending specifically *literary* study. But even though I could do so with a 'canonical' text, I'm going to switch the dice at the outset, and talk about a novel that *should* be a canonical text in American literature but isn't. Its 'value', as I'll construe it, is therefore (for now) independent of its status as symbolic capital, predicated neither on its centrality nor on its marginality to the American canon. You could induct it into the Library of America tomorrow, and I'd still say all the stuff you're about to read.

James Weldon Johnson's *The Autobiography of an Ex-Colored Man* was published in 1912. Its protagonist is nameless, and like the authors of slave narratives, he refuses to disclose his origins: of his town of birth, he writes, 'I shall not mention the name of the town, because there are people still living there who could be connected with this narrative.'[12] And his narrative *is* dangerous: though the narrator is not an escaped slave, he is a black man passing for white, and his story, while claiming to be the unvarnished truth of autobiography, is nevertheless founded on deception. The book's very opening sentence makes this clear: 'I know that in writing the following pages I am divulging the great secret of my life, the secret which for some years I have guarded far more carefully than any of my earthly possessions; and it is a curious study to me to analyze the motives which prompt me to do it.' The narrator, in other words, is writing to out himself as an African American – while keeping his identity secret, of course.

Already, then, after only two pages, the narrator has accomplished something very, very few of my students are prepared to anticipate: he has demonstrated that 'race' is not necessarily readable on the face of things (so to speak). Making this point in detail requires me (or any reasonable teacher or reader of this text) to delve into the legal history of race in the South, at the very least to remind my students that for the purposes of Jim Crow, 'one drop' of 'Negro blood' makes one an African. For instance, should one of your great-grandparents be 'Negroid', I tell these students, you are an 'octaroon', and legally black. Personally, I do not know the ancestry of all my great-grandparents, and if someone wanted to 'out' me as an octaroon I would have a difficult time producing documentation to prove the contrary.

I am borrowing this sense of 'outing' from my gay and lesbian colleagues, of course, and I speak this way in the classroom precisely because it is axiomatic among my students that race and gender are 'given' and visible, but that sexual practice is a 'private' matter unless made otherwise. Dealing with the politics of race as if race were as visibly indeterminate as sexual preference, therefore, usually presents these students with a set of problems they haven't had to grapple with before. When the narrator finally comes to his moment of decision, I try to show, by reference to my government's current policies on the sexual preferences of military personnel, that the narrator's pretense of *not deciding* is simply self-deception: 'I finally made up my mind that I would neither disclaim the black race nor claim the white race; but that I would change my name, raise a mustache, and let the world take me for what it would; that it was not necessary for me to go about with a label of inferiority pasted across my forehead' (p. 139). Don't ask, says the narrator, and I won't tell. But who would ask? Who among you, I say to my students, came into this classroom assuming that I was gay until I indicated otherwise? The narrator knows that whiteness is normative just as heterosexuality is, and that only visible 'deviations' from the norm will be readable as such. As far as he's concerned, though, the decision is not his ('let the world take me for what it would'), and besides, it's really not *necessary* (a nice choice of word) for one to go around as an oppressed person if one has the choice not to.

The unreadability of race, then, is our first point of contact with this text. Allied to this point is a series of corollaries about the intersection between our 'private' identities and the legal/social apparatus in which we take up those identities. What are the relations between our self-understandings and the social contexts in which those understandings become intelligible to us *as* understandings of 'ourselves'? That is, how do we deal personally with identities that are socially constructed, and what part do *we* play in constructing them? What differences make a difference, and how do those differences signify socially? How does this narrator, specifically, threaten and undermine a system founded on the belief that racial difference is absolute and irreducible?

On this last question Johnson's text is altogether clear. Referring to the brutal Atlanta race riot of 1906 (in which the 'police' either stood by or participated), the narrator writes:

Even so late as the recent Atlanta riot those men who were brave enough to speak a word in behalf of justice and humanity felt called upon, by way of apology, to preface what they said with a glowing rhetorical tribute to the Anglo-Saxon's superiority and to refer to the 'great and impassable gulf' between the races 'fixed by the Creator at the foundation of the world'. The question of the relative qualities of the two races is still an open one. The reference to the 'great gulf' loses force in face of the fact that there are in this country perhaps three or four million people with the blood of both races in their veins; but I fail to see the pertinency of either statement subsequent to the beating and murdering of scores of innocent people in the streets of a civilized and Christian city. (pp. 137–8)

Our more recent riots have complicated this picture, since we are now so clearly a nation of many more than two 'races', but the narrator's physical and textual deconstruction of the 'great and impassable gulf' remains crucial to how we understand the complex intersections between subjectivity and social identity. Living in the gulf – whether you're black or Korean or gay or (more to the point) hybrid, multiple and variable – may mean placid waters, or it may mean a gulf war.

Now for the next set of complications. The reason the narrator decides to pass for white is that while he is on a tour of the rural South (a tour we'll get back to), he witnesses a lynching. Rather than feeling outrage and sympathy for the man he has watched burn to death, the narrator is strangely ashamed of the spectacle, and ashamed 'at being identified with a people that could with impunity be treated worse than animals. For certainly the law would restrain and punish the malicious burning alive of animals' (p. 139). Indeed, even in voicing his 'understanding' of terrorized black folk he nonetheless treats them as 'them':

A great wave of humiliation and shame swept over me. Shame that I belonged to a race that could be so dealt with; and shame for my country, that it, the great example of democracy to the world, should be the only civilized, if not the only state on earth, where a human being would be burned alive. My heart turned bitter within me. I could understand why Negroes are led to sympathize with even their worst criminals and to protect them when possible. By all the impulses of normal human nature they can and should do nothing less. (p. 137)

This is explosive stuff in the classroom, needless to say, because there is almost nothing in the education of most American children that tells them about lynching – and certainly nothing that prepares them for the horrific information that during many of the years between 1875 and 1925, the rate of lynchings in the United States easily exceeded one per week. As Ida B. Wells reported in 1892, 728 lynchings of black Americans had been recorded between the years 1884 and 1892 *alone*.[13]

Do I acquaint my students with this stuff just to make them feel bad, to feel ashamed of their country as does the narrator, and to make some politically correct point about how the United States is the root of all evil? Of course not. I don't like confronting the history of lynching any more than anyone else does. But when Patrick Buchanan – or Arthur Schlesinger – crows about the superiority of Judeo-Christian nations (or, for Buchanan, just plain 'Christian' nations) that have abolished slavery and that don't practice evil things like *sati* or clitorectomies, I do think it's important to set the historical record straight. Some of my white students don't see any difference between the KKK and the NAACP, and wonder why white people get criticized for forming white advocacy groups even though they can't criticize black advocacy groups without being called 'racist'. It would be a shame to pass those students through twelve years of compulsory education and another four of college in the United States without informing them that once upon a time, the KKK *performed* lynchings, and the NAACP, especially under Johnson's leadership (1920–30), resisted them. It's also useful to let these students know, as William Andrews notes in his introduction to *The Autobiography,* that the Dyer Anti-Lynching Bill, for which Johnson lobbied vigorously, passed the House in 1922 but never came to a floor vote in the Senate. Perhaps its passage would have disunited America, but now we'll never know.[14]

Finally, Johnson's book may perform powerful corrective work in an era when many nonblack Americans (and nearly all college students) consider it potentially *advantageous* to pass for black, since as 'black' students they would become eligible for minority fellowships and other 'affirmative action' initiatives. The only 'passing' narrative most of my students are familiar with is the 1986 movie *Soul Man,* which bears witness to (and simultaneously confirms) the widespread sense among white students that if only they had the same talents and were black, they'd be at Harvard Law on full fellowship without question. Although 'imagination' is not among our fashionable critical buzzwords of the day, it's crucial that 'imaginative' literature allow such students to 'imagine' themselves in this narrator's shoes, and it's worth allowing such imaginative texts to remind people that once upon a time, 'coming out' as black was as potentially dangerous – and even lethal – as 'coming out' as gay or lesbian is today.

All these are important points about our national and individual histories and identities. But if that's all I were concerned with, I wouldn't be in the business of literary criticism. For once we've understood the undecidability of race and the politics of lynching, our work with Johnson's text has only begun. Of course the book is an anti-lynching book, and of course I don't have to offend my students greatly in order to achieve some kind of classroom consensus that the anti-lynching position is a reasonable and defensible one. But there's more. First, the narrator not only passes for white, gradually becoming a wealthy real estate speculator; worse still, he *marries* white. And how: 'she was as white as a lily, and she was dressed in white', writes the narrator upon first seeing her. 'Indeed, she seemed to me the most dazzlingly white thing I had ever seen' (p. 144). She's blonde, too. Basically, he marries Georgette Mosbacher or Christie Brinkley. He courts her, wrestles with his conscience, and eventually tells her of his mixed ancestry; she cries, leaves him for some months, but eventually comes back and marries him. They have two children. She dies. He drops out of 'social life' and devotes himself to raising his children (p. 153). In his closing paragraphs, our narrator voices his regrets amidst professions of his happiness: 'my love for my children makes me glad that I am what I am and keeps me from desiring to be otherwise', he claims – whatever *that* phrasing might mean. But he remains moved by the vision bodied forth by the black leaders of his day:

> Even those who oppose them know that these men have the eternal principles of right on their side, and they will be victors even though they should go down in defeat. Beside them I feel small and selfish. I am an ordinarily successful white man who has made a little money. They are men who are making history and a race. I, too, might have taken part in a work so glorious. ... I cannot repress the thought that, after all, I have chosen the lesser part, that I have sold my birthright for a mess of pottage. (p. 154)

What's at stake here? The original publishers knew quite well, for in their brief preface to the work they pointed out the heart of Johnson's narrative: 'these pages also reveal the unsuspected fact that prejudice against the Negro is exerting a pressure which, in New York and other large cities where the opportunity is open, is actually and constantly forcing an unascertainable number of fair-complexioned colored people over into the white race' (p. xxxiv). To the white readers of 1912, then, Johnson's book has a chilling 'message': They are among us, and they are invisible – and not *despite* the terrorist practice of lynching, but precisely *because* of it.

Leaders of the old school will remember that lynching, in racist theory if not in racist practice, was supposed to be punishment for rape, or for any specifically sexual transgression against the purity of white womanhood. Though Johnson, like Ida B. Wells before him, knows perfectly well that his brethren are being lynched for any challenge to Jim Crow whatsoever (including the challenge of becoming too successful and/or uppity), he plays the rigged hand he's been dealt. That is to say, if racist whites' justifications for lynching are bound up with their fears about miscegenation, and their refusal to acknowledge three million to four million Americans of mixed ancestry testifies to their unwillingness to admit to the rapes perpetrated on black women by white slaveowners, *then,* says Johnson, I'll take these racial and sexual conundra on their own terms: I'll write a narrative that seeks to demonstrate that lynching is not merely *wrong* (since that argument clearly isn't deterring anybody from engaging in it), but that it's *counterproductive.* In *The Autobiography of an Ex-Colored Man,* then, lynching 'naturally' induces light-skinned African Americans to pass as white – and marry white. If you're a racist white guy, this is your worst nightmare.

But there's still more. As you may have gathered by now, Johnson's book *isn't* an autobiography; it's a novel. Johnson himself could not have passed for white, and clearly did not want to. But Johnson did not claim authorship of the text until 1927; for the first fifteen years of the book's existence, then, there was no evidence that it was *not* an autobiography. So it's a book about passing for white, and the book itself is 'passing' as an autobiography. How then do we read it today, and most of all, how do we read it bifocally as either a fictional or a non-fictional text, so as to gauge the difference between the book as an anonymous artifact and the book as the creation of an author who is definitely not identical to his narrator?

For one thing, the latter possibility obviously opens up for us a question that's unthinkable about a 'true' autobiography: what if Johnson is using the narrator *ironically* – as in some sense he must surely be? If Johnson wanted to suggest that lynching was having the counterproductive effect of inducing people to 'pass' if they could, he might have written an essay on the subject. Why write a novel instead, pass it off as an autobiography, and build it around a narrator who is very likely an unreliable informant – particularly insofar as he makes the 'wrong' decision in the end, choosing the path of least resistance over the road that leads to making history and a race?

I'll just mention a few lines of inquiry here, none of which can satisfactorily 'resolve' the question of Johnson's relation to the narrator any more than critics can decide once and for all the narrator's understanding of 'himself' (or our own self-understandings of our 'selves'). First, one should note the tradition of African American 'pseudo-documentary' in which the book participates, a tradition that extends from the documentary impulses of slave narratives to the more recent quasi-fictions of Ishmael Reed's *Mumbo Jumbo* and Marlon Riggs's *Tongues Untied.*[15] Second, one should historicize the conditions of production and reception for such a text, or, in simpler language, check the side- and rear-view mirrors: as William Andrews writes, 'when the *Autobiography* appeared in 1912, the publication of African American novels by Northern commercial publishers was still a new and risky venture' (p. xv). Johnson's decision to claim the authority of autobiography for his novel (an 'authority' with its own long and complex history from St. Augustine to Benjamin Franklin) was therefore inflected both by the 'authority' historically granted to slave narratives by white readers (especially the white 'underwriters' of those narratives who testified to their documentary authenticity) *and* by commercial/cultural/political considerations about the willingness of white readers and publishers to entertain so confrontational a fiction by a black writer. And, moreover, Johnson's text asks us to consider the relations between 'authentic' autobiographies and forgeries in general, from Harriet Jacobs's *Incidents in the Life of a Slave Girl* (which was considered 'inauthentic' until Jean Fagin Yellin documented its veracity in 1981), to Clifford Irving's famous fraudulent autobiography of Howard Hughes.[16]

There's a more obvious reason for Johnson's forgery, as well. Like Robert Townshend's first film, *Hollywood Shuffle* (1987), or Trey Ellis's first novel, *Platitudes* (1988), Johnson's novel is concerned with the past and present representation of African American representation. That is, the novel responds metafictionally to other texts' strategies of representation – particularly, but not exclusively, the plantation stories of Thomas Nelson Page and his ilk, which depicted slavery as an idyll and insisted that African Americans never had it so good.

In his tour through the rural South, for example, the narrator takes some pains to point out that the culture of rural blacks is not self-evidently 'his' culture. His mother was the sewing girl of a well-to-do Southern family, his father 'an impetuous young man home from college' (p. 30); when his father became engaged to a Southern lady of 'good' family, he set up the narrator (that is, his unacknowledged son) and his mother in a house in Connecticut. When the narrator sees rural Georgia for the first time, then, he may be anxious to distinguish himself from the 'natives', and he even speaks of 'strik[ing] out into the interior' (p. 122) as if he were a character in *Heart of Darkness*. But he's also anxious *not* to represent what he sees, and to signify on the rest of the American lit syllabus:

> This was my first real experience among rural colored people, and all that I saw was interesting to me; but there was a great deal which does not require description at my hands; for log cabins and plantations and dialect-speaking 'darkies' are perhaps better known in American literature than any other single picture of our national life. Indeed, they form an ideal and exclusive literary concept of the American Negro to such an extent that it is almost impossible to get the reading public to recognize him in any other setting; so I will endeavor to avoid giving the reader any already overworked and hackneyed descriptions. (p. 122)

Acutely conscious of how 'black' texts and writers are expected to *represent* 'blackness' in ways no white writer has to worry about when representing 'whiteness', Johnson concludes this passage by remarking on his culture's contemporary conditions of reading, conditions that ensure a partial (both synecdochic and partisan) representation of African American characters: 'a novel dealing with colored people who lived in respectable homes and amidst a fair degree of culture and who naturally acted 'just like white folks' would be taken in a comic-opera sense' (p. 123).

Fair enough. Then what does this narrator mean by 'a fair degree of culture', and why should he equate culture with 'white folks'? Here, a rich tradition of spirituals and oral narratives clearly doesn't count as 'culture'; familiarity with Brahms (or Johnson's contemporary, Proust) is another matter. Though the narrator goes on to render a complex and sympathetic description of a Southern 'big meeting' and its attendant musical and oral performances, he oscillates, like any practitioner of cultural studies, between the Arnoldian and the anthropological senses of 'culture'. Unlike his counterparts in cultural studies, though, he associates the Arnoldian sense of culture with whiteness, and the anthropological sense with blackness.

He is, as I should finally reveal, a classically trained musician himself, and he's travelling in the South in order to scour the region for material that he will transform into symphonies and operas. Having learned ragtime in a fashionable New York 'bohemian' club, where black performers go to jam and white folks show up 'sight-seeing, or slumming' or learning how to imitate black characters for variety shows (p. 78), the narrator has spent much of his time playing ragtime versions of the classics for the amusement and entertainment of white audiences. Upon hearing a German pianist play 'classical' versions of ragtime, he decides to acknowledge his African ancestry, round up some raw material, and make his name as a black composer – knowing full well that 'I should have greater chances of attracting attention as a colored composer than as a white one' (pp. 107–8). Thus, in what appears to be a nearly 'professionalist' gesture, he equates his own self-interest and career ambitions with the advancement of the black community on whose music he will draw: 'I must own that I also felt stirred by an unselfish desire to voice all the joys and sorrows, the hopes and ambitions, of the American Negro, in classic musical form' (p. 108). It's hard to know what to make of this, but my advice would be to seek out a professional cultural critic for commentary.

What a professional critic will tell you is this: Johnson's novel interrogates the relations between 'race' and 'culture' in the broadest sense, asking us not only to determine the way these terms overlap in our cultural imagination, but also to investigate relations of ownership and power between 'cultures'. According to the narrator's wealthy white patron, whom the narrator leaves to embark on his career as a 'black' composer, 'music is a universal art; anybody's music belongs to everybody; you can't limit it to race or country' (p. 105). Many readers might reflexively agree with this, but then many of us know a ripoff when we see one, too. Though ragtime, like blues, jazz, rhythm and blues, rock 'n roll, soul, funk, reggae, and hip-hop, is originally a 'black' cultural form, the narrator knows who's getting paid: 'several of these improvisations', he writes, 'were taken down by white men, the words slightly altered, and published under the names of the arrangers' (p. 73). Meanwhile, black performers who do aspire to 'legitimate' cultural forms find themselves shut out, as in the case of the minstrel who wants to be a Shakespearean actor: 'here was a man who made people laugh at the size of his mouth, while he carried in his heart a burning ambition to be a tragedian; and so after all he did play a part in a tragedy' (p. 77).

How then do we read the narrator's desire to be a black composer in this matrix? Between Pat Boone singing blues and Morgan Freeman playing a chauffeur, how can we configure the relations of power, propriety, and property in race and culture? Most of my students have not heard ragtime – except via *The Sting* (1973) and Marvin Hamlisch's arrangements of Scott Joplin compositions. That seems germane to Johnson's novel, I think. So does the work of Roosevelt Sykes or Jelly Roll Morton. So do Gershwin's *Porgy and Bess,* Langston Hughes's 'Note on Commercial Theater', and John Coltrane's rearticulation of Gershwin's 'Summertime' on *My Favorite Things* (itself a thoroughly multicultural and multiaccentual cultural artifact). So do Marky Mark's version of hip-hop, Living Color's version of cock rock, and Steely Dan's versions of jazz winding up in De La Soul's version of 'alternative rap.' What are those gospel singers and rural black folk doing in Madonna's 'Like a Prayer' and Billy Joel's 'River of Dreams'? Or what happens when Nigerian juju impresario King Sunny Ade uses the pedal steel guitar, or when Django Reinhardt hears Louis Armstrong, or when Chuck Berry hears Hank Williams, or when Melle Mel puts on a heavy-metal leather studded bodysuit?

At one point in the novel, our intrepid narrator-pianist plays a curious trick on his wealthy white listeners:

> I struck up my ragtime transcription of Mendelssohn's 'Wedding March', playing it with terrific chromatic octave runs in the bass. This raised everybody's spirits to the highest point of gaiety, and the whole company involuntarily and unconsciously did an impromptu cake-walk. (p. 87)

Get down, funky well-to-do white persons! James Brown hits the speakers, and the entire Chamber of Commerce gets on the good foot and works it on out. For analogies, check out the fate of white Jes Grew carriers in Reed's *Mumbo Jumbo* – or all those innocent, blow-dried white kids in the 1970s who did the hustle without realizing disco's origins in black and gay subcultures.

What Johnson's after, as I tell my students at the end of the week, is fairly elaborate. He's writing an anti-lynching novel, and he's also drawing on and complicating the tradition of personal narrative in African American letters. In passing as an autobiography, his novel implies, by way of its untrustworthy and self-deceived narrator, that the politics of race are so deeply intertwined with those of class as to render some educated and talented light-skinned black men deeply ambivalent about their loyalty to the rest of 'the race'. Because of his training in classical music, and because of his uneasily held belief that European cultural forms are more advanced and 'legitimate' than African American cultural forms, the ex-colored man winds up with a distorted and partial view of the desirability and protocols of intercultural exchange, and thinks that his project of 'classicizing' rural Southern music will honor the music rather than ridicule or exploit it. To readers like Robert Stepto, the ex-colored man's dream has appeared about as desirable as having Bobby Short make hip-hop into something palatable for Woody Allen's ears. And yet – this is part of the novel's power, and its potential appeal – the ex-colored man's class and cultural biases could make for a musical career worth following, if only he had followed it himself.[17]

We could go on for years. In fact, I hope we do. But I've taken up enough of your time already, and I want to conclude by suggesting a few things Johnson's book can and can't do for us. Though the novel undoubtedly inquires into the circulation of symbolic capital, its own status as an item in that economy is, as I noted above, unclear. Johnson's work will invite us, in what I take to be fascinating and rewarding ways, to read carefully, to interpret its narrator's interpretations of himself, and to deliberate about our cultural heritage; it'll even make us think about what we mean by 'our', 'cultural', and 'heritage'. But it won't represent 'blackness' or 'race' in any simple way, and it won't impress upon our foreheads a handy set of 'values' that we can show to be self-evidently better than the 'values' of Henry James's *The Ambassadors* or John Singleton's *Boyz N the Hood* (though we'll probably close the book with a horror of lynching). It won't allow us simply to celebrate black heroes like Crispus Attucks, Benjamin Banneker or Jack Johnson on some 'wall of fame', but it may get us to think about the social and historical conditions under which James Weldon Johnson wrote and we now read. And maybe it will afford us a few hours, or days, or years, of imaginative work and intellectual enjoyment.

Most of all, it will reward painstaking interpretation. The work of literary critics just is the work of interpretation, and the teaching and training of literary critics is the teaching of and training in varieties and possibilities of interpretation. Historicizing a text, speaking its silences, making manifest its 'latencies', reading its rhetorics, interrogating its implicit assumptions or explicit propositions about race or gender or nation or sexuality or 'culture' – this is what we do, and what we try to interest our students in doing. We make the promise that if you do these things, if you practice the fine arts of textual interpretation, you will 'get more out of' your readings, in terms of your own symbolic economy: you will learn the process of constructing analogies, drawing inferences, making finer and firmer intertextual connections among the texts you've read and the texts that compose your world. In theory, you can do this in nearly any field of human endeavor, from astrophysics to sports commentary, but you can probably do it best in those fields that give the widest possible latitude to understanding the formative and 'productive' aspects of language, where the interpretation of discourses and rhetorics necessarily involves interpretation of the discursive and nondiscursive work that 'discourses' and 'rhetorics' have done in the world.

As Robert Scholes has written, we can envision our critical tasks as methods of negotiating between the mutually implicating practices of textual interpretation and worldly evaluation:

> An ethic of reading can begin only when we are willing to accept some readings as better than others and to say why this is so and to accept some texts as better than others and to say why this is so. ... Such judgments, it should now be clear, require us to connect what is represented in the text with what we see in the world – in a manner that is ethical because it is political, and political *because it is textual*. This is a crucial point. The notion of textuality reminds us that we do nothing in isolation from others. We are always connected, woven together, textualized – and therefore politicized. This is why there can be no ethics of reading that is free of political concerns.[18]

I think Scholes's text is worth weaving into my own, and into the life in which I deal with texts. There can be no satisfactory derivation of ethics from textuality alone, unless we connect intertextuality with intersubjectivity – as we must, if we're to be adequate readers of the literary and social texts of this world, readers capable of sociotextual analyses and actions that are themselves interdependent.

I expect that this conclusion will seem too genteel, too belletristic to some of my readers. I realize that however one may feel about it, there really is a tiny wing of the profession of literary criticism in which 'textuality' itself is a nasty word, where textual hijinx are frowned upon as something merely 'ludic', and where *textual studies* is decried as a bad, apolitical enterprise, while *cultural studies* is set apart as the good stuff that really gets things done (with the further proviso that we stay away from 'experiential' cultural studies, which does no more than describe things, and hew to 'critical' cultural studies, which will redistribute power, wealth, and resources, and stop the insanity in general).[19] Doubtless, the world truly would be simpler to get around in if there weren't all these texts in the way, mediating our access to the real. But until that moment of revelation when we can get past textuality once and for all, no more to peep through lattices of eyes, hear through labyrinths of ears, I suggest we keep reading. For some of these texts do not merely delight; they instruct as well. Or, to elide Horace and Sir Philip Sidney with Michel Foucault and Carol Vance, they afford us power and pleasure in always uncertain measure.

I intend this conclusion, then, not only as a provocation but as a reminder. The contemporary American right finds it alternately ludicrous and appalling that literary and cultural critics should try to be a politically progressive force in the world, but we have long traditions – and many current constituencies – in which the social and political relevance of textual criticism is not only expected but welcomed. Indeed, it is upon these traditions and these constituencies that the right itself depends every time it concocts a manifestly political reading of academic criticism for 'public' consumption. Cultural politics are not 'merely' textual. They involve bodies at abortion clinics, viruses in laboratories, contaminants in the groundwater and appropriations in state legislatures; and however much we may depend on texts to understand these things, they are not texts themselves, not in the sense that *The Autobiography of an Ex-Colored Man* – or *Public Access* – is a text. But if you've read this far in this book or in this world, tracking the practices of legitimation and delegitimation that structure our polity and our lives, and you still think that the 'textual' or the 'discursive' is *not* a crucial site of social contestation for our 'private' identities and the legal/social apparatus in which we take up, claim or transform those identities, then you just haven't been reading carefully enough.

In fact, the crisis of PC and the universities is itself partly a crisis of reading: the PC scandals swept through the press so easily because so few of our 'traditional' intellectuals and mainstream journalists are capable of reading interpretively, reading intelligently, or (in some cases) reading at all. The intellectual right is not dismayed by this, since, as many of their spokespersons have written, reading is part of the problem, not part of the solution. In her reply to Dinesh D'Souza's critics, for instance, Heather MacDonald answered my challenge to link literary theory with incidents of campus 'oppression' by complaining that theory is too hard to read:

> to demand that any analyst of the university first do time with [Toril] Moi, [Eve] Sedgwick et al., is a brilliant strategy. These theorists function as a moat around the university. Anyone from the outside who tries to swim through them will quickly find himself caught in the oozy prose, unable to proceed any further.[20]

In this moat there are dense, complex texts; myriad interpretive modes; engaging and *engagé* cultural criticism; and other monsters too dreadful to speak of. Now, MacDonald knows better than she's letting on here; like Roger Kimball, she's a former Yale graduate student who's now advising her readers not to bother looking at writers whose work demands greater reading comprehension skills than does her own. But what makes the PC crisis truly a 'crisis' is that the resistance to intelligent reading is not confined to MacDonalds. As I've shown time and again in these pages, it's increasingly typical of Schlesingers, Lehmans, Broders and Howes every bit as much as of Teachouts, Thernstroms, D'Souzas and Quayles. To put this impasse another way: while we academic readers have been devising more and more exacting ways of reading our texts, our worlds and our critics, the reading skills and reasoning facilities of the *Partisan Review* regulars (a group that now includes Heather MacDonald) have become cause for national alarm.

Yet public access to academic reading, interpretation and criticism does require bridges – if not necessarily drawbridges. Some of those bridges can't be built by us alone; they require a renewed national commitment to all areas of education, especially the nonvocational forms of education that are supposed to train citizens for democracy rather than for employment at McDonalds. That means, above all, more adequate state and federal funding, as well as more comprehensive institutional support for nontraditional, continuing, or just plain struggling students. As writers, teachers and critics, though, our task should be clear: the critical discourse of 'public access' demands greater public access to critical discourse. Reading for comprehension is one thing, like learning to tell time; reading *critically,* reading for interpretation, is another – more like learning to take the watch apart, inspect its machinery, put it back together, show someone else how it works, and connect what you've learned about watches with the larger machinery of our lives. I'll be the first to admit that we need more citizens who know what time it is, but we need even more than that: not just clockwatchers, but people capable of envisioning – and creating – the coalitions that can turn the century. To have a chance of reaching those people we have to open the public access channel, and we may occasionally have to get textual and ludic about the enterprise: after all, one reason most folks don't do critical reading is that they're too busy punching the clock. For those potential readers, cultural criticism can do cultural work only if it's both critical and entertaining – that is, if it isn't more 'work'. So if cultural critics are going to help people tell time and turn the century, then at some point, it seems, we may have to learn to conduct ourselves as if it were 1999.

Notes

1. Gerald Graff, 'The Unintelligibility of the Humanities', paper delivered at the annual convention of the Midwest Modern Language Association, 6 November 1993, p. 1.

2. Bruce Robbins, *Secular Vocations* (London: Verso, 1993), pp. 84–117. For my more extended (but still brief) take on *Secular Vocations* see 'Egghead Salad', *Village Voice Literary Supplement,* no. 121 (December 1993), pp. 29–30.

3. Hence, to return to an issue I broached in Chapter 5, 'Pop Goes the Academy', Constance Penley's uneasiness about the relations between fans and academics, and her relation to *herself* as academic and as fan.

4. Each of these wonderful testimonies to the publicness of academic work is available in your local library, unless your locals have banned *The Source* for its connection to rap (aka violence). Stacey D'Erasmo, 'The Gay Nineties: In Schools Across the Country, Gay Studies is Coming on Strong', *Rolling Stone*, 3 October 1991, pp. 83–7, 130; Dan Zevin, 'Dancing in the Seats: Roll Over Beethoven, the Professors of Pop Have Arrived', *Rolling Stone,* 17 September 1992, pp. 83–8, and Elizabeth Tippins, 'Mastering Madonna', *Rolling Stone,* 17 September 1992, pp. 89, 111; Michael Eric Dyson, *Rolling Stone,* 28 October 1993, pp. 75–6; David Rakoff, review of *Alphabet Man, Details* (October 1993), p. 189. For the review of Houston Baker's *Black Studies, Rap, and the Academy,* see Bill Martin, 'Connecting the Black Dots', *The Source* (September 1993), p. 26.

5. Editorial, 'Shakespeare for Mere Mortals', *New York Times,* 3 September 1993, p. A22.

6. David Bromwich, *Politics by Other Means* (New Haven, Conn.: Yale University Press), p. 46; hereafter cited in the text.

7. David Denby, 'Does Homer Have Legs?' *New Yorker,* 6 September 1993, pp. 52–69. Denby's article is engaging and broad-minded, yet marred by its reliance on Searlean caricatures of the cultural left as a bunch of folks who want to banish Homer for his glorification of war and his treatment of women as items of exchange. What the upstarts among the cultural left at Columbia had been saying about the core curriculum, in fact, is that in enormous survey courses, it's impossible to teach literary works in their cultural context, as complex conversations with their day and ours, the way we think they *ought* to be taught. The core course, unfortunately, practically forces one to teach a bunch of masterpieces in chronological order and nothing else, and most responsible teachers who've had the experience will admit that it's not unlike rushing a tour group through a museum.

8. J. R. R. Tolkien, '*Beowulf:* The Monsters and the Critics' [1936], in R. D. Fulk, ed., *Interpretations of Beowulf: A Critical Anthology* (Bloomington, Ind.: Indiana University Press, 1991), p. 36.

9. M. H. Abrams et al., eds, *The Norton Anthology of English Literature,* 5th edn (New York: Norton, 1986), p. 26.

10. *Husbands and Wives*. Written and directed by Woody Allen. Columbia Tristar, 1992.

11. See John Guillory, *Cultural Capital: The Problem of Literary Canon Formation* (Chicago: University of Chicago Press, 1993), pp. 15–19 *et passim;* for the relations between Africans, literacy, slavery, and 'Western culture', see Henry Louis Gates, Jr, 'Writing, "Race", and the Difference It Makes', rpt. in *Loose Canons: Notes on the Culture Wars* (New York: Oxford University Press, 1992), pp. 43–69.

12. James Weldon Johnson, *The Autobiography of an Ex-Colored Man* (New York: Penguin Books, 1990), p. 2; hereafter cited in the text.

13. Ida B. Wells, 'Southern Horrors: Lynch Law in All Its Phases', in Karlyn Kohrs Campbell, ed., *Man Cannot Speak for Her: Key Texts of the Early Feminists*, vol. 2 (New York: Praeger, 1989), pp. 389–419.

14. William Andrews, 'Introduction', p. xiii. And perhaps I'm just being divisive today in assigning a text that deals with the subject. As a character says in *Monty Python and the Holy Grail*, 'Come, come! This should be a *happy* time! Let's not bicker and argue about who killed who!' Or perhaps we should take the suggestion offered by former Secretary of Education William Bennett: as Cary Nelson put it in an essay reviewing one of Bennett's television performances, 'Among his more frightening arguments was his assertion that black students should encounter nothing in their education that reminds them of their history of oppression and discrimination in America.' Once again, don't ask, don't tell. See Cary Nelson, 'Canon Fodder: An Evening with William Bennett, Lynne Cheney, and Dinesh D'Souza', *Works and Days*, no. 18 (1991), p. 46. Nelson's article addresses a 4 April 1991, American Enterprise Institute symposium on higher education, an event timed for the release of D'Souza's *Illiberal Education*. Bennett's rationale was that black students would be humiliated by pedagogies that focus on race relations.

15. See Barbara Foley, 'History, Fiction, and the Ground Between: The Uses of the Documentary Mode in Black Literature', *PMLA,* vol. 95 (1980), pp. 389–403; Valerie Smith, 'The Documentary Impulse in Contemporary African American Film', in Gina Dent, ed., *Black Popular Culture*, a project by Michele Wallace (Seattle, Wash.: Bay Press, 1992), pp. 56–64.

16. See Jean Fagan Yellin, 'Written by Herself: Harriet Jacobs's Slave Narrative', *American Literature,* vol. 53, no. 3 (1981), pp. 479–86; and G. Thomas Couser, *Altered Egos: Authority in American Autobiography* (New York: Oxford University Press, 1989).

17. For further information and criticism on Johnson, see Eugene Levy, *James Weldon Johnson: Black Leader, Black Voice* (Chicago: University of Chicago Press, 1973); Houston Baker, *Singers of Daybreak: Studies in Black American Literature* (Washington, D.C.: Howard University Press, 1974); Robert Stepto, *From Behind the Veil: A Study of Afro-American Narrative* (Urbana, Ill.: University of Illinois Press, 1979); Valerie Smith, *Self-Discovery and Authority in Afro-American Narrative* (Cambridge, Mass.: Harvard University Press, 1987); Robert E. Fleming, *James Weldon Johnson* (Boston: Twayne, 1987); Bernard Bell, *The Afro-American Novel and Its Tradition* (Amherst, Mass.: University of Massachusetts Press, 1987); Donald A. Petesch, *A Spy in the Enemy's Country: The Emergence of Modern Black Literature* (Iowa City, Iowa: University of Iowa Press, 1989).

18. Robert Scholes, *Protocols of Reading* (New Haven, Conn.: Yale University Press, 1989), p. 154.

19. See, e.g., Teresa Ebert, 'Ludic Feminism, the Body, Performance, and Labor: Bringing *Materialism* Back into Feminist Cultural Studies', *Cultural Critique,* no. 23 (1992–93), pp. 5–50; Donald Morton, 'The Politics of Queer Theory', *Genders,* no. 17 (1993), pp. 121–50.

20. Heather MacDonald, 'D'Souza's Critics: PC Fights Back', *Academic Questions*, vol. 5, no. 3 (1992), p. 13.

Index

Index

DATE DUE